To. dear Ian,
Best wishes o… y
from Mum & Dad … 994

The History of Thames Rowing Club and Tideway Rowing

Hear the Boat Sing

THE HISTORY OF THAMES ROWING CLUB
AND TIDEWAY ROWING

Geoffrey Page

Geoffrey Page.

The Kingswood Press

First published in Great Britain 1991
by The Kingswood Press
An imprint of Methuen London
Michelin House, 81 Fulham Road, London SW3 6RB

A CIP catalogue record for this book
is available from the British Library
ISBN 0 413 65410 9

Typeset by Falcon Typographic Art Ltd., Edinburgh & London
Printed and bound in Great Britain
BPCC Hazell Books
Aylesbury, Bucks, England
Member of BPCC Ltd.

The publishers are indebted to
ALAN BURROUGH, CBE
whose generosity made possible
the publication of this history

Contents

Preface

This was originally intended to be simply the history of a famous rowing club and the story of the many personalities who have given it its particular character.

The part played by Thames Rowing Club in the development of rowing beyond the confines of the Thames Tideway has been so great, however, that it is impossible to write about the Club without linking it with the progress of amateur rowing generally. Since the Club's foundation, Thames men, with their close neighbours and rivals London Rowing Club, have been involved at every important moment in the history of the sport, so this has also become the story of English rowing seen through the eyes of Thames men and, more recently, women. I have tried to present the Club's own story in this wider context.

I have always felt that there has been an imbalance in the chronicles of rowing in England, the majority of accounts, certainly until comparatively recently, having been written by those involved primarily with rowing at Oxford or Cambridge or with the link between these two, the Leander Club. The Badminton Library's *Boating*, written a century ago by the legendary W.B. Woodgate, included some interesting passages about Metropolitan rowing, and W.H. Eyre contributed a lively account of rowing at Thames from 1874 to 1882 to R.C. Lehmann's *The Complete Oarsman*, but these were exceptions to the rule. Much of the established opinion in the English rowing community until well after the First World War was based on the ideas of the famous Varsity oarsmen and coaches of the second half of the 19th century and the first decade of this century, yet it was London who first introduced sliding seats to Henley in 1872, and between then and 1960, when Thames introduced 'spade' blades into this country, came not only the creation of the Amateur Rowing Association, a direct offspring from the Metropolitan Rowing Association, but many other changes too: developments in rowing technique, the introduction of winter rowing and Head of the River races, as well as a widening interest in international rowing. All had their roots in the Tideway, and had an influence well beyond this country.

This book should have been written by the Club's principal historian and archivist, Dr K.A. Williams. For many years, Bill assembled notes and articles, many of which appeared in the *Journal of the Thames Rowing Club*. These notes were to have been a basis for a history of Thames, originally for the Club centenary in 1960, but Bill was always a busy man and time gradually slipped by and eventually ran out altogether for him. It finally fell to me, as one of a generation that knew many of the old Thames men and yet rowed after the Second World War and so formed the link between the 'Ancient' and 'Modern'. A great deal of what I have recorded has never appeared in print before and results from conversations I have had with men whose memories stretched back into the last century. I have also drawn freely from Bill's notes and happily acknowledge the debt that I and the Club owe to his research. I hope he would have approved of the result.

No doubt much that should have been included in these pages has been washed away by the river of time and has failed to reach me, but I hope the essence of what Thames has always stood for comes through and that I have caught some of the history of the Club and the Tideway that might otherwise have been lost.

I would like also to put on record my thanks to many people who have given considerable help and advice, including Philip Carpmael, President of London Rowing Club, Hamish Hamilton, and Dick Phelps, who are, alas, no longer with us. To John Levy, Peter Kirkpatrick, Alan Burrough and Pauline Churcher, who read the manuscript and offered constructive advice, to Timothy Wilson, who knows as much as anyone living about the Club's past, and to Freddie Beardmore, my special thanks for their assistance.

G.G.H.P.

Acknowledgements

Most of the illustrations in this book are reproduced by kind permission of the author and of Thames Rowing Club. Some appeared originally in *The Field, The Graphic, Illustrated London News* and *Vanity Fair*. Some are almost certainly from the George Bushell Collection though the photographs carry no attribution. Every effort has been made to trace the source of all illustrations but we have not always succeeded: our apologies to those omitted.

However, we are able to acknowledge the considerable help given to us by John Shore (nos. 67,68,69,70,71,73), the Hulton Picture Company (no.8, the endpiece to chapter 3 and the endpiece to the Prologue), Barratt's Photo Press (no.34), P.C.Kirkpatrick (no.36), S.F.A. Miskin (no.58) and Stearn & Sons, Cambridge (no.41). The portrait of Steve Fairbairn by James Quinn (no.9) is reproduced by kind permission of the Master, Fellows and Scholars of Jesus College, Cambridge. We must also acknowledge that no.25 appeared in *Rowing to Win* by Colin Porter (Stanley Paul, 1959) and no.35 in *Henley Royal Regatta* by Richard Burnell (Kingswood Press, 1989).

In the colour section, nos. 6,7,8,9,10 are reproduced by kind permission of the artist who is also the author; no.15 by kind permission of John Shore; and no.1 is reproduced from an oil painting by Dickinson and Foster in the possession of Thames Rowing Club.

Foreword

by Alan Burrough, CBE

I am very pleased that Geoffrey Page has undertaken this great history, born of his long experience of rowing and of the most careful research. He describes an enormously important period in the development of rowing as a competitive sport, reaching out beyond Thames Rowing Club to describe the progress of British and international rowing generally during the last 130 years.

Geoffrey is well qualified for this monumental task not only because he has been a member of TRC for over sixty years (he was put up for junior membership by his father when he was five weeks old) but for much of that time he has been an exceptionally active member. He rowed in the TRC Grand Challenge crew at Henley Royal Regatta three times, for four years was Captain of the Club, and for a long time coached not only TRC but also many other men's and women's crews. Since 1965 he has been rowing correspondent of the *Sunday Telegraph* and latterly of the *Daily Telegraph* as well.

Undoubtedly Geoffrey derived much of his knowledge of rowing from his father, James Houghton (Freddie) Page, a distinguished master at St Paul's (which school both Geoffrey and I attended), who was a member of TRC for many years and also its Captain and coach. I gained considerable help from Freddie during my formative years because I was coached by him at school, at TRC and in the victorious Cambridge Boat Race crew of 1939. Moreover, I was in his form at St Paul's for a short time when ironically he encouraged me to stop trying to learn Latin and to turn to Higher Mathematics. Five years later, when embarked on a business career and rowing in the TRC First VIII I decided to change course and go up to Jesus College, Cambridge. However, there was a snag: although I had passed London Matric at that time, I needed Latin for Cambridge! Freddie stepped into the breach and for a few weeks in the evenings he taught me enough to pass 'Little Go'.

I had two spells of rowing with TRC, two years between school and Cambridge and then four immediately after the war during which I had the privilege of being Captain for two seasons. Like Geoffrey I had some truly enjoyable years with some good crews and many successes. I suppose my most memorable race was one I did not win, the Goblets with 'Sparrow' Morris in 1947, which Geoffrey has described in the book. Afterwards Morris and I were selected to represent Great Britain in the European championships at Lucerne; with TRC's winning Stewards' IV crew we were the first British entries in the European championships. Sadly, neither made the medals, both finishing fifth.

Since 1972 I have been honoured by TRC as their President. With all clubs there are good times and the not so good. Currently TRC is rising rapidly — under the excellent Captaincy of Pauline Rayner, the first time a woman has held this office – from a rather low spell and I'm sure the Club will soon regain its former glory.

Rowing is a sport which has been expanding rapidly in recent years. It encourages the healthy development of character and of mind and body, and so far as I am concerned it has led to many lasting and trusting friendships. Geoffrey's book encapsulates that sense of togetherness which rowing, and particularly membership of a great club like Thames, inspires and I trust it will be bought and treasured by all who are concerned with rowing.

The Oarsman's Song

The willowy sway of the hands away
And the water boiling aft,
The elastic spring and the steely fling
That drives the flying craft.

The steely spring and the musical ring
Of the blade with the biting grip,
And the stretching draw of the bending oar
That rounds the turn with a whip.

And the lazy float that runs the boat,
And makes the swing quite true,
And gives the rest that the oarsman blest
As he drives the blade right through.

All through the swing he hears the boat sing
As she glides on her flying track,
And he gathers aft to strike the craft
With a ringing bell-note crack.

From stretcher to oar with drive and draw,
He speeds the boat along.
All whalebone and steel and a willowy feel –
That is the oarsman's song.

Steve Fairbairn

Prologue: The Gentlemen Amateurs

In the early years of the 19th century the tidal reaches of the Thames upstream of Chelsea retained much of their 18th-century character. There remained many elegant houses spread along the banks between what were still, in effect, villages. The tentacles of the railway system that was to link outlying villages with the City later in the century had not yet materialised and the sprawling suburbia that became the dubious legacy of the later Victorian era had scarcely begun.

There were still very few bridges and the banks of the river had not yet been built up. The Victoria Embankment, which was to take six years to construct, would not be completed until 1870, to be followed a few years later by the Chelsea Embankment. Before this time, the river bank consisted of a series of mudbanks, and dilapidated buildings frequently surrounded their more elegant neighbours.

The river had not been dredged, and above Chelsea it was still possible to walk across it in various places at low tide. There had, for example, been a ford above Chiswick Eyot since Roman times but the building up of the banks caused the level of the river to rise, and eventually the construction of the pound lock at Teddington in 1811, which raised the level further up river, began to lead to new bridges.

In the early 1800s, rowing was just beginning to be taken seriously as a sport by 'gentlemen amateurs'. There had been many races for watermen in the 18th century and earlier and various Coats and Badges were offered as prizes, the most famous being Doggett's, instituted in 1715 and which today is the oldest continuous sporting event still to be contested, predating the Derby and the Oaks.

Eton and Westminster took up the sport, though meetings between these famous schools seem to have been mainly excuses for overindulgence in food and drink! Colleges at Oxford and Cambridge began to institute bumping races. In 1829 came the first University Boat Race. Rowed at Henley, it aroused so much public interest that ten years later the town, as interested at least as much in the commercial as the sporting possibilities, introduced the regatta which is now the world's most famous, if no longer its premier, rowing event.

On the Tideway in the early 19th century there were no big clubs and no clubhouses such as we know today. Small groups of enthusiasts got together and bought or hired boats and rented changing-rooms from boatyards or pubs, and these associations or groups of oarsmen often took their names from those of the boats in which they rowed: *The Shark, The Star, The Arrow* and many others now forgotten.

In 1815, the Shark was the great London club, but the Star and the Arrow were probably the earliest metropolitan clubs. There is evidence that they were in existence at the end of the 18th century, and they survived until about 1820. By then, Leander was in existence and it is often thought to have arisen from the ashes of the earlier clubs, a star and an arrow being two of the principal features of the club shield, though there is little doubt that all three were active at the same time before 1820. In 1913 Guy Nickalls recorded that he had seen a cutting from a newspaper of 1818 which mentioned a six-oar cutter named *Leander*, which was presumably the craft from which the club derived its name.

At all events, Leander was flourishing by 1820

as a small private subscription club with a limited membership, the undisputed 'Cock of the London Water', as the Leander history puts it, boating from Stangate, Lambeth.

There were many other small clubs, most of which faded away after brief lives. One such, in existence about 1820, was the Funny Club, a funny being a type of sculling boat. There was a sculling club, based on Wandsworth before 1830, which might possibly have been the London Amateur Scullers Club, in whose colours T.B. Bumpsted became the first winner of the Diamond Sculls at Henley in 1840. Sculling must have been popular among amateurs at the time since Henry Wingfield was sufficiently encouraged to present in 1830 the silver challenge sculls which bear his name and still carry with them the amateur championship of the Thames.

Other early clubs were St George's, which figured among early Henley winners in the 1840s, and the Thames Club (not to be confused with the present Thames Rowing Club) which lasted for several seasons, during which it won a number of Henley trophies, including the Grand Challenge Cup in 1846. The Meteor Club, Wandle Club, and the Argonaut Club also feature among Henley winners between 1840 and 1850, and their members were to become the founders of London Rowing Club.

In 1843, the Thames Regatta, in which both amateurs and professionals competed, was started. W.B. Woodgate wrote in 1889 that this greatly supplemented the attractions of Henley, but he went on to say that the regatta made the mistake of putting on challenge prizes which became the permanent property of any crew which could win them three times in succession. By this means the Gold Cup for eights, the *pièce de résistance* of the regatta, became the property of the Thames Club in 1848. The regatta, says Woodgate, shorn of its chief glory, lasted for only one more year.

The Thames Club expired at about the same time and many small clubs diluted the rowing talent of the metropolis for the next few years. The best of these were the Argonauts, who absorbed, among others, the Wandle, Thames, St George's, Meteor and Petrel clubs, though they were still numerically small, and Tideway rowing generally deteriorated between 1835 and 1855. The reasons for this are not hard to find. With most oarsmen working in the City and with the lack of quick rail travel to up-river stretches, much of the rowing at that time was carried on between Westminster and Wandsworth, with frequent excursions down to Greenwich. With the appearance of regular passenger steamers to cope with the needs of a new and expanding breed of commuters, however, the Tideway became churned up, and with more bridges being built all the time, rowing from Westminster ceased to be the pleasant sport it had been.

Another reflection on the condition of the lower reaches of the Thames was the comment of a member of Leander who was quoted in 1857 as saying, 'The river for some miles below Putney is the largest navigable sewer in the world.'

It was interference from traffic between Westminster and Putney, over which the Boat Race had been held since 1836, which led to the race being moved to its present course between Putney and Mortlake in 1845.

The old Thames Regatta of the 1840s was also held on part of this course, between Chiswick Eyot and Putney Bridge. Built in 1729 and only the second bridge to be constructed over the Tideway, the old Putney Bridge was, until replaced in 1884–86, a wooden affair of numerous buttresses which made navigation difficult and at times extremely hazardous. At the same time, it had the advantage of restricting commercial and other traffic on the river, so that the reaches above it were more suitable for rowing.

In 1854, a new Thames regatta called the National was founded. It was, however, mainly for professional watermen, though in its last year it introduced amateur prizes as well as the usual bonuses for professionals. It was supported by the Thames Subscription Club, which was not a rowing club but had been established to aid poor watermen and to foster rowing generally. The National died with the club in 1866.

The London Rowing Club was founded in 1856 and transformed metropolitan rowing: Woodgate wrote that it did more to raise the standard of amateur rowing than anything else up to that time. It became a major force to challenge the Universities and also encouraged the formation of other clubs, with Kingston being the first to follow in 1858.

The establishment of London RC, and the eventual building of a club boathouse at Putney, were major developments at a time when all clubs were based on hired premises, and virtually ensured that London would not fade away after a few years. By now, also, there was a regular train service from Waterloo to Putney.

Early rowing successes secured London an immediate reputation. Frank Playford, who had won the Grand in the Thames Club eight, became London's first Captain. Among other founder members were Playford's brother Herbert, who had won the Diamond Sculls at Henley in 1854 as a member of the Wandle Club and later represented the Argonauts, and Josias Nottidge, also a member of Wandle and Argonaut. Nottidge had won the Silver Goblets in 1855 with the outstanding sculler of the day, Alexander Casamajor, winner of the Diamonds in 1855 in Argonaut colours and at the time of London's foundation holder of the Wingfield Sculls.

These and others with proven track records joined London in 1856 but the new club was formed too late for it to compete at Henley 1856.

The following year, London won the Grand and the Stewards' and Casamajor again won the Diamonds, beating another London sculler, James Paine.

Tideway rowing had arrived. London had given notice to the university oarsmen that Henley was no longer to be their preserve and, encouraged by London's successes, other clubs began to spring up: Kingston in 1858, Twickenham and the City of London RC in 1860, Molesey in 1866, Vesta in 1870, Ibis in 1871, and Kensington in 1872. Against this trend to move up-river, Curlew was founded in 1866 at Greenwich, where it remains to this day.

Thames Royal National Regatta, circa 1854,
showing the old Putney Aqueduct in the background

PART ONE
1860–1918

1 The New Metropolis

By the end of the 1860 season, London had won the Diamonds three times, the Grand, Stewards' (rowing over in 1858), and the Goblets twice, and the Wyfold Cup once. Casamajor, virtually unbeatable in a sculling boat, remained the holder of the Wingfields, nobody having challenged him since 1855.

Against this sort of competition, the 1860 founders of the City of London Rowing Club can have had no illusions but they did not set out in opposition to London, though it may well be that the club's formation arose out of an unseemly and much publicised scandal at London which was accompanied by typical Victorian posturing and recrimination. At all events, it involved someone who was to become one of the founders of the City of London RC.

In 1858, Frederick Catty failed to turn up to row in the London Grand eight at Henley, apparently without sending any explanation. Josias Nottidge, the inspiration behind the founding of London was roped in as a last minute substitute, and tow-path gossip, upon which as now the press eagerly seized, implied that Catty had been deliberately kept away because Nottidge was the better oar. Nottidge denied this, saying that he had been so unwell on the morning of the race that he had almost fainted in a Henley chemist's shop. Catty's explanation was that his employers would not let him row at Henley, but this was not well received and a motion to expel him from the club was narrowly defeated, mainly to preserve his honour. Rumours and allegations persisted until the club's victory in the Grand the following year.

Catty, of course, had by then withdrawn from the scene with as much dignity as he could muster. It is therefore interesting to speculate about his appearance in 1861 as the first captain of the City of London RC. Whether it was out of pique because of his treatment by London, or from friendship with some of the other founders, or from a desire to form a club with less competitive aims, it is now impossible to say. No mention of his London connection is made anywhere in the records of the new club.

He was certainly a dominant figure in the early days of the club, the earliest minutes of which are headed 'City of London Rowing Club. Founded 1860', though the earliest recorded meeting is dated January, 1861. The aims of the club were not as competitive or as clearly and eloquently defined as London's. The original rules show the objects to have been 'organised pleasure or exercise rowing'. 'The rowing train will leave Waterloo at 6.35 pm and the crews will be formed at 7.0, Saturdays excepting, when the Captain will decide the time and give notice of the same in the Club room. The Club days throughout the season will be Wednesday and Saturday . . . The only part of the uniform required of members shall consist of a white straw hat and the Club ribbon.' The ribbon is not described.

No big names in the Tideway rowing world followed Catty and the club's aims were modest. The first members were chiefly clerks and salesmen in the rag trade, the big City drapery warehouses in and around Fore Street and St Paul's Churchyard. The club boated from Simmons' Boat House at Putney, which was on the site now occupied by Chas Newens Marine. The club also hired a room during the season at the Red Lion Hotel by Putney Bridge.

After two recorded meetings in 1861 there is a break in the records until February 1862, when at another meeting the name of the club was changed to 'The Thames Rowing Club', Frank Playford, the only traceable member of the old Thames Club of the 1840s, having been approached for permission to assume this title. Playford was thereafter always invited as an honoured guest to the Thames Annual Dinner, which he invariably attended.

By 1863 the Club began to feel the need for its own premises and a special general meeting discussed sanctioning expenditure to find out the cost of building a clubhouse. Catty, still Captain, proposed that the cost should be borne by the promoters of the scheme but he was overwhelmingly defeated and promptly tendered his resignation and withdrew, refusing to change his mind after being asked to do so by the Committee. Various schemes were put forward and efforts were made to raise cash for the building – a 'Dramatic Entertainment' at the St James's Theatre produced £49 6s 5d – but the project disappears without comment from the minutes. Some years were to elapse before a new plan was put forward.

The Club was also beginning to show some interest in competitive rowing, though the constitution remained the same. Perhaps the proximity of London RC and Leander – in 1860 the latter had moved to Putney and was based on the Star and Garter – must have encouraged thoughts of competition and in 1863 Thames held some races for outrigged pairs and fours with coxswain. In July that year the Committee accepted a challenge from the Excelsior Boat Club of Greenwich 'to row a friendly four–oar match in such boats and for such a distance as the members of the Thames Rowing Club wish, on the understanding that the return match take place early next year at Greenwich.' The race eventually took place on 28 May 1864, from Putney to Chiswick Eyot. Thames hired a cutter, or racing four, for the event but the crew were light and Excelsior beat them by 6 lengths, though Thames had their revenge the following year, putting on a heavier, stronger crew to win comfortably and record the first victory by a Thames Rowing Club crew.

In 1864, a committee of Metropolitan Rowing Clubs was formed, primarily to promote an annual Procession of Boats on the Tideway as a 'shewing of the flag' by the rowing clubs along its banks at the opening of the season in March. The following February, Charles Dickens Jnr, the writer's son, organised a meeting of clubs between Teddington and Greenwich to try to arrange that they all opened their season on the same day. The committee also discussed other rowing matters, and it was Dickens who sowed the seeds which eventually grew into a new and important Tideway regatta.

Dickens and Herbert Playford started the process in 1865 by introducing a race for junior eights (which in those days referred to status and not to age, as now) and a race for pairs that summer. Thames, having bought the first eight it ever possessed, at a cost of £12, for the opening of the season, competed in the new event for eights, but lost the final to London RC, the first occasion on which the two clubs had met on the river. The same year Thames also made its first appearance at an up-river regatta, competing unsuccessfully in the junior fours at Walton.

In April 1866, the Metropolitan Rowing Clubs Committee issued a circular deploring the lack of a regatta 'of real importance and national interest in the Metropolis', stating that the Committee considered the time had come for the founding of 'a really grand National Regatta, which it is expected will prove a great attraction to all rowing men.' The result was the introduction that summer of the Metropolitan Amateur Regatta, a direct consequence of Dickens's and Playford's efforts.

Woodgate wrote that:

> its founders expected it to eclipse Henley by dint of offers of more valuable prizes, but it never took the fancy of the University element, and for want of the wider-spread competition

> which strong entries from the UBCs would have produced, it never attained the prestige of Henley. Still the honours of winning eights, fours, pairs, or sculls at it rank, in amateur estimation, second only to Henley.

This no longer holds true today but there is no doubt that it was so in the heyday of the regatta.

A disadvantage from the outset was the perennial one of finance. Writing in 1886, Woodgate pointed out that there are always oarsmen who prefer to be leaders in small clubs than play second fiddle in first-class clubs, and at the time of the founding of the Met in 1866 there were still a number of these small clubs on the Thames. To satisfy them, the Metropolitan eights and pairs for what Woodgate called the 'local second-raters' were established. But as the only large and well-established club, London was soon providing most of the funds. London formed a committee to manage the regatta but it was not until 1900 that the regatta became financially stable.

In 1866, Thames, as one of the smaller clubs, could not hope to do battle with London for the major honours and settled for the Metropolitan Eights (the junior event) and the pairs for 'local second-raters'. At the regatta, held in August, London duly won the Champion Eights and the fours, but Thames proved that, if still only among the second-raters, it was at least the best of them, winning the junior eights with a good crew which included J.E. Catty, brother of F.B. He also won the Metropolitan pairs with T.G. Radmall. These two events were the first ever won by the Club at an open regatta.

At the end of the year the Club moved into new quarters in a recently erected boathouse belonging to Styles of Isleworth, whose manager at Putney was William East. East's son, W.G. (Bill) East, became the English professional sculling champion in 1891 and in 1906 he was appointed Bargemaster to Edward VII. He became a well-known coach of amateur scullers, many of them Thames men, and in his later years he was landlord of various pubs, including the Three Pigeons at Richmond. In this venture he was set up by the Earl of Iveagh, who, as the Hon. Rupert Guinness, had been coached by East to win the Diamond Sculls in 1895 and 1896. The boat in which he did so still hangs on the balcony of the Thames clubhouse. Iveagh joined Thames in order to have a London base from which he could train under East, though he competed at Henley in Leander colours. He became President of Thames in 1911 and remained in that office until his death in 1967.

Tom Radmall became Captain of Thames in 1867 but the Club seems to have had no further successes until J.E. Catty took over in 1869. Among those elected in this year were G.H. Vize and W.H. Eyre, and with their appearance begins the first golden era of Thames's rowing.

Eyre's introduction to the Club came through one of the Club's other activities. During the 1860s Thames became involved in various ventures off the river and the minutes of the time were concerned as much with the various 'Dramatic Entertainments' that the Club staged as with its rowing activities. There was also a swimming meeting in 1866 but one activity that was to have considerable influence outside the Club's immediate circle was cross-country running. The Club oarsmen had realised the value of running as part of their training during the close season and this was encouraged from the earliest days.

Modern track and field athletics are generally traced back to the Exeter College sports of 1850. However, there were hurdle races at Eton before that, but these were closed events, as was the Crick run at Rugby School, a tough cross-country race which is described in *Tom Brown's Schooldays* and dates from 1837. However, a major chapter in athletics history begins in 1863 when England's first open amateur meeting was organised by the West London Rowing Club, whose leading light was W.L. Slater, of whom we shall hear more. The starting date for open cross-country running is given as 1866, when Thames RC held its first annual races. The Club's athletic activities eventually blossomed into the Thames Hare and Hounds, whose own foundation as the first cross-country club dates from November 1867. The Amateur Athletics Association, founded in 1880, had its origin in the Thames Hare and Hounds.

Other running clubs were formed soon after the Hare and Hounds. The Blackheath Harriers (1869) also owed something to a Thames member, F.H. Reed, who became the Harriers' honorary secretary in April 1870 and remained one of their leading lights for many years.

Another Thames member, Walter Rye, one of the founders of the Thames Hare and Hounds, described the first Thames RC run on Wimbledon Common:

> The arrangements were primitive in the extreme, and indeed the whole affair was treated more as a joke than anything else. The race was run in the dark over about two and a quarter miles of the roughest and boggiest part of the Common . . .
>
> Still, there were a dozen starters and the affair being the first cross-country steeplechase (not being at a school) that had ever taken place, attracted much attention in the athletic world. The next race was made an open event and attracted twenty-four starters. Considerable interest was felt in this race, from the fact that two or three old public schoolboys took part in it . . . but, as at most other sports, the native Cockney proved equal to the occasion, and early training did not have the effect of showing any superiority in the old boys over the Londoners.

The fourth annual sports of Thames RC, in March 1869, were held in Putney Park, on a cold and stormy day, with a fall of snow which did little to encourage the spectators to stay. The Thames Handicap Steeplechase was over two miles with twenty hurdles and six times over a water jump that was so stiff that the eight or so starters splashed into the waters, several taking a three-foot dip each time.

Only one more meeting was held after this. The minutes reporting the event originally included the phrase 'and the meeting a success', but, ominously, this was crossed out. This and the previous meeting had both incurred financial loss. So that was the end of the Thames Athletic Sports but they had served their purpose, and it was through the Thames Hare and Hounds that 'Piggy' Eyre was introduced to Thames RC, his proposer being Walter Rye. They were both studying law and later became partners in a firm of solicitors.

Eyre recorded his early years with Thames in his inimitable fashion, in R.C. Lehmann's *The Complete Oarsman* in 1908:

> I was then tremendously hot on athletics in general, going in for boxing, swimming, rugby football, and cross-country running with the Thames Hare and Hounds . . .
>
> This brought me in touch with a small but intensely enthusiastic set of amateur swimmers, boxers, etc., of whom W.L. Slater, known as 'Micky', then of the West London Rowing Club, and G.H. Vize, afterwards heavyweight champion in 1878, and for many years President of the Amateur Boxing Association, were the ruling spirits.
>
> Vize was then considered the best amateur swimmer in England, and I have no doubt he was so, though there was no such thing as a championship. He joined Thames at the same time as I did, and we both went in for the (to us) new sport heart and soul.
>
> In those days the professionals of all sorts used to train very hard indeed, and we were full of the stories and traditions of various 'pros' in the different branches mentioned. But Slater was the master spirit. He was the son of a Yorkshire sporting squire, who married very late in life, after running through a fortune at all sorts of sport . . . He had brought his son up to be a rare hard one, and full of enthusiasm for sport and struggle.

Slater did not immediately join Thames with Vize and Eyre but it is not difficult to imagine the impact of the arrival on the Thames scene of two such enthusiastic extroverts, who wasted no time in trying to impress their training ideas, derived from assorted pros and from Micky Slater, on the Club oarsmen. Eyre always maintained that his hardest race was one of his first. I have in front of me as I write a letter he wrote to my father in 1936, to which he added an account of this race as a postscript:

> I remember myself at the end . . . of the hardest race I ever rowed shutting my eyes and spurting as hard as I could (I was stroke) for the last dozen or so strokes. I nearly fell out of the boat I was so done – it was the Thames trial eights for the Metropolitan junior eights, a year before we first went to Henley . . . The two eights were never clear and we were always behind till the last, say, 10 yards.
>
> We were steered by one Tom Radmall, a fine oar and coach but a fearful bully – he bullied me about my stroking all the way, but he won us the race by it . . . We were ¼ length behind close to the finish when Tom yelled at me, 'Now your hardest row – you have not rowed a d—d stroke all the way!' This roused me to shut my eyes and do all I could, longing to hear 'Easy all!' When it did come, I gasped out to Tom, 'How much did they beat us by?' When he replied, 'Why, you d—d young fool, you've won!' After which he bullied me all the way home about my rowing . . .

George Vize was in this crew and the Thames minutes recorded that the race was considered one of the finest ever rowed on the river, and both winners and losers were awarded 'pewters'.

Such men as Tom Radmall were ideally suited to the temperament of Vize and Eyre, and it was a happy accident of time and fate that drew them together, as was the election of J.E. Catty as Captain the year that these two joined the Club. Catty coached the eight which won the Metropolitan eights later that year. In the same letter from which I have quoted, Eyre described Catty as the best captain and coach he ever served under.

Vize and Eyre were also in a four that won the junior event at Walton in 1869 and Eyre commented that there was as much jubilation in the Club as if they had won the Grand. Nevertheless, the newcomers had trouble persuading the Thames authorities to back them. They had their eyes on the Wyfold Cup at Henley in 1870, but this was regarded by the Club officers as being beyond their legitimate aspirations, but at that moment Micky Slater turned up and, with another West London oarsman, A.J. Lowe, they decided to have a go. Piggy Eyre said that, because the Thames officials would not back them, they rowed from the boathouse of Harry Salter at the Feathers, Wandsworth, a well-known waterman's pub and training place at the mouth of the Wandle. All through the winter, they went out whenever they could as soon as it was light enough, about 6 am, doing very long rows in a heavy boat, and towards the end of March they began regular training for Henley. Piggy wrote:

> We never paddled easily at all. Having little time to spare we used to get into the boat and row hard at a slow stroke up to Putney Bridge. Then we turned round and pegged away down to the West London Railway Bridge, a little over 1¾ miles, as hard as we could lick, turned round, and came back at a hard slow stroke. It did not run to shower baths there, but we used either to have a dive in 'the Cut', the barge entrance to the Wandle, or in the Thames itself at low water (when it was beautifully clear) or have buckets of water thrown over us, rub down, snatch a hasty breakfast, and bustle up to town.
>
> When the day's work was over, we repaired again to the Feathers. If Micky came down early enough, which was very seldom indeed, we went out again in the dark, and again rowed the distance hard, or sometimes down to Chelsea and back.
>
> After [supper] we invariably did a very hard walk together of between four and six miles at top pace, so as to harden the muscles of our

> legs. If Micky did not come down in time for a row, we would do an extra hard walk and not infrequently finish up with a run of about a mile or so . . . We had boxing, too, two or three nights week, a good deal of that, also, in training at Putney in after years . . . On Saturdays, we used to row to Richmond, or, if the tide was flood, down to Westminster and back; and on Sundays we always did a lot of sculling together, there being in those days a sort of unwritten law against rowing in a four on a Sunday.

Their training was so successful that they gained their first objective and were entered for the Wyfold Cup in 1870, still a coxed event. They were steered by a boy, J. Shearman, a nephew of the Catty's.

In those days, the Henley course ran from a starting point on the Bucks side of Temple Island, past a bend at Fawley, to just below Henley Bridge. The sharp bend just above the finish of the present course, above Poplar Point, gave a great advantage to the Berks crew, often a decisive one. It was certainly a sporting course, the source of much controversy until it was altered in 1886, and afterwards, too, since one lot of problems had only been replaced by others. Only when the present course was finally established in 1924 were most of the critics mollified.

Thames, in 1870, did not, it would seem, need any help from the course. The final was between the holders, Oscillators Club from Surbiton, Thames, and the Oxford Etonians. The *Rowing Almanack* says, 'The race was a pretty hollow affair, the Thames crew winning as they pleased from first to last.' The margin was 3 lengths.

After this win, the four made their peace with the Thames authorities and in 1871, with Slater stroking in place of Lowe, they repeated their success, winning from Kingston by 1½ lengths. The Club was emboldened by these victories and in 1872 entered for both the Thames Cup and the Wyfold, winning both.

The success of the 1870 four had laid the foundation of a system of training which became traditional at Thames for the next fifteen years or so. By 1872, Eyre says, Slater's circumstances had changed. He was then able to come down to the Club every night and took the whole Club in hand on his own Spartan lines. Many years later, when chairman of a Thames annual dinner in the 1930s, Eyre summed up the attitude of the early members of the Club to their training: 'Never row slack; never paddle; always row hard at whatever rate you are going at. You will get stale before you are fit, and then once you are fit, you will stay fit.' It all sounds remarkably like what my generation used to call in the 1950s Porterism.

The 1872 Thames Cup crew, which contained, among others, Slater, Vize, and Eyre, included one newcomer who was to become as famous an oarsman and as notable a stroke as any of his contemporaries. This was Jimmie Hastie, who had joined the Club as a novice in 1871. In 1872 he rowed three in the eight and bow in the Wyfold four, which did not include Eyre that year.

Thames again won the Thames Cup in 1873, again at the expense of London, who finished well behind. The crew also carried off the Champion Eights at the Met a fortnight later, though the Club failed to win the Wyfold, losing to the Irishmen from Kingstown Harbour BC. But with such a run of Henley victories behind them, the Thames authorities began to raise their sights towards the ultimate target, the Grand Challenge Cup.

2 A Changing Scene

The 1870s must have been an exciting decade for rowing men. There were some significant technical developments during these years, though the first actually arose from the previous decade as a result of 'Guts' Woodgate's celebrated coxless four at Henley in 1868.

In 1867, Woodgate and other English competitors took part in two international regattas in Paris, held as part of the Paris Exhibition. Kingston and London, among others, took part, though Thames declined the invitation. Among the competitors were a four from the Western Club of St John, New Brunswick. Giving every appearance of being professional watermen, they won two events, but the significant thing was their boat, which carried no cox, being steered by the bowman using a pivoting lever on his foot rest. The advantage of this, at a time when all four-oared rowing in England was in coxed boats, was not lost on Woodgate, who had a reputation for ingenuity and invention, though he seems to have gone too far in Paris, being disqualified for fouling his opponent in the single sculls!

Woodgate entered a Brasenose four for the Stewards' and Visitors' at Henley the following year, announcing that they would race without a cox, but this was rejected by the Henley Stewards after a protest from University College, Oxford, who had also competed in Paris. Accordingly, Brasenose went to the start of the Stewards' with a cox, who jumped overboard immediately the race started, to the immense delight of the large crowd that had assembled to see the fun, and to the extreme danger of the cox, who was rescued only with difficulty. This was Fred Weatherley, later to write the words of the song *Danny Boy*, as well as other such classic favourites as *Roses of Picardy* and *The Boys of the Old Brigade*.

BNC, with Woodgate at three steering with his foot, won by a large distance, only to be instantly disqualified. The result, however, was that the Henley Stewards offered an event for coxless fours in 1869 for which, surprisingly, BNC did not enter, only two crews starting. The Stewards tried again in 1872 but only London entered. Nevertheless, in 1873 the Stewards' Cup was changed into a coxless event, the Visitors' and Wyfold following suit in 1874.

Sliding seats first appeared at Henley in 1872. Sliding of some sort had been already been practised by professionals and some amateurs by the simple expedients of either greasing or polishing the seat and wearing trousers reinforced with shiny leather, though as early as 1857 J.C. Babcock, of the Nassau Boat Club, New York, had produced a version of a sliding seat for his sculling boat. It was used for the first time by a rowing crew in May 1870, on the opening day of the Hudson Amateur Rowing Association at Pleasant Valley by the Nassau Boat Club, and the novelty was brought back to England by a crew of Tyne professionals who had been racing in America.

In June 1872, London raced the Atalanta Club of New York at Putney. Both crews used coxless fours but London, after experiments by F.S. Gulston, had adopted sliding seats and overwhelmed their opponents, who were on fixed seats. A few weeks later, London took their four and eight to Henley with slides and created a sensation during practice, with the result that many other crews adopted them at the last minute. London retained the Stewards' and won the Grand easily from Kingston, who were one of those to make the late change.

In 1873, both university crews used slides for the Boat Race, which Cambridge won in record time. Slides at that time had a movement of only eight or nine inches and it was not until 1885 that longer runners began to come into fashion, though by modern standards their movement of fifteen inches or so still seems ridiculously short. An exception to this rule was Ned Hanlan, the Toronto sculler who was world professional champion from 1880 to 1884. He used a nineteen-inch slide during his best years.

Swivel rowlocks appeared in 1876, again an import from America, but although scullers immediately adopted them, rowing coaches in England, though not in some parts of the Continent, were not convinced of their merits. Although it was many years before they began to come into favour in England, by 1879 they were not uncommon on the Thames. London, Kingston, and Twickenham were trying them at that time, while Avon RC were using them when they won the Thames Cup fours at the Met that year. Magdalen College tried them in 1892 but they were made of inferior metal and twisted. London were on swivels when they won the Stewards' in 1895 and 1896, but the Club later adopted Lowe swivels – a compromise version designed to combine the virtues of both the fixed pin and the swivel – and the real breakthrough did not occur until after the turn of the century.

In 1874, in the midst of all these developments, Thames felt strong enough to enter a crew for the Grand and a second eight for the Thames Cup, the decision being justified when, although the Club did not win the Grand, the second eight recorded the Club's third successive win in the Thames Cup.

Five of the previous year's crew, plus Piggy Eyre, had moved up to the Grand, and it would have been six had not George Vize dropped out through illness. He never rowed again. Eyre said that he imagined his heart had been affected by rowing, though his subsequent career belied this. He turned seriously to boxing, which he had learnt from Ned Donnelly, who produced many amateur champions. Vize was beaten in the amateur heavyweight championship in 1877 by R. Frost Smith, known as 'Bricky'. Not satisfied with this, he fought Smith again the same evening, only to lose again, but the following year he beat Smith to take the title, as well as the West London Boxing Club open championship.

Vize was one of the founders of the Amateur Boxing Association, and was its president for thirteen years. He started the Thames Boxing Club which met at the clubhouse at Putney. It continued to exist until after the First World War, when Steve Fairbairn wound it up because of the damage that was caused to oarsmen's hands. In its early days it was quite famous, professional boxers giving displays in the ring in the Big Room at the clubhouse. Among Thames members well known in the boxing world were Alfred ('Fatty') Allport, who also played rugby for England, Bruce Logan, Sidney Smith, and Karl Vernon ('The Bean').

Vize lost only one of thirteen races at Henley, winning the Thames Cup twice and the Wyfold three times, and his last-minute illness in 1874 must have been as much a disappointment to him as to the Grand eight and Stewards' four.

There were many facets to the extraordinary personality of this truly Victorian character. He was very good at keeping a crew happy, bubbling over with quips, and he used to amuse everybody by writing topical verses and parodies. Many stories were told about him, such as the occasion at Barnes and Mortlake Regatta when he found himself in a crowd gathered round some three-card-trick men, who, unknown to them, were being watched by some policemen getting ready to pounce on them. Vize, sizing up the situation, pushed a bystander into the policemen, who in turn fell into the crowd. The cardsharps left at some speed but the unfortunate onlooker had a hard time convincing the irate policemen of his innocence.

Once, after a Club dinner at the Star and Garter in the winter, Vize insisted on swimming fully clothed from just above Putney Bridge, to the ferry opposite the Club. The river was full of ice at the time.

Vize collected ancient coins but sold these in later life and turned to English pottery and china. Then he collected prehistoric implements, and this is why there is a small arrowhead in the corner of the large cartoon of him by Hassall that hangs in the Club.

Eyre has left a description of the training of the Grand crews of his time. Trial eights were formed at the beginning of April and did long, hard rows in heavy boats from Putney to Chiswick Eyot or Barnes Bridge and back every night at a slowish stroke, with emphasis on leg drive, swing, and the catch. There was a good deal of land work and running, either on Barnes Common or at the London Athletic Club track, and parties were made up for hard walks on Sundays. The heavy boats, Piggy said, hardened up the muscles, the coaches bullying and driving the men unmercifully. Not surprisingly, a lot of men dropped out but it sorted out the real racers and stayers from the weak ones.

The trials were usually over early in May and the eight made up, but the crew kept in the heavy boat until a month before Henley with long rows on Saturdays and the fours from the eight getting whatever practice they could. When they took to the racing boat, they increased the rate of striking but continued for another week to do a long row every evening. The 1878 crew, which Piggy thought the hardest trained of any, did three hard, fast rows from Mortlake to Putney on successive nights, having paddled up in two hard pieces:

> Hastie was really a man of phenomenal strength and vigour. He was so terribly nervous that he often made a hash of the early (or some other) part of a race, but in practice he never seemed to tire. And his great power enabled him to keep his stroke long and work like a horse, when everybody behind him was dead done and rolling from distress. These long fast rows, we thought, got the crew well together – and also got them over the stale stage. We always tried to get our men stale about three weeks before Henley, and these rows did it for us. But we never dropped a night's practice, or slackened the work, but just pegged away, the coach hounding us on – it really was awful – and, of course, rowing got ragged, and the fellows bad tempered – and sometimes we lost a man then, but very seldom.

Three days a week, after the outings, they used to run up the towpath to the Crab Tree, or to the Old Tree, rather more than a mile each way. Piggy said that Hastie and he did this every night. In the last fortnight before going to Henley, they rowed a 'course' every night – seven and a half minutes under the bank against the tide, as hard as they could go.

At Henley, they always rowed the full course, in either the eight or the four, sometimes in both, every day until the day before the race. There was always a three- or four-mile walk after the evening meal, generally up to the Five Horseshoes on Remenham Hill, then down through the wood singing – Piggy said they had a good quartet in those days – and back by the river.

Hastie and Eyre also competed in the Goblets from 1877 to 1881 and they practised in the pair whenever they could, sometimes having an early breakfast so that they could train before the other crews came down to the river.

An unwritten law which lasted until after the Second World War decreed that there was no rowing on Sundays. Instead, the Thames men did a Sunday walk which was invariable from 1874. Piggy said they would stroll in the morning after breakfast via Maidenhead Thicket to the Ray Mead by Boulter's Lock, where they would have lunch and 'some grand old ale' from stone bottles. After a short rest, they would race back to Henley – fair toe and heel walking, Piggy called it – as hard as they could go. In 1879 they ran all the way home – something like ten miles. They used to arrive in a great sweat, and have a bath (Piggy always going in for a plunge) and after a rub down, everybody felt fine. After Piggy's time, the walk was dropped but he thought it stopped the men getting lethargic on lazy Sundays.

Eyre thought that the 1874 crew would have been faster had Hastie and not Slater stroked. While Slater's stroke was regular and even and he always kept going to the end, with great power, doing an immense amount of work on his own oar, Piggy said that:

> Hastie did that too, and was more polished in every way, with a long swing and a very firm catch, and with a marvellous power of keeping his men at a very fast stroke, without their feeling bustled.
>
> I cannot express this properly; but we used to come on shore, thinking we had been rowing 38, when the clockers gave us 40 or 42. I think it was Hastie's wonderfully steady swing out and firm grip, and then the smooth recovery, that made it seem easy. There was not a fraction of a second wasted over any part of the movement. But he could not be relied on to finish as Micky could. He did not lack pluck. He proved that on several occasions by magnificent hard losing races, and one grand win on the post – but then he thought he had no chance, and was only going to make a good show. He rowed far best then. In ordinary races he so fretted and 'needled' while the race hung in the balance that he licked himself before the end: he would make one great effort, but could never make a second. It was sheer 'needle' and anxiety for the lead wore him out during the race. I was as big a funk as he was at the start (surely two such 'needlers' never rowed in a pair, before or since), but as I got really licked in body, the needle vanished, and I never worried over the last part of the course, except to long to leave off.

It is interesting to record these subjective comments along with those of contemporary observers. The famous Victorian coach, Rudie Lehmann, wrote:

> Mr Hastie had enormous power and perfect judgement, and no man ever knew better exactly how and when to crack an opposing crew.

Of Micky Slater, a memoir in the *Rowing Almanack* said:

> Of but middle height, he was gifted with great bodily strength and extraordinary powers of endurance, and though, owing probably to inefficient coaching in his early days, he was never a polished oar, he was an extremely effective one. He was also a sculler of the first class as regards racing, but never had time to practise the art properly or to acquire a really good style . . . It was Slater who, by his enthusiasm and energy and extraordinary power of influencing the younger men, did more than anyone else to raise the Club from a very inferior position in the boat racing world to that which it now occupies. Slater, though by no means an ideal stroke, rowed so evenly and resolutely that he was kept stroke of the Thames first crews for three years.

The 1874 Thames Grand eight were physically strong but not a big crew, averaging just under 11 stone, which in those days was not exceptionally light. However, they were trained to perfection and were extremely well together. In their heat, they drew the favourites, Jesus College, Cambridge, who were about 9 lb a man heavier. Seven of them were either Cambridge Blues or subsequently won Blues, with an eventual tally of fourteen Boat Race appearances between them, most of them victorious. They were technically superior to Thames and were stroked by 'Cabby' Rhodes, the winning Cambridge stroke of that and the previous year. Eyre thought that no stroke he had ever seen could beat Cabby for a sustained spurt – not even Hastie or the famous Oxford and Leander stroke of a later generation, C.W. Kent.

Jesus led Thames by 1½ lengths at Fawley and took Thames' water, but Thames held on. 'Their spurt dying out,' wrote Piggy, 'they sheered out for safety, but still washed our bowside till Phyllis Court wall, when we overlapped and got by them inch by inch round the bend.' Thames' condition told in the end. The crews were level with 200 yards to go and Thames got by to win by ½ length.

It was an auspicious start but it was all to no avail. In the final, with a tearing headwind right down the middle of the river, Thames drew the centre station and never saw Eton or London.

Thames were also out of luck with the Stewards' four, hitting the bank at Poplar Point in the final against London, who were at that time in the middle of a run of eight consecutive Stewards' wins – in fact, they lost the cup only once between 1868 and 1878, an unrivalled record.

Thames did at least come home with the Thames Cup once again, and that 1874 Henley saw the emergence of a new Thames personality in the form of Ayton Safford, who was to achieve a remarkable record as a cox, steering the Thames Grand eight at Henley for no fewer than twenty-six consecutive years from 1874 to 1899 inclusive, and again in 1901 and 1902. He also steered the Thames Cup eight for many years and was doubling up in 1874, thereby winning the Thames Cup on his first appearance.

After Henley in 1874, Thames met London again in the Champion Eights at the Met. London had substituted at six the Cambridge President, Charles Read, for F.L. Playford, then still a youngster but who eventually won nine Henley medals in an outstanding career. Kingston, with a crew full of Blues and who had also lost to London at Henley, also took part in this race. After a hard tussle, Thames came home ¾ length ahead of Kingston with London a further ¼ length behind, Thames once again drawing away in the last quarter through their superb condition. 'A glorious revenge that was,' said Piggy.

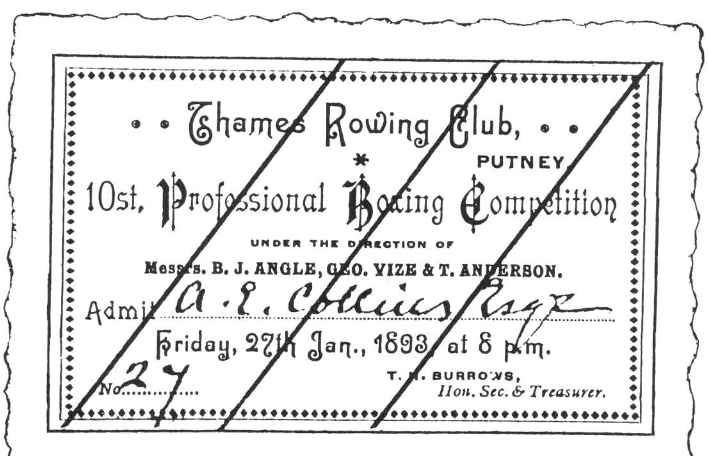

Admission ticket to the
Thames RC boxing competition, 1893

3 Grand Days

In 1875 Slater was unable to find time to row and Hastie stroked the Grand eight for the first time. But at Henley, against Leander and London, he went off far too slowly, 'through sheer funk' said Eyre, and Thames were beaten by Leander, with London third, though the Wyfold four easily won their final from London and Molesey.

It was a different story in 1876. Thames had a very powerful crew, though Mickey Slater, who had 'retired', had changed his mind when somebody had cracked up in training. There was also a youngster in the crew who, in Piggy's opinion, was as strong a middle-boat oar as ever rowed anywhere. This was Clement Chevallier Cream, who had been one of the previous year's winning Wyfold four and had won also won the Thames Cup in 1874. He was well over six feet tall and thin as a lath, though strong and with a very long reach. Piggy said he never saw him again after 1876 until he turned up at a Thames dinner in the early 1900s, a successful insurance 'swell', looking just the same, except for greying hair. He was then 54 years old and looked about 40, still thin and active looking. 'That comes of plain living and hard thinking', said Piggy, 'for he was one of the very few "intellectuals".' He sang a very deep bass in the quartet mentioned earlier and was especially good at old English madrigals and glees.

There was also an Irishman, Paddy Labat, in the crew. He had won a lot of races in Ireland, representing Dublin University Rowing Club, an alternative boat club of Trinity College, Dublin. With Thames in 1876, he competed both in the Grand and the Diamonds, losing the latter in the final to Frank Playford of London. He rowed in the winning Thames eight for the Champion Cup in the Met, but was then recruited by Gully Gulston, along with another of the Thames eight, Joe Howell, to row with London in the Philadelphia Centennial Regatta, at which they lost the fours on a disputed verdict after a series of blatant fouls by their American opponents, Beaverwyck, who would, in any case, have been classed as professionals by the English definition of the time.

Howell later returned to Thames, but Labat, staying with London, went on to win the Goblets with Gulston in 1879, at the expense of Hastie and Eyre. Labat also continued to represent Dublin University RC from time to time, winning the Wyfold with them in 1881. His last competitive appearance at Henley was with London in the Stewards', losing in the final to Thames. After this he became a well-known figure at Henley for many years, driving the umpire's launch, which he owned. He was steering the launch in which King George V and Queen Mary followed the final of the Grand in 1912.

Labat had the reputation of being a very astute judge of form and was one of the first to spot the emerging talent of Ned Hanlan, the Canadian professional, with whom he had become acquainted at the Philadelphia Centennial. Hanlan, relatively unknown until then, won on that occasion with a pair of sculls lent to him by Labat. Four years later he became professional sculling champion of the world.

In 1876, Thames beat London in their heat of the Grand and met a combined Brasenose and University College crew, rowing as Oxford University, and Jesus College, Cambridge. The Oxford Mixture, as Piggy called them, had previously disposed of Kingston and a Leander crew stroked by the redoubtable J.H.D. Goldie, and contained four Blues, including J.M. Boustead, whose son Guy in 1947 presented the Boustead Cup in memory of his father, to be rowed for in an annual race between Thames and London.

The Jesus crew were even more formidable. They were stroked once again by Cabby Rhodes with four other current Blues, as well as Charles Fairbairn, one of several Australian brothers, three of whom rowed at Cambridge, and who won his Blue in 1879. Piggy wrote of the final:

> In that race, Hastie went off in a way that, I think, fairly paralysed the other strokes for the moment. What the rate was I do not know, but we all took it up magically (of course by pure accident) and I never in my life, before or since, felt a boat jump under me like it. We cleared the 'Mixture' in less than two hundred yards, crossed them, and after a sharp tussle, got the Jesus water . . . Then Cabby came at us with a rush. The yells of the Cantabs to him to 'bump' us, I shall never forget. Hastie jerked his head towards Bucks, and Safford, losing his nerve, lugged his right string so hard that he ran us across Oxford again, and nearly fouled the bushes just above the Fawley Court boathouse. When we got straight, we buckled to, and came across gradually, got their water again a little before the corner, and won (easing down a bit, but mortal licked at the finish) by nearly two lengths. Oxford were a long way astern; but, as Jesus eased off, so did we. In the last hundred yards they came up with a rush, and overlapped the Cambridge men just on the post.

After this, the final of the Stewards' was something of an anticlimax. Thames were nearly a length ahead of London just below the Point and attempted to cross in front of them, but London spurted and a foul ensued. Thames were in the wrong and did not persevere.

> Lord, what an evening we had after it, wrote Piggy. I remember Hockin (the Jesus six) leaning back against a rose-bush, and dropping suddenly behind it . . . in the midst of an impromptu speech he was making. His shoes remained sticking out to represent him, but he 'accepted the situation' and went to sleep comfortably, subsequently rousing us all about 2 a.m. to let him into the house. . . . It makes one laugh to think of it now, and one does not win the G.C.C. every day.

Five of this crew rowed again in 1877 but they lost the final of the the Grand to London, who also beat Thames in the finals of the Stewards' and the Thames Cup, but honour was saved when Eyre and Hastie beat LeBlanc Smith and Playford to win the Goblets for the first time.

Micky Slater, whose last Henley this was, also had a go at the Diamonds but survived only one heat. From seven Henleys, he took six medals: three for the Wyfold, two for the Thames Cup, and one for the Grand. He did not lose interest after ending his active career, however, and put a considerable amount of time into coaching the Thames juniors, with whom, as in the rowing world in general, he was immensely popular.

A newcomer in the 1878 Grand eight was a 19-year-old raw-boned youth, G.H. Scales, who was 6ft 3in tall and very strong. He had weighed 12 st 10 lb at the time of the trial eights but the tremendous work done in training pulled him right down and when the inevitable stale stage arrived he said he could not continue and dropped out. The ruthless attitude towards training and any weakness inside the crews is summed up by a remark of Hastie's at the time. Told by someone that Scales would crack under the pressure, Hastie said, 'Well, better crack him up now than let him crack us all up in a race.'

It was learned afterwards that Scales lived with two maiden aunts, who thought an egg and a slice of toast was a nice breakfast or supper for a 'growing boy'. He would never eat with the crew in the evening, so no one had any idea that he was doing his work on utterly insufficient food.

'He was a most simple youth,' wrote Piggy Eyre, 'and no doubt the old ladies ruled him with a rod of iron.'

In his place they picked 'Pongo' Mapleton, aptly known as 'the Missing Link', but he failed to turn up at Henley, sending a telegram to say he would get the sack if he came – shades of Frederick Catty! So they were left with seven men, but as luck would have it, Scales had arranged to take his holidays at that time. He came down that morning to see the crew and he was immediately shoved into the boat for a short outing. He did well and after a square meal he did even better in the evening, so he stayed in the crew. A proper training diet made all the difference and he stood all the hard work.

Thames easily beat Kingston in their heat, to face Jesus once again in the final. Piggy recalled:

> It was this race that Hastie rowed 44 a minute without slackening, and keeping a fair length (as long as any of us could possibly row, I am certain) from the Island right up to Phyllis Court wall, by which time we had cleared the Jesus crew, and were able to slacken the pace a little bit, though we had to keep going all we knew for work to get home at all.
>
> We must have looked a pretty sight for form at the finish, but that race undoubtedly was won by nothing but sheer hard condition, plus the wonderful power of Hastie.

Writing to my father in 1934, Piggy said: 'There were seven winning Blues in the Jesus crew and as usual they were much heavier than we were. I remember I was so done I fell out of the boat in getting up and I shall never forget how wonderfully the cold water revived me.'

The 1879 Grand eight were noticeably weaker. The weather at Henley was appalling, and as it had been raining for a week or more the towpath was many inches deep in mud where it was not actually under water. In these conditions, the stations were critical and Thames had much the worst of it against Kingston, to whom they lost in their heat. Kingston, however, were unable to hold Jesus in the final, and the college at last recorded its first win in the Grand.

Eyre and Hastie, in three events, were also victims of the conditions in the Goblets, losing the final to Labat and Gulston. The Thames pair were nearly blown ashore and then ran into some poles which had been lashed in a line below Poplar Point in an effort to reduce the advantage of the Berks station, but all chance of victory had gone by then, anyway. In the Stewards' final, Thames were equally unlucky when they were involved in one of those incidents which were unfortunately becoming increasingly familiar to Henley competitors. Against Jesus and Lady Margaret, Thames were just beginning to draw away when they ran into a houseboat being towed by a steamer off Remenham and that was that. Jesus got up to win in the end, to bring London's long series of victories to a close.

In 1880 the Thames eight included a Blue for the first time. He was David Brown, who had rowed in the winning Oxford crew that year. Fifty years later, one of the greatest of all coaches, Steve Fairbairn, wrote of him:

> The finer an oarsman's movements, the more easy they will look . . . there was a very good Oxford oarsman, David Brown, who had the same dreamy-looking forward swing. One day I was standing on the bank at Henley, watching him rowing in a pair. He looked to be loafing (but) as he passed me, I saw his blade was driving terrifically hard. This oarsman had done some rowing with Jimmie Hastie, and he got this action from him.

In the 1880 Grand, Thames were as well trained as usual but they were beaten in their heat by Leander in a strong cross-headwind, Leander slipping right away under the shelter of the trees; but with Brown in the four, Thames at last got their name on the Stewards' Cup, beating Jesus and London easily in their heat and winning as they pleased against Molesey in the final.

1. The fourth annual Thames RC athletics meeting, Putney Park, March 1869

2. The Wyfold four, 1870—the first Thames winners at Henley: *left to right*: A. J. Lowe, W. H. Eyre, J. Shearman (cox), W. L. Slater, G. H. Vize

3. The Thames Cup eight, 1872—the first Thames winners of that event: W. G. Giles (bow), H. J. Smith, J. Hastie, W. Page, G. H. Vize, J. A. Cameron, W. H. Eyre, W. L. Slater (stroke), E. A. Safford (cox)

4. *above* George Vize, 1911

5. *above* 'Piggy' Eyre, 1911

Opposite
6. The Grand eight, 1876—the first Thames winners of that event: R. H. Labat (bow), J. Howell, G. C. Gordon, C. C. Cream, W. L. Slater, J. A. M. Robertson, W. H. Eyre, J. Hastie (stroke), E. A. Safford (cox)

7. The winners of the race with Hillsdale in 1882. *Left to right*: H. B. Tween (bow), H. J. Rust, J. Hastie, F. Canton (stroke)

8. Sketches of the Hillsdale Race, 1862

Eyre and Hastie finally buried the painful memories of the previous year, winning the Goblets, Molesey pushing Labat and Gulston into third place.

Thames lost the services of David Brown the following winter through some quarrel with Hastie and they had only a moderate crew for the Grand in 1881, losing to the ultimate winners, London, in their heat. Piggy wrote:

> That was about the hardest day's work I ever did at Henley in a broiling sun, with a neuralgic sick headache all day. It was neck and neck between us and London till past Fawley, when they got away and took our water. Hastie put on a splendid spurt at the White House and drove them out, and round the corner we caught them up gradually till I thought we were going to win. When straight for home, however, they gradually drew away again, and beat us not quite clear. I do not think I ever felt so bad in my life, as on getting out of that crew. Frank Playford, who had stroked London, was very bad too and we lay on the lockers together a good half hour after everyone else had left the boathouse.
>
> Later we had to row Cornell and London in the Stewards', and we were taken right back to the start after a foul between these two at Fawley, we being then a little behind. On the second attempt we were again behind for three parts of the way, but then got by them both, and, having the station, won by 2 lengths.
>
> After that Hastie and I had to turn out to row Leader and Payne, who had done nothing all day, but we really had the best of it, as they had lain about in the sun needling all day and rowed as dead as a nail. They had rowed us hard at two or three regattas previously, and had trained specially for the Goblets and nothing else, but whereas they had previously always led us at the start, that evening with two and (nearly) a half hard races out of us, we ran clean away from them and won anyhow. That again shows how condition will enable men to revive after fearful gruellings.

Eyre and Hastie went on to win the Goblets for a third time, despite fouling the bank a couple of times, but the Stewards' went to a fine Hertford College four which contained David Brown.

Piggy was still rowing in 1882 but he fell ill in the later stages of training and the four did not start. The eight lost to Exeter College but Piggy was back after Henley at the new Marlow Regatta, when the eight lost on a foul to Kingston, whose eight contained Steve Fairbairn, whose highly successful coaching methods were to revolutionise the sport in later years, and earn him the soubriquet of 'father of modern rowing'. Also in the Kingston boat was Gilbert Bourne, who had just won his first Blue as a freshman from Eton and was the author in the 1920s of *A Text-Book of Oarsmanship*, which was to become required reading for any serious oarsman. At this regatta, an American four from Hillsdale easily won the senior fours. We shall hear of them again.

Marlow was the end of Piggy Eyre's serious rowing career, though for many years afterwards his name cropped up at regattas and in scratch crews. Charles Morrell, a Thames member, in a letter to *The Times* in 1938, wrote:

> Piggy rowed his last race in the Thames Rowing Club regatta scratch eights in 1928 at the age of 80, and finished in grand style. As he got out of the boat on to the stool he said, 'That was a magnificent race and I enjoyed every moment of it. Did you see our spurt in the last 50 yards? We nearly caught them, didn't we?'

He died in 1939 at the age of 91. It is true to say that Piggy, Micky Slater, and George Vize between them set the standards of hard training and racing that were to become the hallmarks of all good Thames crews. During the period that Piggy was active, Thames won thirteen Henley trophies and he himself won nine: the Goblets three times, the Grand and Wyfold twice, and the Stewards' and Thames Cup once each. With his retirement, an era came to an end. To say he was an exceptional personality is an understatement. He was, and remains, the spirit of Thames Rowing Club, a true immortal. He is remembered in the Eyre Club, an alternative title under which Thames members sometimes row, and in the Piggy Club, a fund-raising body to help the Club's finances.

Eyre served Thames and the rowing community well. He was on the Committee of Management of Henley for many years until increasing deafness obliged him to resign, and he was on the Committee of the Amateur Rowing Association for a long period. All his life he remained a devoted supporter of the Club. In his old age, he wrote to my father: 'Seeing the practice of the crews over the Henley course I enjoy far more than the Regatta, as then I am in a blue funk about the Thames crew until they row, and am in a state of utter dejection after a defeat; till a possible Thames victory picks me up again . . .'

The encampment of the Thames Rowing Club
– a sketch made from a steam launch at Henley, 1878

4 Amateurs and Americans

By 1879 Thames had its own premises. The foundation stone of the present premises was laid by Mrs J.E. Catty on 22 March of that year, and the Club moved in at the beginning of the autumn. The area at the back was still open land, known as Guy's Fields, and was used mainly for cricket pitches. It was some years before they were built upon.

That year also saw the establishment of the Metropolitan Rowing Association. Up to this time there had been no governing body for rowing, and regattas wrote their own rules. A meeting of representatives of Oxford and Cambridge and the principal boat clubs in London had published some Laws of Boat Racing in 1849 which were adopted by Henley, but these dealt solely with the conduct of racing. Questions of eligibility to compete were left to individual regatta committees to decide.

In 1872, the presidents of the university boat clubs, the captains of Leander and London, the two Henley umpires, and several other well-known university and London rowing men met in Putney to produce a new set of rules, which differed mainly in the laws of fouling. These were adopted that year by Henley but with the appearance at Henley of American crews of uncertain amateur status, and with an increasing number of contests between English and overseas crews taking place in the 1870s, it was becoming necessary to be more explicit in defining the difference between an amateur and a professional.

Until then the question of an exact definition had been delicately avoided. To a Victorian sportsman amateur and gentleman were synonymous. Tradesmen, artisans, labourers, and watermen were not gentlemen and so, by definition, were not amateurs. It was not just a question of competing for money – many so-called 'gentlemen amateurs' had competed for wagers in the first half of the century, and as late as 1868 Woodgate had himself competed against a professional for a £10 prize: it was a matter of how a man earned his living. An amateur did not make a living out of his sport or physical labour, but the question that was beginning to require an urgent answer was: where should the line be drawn?

In 1867, the New Brunswick four, composed of shipwrights and woodcutters, were unquestionably not amateurs by English standards but had rowed against *bona fide* gentlemen amateur crews from England and elsewhere. Three years after the Paris regatta they rowed a Tyne crew of professionals for a large money prize in Canada, losing to the Tynesiders.

A more recent example had been the Philadelphia Centennial Regatta mentioned earlier where London had been fouled and beaten by the Beaverwyck crew. The London crew, according to *The Times*, had soon found that in America 'amateur' was an elastic term, and included coal-whippers, glass-blowers, hewers of wood, and drawers of water who would have been classed as professionals at Putney.

In April 1878, another meeting of distinguished oarsmen was called to discuss the problem, with Frank Playford as chairman, Jimmie Hastie attending as Captain of Thames. The definition they came up with was an unfortunate one in that it committed to writing what had only been inferred until then, barring anyone from competing as an amateur who had 'ever been employed in or about boats or in manual labour' or was a 'mechanic, artisan, or labourer'. This socially divisive rule, adopted a year later by Henley, was to split rowing in Britain into two camps for well over half a century, but at least the position was spelt out to the foreigners.

By this time, the bit was well between rowing men's teeth. Oxford, Cambridge, Leander, Thames, London, Royal Chester, Kingston, Twickenham, and Dublin University formed the Metropolitan Rowing Association; Molesey soon joined them and in 1882 the MRA changed its name to the Amateur Rowing Association.

The original chief purpose – the formation of crews to meet foreign and colonial crews – remained in the ARA's rules but was not acted upon until the 1908 Olympic Games Regatta was due to be held at Henley, which made it necessary for the ARA to select crews to take part. Instead, the ARA concerned itself primarily with becoming the governing body for the sport in the United Kingdom.

One of the first challenges that the ARA had to face, however, was that emanating from the Henley entry in 1882 of the Hillsdale crew from the United States. The previous year considerable controversy had arisen over the Cornell four that had entered for Henley. At that time the entries for overseas crews had to be made by 1 March, but on 25 May the Henley Secretary received a cable which read: 'Cornell University fours entry Visitors' and Stewards' delayed through misunderstanding. Will you accept now? Passage engaged for Saturday next.' The Committee of Management rejected this but the Cornell crew arrived and handed in a formal entry, asking the Henley Stewards to override the earlier decision. The press took the matter up and were strongly in favour of allowing Cornell to row, and a petition from the OUBC and twenty-one Oxford college boat clubs, as well as letters from the Captains of the First and Third Trinity Boat Clubs, London, Thames, and Kingston, eventually persuaded the Stewards, on the casting vote of the President, to allow Cornell to row for the Stewards', though not for the Visitors'.

Cornell were unhappy about not being allowed to compete in the Visitors' and before the regatta challenged Hertford to race them. This was accepted and the race took place the morning after the regatta, at which Hertford had won the Stewards' but had not met the Americans, who had lost to Thames. Jimmie Hastie, who had been rowing in the Thames four, acted as umpire for the challenge race, in which Cornell, already trailing, twice hit the bank before Fawley, Hertford paddling in comfortably ahead.

Cornell later went to Vienna Regatta, where the stroke apparently pretended to faint when his crew were well ahead. He was afterwards accused by his crew of having 'sold' the race and this was generally accepted.

The *Rowing Almanack*, commenting on the Henley entry, states:

> There was a great deal of discussion among rowing men as to the advisability of objecting to the Cornell crew whose members were suspected of not being *bona fide* amateurs, but the crews who entered against them preferred to take their chance of beating them rather than make any objection. This, however, is a matter which should not be left to the clubs themselves, as it is very difficult for persons in this country to procure evidence of the status of the individuals who compose a foreign crew, and in future it is to be hoped that the Henley Stewards, having with due deliberation promulgated laws, will see that they are carried out in their entirety. It is certainly not fitting that postmen, lumbermen, and men who get their living in or about boats should compete as amateurs at the chief regatta in England, and it is not just that the onus of objecting should be thrown upon English clubs, who, rather than throw difficulties in the way of foreign crews, have twice abstained from taking what might have proved fatal objections to their qualifications.

Nevertheless, in 1882 clubs were still having to make up their own minds on such matters and it was with the Cornell affair still fresh in their minds, together with the new ARA's policy and its definition of amateur status, that several crews refused to race against Hillsdale at Henley, at which the Americans intended to enter for the Stewards'. Hertford College had been prepared to race them but pressure from the ARA induced them to change their minds, and others followed suit, so the Americans' entry was withdrawn. They did compete at Marlow, though, beating an inferior Marlow crew with ease.

Since Hertford, the holders of the Stewards', would not race them, Hillsdale issued a challenge to Thames, the previous winners. Not surprisingly, in the circumstances, Thames refused and so Hillsdale issued a challenge to the ARA to produce a composite crew to race them in August, which was also rejected. The next day, however, the Secretary of the ARA received a telegram from Yale, one of three universities – the others being Columbia and Harvard – that the ARA had approached for their opinions on the status of the Hillsdale crew. Yale said that they considered them to be amateurs and would be prepared to race them themselves. The *Almanack* did not share the ARA's confidence in Yale's opinion:

> This was not very much in their favour, as, by all accounts, Yale is not more particular than other American clubs on the amateur question. It is now certain that the National Association of Amateur Oarsmen in America has been in the habit of giving its certificate of amateurship to men who were not amateurs according to the English definition. Two of the Cornell crew had such certificates, and it is well known now that one was an acrobat, and another a swivel rowlock and rigger maker, who were made members of the Cornell University in order that they might row in the crew.

The Yale message was communicated at once to the captains of the leading clubs, and Thames, their misgivings allayed by this, decided after all to accept the challenge, agreeing to row Hillsdale from Putney to Mortlake on 15 September 1882.

Such was the interest and importance attached to this encounter that the *Rowing Almanack* devoted six pages to an account of the crews' training and to the race. Four steamers followed the crews and spectators lined the banks. River traffic was not stopped and several barges were driving up during the race.

On a fine afternoon, Thames won the toss and took the Surrey station. The Americans, striking 49 to Thames's 41, took a slight lead but steered over towards Thames, who gave way. Hillsdale kept forcing Thames towards the bank and the oars overlapped. Eventually, Thames had to hold their course to avoid a barge and a bad foul ensued after about two minutes' rowing. The Americans were the first to get clear and soon after led by over a length, directly ahead of Thames, who pulled out and tried to pass Hillsdale on the Middlesex side off Craven Cottage, but the Americans moved out in front of them. With Thames rolling badly in their wash, they drew away to lead by 3½ lengths at Hammersmith Bridge.

However, the Americans were beginning to get short and ragged and Thames began to pull them back. Responding to the cheers of their supporters in the Club's steamer, Thames gained rapidly at the bottom of Chiswick Eyot. Once again, the Americans pulled over in front and gave Thames their wash, but at the top of the Eyot, Thames spurted and the Hillsdale crew's rowing became very ragged.

At Chiswick Steps, the Americans suddenly stopped, and Thames shot past. The American bowman threw part of his sliding seat away and Hillsdale set off in pursuit, but the race was now over. Thames passed the finishing post 6 or so lengths ahead in 20min 24sec.

The Times commented that the deliberate boring and fouling tactics adopted by the Hillsdale men characterised the match-rowing of the lowest class of professionals. Though the accident to the bowman's slide added to the discomfiture of the Hillsdale crew, reported *The Times* correspondent, no one who watched the race could say the result would have been otherwise if it had not happened, and had Thames finished astern of the Americans, they would undoubtedly have been awarded the race on appeal.

Thus Thames demonstrated the virtues of the 'gentleman amateur' against the American 'shamateurs' and at the same time protected the new fortress that was the ARA. We have come a long way since.

Thames Rowing Club in 1880

5 The Second Wave

Hastie made his tenth successive appearance at Henley in 1883 and ninth as stroke of the Grand eight. The Stewards' four, drawn from the eight, were the same crew that had raced Hillsdale, except for the stroke, Frank Canton, who had retired, J.A. Drake-Smith taking his place.

The eight were beaten in their heat by the holders, Exeter College, but it was a different story with the four. They drew Twickenham, who were in fact the Hertford four that had won the Stewards' for the previous two years and who contained three Blues, including David Brown. The fourth man, J. Lowndes, though never a Blue, won the Diamonds that year for the fifth consecutive time, a record which was not beaten until Stuart Mackenzie's run from 1957 to 1962.

Thames were just over a length behind Twickenham when the latter tried to cross in front to wash them. Drake-Smith immediately spurted and bumped them, Twickenham being disqualified. Fate also favoured Thames in the final against London, who fell victims to the insufficiently marshalled pleasure boats that teemed in disarray all over the river. London twice ran into skiffs and Thames were able to win as they liked for the Club's second victory in this event.

The year 1884 is notable in the Club's history, partly because for the first time three Cambridge Blues rowed for them, but more because one of these was Steve Fairbairn, then 22 years old, who in time became not only one of the most famous coaches in the annals of the sport, but also the architect of many great Thames successes. He had already rowed twice for Cambridge and was subsequently to do so twice again. He had won the Wyfold with Jesus in 1882. He rowed in the Grand for Kingston that year, and for Jesus in 1883.

One of the Blues who came to Thames with Steve in 1884 was Arthur Hutchinson, with whom he had won the Wyfold, and who became a lifelong friend. The third Blue, George Eyre, had previously stroked the Club's Thames Cup eight and became the first man to row for the Club before winning a Blue. He was proposed for the Club by Piggy Eyre, and, although there is nothing to confirm this, he was presumably a relative.

That year, Drake-Smith stroked the Grand eight, Hastie moving to five. Eyre was at two, Hutchinson four, and Fairbairn five. They drew the 'Old Enemy' again, as well as Royal Chester, in their heat but lost a hard race to London, with Royal Chester some lengths behind.

The final was a dramatic race. Twickenham were level with London at Phyllis Court, where London began to go away fast. David Brown, rowing seven for Twickenham, then suddenly collapsed, leaving London to finish alone.

Twickenham were involved in another extraordinary race with Thames in a heat of the Stewards'. The *Almanack* report reads:

> Thames, immediately after the start, came right across the river from the Bucks shore, apparently going for Twickenham, though the wit of such a manoeuvre was not obvious. Fortunately, Twickenham had just drawn clear when Thames dashed into their water astern of them. Warned from the bank, Thames next fetched out again and pegged away in the centre of the river, where they were well out of danger. Half-way over the course they were catching Twickenham fast, though in the worst water, and much cheering and counter-cheering prevailed on the bank, at what was a very pretty race. Suddenly Twickenham fetched right out from under the bank and rowed into Thames in the middle of the river.

> On getting clear, Twickenham paddled ahead, followed by Thames, the umpire (Mr Willan) deciding against the latter. Why he did so is not clear as, however injudicious the action of the Thames crew was in the early part of the race, yet Twickenham had no right whatever to leave their berth, and the best water under the bank, and commit a foul . . . The decision was generally considered by the boating men who saw it to be wrong, and no doubt it was so.

The *Almanack* goes on to say that Twickenham were deservedly punished in the final, where, barely recovered from their gruelling Grand final, they met Kingston, a fresh crew. Twickenham got clear and pushed across but then began to feel the effects of their earlier race.

> The appeals to Kingston to bump them suddenly became frantic, and the response of the Surbiton crew so determined that they gained fast and, overlapping Twickenham, took a shot at them but missed. Coming again, they pinned the latter in against the row of piles in the bay below Poplar Point, and bumped them, Twickenham of course being out of it, and Kingston paddling in first.

Whatever became of the 'gentlemen amateurs'?

No such problems faced the Thames Wyfold four, however, and with Hutch stroking and Steve at three, they were far too strong for their opponents in heat and final, winning both with ease.

Thames also competed in the International Regatta at Hamburg, a two-day event, racing in the eight and two fours drawn from it. The Wyfold four won by ¾ length on the first day from four German fours, and on the second day the other four beat the same crews by a similar margin. The eight also won, beating Germania, Hamburg, by 3 lengths. These wins were the first by Thames at a foreign regatta.

In 1885, Hutch and Steve were back in the Jesus eight, with whom they won the Grand, beating Thames in their heat and then Twickenham, whose third successive losing Grand final this was. Thames reached the final of the Stewards' when London became yet another victim of a spectator's boat, but the final proved to be an anticlimax, the race being all over when Thames broke a blade on the second stroke. Trinity Hall, who had beaten a high-rating Toronto Argonaut four in their heat, went on to beat Jesus easily.

This was Jimmie Hastie's last Henley. The last of the 'Old Brigade', the first wave of successful Thames oarsmen, his great strength and fitness enabled him, in his prime, to row a very fast stroke while keeping it long over the whole course. Jack Angle, who rowed many races with him, remarked that many a light stroke can row a good race with powerful men behind him, without necessarily doing much with his own blade, but Hastie could keep length and power with quite a moderate crew and at the same time do more work than any member of it – with the one exception of Piggy Eyre.

Hastie won over two hundred races on the river, and his Henley tally was the Goblets three times, Grand, Stewards', and Thames twice each, and Wyfold once. Woodgate said of the Goblets pair: 'Among pair oars, for uniform work, few of my time and later could surpass Eyre and Hastie of the Thames Rowing Club in the 'seventies. There were divers stronger and faster pairs at intervals, but none could show a more correct rendering of true pair–oared rowing than they.'

In *A Text-Book of Oarsmanship*, G.C. Bourne paid this tribute to Hastie: 'When I attempt to conjure up out of my memory an ideal oarsman . . . I think of the late Mr J. Hastie of the Thames Rowing Club, whose vigorous and perfectly balanced action, free from all affection of unnecessary ornament, has rarely been equalled and never surpassed.'

Unlike Vize, Slater, and Eyre, Hastie did not live to a ripe old age, dying, after a lingering illness, at the age of 48 in 1897. But like the other three, he is one of the Thames immortals.

The year also saw the end of the Old Course. Complaints about the unfairness of the course had reached such a pitch that it was decided to move the finish down to a point opposite the up-river end of Phyllis Court, roughly where it is now. The start, on the Bucks side of Temple Island, was moved down to keep the course the same length. There were two slight bends, one above the Island and the other at Fawley, but because the starting line was staggered, the stations were theoretically equal. In fact, the advantage moved towards the Bucks station, which was sheltered from the prevailing south-westerly 'bushes wind,' and over the next quarter of a century there were significantly more wins on Bucks than on Berks.

It was also decided to row only two boats in a race to reduce both fouling and the risk of hitting stray pleasure boats, and this meant holding the regatta over three days instead of two, from Wednesday to Friday.

Hutch was back in the Thames Grand eight in 1886, along with Reggie Coke, a Cambridge Blue who had been in the Leander eight in 1885. His life was to be tragically brief: he was drowned at sea in 1891. A Trinity Hall man who had rowed in their winning Stewards' four the previous year, he must have had mixed feelings when Thames drew his old college in the Grand. The Hall, nearing the crest of the wave that was to reach its highest point the following year, were just too good for Thames, withstanding a tremendous late surge from Jimmie Drake-Smith.

Steve Fairbairn was not in the eight but rowed in the Stewards' four with Hutch, with whom he also competed in the Goblets. The four drew the Berliner Ruder Club, the stern pair of which had been in a four beaten by Thames at Hamburg in 1884, and the winners of this race were expected to win the cup. The Germans came from behind to lead briefly after Remenham Rectory but Thames went right away from them after Fawley, to win easily by 3 lengths. The prophets were right. On the second day, Thames went on to beat Kingston, who stopped after a mile, and then turned the tables on Trinity Hall, winning by a length.

The Thames Wyfold four also won, being steered by F.W. Long, who at 9 st 3 lb is the lightest Thames oarsman to have won a Henley medal and the second lightest man to have won the event (C.N.M. Harrison of Trinity College, Oxford, won at 8 st 13 lb in 1896). The Thames Cup eight also reached their final for the third year running, and again lost.

The 1887 regatta is memorable for having seen one of the largest gatherings of royalty to have attended any sporting function. There were the kings of Denmark and the Hellenes, the Prince and Princess of Wales, three other princes and seven princesses, two dukes, and a host of other dignitaries. When the royal party went on the river, the *Rowing Almanack* reported that:

> The immense crowd of small craft, of every description, rendered it impossible to proceed with safety, except at a very slow pace.
> The presence of the Princess of Wales in a conspicuous place in the bows of the leading launch, with the bevy of young Princesses at her feet, to say nothing of the Kings and Princes around her, acted as a magnet on all the fair coxswains who held the tiller ropes of the small boats or else a current of loyalty ran so strong in the river that the boats could not help drifting down upon the Royal flotilla. The result was that of the three launches, the *Princess Beatrice* alone succeeded in taking up her moorings below the winning post before the race for the Silver Goblets was started and upon them. Immediately the race was finished, the *Princess Beatrice*, closely followed by the other launches . . . steamed slowly down the course, a real Royal progress amidst a scene of indescribable enthusiasm. A forest of oars 'tossed or uptilted', was to be seen the length and breadth of the river, handkerchiefs were vigorously waved from the houseboats, and, indeed, from all the fair visitors to the regatta . . . while cheers, loud and spontaneous, gave utterance to the loyal satisfaction the visit to the regatta evoked.

Satisfaction, that is, to all but the competitors and their supporters, since, unfortunately for them, the racing was in progress at the same time. The result was complete chaos and it is astonishing that there were not more collisions and disasters than there were. In the Goblets final, 'Ducker' McLean and his brother Hector ran into the throng at Phyllis Court when less than a length behind the leaders, while Guy Nickalls, in his first Diamonds final (he won the event five times), ran into the royal party and broke a scull, though he would probably have lost anyway.

This Henley, however, was also remarkable for seeing Trinity Hall's greatest triumphs. They carried off the Grand, Ladies', Thames, Stewards', and Visitors', a unique achievement in the regatta's history. It was the *annus mirabilis* of Cambridge rowing generally, 'Jumps' Gardner, of Emmanuel, later to row for Thames, winning the Diamonds, Pembroke the Wyfold, and a Third Trinity pair, stroked by another future Thames oarsman, S.D. Muttlebury, took the Goblets.

Against this unprecedented onslaught, Thames fought hard, the Grand eight coming closest to success. Steve and Hutch were back in the crew, together with an outstanding newcomer, F.E.C. Clark, known as 'The Long 'Un'. They had first to overcome a star-studded Oxford Etonian eight containing six Blues. They were stroked by Laurie Frere, who had stroked the Twickenham Grand eight in 1886 and was to stroke Oxford in 1888. Also among them was Guy Nickalls, whose twenty-three Henley wins in the course of a long career may never be be equalled.

It was a classic race, with Thames, not quite clear at Fawley, being gradually pegged back, but the Club just held on to win by ⅓ length in what was then an exceptionally fast time: 6min 56sec.

The final was another very fine contest and resulted in the narrowest verdict that had yet been given in a final of the Grand. Against Trinity Hall, Thames again took an early lead but the Hall were ½ length ahead at the first signal, then Thames closed up to within ⅓ length at Remenham Farm. Counter-attack followed counter-attack and the Hall were ⅔ length ahead at Fawley, going clear for a short time after that. By the Mile, a challenge by Thames had reduced the deficit to ⅔ length once again, and with a sustained effort all the way home they came back foot by foot, but just failed to get their bows in front before the post, losing by four feet, again in 6min 56sec. It was a race worthy of the royal occasion.

Trinity Hall had also defeated Thames in the Stewards' in a very similar race, though there was never more than ½ length in it either way. The margin was only 3 feet to the Hall at the bottom of Phyllis Court grounds, but at this point the Thames crew were completely rowed out and they stopped fifty yards short of the finishing post.

Later the same day, Hutch and Steve, who had rowed in the four, had to race a heat of the Goblets against Barclay and Muttlebury of Third Trinity, and yet again there was a fierce struggle, both crews rowing themselves to a standstill, Thames stopping first at Phyllis Court and their opponents drifting across the line. It must have been a tantalising Henley for the Club, having come close to winning three events, yet going away empty handed.

Thames mounted another strong challenge for the Grand in 1888, when another oarsman to make a distinguished reputation, W. Broughton, made his first appearance in Thames colours. He had rowed in the Thames Cup for Anglian and came in at five in the Thames Grand eight, a seat he was to hold for five Henleys. He drew high praise from Rudie Lehmann: 'Mr Broughton . . . was another fine example of what a No 5 ought to be – a really slashing oar of wonderful power.'

With Jimmie Drake-Smith stroking, Hutch once again at six and 'Long' Clark at seven, this was probably the best crew that Thames had boated up till then.

It was one of those wet Henleys when the weather never relents, and the only consolation was that the bad weather kept many of the tiresome pleasure boats off the river, though there were still enough to cause trouble.

The course, which had been piled for a few years in an attempt to keep the spectators' boats off the course, had been made narrower, but to little effect, boats often being three or four rows deep on the course side of the piles instead of outside them as people jostled for a view of the racing. The Stewards' report of this regatta said: 'In consequence of these obstructions, the winners of the Grand Challenge Cup had their success jeopardised and other competitors were impeded.'

Leander, just emerging from a long period in the doldrums, had a powerful crew for the Grand, and included Guy Nickalls, Stanley Muttlebury, Ducker McLean and Laurie Frere. They had disposed of London and then the holders, Trinity Hall, before facing Thames in the final, Thames having proved far too good for Kingston. Against Thames, Leander slowly drew ahead to lead by ½ length at Fawley, where Drake-Smith made his effort. The crews were level at the ¾ Mile and Thames drew away to lead by 1½ lengths approaching the finish. The race was as good as decided, but Thames were obstructed by a skiff opposite the press-stand, which was then just below the finish, three's rigger being damaged. Fortunately the crew quickly scrambled clear, to struggle over the line winners by ¾ length.

The Stewards' four lost in their heat but the Wyfold four came through their heats unscathed, Kingston failing to finish after hitting the piles twice in the second round. In the final, Thames beat London by a length, but the Thames Cup eight were beaten in the final for the fifth year running, being no match for Lady Margaret, who won the Ladies' with the same crew. They were never extended in either event and had at bow R.H. Forster, a future Captain of Thames who became one of the Tideway's best known figures. The Forster Cup in the Met is named after him, as are, with Steve Fairbairn, the Forster-Fairbairn Pairs at Cambridge.

There was only one change in the 1889 Thames Grand eight, who beat London before meeting Leander, the latter without Guy Nickalls but stroked by the Cambridge stroke, Jumps Gardner. This race followed the pattern of the previous year's final, though Thames were not impeded on this occasion and drew away to win by 1¾ lengths.

In the final, New College, by virtue of several spurts, led by ½ length at Fawley, but Thames were through at the Mile and retained the trophy by a length. This was Drake-Smith's fourth Henley win as stroke and Safford's fifth as cox.

Thames also won the Stewards', so they finished the decade with the major Henley eight-oared and four-oared trophies. Eleven Henley trophies had fallen to the Club between 1880 and 1889, two more than to London in the same period.

Thames also had many victories at open regattas and in 1889 won the Champion Cup for the fourth year in a row, and for the sixth time in the decade. Better still was the record in the senior fours at the Met, which had in 1889 been won by Thames nine times in ten years. The London Cup for scullers, then ranked only after the Diamonds and the Wingfields, had been won by Thames scullers in 1884, 1885, and 1888.

At the beginning of the last decade of the 19th century, Thames had firmly established themselves on at least an equal footing with their principal rivals and were on the crest of their second wave of success.

6 The Nineties

Steve Fairbairn's last serious appearance for Thames as an oarsman was in 1887 at Bedford Regatta, where he won the senior sculls, senior fours, and coxed pairs, rowing three times in each event, all on the same day. He started in the first race of the day and was virtually either rowing down to the start or racing back all day long, 'and I danced till 4 o'clock in the morning,' he wrote later, 'putting away over thirty miles more, as we danced very fast in those days.'

He was then nearly twenty-five, and shortly after this he returned to his native Australia where, except for a brief spell in England in 1897–8 when he competed none too seriously at Henley, he remained until he finally returned to England in 1904. It is for his coaching from 1905 of, first, Jesus College, then Thames, and ultimately London, that he is best remembered today.

Yet his influence on rowing in the 1880s at Cambridge and with Thames was incalculable. His views on rowing, which to many seemed so radical, were already half-formed by the time he went up to Cambridge in 1881. From the age of 15, in 1877, he had witnessed the conversion of his successful brothers on their return from Cambridge from the orthodox varsity style, which at first they tried to uphold, to the more natural methods in use at Melbourne, based on mileage and leg–work.

He was therefore hardly in a receptive state of mind as far as the coaching at Cambridge was concerned: 'I came to England prepared to find the varsity style not to perfection. I found London and Thames winning most of the races at Henley and rowing differently from the varsity style, much the same as the Melbourne crews, also Jesus College, Cambridge.'

He rowed for Cambridge as a freshman and said that that crew was the worst he had ever rowed in. He then rowed in the Jesus May boat in which all the old oars had gone except one: the Captain, Arthur Hutchinson. It is recorded that on the first outing in the eight, Steve said to the coach: 'Do you mind not talking to the crew? Your talking is upsetting their rowing.' The next day, Steve coached from the boat and took them on a long trip to Ely. They went Head of the River.

It was not an easy state of affairs, but it says a lot for Steve's personality that he won the support of many of his contemporaries. He rowed for Cambridge again in 1883, finding the coaching even more against the grain, and refused to row the following year, rowing instead for Thames at Henley. He returned again in 1885 and won the Grand with the Jesus May boat, the lightest crew ever to do so, but what was more important to Steve was that the Leander crew, who lost in a heat, contained the six best men from that year's Cambridge crew, and his methods were being proved on a tough battlefield.

From his freshman year he coached all his Jesus crews from the boat and they were Head of the River in the four years he rowed for them. He wrote in one of his books: 'I do not claim to have come to England and taught the English rowing, but finding the Jesus men were rowing differently from the other colleges, I carried on their ideas of leg-work and blade-work ... so I started with my two maxims: "get the crew to concentrate on working the oars" and "mileage makes champions".'

Besides having broken away from the orthodox university style, Steve lengthened the slides in the Jesus boat from eight inches to fourteen.

There was the usual outcry that accompanies all departures from the traditional, which Steve found surprising since London and Thames were successful with long slides at Henley at that time. After Jesus won the Grand in 1885 on long slides, both universities used them in 1886 and broke all records in training on the Isis and the Cam.

The essence of Fairbairnism, as it came to be called, was method rather than style. Steve emphasised the vital importance of allowing the subconscious mind to solve problems, realising that the subconscious mind knows better than the conscious what it should do in any given situation. This is very important when applied to skills, and Steve taught his oarsmen to think of the end product and not a pre-determined conscious pattern of movements. In this, and in his understanding of the psychological aspects of coaching, he was light years ahead of his contemporaries.

Steve's poem, *The Oarsman's Song*, printed at the beginning of this book, with its many evocative phrases – 'willowy sway', 'elastic spring', 'lazy float' and others – admirably conveys what he sought to inculcate, with considerable success, into his crews. One of his best known phrases, 'If you can't do it easy, you can't do it at all', encapsulates his whole philosophy. Above all, he taught his oarsmen to enjoy their rowing, win or lose.

Steve did not confine his coaching to Jesus, and the extent of his influence can be judged by the remarkable results at Henley in 1886 and 1887. Steve claimed that, in these two years, the winners of every race at Henley, with the sole exception of the London eight that won the Thames Cup in 1886, had been through his hands and were all rowing on the principles he taught. He did not claim all the credit.

> 'McKenna and Bristowe were mainly responsible for Trinity Hall's successes at Henley and Cambridge . . . I coached the Hall in '86 before the May Races and laid the foundation of leg-work and blade-work taught me by Jesus men, a style started by Joe Sadler.'

Sadler, the world professional sculling champion from 1874 to 1876, had coached the Jesus crews in the 1870s on blade-work and not on body form. These crews were outstandingly successful on the Cam and at Henley.

Reginald McKenna won the Grand and Stewards' with Trinity Hall, and joined Thames on the same day as Steve in April 1882. A Blue, as was Bristowe, he never rowed for Thames and the only references to him in the Thames minutes are the not uncommon ones of arrears of subscription (which he paid), which have rather more point than usual since he was to end a distinguished political career as Chancellor of the Exchequer in Asquith's government in the First World War, with the unenviable task of finding the money to pay for that holocaust.

Steve's influence was equally powerful at Thames, where he found a ready audience of men brought up in the school of Slater and Eyre. He learnt something in turn from Thames men, not least Jimmie Hastie, whom he quotes frequently in his writings. In the years he rowed with Thames, he coached, as usual, from the boat, and even after he had left for Australia, so missing the Grand wins of of 1888–89, his influence persisted, the captains of both these crews writing to him to say that it was all because of his work with Thames from 1884 to 1887 that these wins had come about.

In 1890, Steve's teaching was still bearing fruit. Not only were there men who had rowed with him at Thames, but there was still an influx of his friends from the Cam and elsewhere.

After the previous two years' successes, the Thames eight ought to have been close to winning again, but at Henley they lost to an exceptionally strong and fast London crew which went on to win the final. The Thames Stewards' four had their revenge later, being able to paddle in ahead of London, easing off, but they lost the final after being two lengths ahead of Brasenose at Fawley. The BNC stroke, C.W. Kent, spurted hard all the way home and the College went through, to win by ¾ length.

However, the Thames second eight, after several years as losing finalists, at last won the Thames Cup which the Club had not held since 1874.

A further influx of Cambridge men arrived in 1891 in the shape of two outstanding oarsmen, both Blues, S.D. Muttlebury and J.C. Gardner. 'Muttle' rowed five times for Cambridge, from 1886 to 1890, winning in all but the last year, and had won the Goblets three times with different partners, the most recent being Gardner in 1889. A close friend of Steve's, he was also a staunch believer in long slides and leg-drive, though he had been taught in the orthodox nursery of Eton, with whom he twice won the Ladies'. An enormously powerful heavyweight, he drew these lines from Rudie Lehmann:

> His blade sweeps through the water, as he swings his 13.10
> And pulls it all, and more than all, that brawny king of men.

When he died in 1932, many tributes were paid to him in *The Times*, among them this from R.P.P. Rowe:

> Muttlebury had a natural aptitude which amounted to genius for rowing, and, as he was not only massively large and full of courage, but Herculean in muscular strength, it was inevitable that he should be an outstanding exponent of oarsmanship. Added to this, he came to his prime when rowing was in a transitional stage, when the old methods of the straight back and the body catch, suited to the fixed seat and the short slide, had necessarily to be superceded by methods required by the long slide. I consider that long-slide rowing sprang suddenly to perfection in Muttlebury . . .
>
> He had the most charming 'good manners'. It was a trait natural to him which all must have noticed. Moreover, no friend of his can have failed to enjoy his quiet dry humour, with a spice of real wit. But with this, somewhat unusually, went a refusal to hurt.

The *Rowing Almanack* describes him as a giant among giants whose prowess and feats of strength had become legendary even in his own lifetime. On the Cam they used to tell how one day he took a brand new set of oars down to a bank tub and broke every one of them. He was to become for many years one of the mainstays of Thames.

'Jumps' Gardner had won the Diamonds in 1887 when Guy Nickalls hit the royal party, but Gardner had been leading at the time. He was a fine sculler and won the Wingfields in 1890 when his opponent was again Guy Nickalls, who thought him 'the finest I have seen of amateur [scullers]. He was quite the best stripped man I have ever seen, his muscles standing out like bars of steel all over his body.' He stroked Cambridge to Boat Race wins in 1888 and 1889, though he lost in 1890.

There were now four winning Cambridge Blues in the Grand eight, with Gardner stroking. Henley 1891 began with a gale blowing from the south-west, accompanied by some of the heaviest rain showers ever seen at Henley, summer returning only for the final day. However, the racing was magnificent and went a long way towards making amends.

The first heat of the Grand, the first race of the regatta, gave some idea of what was to come. Thames faced Leander, who were all Oxford Blues, six of them from that year's winning Boat Race crew and stroked by Kent. Their boat was something of a novelty, with the stern cut down to the size of that of a sculling boat and with a fin rudder, something like a Donoratico hull of the late 1950s. Lehmann says he never saw a faster boat but strangely nothing more is heard of it, so apparently the design did not catch on.

Leander, on Berks, had to row against the full force of the gale while Thames had some shelter from the Bucks station. Nevertheless, it was Leander who led by ¾ length at Fawley. Thames then came back and the lead changed hands several times. Thames were leading by a few feet a few strokes before the finish but Kent made one of his demon rushes to force a dead heat.

The re-row did not take place until the following day during a period of calm after the first storm. The crews were level at Remenham Rectory but Leander then drew ahead and, in fairer conditions, Thames had no answer, Leander going away to win by 2 lengths.

Leander went on to beat London in the final by a length after another tremendous race, setting a record time of 6min 51sec, which was not beaten until 1934, when the course had been changed to the present straight one, which is the same length. John Cooper, Secretary of the Regatta for thirty-seven years, thought the 1891 Leander crew was the strongest he ever saw. This year marked the revival of Leander rowing and they were to win the Grand twelve times in the next fifteen years, a performance unlikely to be equalled in view of the standard of modern competition.

Thames had, however, other strings to their bow, notably a fast Stewards' four, stroked by Gardner. Thames met Magdalen College, Oxford, with the Nickalls brothers, on the second day, Magdalen having beaten Brasenose by 2 feet. Thames gained a ¾ length lead by the top of the Island but then hit two posts and Magdalen were able to draw level, only for Thames to pull away again. However, Magdalen came across at the White House, having made a spurt, and the oars clashed, Thames getting the better of this and going away to win by 1¾ lengths. In the final, Percy Landale at two was up against his younger brother, Walter, also a Blue, rowing for Trinity Hall. Thames won easily but the Hall had their consolation prize when they won the Visitors' with the same crew.

The Goblets involved a series of close races, Hutch and Clark losing by a ½ length to Lord Ampthill and Guy Nickalls, while Gardner and Muttlebury failed by only a ¼ length against two Oxford Blues, Fletcher and Wilkinson. In the final, the latter were leading by ¾ length at Phyllis Court with both pairs seemingly rowed out when Nickalls put in a tremendous spurt and won by one foot.

After Henley, Thames recaptured the Champion Eights in the Met, London having won in 1890, and took the Thames Cup for fours for the tenth year in a row. The second eight won the senior event at Kingston, avenging their Henley defeat in the Thames Cup final by beating Molesey by ¼ length. They beat Molesey again at their own regatta, this time by 1 length, and when Molesey put Kent in to stroke at Reading it was to no avail, Thames winning by ½ length to take this event as well.

Thames were without Gardner, Hutchinson, and Landale in 1892. Drake-Smith went back to stroke and still had the powerful oars of Clark, Muttlebury, and Broughton behind him. Alfred Allport was a newcomer to the crew.

The weather at Henley was almost as bad as it had been the year before and once again produced inequality in the stations. It rained without intermission for the whole of the first day, then when it stopped early on the second day, a gale sprang up and blew straight down the course against the crews. On the third day it was even worse, the wind swinging across and blowing even more strongly, giving the boats on the Bucks station an immense advantage. Only three finals were won on Berks, one of these on a foul.

In their heat of the Grand, Thames had the race given to them after half a minute when London caught a substantial crab and they were never in with a chance thereafter, but the final was as good as lost when Thames drew Berks against Leander. With five of the previous year's record-breaking crew, Leander won by three lengths.

It was not a good Henley for Thames, Clark and Muttlebury putting themselves out of the Goblets by hitting a moored skiff, but the Club had better fortune in the post-Henley regattas, the Met proving to be unusually successful. The Champion Eights, Thames Cup fours, and the London Cup (won by W.H. Cumming for the fourth time) all came to Thames, as well as the Metropolitan pairs and the senior-junior fours.

Jimmie Drake-Smith retired at the end of the 1892 season after ten consecutive seasons in the Grand eight, all but two of these at stroke, during which period he won the Grand and Stewards' twice each. He had been Captain of the Club in 1887 and 1889. In 1893, his place at stroke was taken by L.H.K. Bushe-Fox, who had won the Thames Cup and the Ladies' in 1888 with Lady Margaret and had rowed in the Thames second eight and the Wyfold four in 1891 and 1892.

Another newcomer to the crew was A. Bogle. 'Bogie' was one of the more colourful characters to have rowed for Thames, and there have been many in the history of the Club. He had won the Thames Cup in 1892 with Jesus and was also a fine boxer, though much of his fighting was done outside the ring! He was well-known in his rowing days for his performances in the Fair after Henley. The police were always on the lookout for him as soon as it was known that he had finished racing and a message would come to the Club that 'we have got your Mr Bogle safely.'

Bogie remained one of the Club's great characters to the end of his days. In his old age he emerged from a bath at the Club through a cloud of steam, a plump Colonel Blimp, to find the boatman collecting chairs for the Big Room. Bogie asked what was going on and was told that there was to be a lecture by the Oxford Blue and coach, Dr Pat Mallam, on 'The Economy of Muscle'. 'Muscle! Muscle! They haven't got any muscle', he exclaimed.

French crews competed at Henley for the first time in 1893, though a sculler, G. McHenry, had competed for the Diamonds in the colours of the Cercle de l'Aviron, Paris the previous year. In 1893 he competed in Thames colours. SN Basse-Seine, with whom Thames were to establish close links in years to come, entered for the Grand and Stewards', drawing Thames in the Grand and in the second round of the Stewards', the latter event producing a *contretemps* which came near to being an international incident.

The previous October, Basse-Seine had beaten London by two lengths in Paris and their 1893 eight were reputed to be faster. In their Grand heat against Thames, they took a slight early lead but Thames were ½ length up at Fawley. The French stroke then mounted a series of spurts but his crew fell to pieces under the pressure and Thames crossed the line ¾ length ahead. In the next round Thames went out to London, who in turn lost to yet another fast Leander crew stroked by Kent.

The Stewards' race which caused so much fuss occurred on the second day. Basse-Seine having drawn a bye, Thames qualified to meet them by beating Brasenose, the latter stopping at the White House. Against Thames, the French led by a foot or two at the ¼ Mile when Thames steered out towards them, Basse-Seine giving way to such an extent that they ran into one of the piles. Before they could get clear, Thames were a length up. The French never recovered and were eventually beaten by two lengths.

The French claimed a foul, withdrawing this later after strong pressure from the Baron de Coubertin, the President of Basse-Seine, who later founded the modern Olympic movement, but the umpire reported Thames to the committee for 'unfair conduct'. This seems unfair in itself since similar things had been happening every year at Henley and one presumes that it was more because a foreign crew were involved than because of any particularly diabolical act by Thames.

Thames, summoned before the committee the next day, assured them that their deviation was not intentional and this was accepted, but the matter was taken up by the press. Some correspondents thought Thames's act disgraceful; others described the committee's action as 'disgusting'; but all felt the umpire had no right to bring the matter before the committee in the first place. A special meeting of the Club at Henley resolved that, should the regatta committee not clear the Thames four of unsportsmanlike behaviour, an apology from the umpires should be demanded, but in the event the four were exonerated by the Henley Stewards.

Despite the furore, the Stewards' four still had to row the final against Magdalen, but this proved to be something of an anticlimax. Though it was a hard-fought race, the college got home by ¾ length.

In the Diamonds, McHenry won his heat when his French opponent stopped at the ¾ Mile and then met another Thames sculler, Frank Beddington, the latter coming from behind to lead by one length at the Mile. McHenry stopped soon after and had to be lifted out of his boat, a victim, apparently, of the hot weather. Beddington went out in the next round.

Meanwhile, the Thames Cup eight had easily beaten Vesta, whose first Henley appearance this was. 'The Vesta crew', stated the *Almanack* somewhat patronisingly, 'struggled gamely to the finish.' The final against Eton Excelsior also resulted in an easy win for Thames, which no doubt mollified 'Fatty' Allport, who had been demoted from the Grand eight.

In 1894, the ARA issued new rules for regattas and boat-racing, which were immediately adopted by the Henley Stewards where applicable and they were in effect for the regatta that year, fortunately, as it turned out.

This year saw the return of Gardner as stroke of the Grand eight and Stewards' four. The old firm of Muttlebury (Captain of the Club this year), Broughton, and 'Long' Clark were still there, plus the addition of Joe Orford, a Cambridge Blue. They were a fast crew, defeating Trinity Hall in their heat, coming home very easily, although the verdict was ¼ length. Leander, stroked yet again by Kent, easily defeated London, to meet Thames in the final. There was little in it to the Mile, where the crews were level, but once again it was Kent who made the vital last spurt, Leander winning a fine race by ½ length.

McHenry did not go for the Diamonds that year and steered the Stewards' four, who were involved in another incident, though without any of the unfortunate repercussions of the previous year. In their opening heat against Leander, Thames were just ahead at ½ Mile when Leander ran into the inevitable pleasure skiff and badly twisted a rigger. The umpire, John Goldie, one of the ARA sub-committee that had drawn up the new rules, took advantage of these and ordered a re-row after the last race of the day. The new rule which he applied read: 'Every boat shall abide by its accidents; but if during a race a boat shall be interfered with by any outside boat, the umpire shall have the power, if he thinks fit, to re-start the boats according to his discretion, or to order them to row again on the same or another day.' Readers of these pages will have realised that this rule had been long overdue at Henley.

In the re-row, Leander were rowed out and eventually stopped opposite the grandstand, leaving Thames, who were almost as exhausted, to struggle over the line. Molesey went out to New College but in the final the latter were no match for Thames, who won easily by 1¾ lengths. Surprisingly, this proved to be Muttlebury's only Henley win in Thames colours.

The bow four of the Grand eight, with Bogle stroking, took the Wyfold, and the Hon. Rupert Guinness, a member of Thames but in Leander colours, made a notable début in the Diamonds. Guinness was deliberately 'washed' by Vivian Nickalls for much of the race, but he forced Nickalls out with a determined spurt and all but caught him, going down by only ¾ length. Guinness went on to win the event in the following two years, beating Guy Nickalls, the holder, who had already won the Diamonds five times, in the final in 1895, and then getting his revenge over Vivian Nickalls in 1896, sculling his opponent to a standstill in a heat.

This was Frank Clark's last season. Captain of the Club in 1892–93, he rowed in the Grand for eight seasons, winning both this event and the Stewards' twice each. Nearly 13 stone in weight, 'Long' Clark's high standard of oarsmanship placed him firmly in the ranks of the Tideway greats. He combined size, strength, skill and staying power, indispensible qualities in a first-class oarsman, and among his many regatta wins he could count six victories in the Champion Eights.

'Jumps' Gardner also retired from the Henley scene in 1894, though his name continued to appear in the records at lesser regattas for a year or two longer, so only Muttlebury and Broughton were left of the anchor men in 1895. Bogle was moved up to stroke the eight and the Stewards' four.

At Henley in 1895 a strong 'bushes' wind again heavily favoured the Bucks station and the majority of winning crews came from this side. The Grand was notable for an entry from Cornell University and for a very fine Eton eight stroked by Harcourt Gold, who later became Chairman of the Regatta and also of the ARA. He was knighted for services to rowing in 1949.

The racing was full of excitement but was marred by a notable fiasco: Leander drew the Americans in the Grand but were left standing at the start, having been paddling on with two and four, while seven and five were backing down, as the umpire said 'Go' despite their calling out 'No' when asked if they were ready. Cornell, on Bucks and sheltered from the strong cross-wind, were able to get off without difficulty. Kent, stroking Leander, had his hand up at the time and so made no effort to row, but the umpire allowed the race to continue and that was that, Leander's protest to the committee being disallowed.

In the previous race, Thames had lost to Eton. Trinity Hall rowed Cornell to a standstill in the next round and went on to beat New College in the final, but the real loser, because of the muddle in the first round, was Kent, who was deprived of his chance of a fifth win in succession at stroke.

Broughton and Muttlebury met the Nickalls brothers in the final of the Goblets, but the Thames pair hit several rowing boats which had, as usual, strayed onto the course and London finished alone. The Stewards offered to row the race again but Thames declined. The Wyfold four had also stopped in their heat after hitting a post, and with a very light Thames Cup eight losing their heat, it was not a good Henley for the Club.

Things were no better after Henley. Rupert Guinness, now in Thames colours, recorded the Club's only win in the Met, when he beat Guy and Vivian Nickalls, the Toronto sculler E.A. Thompson, and Harry Blackstaffe, the future Olympic champion, in a five-boat final for the London Cup.

Muttlebury had retired in 1896 and although Thames reached the final of the Grand again, they were lucky to do so and were no match for Leander.

The Stewards' four lost to London in the final and Thames crews generally were showing evidence of a decline, though the Club had an excellent post–Henley season. Rupert Guinness beat Vivian Nickalls to win the London Cup.

Guiness and his younger brother, Ernest, rowed in the Thames eight for the Champion Cup, losing to London, but the eight won at Walton, Kingston, Staines, and Molesey, while the Stewards' four also won at these regattas and also regained the senior fours at the Met. At this regatta, the name of J. Beresford, then of Kensington RC, appears on the roll of winners for the first time: he won the junior sculls.

A victory abroad was that of R.P. Croft, a former Trinity Hall man now in Thames colours. He won an international sculling race in France on the Marne at Nugent, beating François Boudin of the Société d'Encouragement by 1¼ lengths. This was the first race for the Coupe de Paris, for which McHenry competed unsuccessfully the following year. Boudin had rowed for 'Encou' in the 1896 Thames Cup final.

Despite these successes, all was not well with Thames rowing. Broughton and Bogle were not rowing in 1897 and at Henley no Thames crew survived the opening round. The scandal of the regatta was the acceptance of an entry for the Diamonds of a young American, Edward Hanlan Ten Eyck, who had been named in honour of the former professional world champion. The son of a professional oarsman and sculler, who coached him, he did all the wrong things at Henley, such as associating with professionals on an informal basis, and he was regarded with deep suspicion. The *Rowing Almanack* did not approve:

> Notwithstanding the fact that information as to Ten Eyck's having been employed as a jack-in-the-water on Lake Quinsigamond, Massachusetts, was made public in both the American and English Press and the very strong presumption from his parentage, his associations, and his appearance, that he was by no means of the British type of amateur, still less a gentleman amateur, the Henley Authorities let him come, made inquiry of a more or less superficial and inconclusive character into his antecedents, and, at the eleventh hour, viz, on the day of the draw . . . decided, by a majority of one vote, 'that at present there was no evidence to disqualify him as an amateur.'

This was apparently because there was no proof that he had ever received money or wages for the work he did. Ten Eyck, as was only to be expected of a true professional, won by boring and washing his opponents, but anyone who has followed the tactics of the 'gentlemen amateurs' at Henley and elsewhere will recognise that they, too, were often guilty of such unsportsmanlike actions.

Far more damning, in the eyes of E.D. Brickwood who, as 'Argonaut' (he was a member of London), edited the *Rowing Almanack* for many years, was the fact that after Henley Ten Eyck had attended a dinner given in honour of himself and his father at the Half Moon at Putney by all the best known English professionals. This surely was an open confession of guilt. The following year, Ten Eyck's entry for the Diamonds was refused, despite the fact that he was the holder, having beaten Blussé of De Hoop, Amsterdam (who had to be lifted out of his boat soon after Fawley), Ben Howell, and finally Blackstaffe.

For Thames, the post-Henley regattas were as depressing as their Henley results, the majority of wins coming in sculling events. Steve Fairbairn, now 35 and back in England for a year, was in the senior four at Kingston, losing to London in the final, while another reappearance was that of Piggy Eyre, who could still be found, at the age of 50, competing here and there in a pair, though without success, but he did win the pairs in the Club Regatta that year and later dead-heated in the final of the Club eights in October.

Bogle and Broughton returned in 1898, and with them came two powerful Cambridge Blues who had won the Grand with Trinity Hall in 1895, William Bieber and William Fernie.

Henley entries for some years had been steadily increasing in number and there were thoughts of introducing a third day. The standard, however, was not considered to be very high generally, and there was even a proposal in the autumn of 1898 to revert to fixed seats for the Thames Cup because of the low quality of this event. Fortunately, wisdom prevailed and no change was made.

Thames, stroked by Fernie, lost a hard race in the Grand by ½ length to the holders, New College, but Leander won the event. In the Stewards', Thames hit a pile below Remenham and went out to Leander, and the Club seemed to be doing as badly as in the previous year until the situation was rescued by an extraordinary performance in the Goblets by Bogle and Fernie, who became only the second Thames pair to win the event, Eyre and Hastie having been the winners on the other three occasions.

The pair beat Stout and Lowe of London easily and then in the final met somewhat unexpected opponents in Hutchinson and Fairbairn, who were rowing for Jesus. Bogle was always a very difficult and aggressive crew member and it is said that on the day of the final he was not on speaking terms with Fernie. All the way down to the start they tried to each pull other round and they pursued the same tactics in the race, quite without reference to their opponents. The Jesus pair set off at a high rate and led by 3 lengths at the Rectory, but it was a suicidal pace. Bogle and Fernie took the lead after the ¾ Mile and the outcome was no longer in doubt.

They did not stop at the line. Legend has it that they continued to Marsh Lock, where they got out and fought it out on the bank. It is not recorded who won the fight, but the boat was left for the boatman to collect.

The pair rowed together once again at Kingston, where, presumably still trying to pull each other round, they were disqualified against Hutch and Steve. This seems to have been the last straw, Fernie, in Trinity Hall colours, appearing with a new partner at Staines, where they beat Hutch and Steve in the final. Two days later, at Walton, Piggy Eyre popped up in a pair, only to go down to Hutch and Steve, who went on to win the final. It seems to have been quite a year for the evergreens. Steve also won the Garrick Pairs at Molesey in Thames colours, Piggy Eyre, for some reason representing North London RC, being a losing finalist.

Also remembered from 1898 is a long row on 25 September from Putney to Gravesend and back by a four consisting of R.C. Whiteing, W.F. Folliott, Piggy Eyre (then 51), and C.F.H.Greenwood. A well-known riverside character, 'Doggett' Cobb – he earned his nickname through regularly beginning sentences with phrases like 'When I won Doggetts' or 'I remember, in my Doggett days' – was to have steered them but he was ill and instead the four took another Putney waterman from the same family, George Cobb.

They set off against the tide just after 9 a.m., reaching London Bridge in an hour, and made good progress to Greenwich. Here the wind rose and they began to ship a lot of water, so they rowed inshore to a gravelly beach below North Woolwich Gardens and emptied the boat. Conditions improved, but the last piece was against the tide. They left the boat at 2 p.m., had a cold shower at the Clarendon, where they disposed of a leg of mutton, a quart of bitter ale each and, after a decent interval, an excellent bottle of old port. Thus fortified, and after a short rest, they started back at 3.55 p.m.

At Erith, W.H. Cumming, who had been looking out for them, came out with tea and a small bottle of cognac, for which the senior member was known to have a partiality with his tea.

After this, the crew rowed the rest of the distance, about 25 miles, with only three or four short easies. They rattled it in for the last quarter mile at 33 strokes to the minute and were back at the Clubhouse at 8.15 p.m. having covered 65 miles. They then did full justice to an excellent Irish stew and a judicious allowance of champagne.

Their actual rowing time was 8½ hours and

this was the longest row down river and back at the time. In 1966, another Thames four repeated the row, starting at 6.30 a.m. and returning at 5.40 p.m., though the total rowing time was just under 8 hours.

In 1899 a feature of Henley was the booming of the course, and this cured the problem of interference from the straying pleasure boats which had for years ruined many races. The entry was now so large that preliminary heats were rowed in some events the day before the regatta began. There were also entries from four overseas countries.

There were wholesale changes in the Thames crews, one new name being that of Harold Greenwood, the cox of the Thames Cup eight. 'The Little Moke', as he became known to generations of rowing men, became President of the Club some seventy years later. It was, however, a disastrous Henley for the Club, with one redeeming feature, Ben Howell putting up a fine performance in the Diamond Sculls, in which St George Ashe made his first appearance. Howell, an American who learnt his rowing at Cambridge, had won the Grand with Trinity Hall in 1895, and his Blue in 1897. He had given Ten Eyck his closest race in the Diamonds in 1897 and won the event in record time in 1898, beating Blackstaffe of Vesta by some distance in the final. In Thames colours in 1899, he beat a Canadian and a German with ease on his way to the final, where he sculled Blackstaffe, who was using an unusually short boat, to a standstill, to retain the trophy and give the Club its first win in the event. He later won the Wingfields, once again at the expense of Blackstaffe, the holder, but did not go for the London Cup, which 'Blackie' won for the third year running.

So the 19th century ended for Thames with a Henley win and the Club had now won every Henley event open to them, but the signs of a decline in their rowing were still evident, with no wins in the Met and only limited success elsewhere. All traces of Steve Fairbairn's coaching and the old ideals of Slater, Vize, Eyre, and Hastie seem to have disappeared with the dying century.

7 Berry, Bean, and Belgians

If Thames rowing had lost its way at the end of the 1890s, so in some ways had English rowing as a whole, though it was not apparent at the time. Despite the introduction of European Championships in 1893, rowing in Britain still focused on Henley and the Boat Race. The latter was dominated by Oxford, who were unbeaten in the decade until an exceptional Cambridge crew triumphed in 1899. At Henley, Leander, based mainly on Oxford men, won the Grand seven times in the same period, and Eton completed an unprecedented, and so far unequalled, run of seven consecutive victories in the Ladies' Plate in 1899. During this period, Etonians won 65 Blues at Oxford and 27 at Cambridge, one third of the total available. It was certainly the Golden Age of Orthodoxy, but the bubble was soon to be burst by the arrival at Henley of the far from orthodox Belgians.

In *A Text-Book of Oarsmanship*, Gilbert Bourne, himself an Etonian Oxford Blue and an exponent of the 'true art' in the 1880s, pointed out that the average winning times in the Grand in the 1890s were slower than those of the late 1880s. Looking for an explanation for the apparent decline in speed during the Golden Age, he picked on boat design, contending that the shorter boats of 56 feet in length in vogue until the early 1890s were faster than the longer boats of up to 63 feet in use from the middle of the decade.

This would seem to be confirmed by the modern tendency towards shorter boats, but Bourne also commented that at the same time rowing style had altered, with less sharp beginnings, longer finishes and a slower recovery creeping in. More marked was a tendency to paddle at abnormally low rates, accompanied by an exaggerated over-reach and a pronounced lie-back at the finish.

However, a Tideway-trained oarsman might have come to other conclusions about the slower speeds in the 1890s. Despite some outstanding oarsmen such as Muttlebury, there was a definite dropping off in the standard of both London and Thames. From 1885 to 1892, when Steve Fairbairn's influence on both the Tideway and the Cam was considerable, even for a few years after he had returned to Australia, the Grand went once to Jesus, Cambridge, once to London, twice to Trinity Hall, Thames, and Leander (the latter in the last years of this period), and the Stewards' went three times to Trinity Hall and Thames, once to Brasenose, and once to Royal Chester. From 1893 to 1900, only Trinity Hall and New College, with one win each, broke into Leander's long run of victories in the Grand. This could have been due as much to a falling off in the standard of Tideway rowing as to the quality of orthodox crews.

This is of course debatable, but Bourne nowhere suggests that Steve's coaching might have had as much influence on the faster times from 1886–92 as the shorter boats. After 1892, those who had either rowed with Steve or had been coached by him were gradually disappearing from the active rowing scene, and rowing on the Tideway and the Cam began to fall back into the bad ways that Steve had tried to eradicate.

Steve began coaching again regularly in England in 1905, mainly for Jesus, who reached the final of the Grand four times between 1906 and 1914, the winning times being markedly faster than those of the later 1890s. Cambridge colleges also began to win the Ladies' again, having last won in 1892.

It is easy, of course, to explain almost anything by manipulating statistics, and there were several other factors affecting rowing in the first decade of the 20th century, but it is difficult to deny not only Steve's influence when he was actively involved, but also the negative effects resulting from his absence.

In 1900, Tideway rowing was at a low ebb and both Thames and London were experiencing particularly bad runs. At Henley that year no Thames crews survived a heat, though Howell managed to reach the Diamonds final again, despite suffering from malaria. In the final, he came back from being two lengths down to E.G. Hemmerde of University College, Oxford, and lost by only ¾ length. He then blacked out and fell in but the sudden immersion revived him and he was quickly rescued. He did not compete again.

Ashe took part in the Olympic Regatta in Paris in 1900, the only British competitor to do so. It was a pretty informal affair and he finished behind two French scullers.

More significant to English oarsmen in 1900 was the decision by the Henley Stewards to place the Belgian Rowing Federation on the same footing as those of France, Holland, and Germany, with whom Henley was 'in agreement'. This allowed these countries to enter for Henley later than other foreign crews which had to be vetted first. Thus, in 1900 there was a Belgian crew in the Grand for the first time.

Belgian crews were a powerful influence in European rowing at this period and since the introduction of the European Championships in 1893, Belgium had won 14 of a possible 29 gold medals by the end of 1899. However, observers at Henley were not impressed by the Ghent crew, who were using swivels and broad blades, and what the *Almanack* described as 'their peculiar style of rowing', but the writer grudgingly admitted that their boat ran remarkably well. There was some dismay in their heat against Leander when they held the lead to the bottom of the enclosure, but then Leander got past to win by ¾ length and English supporters breathed again. To put this Leander victory in perspective, however, it is necessary to point out that seven of the Ghent crew were in the Belgian eight that lost by 5 lengths that August in the final of the Olympic eights to the Vesper Boat Club of Philadelphia.

In 1901, a foreign crew reached the final of the Grand for the first time. The University of Pennsylvania defeated London and then Thames, who were no match for the Americans, the latter meeting Leander in the final. This aroused enormous excitement and Henley was swamped with American supporters. Like the Belgians, Penn used swivels and it was as much a battle of styles as an international match, but Leander, in the full flood of their winning tide, held the fast-starting Americans to ¼ length at the Rectory and then went through, amid tremendous enthusiasm from the vociferous crowd, to win by a length. Once again the 'true art' had been vindicated.

Thames continued in the doldrums, though Ashe reached the Diamonds final, where he was well beaten by C.V. Fox.

In the autumn of 1901, Dr Edmond Warre, a famous Eton headmaster and rowing coach, tried to persuade the Henley Stewards to close the regatta to foreign crews, contending that allowing all the world to compete was not in the best interests of amateur rowing, but after a referendum of the views of the universities and leading clubs, the Stewards rejected the proposal. Nevertheless, there remained a strong suspicion that foreign ideas of amateurism were still some way from the English ideal of the 'gentleman amateur', and from December 1902 the Stewards barred professional coaches and managers.

At all events, in 1902 the foreign challengers, including a Ghent pair and the Toronto Argonauts in the Grand, were repelled, though Leander suffered one of only three defeats in fifteen years in the Grand, losing to Third Trinity in the final. Thames had one of their slowest crews for many years and never saw London after the Rectory. For the second year running they did not put on a Stewards' four, but the Thames Cup did at least survive a round. This was the only Henley appearance of R.F. Reeve, a Jesus man and a close friend of Steve's, who, despite his limited success as an oarsman, became an outstanding coach of beginners.

The next year, 1903, saw Thames constructing a rowing tank, built to the design of the Club's Captain and instigator of the scheme, A.F. Johnstone. It quickly paid dividends.

Also in 1903, initiated by Thames and London, the Thames Amateur Rowing Council was created with the objects of upholding the standard of amateur oarsmanship and to help the organisation and promotion of amateur regattas on the Thames. C.W. Kent was elected Chairman of this new body.

Thames had only two crews at Henley, for the Grand and Thames Cup. They failed to survive their opening heats, the Grand eight going down to Leander by an ignominious 6 lengths. This marked the lowest point in the Club's fortunes; according to the brief history which was produced in 1910 to mark the Club's jubilee year, the effect of the new tank was immediate and the summer of 1904 saw a great revival, though the Grand eight were unable to appear at Henley. Hugo Borrmann, a German from the Viking RC, Berlin, had joined Thames and was put in at six in the Grand eight, but at the last minute he was unable to get away for Henley and so the crew did not leave Putney.

The extraordinary efforts made in an attempt to get leave for Borrmann were fully reported in *The Field*:

> He was about the best man in the crew, and it was not practicable to find an efficient substitute. A German . . . engaged at the German Consulate, he had arranged for leave during the Henley week, but unexpectedly received instructions to proceed to some other city at the end of July. His chief, therefore, cancelled his leave, having, he stated, an objection to all forms of sport in which there was racing. A telegram was then sent to the Kaiser, appealing to him to grant Borrmann leave. The Emperor, however, was at Kiel Regatta at the time, and no answer was received. So Mr R.H. Forster, the Captain of Thames, wrote to Lord Lonsdale asking for his good offices in the matter. He replied that the Emperor was so busy at Kiel that he had not approached him, but had communicated with the German Foreign Office. The first result of this was that he was told he could take leave as soon as his successor arrived . . . On the day after the regatta was over, Borrmann received his leave.

This was the first time since Thames first entered the Grand in 1874 that they had not been represented in this event. The crew competed in other regattas, however, losing to London by 1 foot at Walton, ¾ length at Kingston, and ½ length at the Met, but at Staines they won by 3 feet for the first victory over the London first eight since 1896, and the win was repeated at Molesey, where the margin was 1¼ lengths. Other wins began to come the Club's way, and Ashe won the Wingfields at his fourth attempt.

This was the year in which Steve Fairbairn finally returned to England, where he was to spend most of the rest of his life. He began to coach his old college, Jesus, and success for them was immediate. The Headship of the Lents was regained in 1905 after an interval of seventeen years and the college went Head in the May Races in 1909 after a lapse of twenty-three years. From Steve's return until the outbreak of war in 1914, the college was Head of Lents eight times out of a possible ten and Head of the River five times in the Mays.

Rowing in England at this time was undergoing some radical changes, few of them beneficial. Steve described the state of college rowing in 1905 as 'really shocking'. The 'lively recovery' and other exaggerations had made the sport an agony, and he set out to rectify this. At the same time the appearance of the Belgians had begun to arouse arguments between orthodox purists and the more adventurous rowing men. The influence of the Belgians on English clubs, not least Thames, was soon to become evident.

In 1904, Julius Beresford had won many sculling trophies, though he failed in his attempts for the Wingfields and the London Cup. There was a close camaraderie on the Tideway between the scullers of the time, amateurs and professionals. 'Berry' was particularly friendly with Harry Blackstaffe of Vesta and Hamilton Cloutte of London, and 1904 he tried a pair with Blackie in the combined colours of Kensington and Vesta but surprisingly for two such skilful scullers they had limited success. It was becoming clear to Berry that, with a weight of barely 10 stone, he could not get much further as a sculler, but at a time when most oarsmen would call it a day, he decided to move to a larger club and try rowing seriously, so he joined Thames, which he felt suited his temperament.

About the same time Karl Vernon joined Thames. A vegetarian, he was immediately nicknamed 'The Bean'. He had no previous experience but he was the ideal type to fall in with Berry, who took him under his wing. Two other newcomers to the Club were C.J. Sprague, who had stroked the St Paul's School first four, and G.L. Thomson from University College School. Thames had had no Henley wins in eights or fours for ten years but in 1905, with Sprague at stroke and Thomson at six the Thames Cup eight at last broke through and the trophy came back to the Club for the first time since 1893, though the Grand eight were still well below the class and went out to SN de Gand in the first round. The Belgians were far too fast for Thames and were clear at the top of the Island, to win easily by 5 lengths.

This was the year of the controversial entry of the Vesper eight for the Grand, which was to lead to such heartaches for John B. Kelly many years later. Three of this crew had won the Olympic eights of 1900, but at Henley they were beaten by Leander by 1 length in the second round, Leander going on to beat the Belgians in the final. Subsequent investigations revealed that the Americans did not conform to Henley's amateur definitions and so Vesper were barred from competing again at Henley.

Berry had been put in at bow to steer the Thames Stewards' four, the other three men being drawn from the Grand eight. Despite their mediocre performance in the Grand, form was confounded by a magnificent race in a heat against Third Trinity. The college crew contained three Cambridge Blues, two of whom, Peter Haig Thomas and the Cambridge stroke, R.H. Nelson, won the Grand with Leander that year. In the Stewards' heat, Thames were ½ length down at the Mile, where R.V. Powell was showing signs of distress. Trinity held on, however, to win by ½ length. Powell was lifted out of the boat and Trinity had to scratch from the final.

The year 1906 was Duggie Stuart's. He was the stroke of the Cambridge eight which won the Boat Race having adopted a controversial 'sculling' style, for which he was largely responsible. Cambridge paddled in 3½ lengths ahead of Oxford, though Cherry Pitman in his *History of the Boat Race* (1909) wrote that they 'rowed in a style which found little favour with any but a few professional scullers. It was described as a 'sculling' style but was not very complimentary to the sculler, if there was one, upon whom it was modelled. They had no beginning, no lift of the bodies, but a hard, simultaneous thrust of the legs during the second half of the stroke', the latter being one of the characteristic features of the Ghent crews. But whatever the purists thought of Stuart's 'style', he stroked three Cambridge crews to Boat Race victories.

At Henley there were so many entries that a fourth day had to be introduced. Sprague and Thomson were promoted to the Thames Grand eight and 'Bean' Vernon appeared at Henley for the first time, rowing in the Thames Cup eight, along with another newcomer destined to play a major part in Thames rowing, Bruce Logan. The Bean and Berry also went for the Goblets and St George Ashe made his last appearance in the Diamonds.

The Grand eight drew the Argonaut RC, Toronto, but Thames were never in the race. However, Trinity Hall, stroked by Stuart, defeated the Canadians by ½ length in a fierce semi-final which aroused tremendous excitement among the spectators. But this time the Belgians were not to be denied, the Grand going abroad for the first time, to the intense chagrin of British oarsmen, though it was the ease of the Belgians' victory over the Hall that really upset the pundits. It is true that, for the first time for many years, Leander had been unable to raise a crew for the Grand, but by winning as they liked, the Belgians really set the cat among the pigeons and their victory sent shockwaves right through English rowing.

To orthodox-trained eyes, the Ghent crews looked very strange. To those used to judging form by the actions of the bodies rather than the blades, and familiar with the controlled squaring of the fixed pin, the late flick square of the Belgians' blades and a restricted swing forward gave the impression of a short, even hurried catch, but the Belgians let their boat run well and the shortness and hurry were illusions. This apparent shortness was partly a result of the Belgians beginning to move their bodies back before the blades entered the water, the blades travelling back slightly before the catch, the slides starting to move at the moment the blades connected. The Belgians claimed that this produced a harder catch and prevented them from reaching out too far and 'pinching' the boat at the catch. Their stroke may have looked short but, as Steve Fairbairn was always saying, 'It's the quickness of the hand that deceives the eye.' He wrote: 'My reply to the query, "Why were the orthodox oarsmen longer than the Belgian and Jesus oars?" was, "The answer is the same as the answer to the riddle, "Why does a married man live longer than a bachelor?" and that is "He does not, it seems longer."'

Stuart, who tended to dominate his crews, came in for a lot of unfair criticism. In a letter to *The Times* in 1932, he wrote:

> It has often been said that it was due to the failure to row in the orthodox way that foreign crews were able to take away the Grand Challenge Cup, but that is an exaggeration, for nearly all Oxford crews and most of Cambridge, to say nothing about the Metropolitan crews, all of which were still floundering in orthodoxy, were unable, in spite of all, to put up any crews capable of keeping the foreigner out.
>
> How was it that all the old-style coaches and all the old-style oarsmen were unable to turn out first-rate crews? The answer is that the orthodox style is an impossible and artificial one, possible indeed to men after long experience and, above all, of fine physique, but impossible for most men and clubs where the pick is limited and time inadequate.

Bean and Berry were also victims of the Belgians in 1906, losing their Goblets' heat to Molmans and Visser, who were also in the Ghent eight. The Belgians reached the final but unaccountably only paddled over against Third Trinity, presumably content with their win in the Grand. Ashe lost to Duggie Stuart in the Diamonds, though Blackstaffe at last won the final to record Vesta's first Henley victory.

After Henley, Thames won the Champion Eights for the first time since 1896, beating London, who were stroked by Stuart. They also won at Walton, Molesey, and Kingston, beating London whenever they met.

Cambridge were challenged by Harvard, winners of their annual race with Yale, and raced the Americans over the Boat Race course on 8 September. The Cambridge eight, with Muttlebury again one of the two coaches, differed only slightly from their Boat Race crew and were again stroked by Stuart, whose sculling style resulted in another victory, though Cambridge could not shake Harvard off over the second half of the course. Harvard had also been trained in a sculling technique by the Australian professional, Jim Wray. This was similar to that used by English professionals in the previous century, the blades being sliced in at the catch, the pressure of the water flicking them square. This could be done only by a crew using swivels, since the blade is turned automatically at a certain point on a fixed thole. It was a technique that was carried over to Seattle by the Eton professionals and boatbuilders, the Pocock brothers, in the early 1900s, and which was last seen in this country when crews from the University of British Columbia, Vancouver, rowed at Henley in the 1950s.

The ultimate humiliation for English rowing come in 1907 when the Belgians beat Leander in the Grand. It is true that Leander were stroked by the unorthodox Stuart, but with one Oxford and seven Cambridge Blues aboard, their defeat could not be dismissed lightly. The margin was only ⅓ length, but the injury to British pride was immense. With the Olympic Regatta due to be held at Henley the following year, the threat was obvious.

Thames rowing, though gradually improving, had not succeeded in bridging the gap that had opened up at the end of the previous century. One reason for this had been the reliance on ready-made university oarsmen to man the Grand eight and the neglect of the lower crews, so that when the supply of university oarsmen dried up and the older Grand oarsmen retired there were too few men of the requisite standard in the Club to replace them. At this point, Bill Forster came onto the scene and helped to revive Thames and Metropolitan rowing generally by concentrating on improving the standard of the lesser crews and by training the second eight and juniors with the first eight. Nevertheless, Vernon said that at the time Berry and he joined Thames, selection for the Henley crews was based mainly on body form and a lot of good men were being passed over because of this. The 1907 season was therefore a significant one because at the end of the year, Thames oarsmen decided to adopt some of the Belgian methods, as well as their rigging and short oars.

For Bean and Berry though, in their pair, 1907 had been a very good year. They were the only Thames crew to take a trophy in the Met, and they also won at five other regattas. At Goring and Streatley they easily beat another Thames pair, R.A. Sparks and G.L. Thomson. Thomson had been spare man for Cambridge that year and had won the Ladies' with Trinity Hall, who had also adopted Belgian methods and rigging. At Henley, Bean and Berry had a straight final but had to concede two stone a man to two redoubtable Cambridge Blues, B.C. Johnstone and R.V. Powell. Though well beaten, the Thames pair drew praise in the *Rowing Almanack* for their 'plucky rowing'.

The Thames Grand eight, still stroked by Sprague, had lost to Christ Church (another crew attempting Belgian methods) by several lengths, but they did have two regatta wins later on.

Berry popped up everywhere after Henley, not only in the pair, but also in various fours he had got together. By the end of the season he was rowing in the senior eight, which included a promising oarsman, Charles Rought. He won at Staines with a four containing Bruce Logan, whose first win this was.

Despite their successes, Bean and Berry never seemed to impress the Thames coaches, including Bill Forster, who had been Captain of the Club since 1903. This was not altogether surprising since Berry was now in his fortieth year and very light, while Bean, never a stylist at the best of times, was still a comparative novice. Eventually, in the autumn of 1907, Berry decided that the only way he was going to get anywhere was to buy his own boat and form his own four. This consisted of himself, Bean Vernon, Charlie Rought, and Bruce Logan. In 1952, writing in the *Thames Journal*, Bean said that Rought had been dropped from the second eight and was about to leave the Club, while Logan did not want to row in a Henley eight. Logan was put to stroke the four and Berry coached from the bow seat.

This four used swivels, like the rest of the Thames crews at this time. Berry once told me that, when Captain of Kensington RC, he had been bold enough to order a set of swivels for a four but he had been severely reprimanded at a General Meeting for his audacity. The swivels were removed and remained on top of the lockers for some years.

Thames's adoption of the Belgian rig was the result of an invitation from Bill Forster to the Belgians' cox, Raphael van der Waerden, to talk to the Club following Ghent's win in the Grand in 1906. The Belgian oars weighed only 6 lb compared with the 9 lb English oars, and were shorter overall, with shorter inboard length, while the rigger spread (thwartship distance) was slightly greater than was usual in English crews of the period. The Belgians also used 'unlimited' slides and sat lower in the boat. Berry was quick to adapt his four's rig and oars towards the Belgians', though he did not quite go the whole way.

The four trained right through the winter – another major departure from the normal custom – rowing on Sunday mornings, while Logan and Vernon played rugby on Saturdays, though later Berry dissuaded them from this as they were suffering too many injuries. They constantly rowed the Boat Race course, paddling one way and rowing back hard. In the Christmas Eights that December, the winning crew included Rought, Logan, and Berry. The Bean was playing rugby that day.

8 Recovery

The Olympic year of 1908 offered a challenge to English oarsmen. Leander, smarting from their defeat by the Belgians, were determined to put matters right, calling together a crew of stars and distinguished veterans such as Don Burnell, then retired from active rowing, and Guy Nickalls, aged 40, who had also retired but was suddenly to be found digging his garden over and over again. He also gave up wine and beer. The British were taking the matter seriously.

Duggie Stuart won the Boat Race for the third year running and Gordon Thomson was spare man for Cambridge once more, while 'Muttle' was again one of the light blue coaches. Cambridge were later to form Britain's second line of defence at the Olympic Regatta, for which each nation was allowed two entries for each of the four events. This meant that defeat at Henley, three weeks before the Olympic Regatta and restricted that year to United Kingdom entrants, would not mean losing a chance of being selected for the Olympics. This proved fortunate for some, notably Harry Blackstaffe, another 40-year-old veteran, who managed to get himself disqualified in the Diamonds but later won the Olympic title.

At Thames, Berry's plans were eventually thwarted in a way which he cannot have foreseen. In the spring, his four competed in Amsterdam and to the surprise of the Thames establishment, they won the coxless fours, beating a Ghent four drawn from their 1906 and 1907 Grand winners. When the four returned from Amsterdam, Thames had made up provisional Stewards' and Wyfold fours, so Berry's crew were tried against the Stewards' four, winning easily. They were then picked for the Stewards' and the other four became the Wyfold four.

Unfortunately, Logan and Rought were also put into the Grand eight, so Bean and Berry went again for the Goblets. This, in an Olympic year, proved to be their undoing, and Bean and Berry believed to the end of their days that had they concentrated on the four alone, they would have won both the Stewards' and the Olympic fours.

At Henley, the eight had first to deal with London, whom Thames had not beaten in the Grand since 1892. Taking a leaf from the Belgian book, Thames shot away at the start and were clear at the first signal, stretching their lead to 2 lengths at Fawley, after which they dropped their rate to 32, to win comfortably. This was the first Grand heat the Club had won for twelve years. The next day, however, they lost to a fast Eton eight, one of whom was Eugene Millington-Drake, later an Oxford Blue and a remarkable, if somewhat eccentric, character. He achieved fame when British Ambassador to Uruguay at the time of the Battle of the River Plate in 1939. It was 'Millers' who brought about the scuttling of the German pocket battleship *Graf Spee* in Montevideo harbour.

Eton beat Thames after what Bean called a 'terrific race', the crews being level at Fawley, after which Eton gradually drew ahead. Thames came in at 40 up the enclosure, but the boys won by ¾ length.

Later the same day, Berry's four raced a fresh Magdalen four in the Stewards'. This was another fine battle, Thames taking an early lead of a length, only for Magdalen to haul them back. The crews were level at the ¾ Mile but Rought and Logan were feeling the effects of their earlier race and Magdalen pulled clear to win by 1½ lengths, breaking the record with a time of

7min 28sec. They went on to win the final in a much slower time and later won the Olympic title comfortably.

Only two pairs entered for the Goblets, Bean and Berry being beaten, after a close race to Fawley, by Harold Barker and Albert Gladstone of Christ Church. Bean wrote later that, because Gladstone was in the Olympic eight, which did not compete at Henley, Beresford and he were invited to row in the Olympic pairs, but added that, unfortunately, their entry was withdrawn in error. He did not elucidate further, but one can imagine the reaction of the volatile Berry, who was never at a loss for words to suit an occasion!

Thames ought to have been chosen as the second British Olympic four, and this was generally expected after their fine race with Magdalen, but to everyone's astonishment a new Leander crew were put together instead. There was an immediate uproar in the press, one anonymous correspondent writing:

> The proceedings of the sub-committee of selection require some explanation. The Thames four which won the international race in Holland and has won all the senior races since Henley, rowed the Magdalen College four a most desperate race, right up to the finish in the first heat of the Stewards' Cup, which was accomplished some three or four seconds within record time. As Thames were beaten by under a length, they too must have been inside record. Yet the selection Committee have absolutely ignored the Thames crew, as British second string in the fours, and have, since Henley, been devoting themselves to knocking up scratch fours under Leander colours, with a view to putting up something which cannot possibly turn the tables on Magdalen, but might make a good race with the less expert of the foreign entries.
>
> In the pairs, a Tideway combination which has done very well indeed at many regattas has been absolutely ignored in the persons of Beresford and Vernon of Thames. The pair were beaten at Henley only by Gladstone and Barker in really splendid time. Gladstone was then requisitioned (quite wisely) for the Leander eight, so it was decided he must not start to row in the pairs. Once again, ignoring the Tideway, the selectors knocked up a couple of scratch Leander pairs, composed (will it be believed?) of four men, none of whom has ever won a first-class pair-oared race at any regatta on God's earth . . .
>
> The reason, I suppose, is that Beresford and Vernon row in 'bad style'. I grant that, but they are such good watermen, and are so splendidly together, and have practised so long and assiduously that they are all the more assuredly very hard to beat. Though my usual bet is a 'tanner', I am ready to wager a fiver they will 'down' either of these Leander pairs over the Olympic course, if this, or any other criticism (and there have been many) can provoke the 'Brilliants' to taking up the challenge.
>
> It is a pity that the Committee should show such marked bias against Tideway men, who alone keep up the best amateur traditions among metropolitan athletes.

No such challenge was taken up, however, and so no Thames crew found a place in the 1908 Olympics, though another Thames man, Gordon Thomson, who had stroked Trinity Hall in the Grand, and J.R.K. Fenning, from the London Grand eight, proved they were not quite as hopeless as their critic had implied by winning the Olympic title from the other Leander pair, Steve's nephew Eric Fairbairn (another Thames member) and P. Verdon. Two more of that year's Henley losers thus won an Olympic title, Thomson before gaining his Blue the following year.

Leander achieved their objective when the 'Old Men's Eight', coached by Harcourt Gold on traditional orthodox lines, won the Olympic title surprisingly comfortably from the Belgians, who included the same stern four that had won the Grand in 1907, though it was not the best crew that they could have put on because of some internal dispute between the two Ghent clubs.

The Olympic Games were still in an embryonic

stage, and only eight nations took part in the rowing events, partly because the ARA insisted on applying their strict amateur definition, so that absentees included the United States, France, Holland, and Switzerland, and Italy entered only a sculler. Nevertheless, British traditionalists were able to hold their heads high once again. The insularity of British rowing may have led to most British rowing men not knowing or caring about such things, but the Belgians had only once lost the eights in the European Championships (to France in 1905) since first winning the title in 1897. They won it again in 1908, so Leander's Olympic win was that much more commendable.

Thames did have a Henley success in 1908, however, when the original Stewards' four, stroked by Sprague, won the Wyfold without difficulty.

In the spring of 1909, an unfortunate incident occurred when Sprague, who had been elected Deputy Captain, was suddenly expelled from the Club with ignominy. No reason is given in the Club minutes, but Sprague admitted the offence, whatever it was. He had been stroking the eight until then, so Logan took over, with Rought also in the crew once again.

That year, Duggie Stuart's bid to become the first man to stroke four winning Boat Race crews was thwarted by the son of Gilbert Bourne, R.C. Bourne, who stroked his first Oxford crew to victory with five Magdalen men behind him. Ultimately it was he and not Stuart who achieved the distinction of four Boat Race wins as stroke.

At Henley, foreigners were reinstated and there was another formidable challenge in the Grand from the reunited Belgians. Thames were unlucky to draw a powerful Magdalen eight containing their Olympic four and were well beaten, but this did at least help Berry's four, who did not have to race until the following day, when they easily beat Trinity Hall. This put them up against the famous Magdalen four once again in the final. The *Rowing Almanack* account of this race says:

> Magdalen rowed 19 and 36 to Thames's 23 and 43. For a few strokes Magdalen seemed to go the faster. The two crews made for the centre of the course, and nearly collided halfway up Temple Island. Magdalen steered across under the Island and Thames went away fast, leading by over a quarter of a length at the top, by half a length at the quarter mile post, and by two lengths at the half mile . . . At the mile post, Thames were still two lengths in front, and, in spite of some hard spurts by Magdalen, easily held their advantage, finishing one and a half lengths ahead in 7m 38s.

It was a famous victory and Thames's first Stewards' win in fifteen years. It also emphasised the shabbiness of the four's treatment the previous year by the Olympic selectors.

Bean and Berry also reached the final of the Goblets, losing to the Cambridge Blues 'Soccer' Williams and 'Bush' Johnstone, who had previously disposed of Steve Fairbairn and his partner, B.M. Arnold, Steve – now approaching 50 and weighing 15 stone – having decided that half a mile was about as far as he could manage at his age and weight!

For Leander, Henley 1909 was as miserable as the weather that marred the whole summer. The Belgians, their differences settled, were back at full strength with the prestigious prefix 'Royal' added to their title in recognition of their earlier achievements. They were at full throttle in the Grand and so were Jesus, now beginning to reap the full benefit of Steve Fairbairn's coaching. They had won the Ladies' in 1908, their first victory in this event for thirty years, and in the second round of the Grand they won a hard duel with Leander by ⅓ length. Leander were stroked by the rising star, R.C. Bourne, who had four Cambridge and two other Oxford Blues behind him. For Jesus to beat a crew full of Blues was to bring particularly sweet music to Steve's ears!

But in the end, the Belgian eight were again too strong, though Jesus went down by only 1 length after a magnificent race.

That the more conservative elements were beginning to take notice of the Belgians' methods is shown by comments in the 'Review of the Season 1909' in the *Rowing Almanack*:

> It is interesting to view, as it were, our oarsmanship through their eyes, as may be done by reading further on the Belgian experts' remarks on the most glaring faults of English rowing. Apparently their doctrines vary little from those our best coaches endeavour to inculcate, and it behoves us to take a leaf out of their book and eradicate habits which tend to exhaust the oarsman rather than to improve the pace of the boat. The worst of these faults, they point out, are using the arms at the finish of the stroke and overreaching with the shoulders.

Steve praised the Belgians, yet their rowing was contrary in several ways to his later theories, which he had not fully developed at that time. While they believed, with Steve, in 'rowing the blade in', they held the slides until the bodies were vertical, claiming that all the work of the thighs and legs is wasted if the slide is allowed to go before the body. Nor did they allow the arms to bend in the way Steve did: 'But, above all, the arms must not be employed; they must be kept rigid until the moment of the finish' – which reads strangely today and was heresy to a Fairbairn-trained oarsmen. However, the Belgians cleared away some of the dead wood in English rowing. They did not appear at Henley in 1910 and were beaten in 1911, so their win in 1909 was to be the last by a Belgian crew until Piessens and Collet won the Double Sculls in 1948.

After Henley in 1909, Thames continued to be successful up and down the river. Nobody could touch Berry's four and his pair with the Bean went on winning. During their partnership in the pair, Berry and Bean won thirty out of the thirty-six races in which they started, but though they were four times finalists at Henley, the Goblets eluded them.

Thames celebrated the Club's Jubilee with a dinner in February 1910, at which Piggy Eyre was in the chair. The following day he wrote, in his inimitable style, to Berry:

> My dear Beresford,
>
> I feel I must write and apologise to all the members of your Stewards' four for my unpardonable forgetfulness in saying absolutely nothing about what was really the greatest thing Thames have ever done. But you've no idea what a wool-gathering idiot I am when I am on my legs. All sorts of stuff runs through the space where one's brains should be, and I invariably forget something important that I had intended to say. This slip was the worst I ever made, for you fellows, by your determination, and splendid training, had given an object lesson worth all the precept I have bungled over. Moreover I had thought out and worked it all up to something that would have brought down the house, and I clean forgot the lot. It's awful. You must not reply. It's a subject that will be a very sore one with me for a damned long time, and I don't want to hear anything about it. I only feel I must do penance to you fellows by writing this letter, which I hope you will show the others.
>
> I want to say that without doubt yours was the best thing Thames ever did. Damme, it was! You beat decisively the four which had won the World four-oared championship. And you did it by sheer self-denial, resolution and all the other essentials I jawed about. I was going to hold forth on your rows to Richmond and tremendous work; your individual watermanship; and the good fellowship between you. But that's enough of it, and you must not reply,
>
> Yours ever,
>
> W.H. Eyre

T.D. Richardson arrived at the Club in 1910. 'The Tyke', a lightweight of under 10 stone, had rowed Head of the River at Cambridge with Trinity Hall behind Stuart and Thomson,

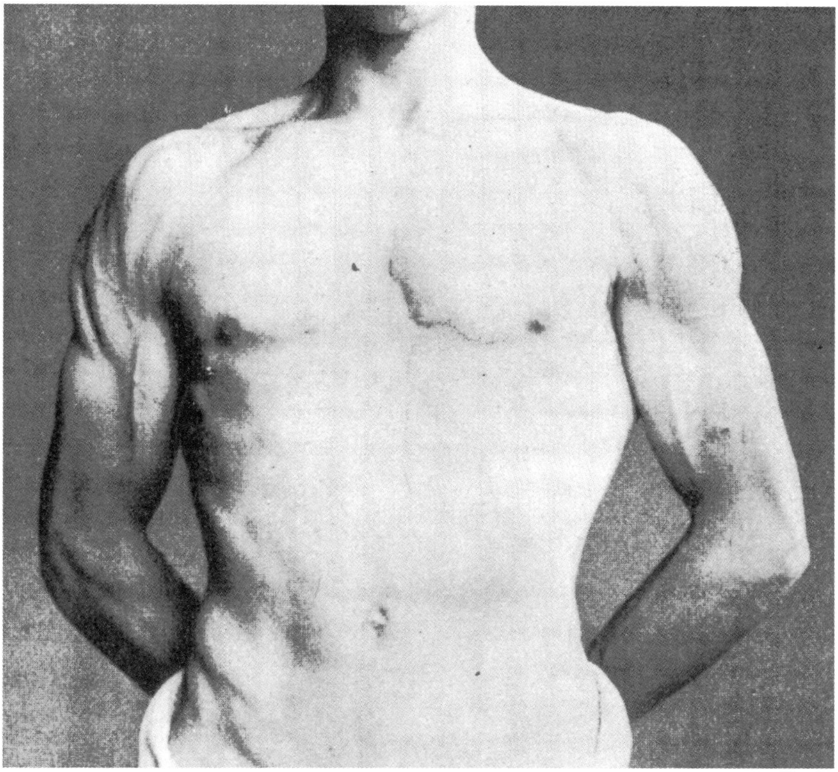

9. Described by Guy Nickalls as
'the best stripped man I have ever seen',
the torso of 'Jumps' Gardner, circa 1890

10. 'Muttle' (S. D. Muttlebury), who joined Thames in 1891

11. A future President of Thames—the Hon. Rupert Guinness, winner of the Diamond Sculls in 1895 and 1896

12. The Belgian winners of the Grand at Henley, 1909

13. 'Berry's four'—winners of the Stewards' Cup in 1909 and 1911: Julius Beresford (bow), Karl Vernon, Charles Rought, Bruce Logan (stroke)

14. Thames RC beating Trinity Hall in the semi-final of the Stewards', 1909

15. Julius Beresford (bow) and Hamilton Cloutte (stroke), winners of the Silver Goblets, 1911

and also won the Ladies'. The Hall's ideas at that time were very much in line with those of Thames, and despite his lack of pounds and inches, Tyke stroked the Thames Grand eight in 1910.

The weather that year was wretched. The one breath of summer was at Walton and it brought an unusual victory for Thames, Berry's four becoming the wettest crew in almost the only dry regatta. In fact, it was not at that moment Berry's four, his place having been taken by Albert Snellgrove. According to Berry, Bill Forster, the Club Captain, had been dropping heavy hints to Berry that he should retire, and Berry said that he was 'artfully taken out of the four' for Walton, despite the fact that he owned the boat in which the crew rowed.

Thames met a Winnipeg four who were preparing for Henley and they were fouled by the Canadians when leading. Thames capsized and were awarded the race but the crew gave their tankards to the Canadians while keeping the trophy. 'This resulted in great friendliness,' wrote the Bean, 'and Winnipeg gave us a dinner at the Ritz before they went back to Canada.'

Berry was hastily reinstated in the four but at Henley he also joined Logan and Rought in the Grand eight when someone fell ill, though Bean was still left out. Because of Berry's commitments, the pair did not row at Henley.

As luck would have it, Thames drew Jesus in the Grand and there was a titanic struggle. Jesus, stroked by Steve's nephew, Eric Fairbairn, were leading by ¼ length at the Mile, and in a desperate row in, the crews were level at the grandstand, but Jesus just got home with 2 feet to spare. Jesus went on to beat London but lost in the final to Magdalen.

The Stewards' had drawn entries from Canada, Germany, and Holland. Thames met Winnipeg again in an event that had never yet gone overseas. This time the Canadians won by a length, going on to win the final from the Germans.

Tyke Richardson and his equally diminutive brother had a close race in the Goblets with G.W.H. Walker and George Drinkwater, an Oxford Blue. Drinkwater became a famous rowing journalist and Boat Race historian. An architect and sculptor by profession, it is his bust of Steve Fairbairn that is the trophy for the Head of the River Race. Sadly, he was killed by a bomb in London during the Second World War.

Berry's four had the usual crop of post–Henley successes but the eight lost a few times to London, though they retained the Champion Cup after clashing blades several times with London. In the Thames Cup fours, London ran into Thames just after Harrods when Thames were ½ length ahead. Rought's blade went through the skin of the London boat, which sank, and Thames finished alone. Thames also took the two other four-oared events at the Met.

In 1911, the Remenham clubhouse was built between the ¾ and 1 Mile marks at Henley. The Club had been founded in 1909 by London, Thames, Kingston, Vesta, Molesey, Twickenham, and Staines for their members. It was intended as a meeting place away from the crowds of the main enclosure during the Regatta and had a unique view of both start and finish. The subsequently constructed Remenham 'mound' maintains this and provides a fine vantage point at what is often a critical part of a race. Today, the Club still exudes that spirit of cheerful camaraderie which is one of the bonuses that past and present club oarsmen enjoy.

The Bean married in August 1910 and claimed to have retired from rowing, but it could not last, of course. Berry persuaded his old friend Hamilton Cloutte, the London sculler who had competed many times, unsuccessfully, in the Diamonds and Wingfields, to take Bean's place in the four, but the crew did not go well with Cloutte and in the spring of 1911 Bean was persuaded to return.

None of the four rowed in the Grand eight that year, Berry and Cloutte going for the Goblets, as did Rought and Logan.

Unlike the previous year, 1911 produced marvellous weather and there was a record heatwave throughout the regatta season. In the spring, a challenge race, engineered by Steve Fairbairn, took place between Jesus, Cambridge, and the Ghent clubs at Terdonck, the Belgians' home water. The race aroused tremendous interest and the college oarsmen were lionised and treated like stars wherever they went. Over a 2,000-metre course, Jesus won by 2 lengths against a crew that contained only two previous winners of the Grand, but it was still a notable success.

The Belgians reorganised after this and brought to Henley what they considered to be their fastest eight of all. Another overseas entry for the Grand came from Ottawa RC, who also had a four from the eight in the Stewards'. In the Grand, Ottawa drew the Belgians, whose stern pair were Visser and Molmans, who had beaten Bean and Berry in the Goblets in 1906. In a high-rating battle, the crews were level at the Mile, the Canadians then taking a slight lead. The race came to a dramatic end when, coming along the enclosure at 39, the Belgians suddenly stopped, Molmans having torn an abdominal muscle.

Jesus had earlier beaten a light Thames eight, while Magdalen, with an average weight of 12 st 10 lb and at that time the heaviest crew to have rowed in the Grand, beat the fighting Ottawa crew in a time close to the record, drawing adverse comments, not for the first time, for crossing in front and washing the Canadians. This put the two Head crews of their respective universities together in the final, Magdalen winning. Despite the fierce racing in the Grand, an exceptional Eton eight won the Ladies' in a time six seconds faster than Magdalen's winning time in the Grand.

In the Stewards', Berry's four were in cracking form. Against Magdalen, with only Angus Gillan left from the Olympic four, Thames showed a remarkable turn of speed. They led by 1½ lengths at the first signal and won in a paddle. Third Trinity, all Blues, fared even worse, being two lengths down at the ¼ Mile, though they hung on better than Magdalen. Trinity Hall met Thames in the final, having removed Ottawa. Gordon Thomson, stroking the Hall, could not match Logan's pace off the start and Thames led by a length at the top of the Island, after which Logan was content to do just enough to win by 1¼ lengths, since three of the four had reached the semi-final of the Goblets. Cloutte was in a pair with Berry, but was not in the four, in which Vernon rowed. The *Almanack* account of the latter race says:

> Beresford and Cloutte rowed 41, Logan and Rought 38, the former leading by a few feet. At the top of the Island, Rought caught Cloutte and led at the first signal by a quarter of a length. At the half mile Logan and Rought led by two thirds of a length, Fawley being reached in 3m 58s, and Rought being half a length in front. It was a good race to the mile, less than half a length dividing the boats. A very fine race ended in a dead heat in record time 8m 8s. Afterwards Cloutte and Rought tossed to settle the result of the dead heat, Beresford and Cloutte being the winners.

The pairs tossed because the final of the Stewards' was still to come. The record set by these men was equalled twenty-seven years later but was not beaten until 1952, when one of the successful pair was another Thames oarsman, Tom Christie. There was a strong following wind on this occasion and I can still hear Berry complaining that records should not be allowed in such circumstances, asserting that they never had such helpful conditions in his day!

Despite Berry's memory, conditions were certainly fast in 1911, though in winning the final against Bruce and Gladstone of Christ Church by 1½ lengths they could not match the previous day's time, but they equalled Muttlebury's old record of 8min 15sec.

Berry, at 43 the oldest man competing in the regatta, was also the only man to win two finals when everyone found the sultry heat exhausting. These, despite his age, were not to be Berry's last Henley wins, but they provided the greatest moments of his long career.

After Henley a new Thames sculler began to make his mark, Laurie Tann winning the junior-senior sculls in the Met by 4 feet, having earlier won the junior event at Walton. He continued his meteoric climb to the top by winning the senior sculls at Kingston, though he lost at Marlow to Jock Wise of London, later to be that Club's President from 1951 to 1971.

The Olympic Regatta in 1912 took place in Stockholm. There was no event for coxless fours (this event was not introduced to the European Championships until 1925) and there were coxed fours instead. Berry, intent on being selected after the disappointment of 1908, recruited a former Anglian cox, Geoffrey Carr. The four used a twenty-year-old coxed four, but continued to train in the coxless four as well, while both pairs also carried on.

Earlier in the year, Bourne had established what is still a Boat Race record, stroking a winning Oxford crew for the fourth time, though both crews sank at the first attempt and the race had to be re-rowed two days later.

It was an interesting year. Ernest Barry brought the World Professional Championships back to England for the first time since Joe Sadler lost it in 1876, and the King and Queen attended Henley and followed the final of the Grand.

Harold Messom stroked the Thames Grand eight, almost a new crew, but coxed again by the 'Little Moke.' In the Grand, Sydney RC, the first Australian crew to row at Henley, beat the Toronto Argonauts. They rowed smoothly and were perfectly together and went on to beat New College. Leander, with only one man rowing who was not subsequently in the Olympic eight, were far too good for Thames, but they lost a very fine race with Sydney by ¾ length in the final.

Berry's four had a bye to the Stewards' final, where they met New College, stroked by Bourne. Thames were clear at the top of the Island and by Fawley, with the College rolling and Thames still 1¼ lengths ahead, the race looked over but Bourne then started a series of spurts. Despite erratic steering, they were overlapping at the Mile, and Bourne made even greater efforts, finally getting his bows in front at the bottom of the enclosure. Thames were done and New College went away to win by 2¼ lengths. Bean was convinced that this defeat was due mainly to their having practised so much with a cox, though doubling up in the pairs again cannot have helped.

Both the pairs reached the final, the first occasion at Henley on which two Thames crews had done so. This time the advantages of relative youth and greater weight told against the veterans Beresford and Cloutte, though there was another great race. The older pair had to row a faster stroke to hold their rivals but there was only ¼ length in it at the Mile. After their race in the Stewards' earlier in the day, this pace was bound to tell on the older pair first and Berry began to have trouble holding the boat straight. In the end Logan and Rought won by 1¼ lengths, which was poetic justice after the dead heat of the previous year when the toss had gone against them.

The lesser Thames crews failed again, though the Thames Cup eight did at least go out to the eventual winners, the Rowing Club of Paris. The latter rowed in a way similar to the Belgians and became the first French crew to win at Henley.

The Thames four were selected for the

Stockholm Olympics but the main events in British eyes were the eights and sculls, both of which were retained, Leander reversing Henley form in the eights and beating Australia, represented by Sydney, in their heat, and then beating the second British crew, New College, by a length in the final. Jock Kinnear, of Kensington RC, though beaten at Henley by Duggie Stuart's younger brother, Colin, was not extended in winning the single sculls.

British observers were surprised by the high standard of the coxed fours, which, since Woodgate's days, had been regarded as a second-class type of boat. The Belgians put on a four instead of an eight but lost to the Norwegians, who cracked them near the finish, Thames then beating the Norwegians by ⅓ length after another hard race. In the final against Germany, the Bean was suffering from a boil and Bruce Logan had been stung by a wasp. The Germans had a slight lead at 500 metres and then gradually drew away to win by 2½ lengths, so Thames had to be content with the silver medal, the first international championship medal to come to the Club and an especially praiseworthy achievement by Berry at the age of 44. Surprisingly, this was to be the only medal won by Britain in the Olympic coxed fours until an outstanding composite crew won the gold in 1984.

In 1913, Stanley Bruce, an Australian and former Cambridge Blue, selected and coached the Thames Grand eight. The Bean decided to retire once again, but Berry and Cloutte had another go for the Goblets. Logan and Rought were back in the Grand eight and the four disbanded.

Leander produced a very fine eight which included five of their winning Olympic eight. They equalled the course record, set by New College in 1893, in beating the Toronto Argonauts and then raced Thames in the next round. This was a much better Thames crew than their immediate predecessors and they were a canvas ahead at the ¼ Mile, holding this to Fawley. Leander then lengthened out and gradually drew away to win by 1¼ lengths. In the final, they recorded Leander's first Grand win since 1905, beating Jesus, who were in their fourth Grand final in five years.

Berry and Cloutte found Buxton and Gladstone too strong for them in the Goblets and the other Thames crews were again unsuccessful, though E.L. Watts had his moment of glory in the Diamonds when he comfortably beat a Russian, H.M. Kusik from St Petersburg.

Stanley Bruce was elected an Honorary Life Member of Thames after Henley. He became a distinguished Prime Minister of Australia and maintained his interest in the Club. As Viscount Bruce of Melbourne, he was a guest at the centenary dinner in 1960.

In 1914, only Bruce Logan remained from the 1913 Grand crew and there was talk of not entering for the Grand but this horrified the older members, so a stopgap crew was produced with Berry, now 46 and the oldest competitor at Henley, at stroke, and Bean Vernon was included at five for his first appearance at Henley in an eight. Berry's brother, Pandy, a mere 9 st 6 lb, was at bow, and only two men were over 11½ stone.

The Grand was a chastening experience for the home crews, all four semi-finalists being foreigners for the first time, while the ultimate winners, Harvard, were not even their first crew but their Junior Varsity eight. Thames, London, Leander, and Jesus were the four home defenders and none survived a heat, Thames going out to their old antagonists and friends, Winnipeg. It was a black day for English rowing.

In the Stewards', however, the foreign challenge was repulsed by Leander, stroked by Bourne and with Thomson at two. Three of Berry's old four got together for Henley, with Watts in Rought's seat at three, but they lost a good race with Leander. In the final, Leander cracked a German four from Mainz after the Germans had led by a length at the Mile. The German three collapsed opposite Phyllis Court and Leander finished alone.

The Diamonds were won by a giant Italian from Como, Guiseppe Sinigaglia, who was twice European champion. The deaf and dumb Donald Gollan made his first Diamonds' appearance, losing in the second round, and Laurie Tann also won a heat before losing by a bare length to Bob Dibble from Toronto Don RC. The Italian beat Dibble, whom he washed most of the way, but in the final against Colin Stuart, who had put Gollan out, he hit the booms, presenting Stuart with a two-length lead, though Sinigaglia got through in the end, Dibble stopping, sculled out, before the finish. It was Sinigaglia's last race.

Gollan lost to Stuart in the London Cup, but Laurie Tann beat Stuart in the final, having eliminated Jock Wise in a heat. He confirmed this form by beating Bourne and Gollan in a heat of the Wingfield Sculls and followed this up by again beating Wise, the holder, in the final. It was unfortunate for Tann that he should have been approaching his peak form as the fury of the First World War was about to be unleashed. He did not compete at regattas after his Wingfield success and though he was to reappear after the war as one of the mainsprings of Thames's revival, it was to be as an oarsman rather than a sculler.

The Stewards' four retained their event in the Met and the first eight retained the Champion Eights after being led by London for most of the way, Berry's final spurt getting Thames home by 1 foot. Wins continued to flow in after this, Berry's four having their usual successful run, though the eight lost several times to London, albeit narrowly.

But the summer of 1914 became darker as the clouds of war began to gather, though the regatta season was virtually over by the time the thunderclap came, and only the later skiff events and club regattas had to be abandoned. The youth and manhood of England marched to fight in the war that was to end wars and among them were most of the oarsmen whose names had filled the regatta programmes of the previous few years. After 1914 the world was never to be quite the same.

It also marked the end of an era in the Club's history with the deaths, the fullness of their years, of George Vize, Micky Slater, and Pat Labat. Not only were many of the younger men never to return, but some of the main links with the early days, especially Vize and Slater, who had continued to help and encourage the Club in their later years, had also gone for ever.

The war took an enormous toll of a whole generation. Among those lost were the Leander oarsman and sculler, F.S. Kelly, who was also a noted concert pianist; the Italian sculler Sinigaglia; and the poet, Julian Grenfell, winner of the Wyfold Cup in 1909. The son of a famous oarsman, W.H. Grenfell, later Lord Desborough, his *Into Battle* can be found in many anthologies of war poems. His younger brother, Billy, another poet, was also killed, and the Desborough title eventually became extinct. Among Thames members to fall was Eric Fairbairn, Steve's nephew, and another casualty was one of the Club's first Vice-Presidents, F.G. Naumann, who lost his life when the liner *Lusitania* was torpedoed.

The unluckiest of all, however, was probably Charles Rought. A prisoner of war almost from the beginning, he died after eating a bad oyster while waiting to be demobilised after his release, and so technically his death occurred while on active service. *Requiescant in Pace.*

PART TWO

1919–1939

9 Steve Fairbairn and the Post-War Revival

What little rowing took place during the Great War from 1914 to 1918 was mainly at the public schools, although there were a number of charity regattas. Thames promoted a four–oared race for schools in 1916, presenting handsome silver cups to the winners, and members of the boat clubs of St Paul's, Bedford and Westminster schools were made members of Thames for the duration of the war, a circumstance which was to pay dividends later.

Despite the disastrous toll exacted by the war, rowing made a quick recovery. In 1919, rowing at the universities was numerically, if not technically, almost back to pre–war level, though the Boat Race was not revived until 1920. Clubs were soon back in action and competitors in the Thames Opening Eights on 12 April included Steve Fairbairn, Berry, the Bean (who had won the Military Medal with the RAMC), Laurie Tann, Bogie, Jock Kinnear, and Harry Blackstaffe, as well as Steve's son, Ian, who had received a bad leg wound in the war which left him with a pronounced limp for the rest of his life.

A five-man committee, which included Berry, had managed the Club during the war, and in February 1919 they invited Steve Fairbairn to take on the Captaincy, which he willingly accepted and which was confirmed at a General Meeting in April, Berry becoming his Deputy.

A special Peace Regatta was held at Henley in 1919, with special trophies. Among these the King's Cup, for all who had fought with the Allies, was the top eights event; there were also the Fawley Cup for senior eights from the United Kingdom, and the Kingswood Sculls. Such was the support that an intended two–day affair ended as a full four–day regatta.

With experienced veterans and a new generation of younger oarsmen, several of whom had rowed for their schools in wartime, Steve decided at Thames to put the veterans together and keep them rowing until the younger men could catch them up. Bean, Berry, Tann, and Logan rowed in a four which won at all regattas except Henley, and the 'Old Men' were put into an eight for the Fawley Cup. Berry, now 51, was brought in to stroke the crew after they failed in the final at Marlow. In this crew were five other men who had represented the Club at Henley before the war: Vernon Teale, George Kelly, Laurie Tann, Karl Vernon, and Bruce Logan. Ian Fairbairn, at seven, had rowed for Eton in the Ladies' in 1913 and 1914, and C.K. Roylance at five had stroked Bedford School in the Ladies' in 1914. With the exception of 'Ginger' Roylance and Ian Fairbairn, who were nevertheless veterans of the war, the average age of the rest of the crew was over 35.

In the Peace Regatta, Thames had a hard opening heat against Marlow, who had at two George Eyston. He was also a member of Thames and later became a famous racing driver and holder of the world land speed record. Marlow had won at their own regatta, beating Thames, and the crews were level at the Mile, but Thames's final burst along Phyllis Court wall saw them home by ¾ length. They then beat Kingston more easily, and in the final against Christ Church the crews were again level at the Mile, where Christ Church faltered and Thames gained a few feet, which was all Berry needed. Spurting along the enclosure, he took Thames to a remarkable 1-length victory.

In recognition of this exceptional achievement, the Club presented the Fawley Cup to Berry. In

1960, the Club's centenary year, and shortly after Berry's death at the age of 91, his sons Jack and Eric gave it back to the Club's safe keeping.

The King's Cup, won by the Australian Services eight, who had been coached by Steve at Thames for a month before the regatta, became the Australian Inter–State Trophy.

Although he did not compete at Henley that year, Berry's son Jack was beginning to make his mark. He had stroked Bedford School during the war and had later been wounded in the leg on active service. At 19 he made his first appearance at Marlow, winning the junior sculls. He followed this up by winning the junior–senior event at Kingston and the senior event at Molesey. He then stroked a four and a Thames Cup eight, both of which won at Staines.

Steve, still Captain of Thames in 1920, used his veterans as pacemakers for the younger men and the crews were successful at all levels, Steve himself coaching from the novices upwards. As usual, he had his finger in many pies, coaching the Cambridge crew for two weeks in February and he was still heavily involved with his old college, Jesus. Cambridge won the first post–war Boat Race, while Jesus went Head of the River at Cambridge. During the 1920s Jesus were Head in the Mays six times and in the Lents five times. They won the Ladies' twice and the Wyfold and Goblets once each, as well as twice reaching the final of the Grand.

But Steve's main ambition now was to revive Metropolitan rowing, and Thames was his chosen vehicle. In May 1920, signs that Steve's plan was beginning to work came with a race between the Old and Young eights, the Old – still stroked by Berry – beating the Young, into which Ian Fairbairn had been moved, by only ¾ length in a 'bridger' between Hammersmith and Putney.

At Marlow, the younger men, stroked by Reggie Bare, who had been Head of the Water at Westminster in 1917, won the Marlow Eights from Jesus by ½ length, and a four from this eight – Kenneth Wilson, Count S. Wachtmeister (a Swedish diplomat), Ian Fairbairn and Charles Rew – also won the senior coxless fours. Jack Beresford easily won the senior sculls, while Ian Fairbairn and Bruce Logan took the senior pairs at the expense of Vernon Teale and the Bean. Bare, 'Cherub' Chandler, and Rew also rowed in the winning junior eight, which was coxed by the evergreen 'Little Moke', Harold Greenwood. In all, Thames took six trophies; the outstanding performer was Rew, who won one junior and two senior trophies on the same day.

At Henley, Thames entered three eights for the first time, the rules having been changed to allow clubs to enter more than one eight for the Thames Cup. This rule was rescinded in 1924 because of the increasing size of the entry. The Old Men, with Berry still at stroke, went for the Grand, but this was very much a holding operation. The main hopes were on the better of the Thames Cup eights, based on the Marlow winners with some from the junior eight, and the Wyfold four drawn from it. There were also a Stewards' four containing Logan and the Bean, but without Berry, whose age now precluded doubling up, two Goblets pairs, and Jack Beresford in the Diamonds. It was the largest Henley entry yet from Thames.

The *Almanack* says that everybody there agreed it was also the worst ever seen at the Regatta, which, looking back over past records, with the bad days veiled by fond recollections of happy Edwardian and Victorian meetings in the golden haze of the years before the war, might seem something of an exaggeration.

The Grand eight drew Leander, stroked by Gordon Thomson, who also stroked their Stewards' four for his last Henley. The eight were not very distinguished but were too good for the Thames veterans, winning comfortably. They were well beaten later by Magdalen, who included Guy Nickalls's son, 'Gully'.

However, the Thames Cup and the Wyfold were both won. In the former, the B crew went out in the first round, but the A crew beat three Cambridge colleges and the Magdalen second eight, before beating Caius College, stroked by the future publisher, Hamish Hamilton, in the final, Thames's greater fitness enabling them to win by 1 length. The Wyfold four were unpressed in all their races.

Ian Fairbairn also reached a third final, the Goblets, but, with Bruce Logan, was well beaten by Nickalls and Lucas of Magdalen. In the Diamonds, Jack Beresford raced four times, winning easily on each occasion, before meeting Donald Gollan, sculling for First Trinity, in the final. Beresford took the lead at once and won by three lengths, for Thames's third Henley win that year.

Beresford, still only 20, was selected for the single sculls in the Olympic Games to be held in Antwerp at the end of August. Leander were chosen for the eights and set out to find a new crew. These were the only two British entries, since the ARA still considered these to be the only first-class Olympic events.

Thames overwhelmed everyone in the post-Henley regattas, winning six events in the Met and rowing over in the senior fours. Jack Beresford won the London Cup and then the Wingfield Sculls, beating Gollan once again.

There were now five events in the Olympic Games – eights, coxed fours and pairs, double and single sculls – but only two crews competed in each final. Interest was aroused by the thorough preparations for these Games made by the Americans, and, in view of the subsequent development of international rowing, the comments of Leander's coach, Cherry Pitman, who was also Honorary Secretary of the ARA, are interesting:

> The result of the [eights] race was a triumph for American organisation and for the business spirit in which the American people undertake amateur sport. English amateur rowing has always been a form of sport which can be indulged in without unduly interfering with a man's ordinary school, university, or business career. The Leander crew consisted of six university men, a barrister and a clergyman, who devoted five weeks of their holiday to training. In form and in pace they were as fine a crew as ever sat in a boat. The officials of the British Olympic Association did not even know until a week before the crew started that the regatta was to be held at Villevorde and not at Antwerp. When they made this discovery they housed the crew at a station hotel in the middle of Brussels no less than seven miles by dusty road from the course . . . The long daily drive took a lot out of the men, and it was impossible to provide them with suitable food. Their boat was sent from Antwerp by rail instead of by canal, and the crew themselves had actually to carry their own boat two miles from the station to the boat tents, the Americans kindly lending a car for the transport of oars and riggers.
>
> The American Navy, on the other hand, selected twenty-five rowing men as long ago as January last, and employed them in the exclusive business of preparing for this regatta. From the beginning of February the crew were ground into one uniform whole by long, steady rows of upwards of twelve miles. During the summer they rowed more than thirty races. They came over in a cruiser fitted with rowing machines, and arrived at Villevorde three weeks before the race with a complete second crew to act as pacemakers, four spare men, the ship's doctor to look after their health, men to rub them down, cooks to prepare their special food, a trainer, and a staff of servants. They were quartered on the banks of the course, and had continual practise in racing against their second crew.

In the circumstances, it was a remarkable performance by the British eight to lose by only 1 second. The course was on the ship canal between Brussels and Antwerp, and to those many Thames oarsmen with memories of Ostend Regatta, Cherry Pitman's description will sound a familiar note:

> The surroundings were not picturesque.
> On the right bank . . . is a rough *pavé* road, bounded on the right by a dreary dusty wall and an odiferous ditch. On the left bank . . . is an almost continuous line of factories, some of which discharged streams of hot water from their condensers into the murky waters of the canal.

The final was a remarkable race between two crews of totally contrasting styles. Pitman wrote:

> The Americans, with their exaggerated swing back, looked as if they had to take more out of themselves in paddling to produce the same pace as was produced by Leander. The latter, with their long, steady swing, sharp beginning, and well held out finish, were perfectly together and looked the picture of what an English crew should be.

Leander were on fixed pins while the Americans, as usual, used swivels. Nevertheless, it was the Americans who won after a terrific race rowed at top pressure throughout, Leander leading by nearly ⅔ length at 1,000 metres and holding this to 1,700 metres, when, in what was to become a familiar pattern over the years, the Americans slowly hauled them back. They were still behind with a few strokes to go but sheer physical strength took them ahead to win by about 10 feet, to begin the American domination of this event which was to last forty years.

Jack Beresford was also learning the harsh realities of Olympic rowing in the new era. He easily won his heat against the Swiss European champion and the Czech, then beat Frits Eyken of Holland, whom Gollan had beaten at Henley. In the final, Beresford met the American, John B. Kelly, who had been given a hard semi-final by the New Zealander, Hadfield, winner of the Kingswood Sculls at Henley Peace Regatta.

Kelly's entry for the Diamonds in 1920 had been rejected and it is often said that Kelly, originally an immigrant Irish bricklayer, was barred under the old rules concerning manual labour, but this is an over-simplification. In a letter to Jack Beresford in the 1950s, Kelly wrote:

> Russell Johnson, secretary of the NAAO [the American rowing federation] had an arrangement with the Henley officials that they would approve all entries from the United States, which he had made during his visit to England in the winter of 1919–20 . . . I asked him to check with the Stewards to see if they would accept my entry because in my earlier days I had served an apprenticeship as a bricklayer.
>
> He contacted four of them and they told him to send my entry in; the war had changed the old rule and everything would be all right.

However, Kelly was a member of the Vesper Boat Club, which had been barred from Henley after infringements of their amateur status had come to light in 1905. The ban still stood in 1920 and it was for this reason that Kelly's entry was not accepted, though in explaining this to the American club, the Stewards questioned, for future reference, whether Kelly was an amateur under the then ARA and Henley definitions, and which had not, in fact, been changed since the war. The bar on Vesper was removed soon afterwards but Kelly never competed at Henley. In 1920, the press made capital out of all this, setting up Kelly as a man with a grievance bent on revenge against the Diamonds winner, and certainly both had something to prove.

The final lived up to the occasion, there being very little in it throughout. Beresford had a slight lead at the end of one minute and held it until the last 100 metres. Neither man cracked, but the 6 foot 5 inch American, weighing over 14 stone against Beresford's 11 st 4 lb, and at 30 years of age Beresford's senior by ten years, proved to have that vital bit of extra strength and won by 1 second.

Far from there being any bitterness between the two men, this epic race helped to establish a lifelong friendship. Kelly became a millionaire and lived to see his son Jack win the Diamonds in 1947 and in 1949, when he also won the European title, though he failed in the Olympic Games. Jack's sister Grace, the film star, became Princess Grace of Monaco and gave away the prizes at Henley in 1981, two years before her tragic and premature death. Jack also died prematurely in 1985 while jogging, having just been elected President of the US Olympic Committee.

The 1920 Thames crew which won the Thames Cup went on to win everything for which they entered after Henley, but they were still young and though they were to provide the nucleus for future triumphs, they were not ready for the Grand in 1921. This was a year of surprises, the first being when Oxford, with four Magdalen men from the Olympic eight, lost the Boat Race by 1 length after having led by ¼ length at Barnes Bridge. Magdalen provided the second surprise when they lost the Headship at Oxford to New College. There were, however, no upsets on the Cam, where Jesus stayed Head with a lightweight, Leigh Holman, at seven.

Magdalen strengthened their crew for Henley by bringing in the veteran Horsfall, but Holman, weighing under 11 stone, had lost his place in the Jesus eight and instead rowed three in a very light winning Jesus Wyfold four.

The Thames veterans were again put in for the Grand and still included Berry, now 53, Bean Vernon, Duggie Douglas, George Kelly, and Laurie Tann, all of pre-war vintage, though Bruce Logan had finally retired. Also in the crew at bow was Charles Morrell, who had been a prisoner of war in Holland. Not too much was expected of them but they put up a remarkable performance against New College in their heat, coming back from ¾ length down at the ½ Mile to pull back to within ¼ length at the Mile, but this time age proved too much and Berry's final spurt could not prevent the college drawing away to win by ¾ length. However, Magdalen beat New College by a length and then beat Jesus by the same margin in the final, when, with very little stream after some exceptionally dry weather, they were only three seconds outside the record.

The other Thames crews were not successful but Beresford again reached the Diamonds final, where he met the Dutch sculler, Frits Eyken, whom he had beaten at Antwerp. Beresford destroyed his chances through an exceptional gesture of sportsmanship. The scullers were level at the top of the Island when Eyken hit the booms. Beresford stopped until the Dutchman was straight again and led by only ½ length at the first two signals. At Fawley, they were level but Eyken lasted the better, to cause one of the major upsets of the regatta in winning by 1½ lengths, but Jack had at least put the word 'gentleman' back with 'amateur'.

Eyken later won the European title, and he and the Christiania Roklub, Norway, who won the Thames Cup in the Leander 1908 Olympic boat, were the first overseas winners at Henley since the war, receiving their trophies from the Prince of Wales.

Jack Beresford retained the Wingfields, though the issue was settled by a foul. The only contestants were Beresford and Gollan, with each being 'shown up' by their respective fathers. This tradition went back to the early days of wager racing, a cutter following each contestant, one man sitting in the bows facing his sculler, directing his course by waving a flag, or, more usually, a handkerchief. On this occasion, Spencer Gollan was in a boat rowed by watermen, while Berry had a crew of Thames men, and since both the scullers and their fathers knew the course intimately, it is hard to know why Gollan, on Middlesex, came across after the Crab Tree, causing several clashes off Harrods Wharf. Beresford made no claim and the scullers were level at Hammersmith Bridge when Gollan again pulled right into Beresford and put a crack in the latter's boat. This time Beresford appealed and both scullers stopped, but before any decision was made, Gollan set off again, followed several lengths behind by Beresford, who eventually finished with his boat waterlogged, to be awarded the race.

By 1922 the younger Thames men were ready to take over and the Bean was the only one of the veterans to row at Henley that year. Leigh Holman had joined the Club and there was some concern when Steve Fairbairn placed him at seven between Ian Fairbairn and 'Nougat' Southgate, both much heavier men, but Steve had an instinct for placing his men in the right seats and Holman was to prove an outstanding seven.

It rained every day and there was a strong south-westerly wind, but there were a large number of unusually close races, which was some compensation. The nine Grand entries included three foreign crews: SN de la Marne, Christiania Roklub, and the 1921 European champions, the Grasshopper Club, Zurich.

Thames drew the Swiss and were leading by ¾ length approaching Remenham Club when they suddenly went right away to lead by 2 lengths at the Mile, and won comfortably by that distance. They then beat the Norwegians by ¾ length after being led by ½ length early on, to put the Club in the final of the Grand for the first time since 1892.

Their opponents were Leander, composed entirely of Blues and stroked by the redoubtable Dink Horsfall. Thames were giving away half a stone a man but both crews struggled with the headwind, with Leander edging out to lead by 1 length at Fawley. Both strokes spurted and counter–spurted for the rest of the course, but Leander held on to win by 1 length. However, a four from the Grand eight, stroked by Rew, won all their races in the Wyfold with ease.

For the third year running Jack Beresford reached the final of the Diamonds but for once he was outclassed, probably the only occasion this happened. His opponent was an extraordinary American sculler, Walter Hoover, who had beaten a fast Australian, A.A. Baynes, in his semi-final. Theodore Cook, the editor of the *Rowing Almanack*, recorded:

> Great interest centred on the American sculler. A greater contrast to orthodox methods than Mr Hoover has never been seen in a winner of the Diamonds. His victory (by nearly half a minute) over Beresford was even more astonishing than our own F.S. Kelly's victory over Blackstaffe: for both the beaten men were sound, resolute scullers, whereas Kelly was perfection of form (as we believe in it) and Mr Hoover broke nearly all the rules. The American must have been extraordinarily strong, and no doubt developed, in practice, different muscles from those in ordinary use. His body and his boat as well were carefully and precisely calculated to suit his natural style. He went away after the sixth stroke. Nobody could ever get near enough to throw him out of his stride, and his defeat of Baynes was almost as conspicuous a proof of pace as his victory over Beresford.

As in the 1920 Olympics, the New World was again bringing the message to an Old World which seemed singularly reluctant to receive it, though for Beresford to fall victim to foreign scullers in successive years was a considerable shock. What Steve Fairbairn thought about it is not recorded, at least by Theodore Cook, who was so enraged by the coaching heresies propounded by Steve that he would not allow his name to be mentioned in his office.

Henley had one more surprise in store for Thames in the form of Vernon and West in the Goblets. They first easily beat a pair from Rotterdam, to whom they were conceding nearly 2 stone a man, and then beat Craig and Ivory, though the latter hit a pile near the second signal when only ¼ length down. So fifteen years after reaching his first Henley final, the Bean was there again. That Nickalls and Lucas, who had earlier eliminated Chandler and Fairbairn, would prove too strong for them was a foregone conclusion, but it was an achievement for the pair, averaging 10 st 10 lb, and with Bean over 40, to get there at all.

The 1922 Thames Grand eight won all their races except the final of the Grand, and the winning Wyfold four were unbeaten until two changes were made. Beresford repeated his wins in the London Cup and Wingfields, the unfortunate Gollan again being the victim, though, in Jack's absence, he won at Marlow, Staines, and Kingston. Jack broke the Wingfields record, which had stood since 1900, by 41 seconds, but Gollan, though a long way astern since Jack scented record conditions, also beat the old record.

Someone else began to emerge on the sculling scene, and from an unexpected quarter. London, still not back to their old form, were nevertheless beginning to expand at the lower end of the club and in 1922 had a useful junior eight which won two close races in the Thames Cup at Henley before going on to win the junior eights at Staines. At five in this crew was M.K. Morris. Morris, however, had resolved to become a sculler and won the junior sculls at the Met on his first appearance, beating Reggie Bare in the final. In the absence of Gollan and Beresford, he went on to win the senior event at Molesey with some ease, attracting considerable attention. The *Almanack* singled him out as someone to be watched.

10 New Heights

In England in 1923, more people than ever were rowing and there were record entries for regattas. It was the year of the new 'streamline' boats designed by Gilbert Bourne, and a new experimental straight course was tried out at Henley, the start being a little way down Temple Island on the Berks side, which reduced the length by about fifty yards. The hope was that, if this new course worked satisfactorily, some of the Island and the bank would be cut away to bring the start back to the bottom of the Island. The new course was a success and by 1924 the necessary excavations had been completed and the present course introduced.

Dr Bourne's new boat was the product of experimentation dating back to before the war. He had studied the shapes of fast-swimming fish, in the belief that natural evolution would have solved the problems of water resistance. He discovered that, whatever their proportions, the lines of entry fore and aft of fish always gave a curve of a certain character, and by 1914 he had evolved a new hull shape for an eight, which he gave to his old college, New College. They mistrusted this gift-horse, however, and did not use it at the time.

New College went Head of the River in it in 1921, though. Bourne then modified his design and in 1923 Oxford won the Boat Race with this new boat. The same boat also won the Grand in 1924.

The Bourne boat had its widest section nearer the bows than usual and tapered off to a narrow V towards the stern. Despite often inexplicable lurches which occurred from time to time and caused the cognoscenti to shake their heads in disapproval, it was undoubtedly very fast. The boat was built at Putney by 'Bossie' Phelps, and Steve Fairbairn promised Thames a similar boat if Oxford won the Boat Race. This was presented to the Club by Steve's brother, George, an Australian Senator, the boat being christened *Senator George*. The bows are still preserved in the Club and whatever the pros and cons of Bourne's design, the *Senator George* was extremely fast.

The 1923 Thames Grand eight were one of the fittest and lightest ever to represent the Club in the Grand, averaging 11 st 3 lb. Ian Fairbairn and Leigh Holman, the latter now down to 9 st 11 lb, filled the stern seats again; Chandler, Bare, Rew, and Wilson, who, like Ian, were all from Steve's 'young' 1920 Thames Cup winning eight, were also in the crew, together with 'Bones' Long from the 1922 Grand eight. Southgate was originally included but eventually lost his seat, while Jack Beresford, always quick to spot a good thing, came in at three.

In May, the crew won the senior eights at the De Hoop Regatta, Amsterdam, where a senior four, got together by the 55-year-old Berry, consisting of Berry, Richard Barrett-Lennard, Duggie Douglas, and stroked by the Bean, also won. Jock Lane and Harold West won the senior pairs, but Jack Beresford, in the senior sculls, paid the price for doubling up when he was beaten by a Swiss sculler, R. Bosshard of the Grasshopper Club, though Donald Gollan was the beneficiary of this, beating Bosshard in the final.

Kenneth Wilson replaced Southgate after Amsterdam and the Grand eight and the Stewards' four drawn from it both won at Marlow, where Jack Beresford beat the up-and-coming Morris by three lengths to win the senior sculls. The pair of West and Lane were also successful, but all this came at the end of a week in which Thames had endured a major domestic crisis, about which more will be said later.

At Henley, the opposition in the Grand included the Norwegians and the Rowing Club of Paris. Thames easily beat Christ Church and Pembroke, Cambridge, with three Blues, and with R.A. Nisbet at bow, disposed of the Norwegians, and went on to reach the final. In their semi-final, Thames had no difficulty with BNC, to reach the final for the second year running.

In the final, Pembroke led by a few feet at the first signal but Thames were ½ length ahead at the second and had ¾ length at the third. A tremendous fight now developed, Pembroke inching back, but Thames still had ½ length at the Mile, and with both crews sprinting in from there, Thames held on to win a great race by ⅓ length. This was Thames's first Grand win since Drake-Smith's crews of 1888–9.

It was a great triumph for Steve, of course, since he had built up the crew from scratch since 1920. The only lighter crew to have won the Grand, before or since, were Steve's own Jesus crew in 1885, which averaged 11 st 1½ lb, but taking into account the bigger entry and higher standard in 1923, the achievement of the Thames eight was the more remarkable.

The Thames Cup eight, stroked by Harold West, backed by Nougat Southgate, Jock Lane, and Bill Killick, lost in the third round to the ultimate winners, First Trinity, by a length.

Thames had two fours in the Stewards': Berry's, which had won at Amsterdam and Reading, and one from the eight, the Marlow winners, but as luck would have it, they drew each other. Berry's four were no match for the younger crew but Bare did just enough to win by a charitable ¾ length. This was the last of Berry's many Henley appearances, the first of which had been as far back as 1896, a remarkable span of twenty-seven years, one less than Safford's, but the latter was a cox.

The A crew were not able to hold the exceptional Third Trinity four, who won all their races easily. This was the famous four of Old Etonians who had won the Stewards' in 1922 as Eton Vikings and the Visitors' as Third Trinity – Eley, Macnabb, Morrison, and Sanders. A classic coxless four, they won the Stewards' again in 1924 and then crowned their distinguished career with the Olympic gold medal that year. Morrison continued rowing in 1925, winning the Stewards' and Visitors' again with different Third Trinity partners, and also took the Goblets from the redoubtable Nickalls and Lucas.

The new star, M.K. Morris, was in sensational form in the Diamonds, though the first shock came when Gollan beat the hitherto invincible American, Hoover, who came back from a 3-length deficit after hitting the booms to lose by only ¾ length. Beresford met Morris in the semi-final but again suffered from doubling up in the eight, the London sculler reversing the Marlow result, winning by 3 lengths. Morris had a hard struggle with Gollan in the final but won the event at his first attempt by a length. 'Geoffrey' Morris, as he was always known, was so exhausted he fell in after the race and had to be rescued. He claimed to have lost a stone in weight during the four days' racing. It was London's first post-war Henley win.

The crowning achievement of Steve's years with Thames since 1919, the winning of the Grand, was marred, however, by rumblings and bickering emanating from the second eight led by Southgate and Bill Killick, arising from one of the crew, A.P. Dawes, not being available for Henley. Steve had procured a replacement but the crew, against his wishes, brought in F.R. Barker from the junior eight instead. Steve was furious and on 17 June he wrote to the Honorary Secretary, E.E. Hughes, a letter which gives every indication of having been penned in haste:

> Dear Hughes,
> I think it would be best to elect another Captain as I am not up to it. My health is troubling me very much so I am sorry to say I must resign. Anno Domini tells me very plainly I must give it up. It has been a great pleasure to work with you and Reeve but I must give it up . . .

On 19 June, he wrote again:

> Ian tells me he is willing to run affairs till after Henley unless it is the wish of members to elect a new Captain at once. If you think that will meet the situation best you might put up a notice to that effect as I don't want to be bothered with a lot of questions, they worry me.

With feverish activity clearly going on behind the scene, he wrote again on 20 June, giving the real reason for his wishing to resign:

> I am sorry to say my resignation is irrevocable. It is not fair to my health to go on but on your letter I would have stretched a point and nominally remained if it had not been for the Thames Cup eight refusing to row the man I had got for them to take the place of Dawes at Henley. As they chose to take this step I feel it quite impossible for me to remain Captain. As the oarsman they intend to take in for Henley instead of Dawes is in a junior eight their action will do harm to that eight, also he will not be up to Thames Cup form, whereas the man I have got for them is an oarsman who is better than any of them and who would have improved their eight.
> Their action, besides being distinctly mutinous, is also doing harm to the Cup eight and the junior eight.

It is strange to find Steve writing like this since, as a champion of juniors and underdogs, he would normally have jumped at the chance of promoting some rising young hope, but presumably he had already promised a place to some oarsman from outside the Club, probably a Jesus man, without discussing it with the second eight. It was then only three days before Marlow and no doubt pre-Henley nerves were beginning to tell on everyone. The problem of stress at this period is well known to anyone who has rowed in or coached a Henley crew. Steve himself was also in some ways a surprisingly nervous man. In his introduction to *Steve Fairbairn on Rowing*, Ian wrote of his father:

> Probably many of his friends in the rowing world, even some of those who knew him best, were not fully aware of how desperately, almost morbidly, nervous he was. He was nervous to the point of being neurasthenic and this caused a great deal of unhappiness in his life.

In the 1920s, he was also in constant pain from his back, the result of an injury sustained while sculling in his first term at Cambridge when another sculler ran into him. Splinters from the bows of the other boat were not properly removed from his back and this led, over the years, to a painful cyst. Towards the end of the 1920s this and recurrent bouts of jaundice forced him to stop coaching altogether, so that with a mutinous second eight, a bad back, and tension with Henley looming up, it is hardly surprising that a relatively small incident should lead to rather drastic explosions of temperament.

Somehow – and one suspects it was Ian's doing – some sort of peace was restored and the Grand was duly won. Then, immediately after returning to Putney, the Club Committee met to sort it all out. Dawes and Killick, who were both on the Committee, said that they had no intention of being mutinous and a resolution was passed assuring Steve of the Committee's full support. Two days later, the meeting was resumed with Ian in the chair. Ian reported that Southgate had come up with other grievances and Ian replied that it must frequently happen that the second eight would be used as a wastepaper basket to receive men turned out of the first eight – a choice of words that can hardly have endeared him to the members of the second eight – and that the best men in the second eight would be taken for the first eight. Men who were not prepared to row where they were put were not wanted.

One can imagine what the bar talk was like during this period. In the end, after yet another meeting, the whole unpleasant affair petered out with Steve apparently placated, since he did not resign and took on the Captaincy again the following year, with Ian again his Deputy.

Despite all the bickering, the post-Henley regattas were once more highly successful for the Club. Gollan had a rare success against Jack Beresford in the London Cup, when it was the latter's turn to be disqualified.

In the Wingfields, with Morris again absent, Jack put Gollan back in his place and took the title for the fourth year running.

The winner of Doggett's Coat and Badge that year was Richard William Phelps, whose brother Tom had won the previous year. These two members of a distinguished family of watermen, eight others of whom also won Doggett's, were to become widely known throughout the rowing fraternity as watermen to Thames and London Rowing Clubs respectively.

After Henley, Leigh Holman was chosen as spare man to accompany a Leander crew which Cherry Pitman coached and took to Toronto in August for a regatta which was part of the Canadian National Exhibition. This was a great success for Leander, who beat the United States champions, Undine Barge Club, by 1½ lengths in the final. Holman did not row again and later married the young actress, Vivien Leigh, who took her stage name from her husband's second name, by which he was generally known; later she left Holman to marry Laurence Olivier.

For the Paris Olympics in 1924 what were to become until 1976 the standard seven international events – eights, coxed and coxless fours and pairs, and single and double sculls – were put on. Selection for these Olympics was complicated for the ARA by the existence of the National Amateur Rowing Association, which had been created in 1890 because of the restrictive ARA definition of amateurism. The NARA did not bar 'mechanics, artisans, or labourers' from their clubs and ran regattas and their own championships, but although their members could not compete at Henley or ARA regattas, they were eligible for the Olympic Games under the latter's rules. The ARA decided to organise trials in certain events between ARA and NARA crews. This was quite an advanced move by the ARA since it meant that their own chosen crews would be competing, with their blessing, against crews who were not, to their thinking, amateurs, though this could apply equally to many competitors in the Olympics.

The first problem for the ARA was to find an eight in time to be ready for the Olympics in July. Thames had already announced their intention of trying for selection, but Cambridge, winners of that year's Boat Race, declined to row a trial against Thames, while Leander, were not eligible with their American stroke, 'Pussy' Mellen, and were not prepared to change their crew. In the end, a rather farcical trial between Thames and Weybridge, then an NARA club, was held on 12 June over the Henley distance on the Surbiton reach. Weybridge, inevitably, were nowhere near the class and Thames won easily, to be selected for Paris. Weybridge were, however, selected for the coxed fours. Earlier the same day, over a mile course at Putney, Jack Beresford overwhelmed the NARA candidate, G. Roberts of Oxford House, and he, too, was selected.

The casual way in which the ARA went about these trials arose from their continued apathy to the whole idea of organised sport at international level. When a new constitution of the British Olympic Association had been put to the ARA for consideration in 1921, the following resolutions were carried unanimously:

1. That the Committee of the ARA are of the opinion:
(i) That organised international athletic competitions to take place at regular specific periods, and the expenditure of time and money which such competitions must necessarily entail are entirely contrary to the true spirit of amateur sport.
(ii) That the exaggerated importance which is attributed to success in such contests endangers rather than stimulates the friendly relations which ought to exist between rival competitors and their respective fellow-countrymen.
(iii) That the inclusion in the Olympic Games of all kinds of games and sports, irrespective of their value for athletic purposes, does not provide a true test of the comparative athletic merits of the competing countries.
2. That for the reasons stated in Resolution 1, the ARA declines to approve the objects or the proposed constitution of the British Olympic Association or to associate itself in any way therewith.

In 1924, however, the ARA had to form a committee, one of whom was Berry, the Thames representative on the ARA Committee, which would find crews for the Paris Olympics. But the ARA's lack of enthusiasm for the whole idea explains why no attempt was made to press Leander or the Universities to form potential Olympic eights that year. Hence the ease with which the Thames eight and Jack Beresford found themselves selected by early June.

That year, despite his continued involvement with the Grand eight, Steve coached all the junior boats and the second eight, which was to pay dividends in due course. On 9 June, the second eight and Jack Beresford competed in Ostend Regatta and forged the link with that regatta that was to strengthen over the years. The eight finished second to a Ghent crew, but Jack easily won the sculls. The eight then went on to win at Reading and Marlow. Records fell in all events at the latter regatta, the Grand eight taking 27 seconds off the record Thames had established the year before.

At Henley, the Grand eight, with five of the 1923 crew and the cox, Jack Godwin, drew a bye and eventually met Leander. The weather was bad for most of the regatta, with a strong stream and a blustery wind, so that times over the new full length straight course were exceptionally slow. Leander, stroked by Mellen and backed by Nickalls and Lucas, were, with one exception, all Blues. Thames led by a canvas at Fawley and, at the higher rate, were ⅓ length ahead at the ¾ mile. Both crews spurted repeatedly all the way home, Leander finally getting by to win by ½ length. In a desperate final, Leander beat Jesus by only 6 feet.

It was generally a disappointing Henley for Thames, but Southgate and Killick, the malcontents of the previous year, who were still rowing in the second eight, were also in the Goblets, in which they accounted for Chandler and Rew from the Grand eight before going out to the ultimate winners, Eley and Macnabb. As the latter were in the Third Trinity four that won the Stewards' and were chosen for the Olympics, the Thames pair, spare men for the Thames Olympic eight, were nominated for the Olympic coxless pairs.

Thames's morale at Henley was finally boosted by Jack Beresford. Geoffrey Morris did not defend the Diamonds and Jack beat in turn Gollan, Sebastian Earl, R.S. Muttlebury (Muttle's son), and in the final Kenneth Craig. His race against the immensely powerful but hardly stylish Seb Earl was his hardest. Earl pulled Jack back from 1½ lengths at the ½ Mile until he was almost level at the Mile. He could not quite get past, though, and it ended when he suddenly capsized opposite Phyllis Court.

The organisation of the Olympic Games in 1924 was, by all accounts, very poor. Conditions for the oarsmen were particularly bad and the course, on the Seine, was constantly being chopped up by launches and other craft. The umpire's boat was a punt driven by an aeroplane propeller which drowned all possibility of hearing anything either on board or outside, and this craft went round the crews at the start, creating a persistent wash.

Fortunately, the eight found fairly good conditions in their heat and qualified comfortably enough for the four-boat final, where they met Yale, representing the United States and for whom Benjamin Spock, the famous baby doctor, was rowing, Canada, and Italy. The race was rowed in a strong headwind and the water was very rough. Thames, realising that their only chance against the heavy Yale crew, with an advantage of 1½ stone a man over them, was to get an early lead, got in front initially but the rowing was rushed. The powerful Yale crew, who had beaten the full 1920-winning Navy crew in Trials, soon went by, as eventually did Canada and Italy, leaving Thames to finish a disappointing last.

The pair had even worse fortune, Southgate suffering from lumbago, and they could only paddle over. Once again, however, Jack Beresford excelled. He lost his heat in the single sculls to the American champion, Garrett Gilmore, by a very small margin, mainly because of some poor steering, but qualified for the final as the fastest loser. In the final, Jack produced his best form, going right away from Gilmore to win by 5 seconds and take the gold medal that had so narrowly eluded him in 1920. With this title went the Philadelphia Gold Cup which had been presented in honour of Kelly's 1920 Olympic win. A condition of presentation was that every four years the cup should go to the winner of the Olympic title, who would be subject to a challenge from any amateur sculler.

The best crew at the regatta were probably the Third Trinity four, though they were pushed fairly hard in the final by the previously unbeaten Canadians, winning eventually by 1¼ lengths. John B. Kelly and his cousin, Paul Costello, retained the double sculls which they had won in 1920, to give Kelly his third gold medal. Because of the Olympics, the Wingfields were not held until August, Jack paddling home ahead of Kenneth Craig for his fifth consecutive success.

At the Club Regatta, a Westminster School member of the Club won the handicap sculls, in which Denis Guye, a future Wingfields winner, finished second, and Berry fourth. The winner was H.R.A. Edwards, a school member since 1922, who was to become an outstanding London oarsman. At the other end of the age scale, in the invitation eights at the Richmond Charity Regatta on Boxing Day, Piggy Eyre, aged 76, scored yet another win.

THAMES ROWING CLUB.

GRAND CHALLENGE CUP

Commemoration Dinner

to be held at

THE THRONE ROOM,

HOLBORN RESTAURANT,

Tuesday, 9th October, 1923, at 7 for 7.15 p.m.

*Price **7s. 6d.***
(without Wine.)

Evening Dress Optional.

Ticket for the Grand Challenge Cup
Commemoration Dinner, 1923

11 Heydays

In 1925 a subtle change began to affect Thames, for that year saw what was virtually the end of Steve Fairbairn's active coaching at the Club. Not that much changed on the surface: Steve remained Captain, though Ian retired from rowing, having been selected to stand for Parliament, an ambition in which he was unsuccessful.

Steve was not well for much of the year, suffering from one of his periodic attacks of jaundice, and his visits to the Club became less frequent. He was also preoccupied in writing his first important book on rowing, *Rowing Notes*, which was to have such a wide influence at home and on the Continent when it was published in 1926. He wrote the book mainly because of misconceptions of his aims in some quarters. Controversy had surrounded his coaching for years and with his recent successes, now was the chance to answer his critics.

He was frequently accused of ruining English rowing, mainly by what he termed the 'Orthodox Brigade'. He always had a ready answer to his critics, of course, and in one of the many letters he wrote to my father between 1923 and his death, he said: 'People have said to me: "If that is rowing I don't know anything about rowing." To which I have replied: "I never said you did".'

In later years he became more extreme in his ideas but by then many of his battles had been won. Above all, it was the man himself that counted. It is no exaggeration to say that Steve was a genius as a coach. His followers were devoted to him, and his crews, more often than not, won. It was because they won rowing in the 'wrong' way that he was not forgiven by his opponents from the old school.

Ill-health eventually forced him to resign the Captaincy in May 1925, 'Bones' Long taking over with Jack Beresford as Deputy. Chandler, Long, Debenham, and Rew, and the cox, Godwin, all remained from the 1924 Grand eight, and a newcomer was 'Felix' Badcock, whom Steve had been nursing for a couple of seasons, and who came in at six. Bill Killick at last found a place, while a surprise inclusion at two was the veteran Bean Vernon. Jack Beresford concentrated on the Diamonds.

Both the Grand and Thames Cup eights arrived at Henley with Marlow wins behind them. The Grand eight had beaten Jesus, Head of the River at Cambridge, by ½ length and there was a needle match when the two crews met at Henley. In glorious weather, Thames led by a length at the Mile. Jesus spurted hard all the way home but Thames won by ½ length. Thames then beat the Oxford Head crew, Christ Church, by ¾ length and so reached the final once again. Leander were rather more formidable than their immediate predecessors and, in very fast conditions, set a new record to Fawley (3min 17sec), where they led Thames by a length, and despite determined efforts by Rew, they held on to win by ¾ length in 6min 53sec, two seconds outside the record. Nickalls and Lucas, in the Leander eight, were recording their fifth Grand win, while the five Oxford men in the crew, one of whom was the cox, Jock Clapperton, were the only Oxonians to win at Henley that year.

Third Trinity, a new crew, were too strong for everyone in the Stewards', but the Thames Wyfold four, stroked by Badcock, won their final against Selwyn, equalling the record.

Hoover, the 1922 sensation, entered the Diamonds again and put out Geoffrey Morris before meeting Beresford in a semi-final. In view of the drubbing the Thames man had been given in 1922, this race was keenly anticipated. The *Almanack* says that it was perhaps the finest thing at the whole meeting:

> Both men went for the lead from the first stroke. Neither could quite certainly attain it. By the half mile they had given up that particular ambition, but were still going full steam, watching each other carefully. Neither showed the least sign of faltering, and there was very little in it at the Mile. Beresford, magnificently trained and showing splendid form, which he kept to the very end, began his spurt about 200 yards from the finish and came home like a lion. Hoover, outpaced and never admitting defeat, worked himself right out to the last ounce, and the two best amateur scullers now racing received a tremendous ovation as the flag fell, which they most thoroughly deserved.

Jack won by three lengths and it was, in effect, the final. The next day, he recorded yet another easy win over Donald Gollan, who never knew how to cope with his rival. Jack, on the other hand, always knew exactly what to do to beat Gollan. The latter, weighing over 13 stone, was magnificently built and ably coached by his father Spencer Gollan, who used hand signs since his son had been born deaf and was therefore also dumb. Jack said that if Gollan could have pushed himself when it mattered he could have beaten anyone, but he never could and Jack knew exactly when to apply the pressure to settle the issue.

After Henley, Beresford again met Hoover, who had challenged him for the Philadelphia Gold Cup, the race taking place at Putney on 13 July over a course from the University Stone to Harrods Wharf. Fortunately, from the American's point of view, conditions were perfect and the water calm. Beresford, on the Surrey station, was ½ length ahead after 30 seconds, but they were level again as they passed the Thames clubhouse. Jack then put in a hard burst and he was clear at Beverley Brook, where Hoover made a desperate effort to get on terms. However, he came across and touched Beresford's boat, both scullers stopping for a stroke or two. On being told by the umpire, Fred Pitman, to continue, Beresford got away the better. He had two lengths at Craven Steps and pulled further ahead to win by 3½ lengths in 6min 47sec. Jack later won the London Cup and, for the sixth time in succession, the Wingfield Sculls.

That autumn there was a contested election for the Captaincy, the Committee having failed to agree on a candidate. Steve had proposed Bones Long, and Jack Beresford his father. Considerable ill-feeling existed at that time between Berry and Steve, mostly on Berry's side, the result of some row of epic proportions probably emanating from the 1923 'mutiny' by the second eight, which Berry had coached. What it was all about has long been forgotten, but even in my own rowing days in the 1950s and 1960s it was still referred to as 'The Row'. Whatever the cause, Berry never made his peace with Steve. So there was an election, Berry winning by 41 votes to 33.

It was from this moment that Steve began to turn his attention towards helping London. Archie Nisbet, who had been Captain of London since 1924, had given him a permanent invitation to coach London if he ever found himself in a position to do so, and took the offer up in 1926. Nisbet had been a member of Thames, having been proposed by Steve, but he resigned in 1923. It was said that, having been in the Pembroke eight who were narrowly defeated by Thames in the final of the Grand in 1923, he immediately joined London to get his revenge. Archie's version was more prosaic: one day after rowing at Thames, he found that the first eight had used up all the hot water in the showers, so he had gone down to London in a huff!

Archie's capture of Steve, and his own efforts as well, were to lead a London revival comparable to that earlier enjoyed by Thames. Steve's move inevitably led to ill-feeling between the clubs, and a few Thames men followed him down the road, the main defector being Charles Rew, but in the end he was the only one to row for London at Henley. Felix Badcock wrote:

> It must not be supposed that when Steve left us the Fairbairn style died in Thames; there was still his second line of defence to carry out the tradition of 'driving off the stretcher'. The 1924 second eight and junior boats had all been coached at some time by Steve and they were only just maturing into first-class boat movers. It is interesting to note that during the latter part of his coaching at Thames he was rather emphasizing a long swing and hard finish, possibly because the 'leg-drive' was already there.

To be fair to Steve, he had long felt that for the good of Tideway rowing as a whole, Thames needed more competition. He was able to coach London only until 1928, however. Ill-health again forced him to give up, but he had laid the foundations for London's resurgence, and the coaches that followed him were all his disciples.

Meanwhile, at Thames, the main burden of coaching fell on Berry. Different as he was from Steve in temperament and personality, he, too, was a brilliant coach, with a canniness that even Steve to some extent lacked.

Moreover, 1926 was a difficult year for other reasons, not least the General Strike, which seriously disrupted summer training. Then Bones Long, who, despite his defeat at the Captain's Meeting, had continued to row, had to drop out with appendicitis. He eventually followed Rew down to London but he never rowed again in a Henley crew.

This was also the year in which the 19-year-old-freshman, H.R.A. ('Jumbo') Edwards, rowing five in the Oxford crew, collapsed at Chiswick Eyot in the Boat Race and stopped rowing for a stroke or two. The crews were virtually level at the time and Jumbo came in for some unfair criticism, but Steve came to his defence in print, saying that had the rest of the crew rowed as hard, Oxford would have had the race won long before this point. But the mud stuck and it was some years before Jumbo restored his reputation with some outstanding triumphs.

That summer, Jumbo came down to Thames looking for a place in a Henley crew, but the crews had already been made up. The following year he rowed in the London Grand eight and so, with one notable exception when he came into the 1932 Olympic four, he never rowed with Thames.

With Rew's departure to London, Berry put his son Jack to stroke the Grand eight, and Jack also doubled up in the Diamonds again. Thames had been beaten in the Grand in the previous two years by Leander and in 1926 they drew them in the first round. With four of their 1925 crew, and stroked by the Cambridge Blue, David Collet, Leander were clear favourites from the start, but Thames made a great race of it, coming from behind to draw level at the Mile. Both crews were flat out along the enclosures but Leander got home by ½ length. In the final, Leander were far too good for Lady Margaret, equalling the record to Fawley before easing off for their third consecutive win in the Grand.

The Thames Stewards' four, stroked by Felix Badcock, reached their final, to meet Leander once again. Leander led by a length at the ½ Mile, but Thames were rowing well within themselves and when Felix applied the pressure at Fawley he gained at once. Thames were a length ahead at the Mile and eventually won easily. This was the Club's first Stewards' win since 1911.

Collet, a very fine sculler, had also entered the Diamonds, but Jack Beresford, having disposed of Gollan yet again, comfortably beat him in the next round and then beat another Cambridge Blue, Goddard, in the final for his fourth Diamonds win and his third in successive years.

Jack beat Collet again in the London Cup and then met him in the Wingfields, which was again marred by a foul. Collet was being shown up by Guy Nickalls but his cutter could not keep up and Collet had to steer without help. Jack was leading when Collet crossed behind him approaching Harrods where, to his surprise, he found himself in Jack's wash and on the wrong side of his boat. His scull put a four-inch crack in the stern of Jack's boat, which began to take in water. Collet carried on but Jack was still leading at Hammersmith Bridge. Collet then passed him and eventually won by six lengths. Jack claimed a foul and Harry Blackstaffe, the unpire, awarded him the race. In this unfortunate way, Jack beat Casamajor's record with a seventh successive win.

Because of the nature of this result, the two scullers arranged a private match over the full championship course twelve days later, a sporting gesture on Jack's part which was much appreciated by the rowing world. The two men were shown up by Berry and Cherry Pitman in launches, to avoid a repetition of the previous problem. Even so, Collet wandered about on the course but had established a sufficient lead by Hammersmith to keep out of trouble. Soon after the bridge, he was directly in front of Jack, who then went for him, but Collet held him off and Jack began to show signs of tiring. He was, however, only 1½ lengths behind at Barnes Bridge. Collet, who had never been below 30 at any stage, was now also near exhaustion. Jack made a tremendous effort to catch him, but Collet, rolling and desperately tired, somehow held on to win by a length. His time of 21min 32sec was 41 seconds better than the amateur record set by Jack in 1922. It had been an exceptionally fine race and both men were loudly cheered. Jack did not go for the Wingfields again.

Steve's influence at London was now beginning to be felt and the already strained relationships between the two clubs took a turn for the worse as the result of an unfortunate decision in the Met, where London had several wins, though in the final of the Champion Eights, London and Thames dead-heated, sharing the trophy. The trouble occurred in the senior fours for the Thames Cup, which Thames had lost only once (1912) since 1908. Thames had their winning Stewards' four against a London four containing Gully Nickalls at three. The crews clashed and the race had to be restarted twice, with the agreement of both crews. Thames crossed the line first, there having been no further incidents, but were then disqualified. Needless to say, this totally incorrect decision by the umpire incensed Thames members. The Thames Cup eight, who had won the Old Barnes Cup, refused to go down to London to collect their medals, and the Club appealed to the ARA over the validity of the decision. Inevitably, the ARA had to support Thames's argument that, since the umpire had restarted the race without disqualifying either crew, what had gone on before was irrelevant, but though Thames won their point, the club had already said that, notwithstanding any ruling by the ARA, they would let the umpire's decision stand, so London kept the trophy.

In December 1926, Steve Fairbairn organised the first-ever Head of the River Race, a processional race against the clock. This has since become a major event in the rowing calendar and other Head races all over Britain and abroad have been established. The first, over the reverse Boat Race course, was held on 12 December, with twenty crews participating, though absentees prevented the top two Thames eights from entering, while the third eight were disqualified for being paced, presumably by one of the non-competing Thames crews. London won by 51 seconds from a business house club, Gresham, which Steve had helped to coach. A second Head was held the following March, forty crews taking part. Thames and London dead-heated for the title, with Jesus third. The race has been held in March ever since.

In the spring of 1927, Jack Beresford suggested tactfully to Spencer Gollan that his son's future as a sculler was limited and that rowing in an eight might bring out the best in him. The old man leapt at the idea and in no time at all Donald was installed at five in the Grand eight.

Another recruit was Jamie, better known as Hamish, Hamilton, a former Caius stroke who had not rowed at Henley since 1922. He wrote to me in 1984:

> After leaving Caius . . . I went to America to learn publishing. Returning to the UK, I happened, Heaven knows how, to go down to the TRC one day in 1926 . . . How often I rowed there I can't remember but that year, in a race from Hammersmith to Putney, I was stroking the Thames eight. Passing the boathouse we were about ¾ length down and I put in a terrific spurt, to dead-heat. Gully Nickalls, rowing seven in the London RC boat (the other finalists), wrote me that it was as unpleasant to row against us as it must have been dramatic to watch.
>
> Old Berry, Jack *et al* were most enthusiastic and made me promise to stroke them in 1927.

Hamilton had earlier stroked the second eight to win at Molesey and on the strength of this had been put into the first eight for the Met, Jack having dropped out to concentrate on sculling. The crew went on to win at Staines with Hamilton still stroking.

Jack did not row in the eight in 1927 but five of the 1926 Grand eight were included. At Henley, Thames again drew Leander, a crew consisting entirely of Blues and with the perennial Gully Nickalls at seven. Three inches of rain fell during the week and the weather was at its worst for this race, with a strong following wind against a strong stream. Leander had a few feet at the first signal, but Thames quickly drew ahead to lead by 1½ lengths at Fawley and went on to win by 2 lengths to end Leander's run of three Grand wins.

In the final, Thames met London, who had beaten Jesus by ½ length. This was only the second occasion (the first being in 1877) that the two clubs had met in the final of the Grand. On a misty day with fine drizzle and gusts of following wind, Thames led at once and were never headed. The *Almanack* says their pace at the Barrier was quite extraordinary. They increased a lead of ¼ length at the first signal to 1¼ at the second. London sprinted home at 40 while Thames came home at 36 to win by ¾ length. The *Almanack* commented:

> Thames must be judged to have been a very fast crew and under favourable conditions it would have been hard to deny they could have approached record time. Their pace must be attributed to the fact that their stroke, J. Hamilton, set them a very good rhythm and knew at all the points of the course exactly their best pace. To this must be added that the crew were very well trained and rowed with almost perfect uniformity . . . J. Beresford, senior, had adapted and extended the Fairbairn style on which they were grounded originally until it was almost in line with what is known as the orthodox, the main difference being that they were not quite so quick into the water as the idealist would desire, largely, perhaps, owing to the fact that they used swivel rowlocks.

There were twenty-five entries in the Thames Cup, with Kent School, USA, making the first of many Henley appearances. Kent were the heaviest crew at Henley that year and Thames, who drew them in the first round, were conceding 21 lb a man. The crews were level at the Mile, there never having been more than ¼ length in it to that point, but Thames, stroked by Berry's younger son, Eric, rowing more smoothly than Kent, just had the edge to win a fine race by the same margin.

Thames continued comfortably through the next three rounds but the final against Twickenham was a hard one, with the crews level at the bottom of the enclosures, but again Thames had enough in reserve to pull ahead to win by ¼ length. This was the first occasion on which the Club had won the Grand and Thames Cup on the same day, a feat achieved by a single club only seven times in the regatta's history.

The Stewards' four beat London easily, and then came from 2 lengths behind in the final to row through Leander after the Mile, after which they went away fast to retain the cup by 2 lengths. Thames also took the Wyfold Cup, beating their next-door neighbours, Vesta, by 2 lengths in the final. This was a remarkable achievement for Duggie Douglas, who stroked this four. He had first rowed for Thames seventeen years earlier, in the Grand. He had won the Thames Cup in 1920, making up the numbers in Steve's 'young' eight, and in 1927 he was also doubling up in the Goblets with an even more senior member of the Club, Bean Vernon, whose first Henley appearance had been twenty-one years earlier. This was the last Henley for these two Thames stalwarts, who had little chance in the Goblets, going out to the eventual winners, Archie Nisbet and Terence O'Brien of London.

The only real disappointment for the Club at this otherwise highly successful Henley was Jack Beresford's defeat in the Diamonds. He was comfortably beaten by an unknown from Worcester College, Oxford, R.T. Lee, but the real surprise, not least to Lee himself, was his win in the final. There was an exceptionally strong entry, which included Collet and a fast Canadian, Joe Wright. Wright beat Collet, who stopped suddenly when leading a few lengths short of the finish. That was generally regarded to have been effectively the final, but Wright was leading Lee by 3 lengths with fifty yards to go when his arm gave out and he ran into the booms, to allow an astonished Lee to go by to win.

For Thames and Berry, it was a most triumphant Henley. Thames had never before won four Henley events in one day and there had not been a clean sweep of the open fours and eights since Trinity Hall's successes of 1887. There were a lot of very happy Thames men after this Henley, but none more so than old Spencer Gollan, who had so patiently coached his son for so little reward for so long. Donald had been unlucky in that such an outstanding sculler as Jack Beresford should have been on the scene during his own sculling days and it was fitting that it was Jack's persuasiveness that finally brought Donald his long-sought Henley medals. The irony was that, while he was winning the Grand and the Stewards', Jack was losing in the Diamonds.

The Thames Grand eight was changed after Henley, and London once again began to pick up post-Henley trophies. At Molesey, they beat the full Thames Stewards' four, and they won several events at the Met, including the Champion Eights from a scratch Thames crew. David Collet won the Wingfields, being shown up by Jack, who had resigned his title. Jack did not compete in the London Cup, which went to Collet, who went on to retain the Championship of the Seine, which he had won the previous year.

All through 1927 and the beginning of 1928 the threat of a new electric power scheme at Chiswick hung over the Tideway. The power station would have meant 2,000 tons of coal a day being brought up the river by tugs, and water drawn from the river would have had to be pumped back, making rowing in the area almost impossible. Berry, as the Club's ARA representative, organised a petition from the Tideway clubs and attended the House of Commons as a witness to the enquiry before a Bill was to be put to Parliament. Mainly through Berry's pressure, the Bill was dropped, one presumes after the Prime Minister, Stanley Baldwin, had been given lunch at Thames in March with other interested parties!

The Olympic Games were to be held in Amsterdam in 1928 but the ARA continued to express its antipathy to the Olympic ideal. In 1926, the Canadian Association of Amateur Oarsmen had asked the ARA to get together with them and the American NAAO to try to get the management of Olympic rowing into proper hands. The ARA replied that it had never been in sympathy with the Olympic Games or Olympic Regattas; that it had not hitherto taken any active part in promoting British entries for such regattas, and had merely acted as a body of reference to receive, examine, and pass on entries to the Olympic authorities, though the ARA was perfectly willing to consider proposals from the CAAO.

This attitude still prevailed in 1928, but the ARA did form a selection committee, chaired by Cherry Pitman, with two members each nominated by Thames, London, and Leander, which can have been nothing if not biased.

Once again, they went through the motion of holding trials with NARA crews, in which the Thames eight and David Collet were easy winners, and Nottingham and Union easily beat Clapton Warwick, a Lea club, in the coxed fours, to become the first provincial crew to gain international selection. Further selections were to be made after Henley.

After they had been beaten by Thames in 1927, Leander had asked Hamilton to stroke them in 1928, but he remained faithful to Thames and turned the tables on Leander by making it a condition of rowing for Thames that the Club got Gully Nickalls to row seven for them. Gully agreed to this, but he was practically expelled from Leander for this move. Apparently it was all right for Leander to poach men from Thames but unforgiveable for the reverse to happen! Gully, however, was always quick to see where his best chance lay and he did not regret his decision. He was soon forgiven by Leander and became their President from 1962–66.

Six of the 1927 Grand eight were rowing again in 1928, and Jack Beresford, now Captain of the Club, realising that his chances of beating Collet were slender, had come into the eight. There was also a new cox in Arthur Sulley, who steered the winning Cambridge crew in the Boat Race that year. A member of Thames, he had been coming down to the Club from Cambridge on Sundays to get Tideway experience. After the Boat Race, Jack asked him to cox the Thames Grand eight at Henley.

Eric Beresford again stroked the Thames Cup eight, and at seven was Charles Allanson-Winn who, from 1923, had been in the Twickenham eight. He had rowed in the 1927 crew that had pushed Thames so hard in the final.

It was a powerful Thames contingent and the only relatively weak crew were the Wyfold four, three of whom were not yet seniors. My father, Freddie Page, had rowed in this crew but could not get time off for Henley from St Paul's School, where he was teaching. His place was taken by F.E. Cameron-Cox from the 1927 Thames Cup eight. As a result, my father began to concentrate on coaching and became Captain of Juniors that autumn.

The Grand eight arrived at Henley having won the Marlow Grand once again, though Charles Allanson-Winn must have been somewhat put out when Thames were beaten by his former club in the final of the Marlow Eights. The Stewards' four had also lost to London, but Beresford and Killick had won the pairs.

The entry at Henley had now grown to the extent that eliminating races in the Ladies' and Wyfold had to be held on the Saturday before the regatta, though Thames were not involved. In the Grand final, Thames met the Cambridge Head crew, First Trinity, who had beaten a poor Leander eight. Thames led by ½ length at Fawley, where they were only one second outside the record, and eventually won unpressed by 1½ lengths. This gave Gully Nickalls his seventh Grand win, a record to this day.

The Stewards' four beat Third Trinity comfortably but in the final they had a desperately hard race with London, who were stroked by Charles

Rew. London led by ½ length at the ¾ Mile. Badcock then raised his rate and began to close. Thames were a canvas down at the Mile, where Rew went to 40, holding this rate to the finish, but Thames, at 37, came through to win by 2 feet by virtue of a tremendous last twenty strokes.

The Thames Cup was retained, again at the expense of Twickenham in the final. The crews had been level at the Mile and it was only halfway up the enclosures, with the crews rowing stroke-for-stroke, that Thames got their bows in front and then drew away to win by ¾ length.

The Wyfold four lost in the second round but Thames improved on their previous year's performance by taking the higher-ranked Goblets, Killick and Beresford having beaten the holders, Nisbet and O'Brien, by 5 lengths in their heat. They easily beat a Quintin pair in the final.

As a result of these performances, the Stewards' four and the pair were invited to row in the Olympics, but as the eight had already been selected, they declined to double up and by mutual agreement Nisbet and O'Brien went for the coxless pairs, First Trinity, who had won the Visitors', being selected for the coxless fours.

The Olympic Regatta, on the Sloten Canal, Amsterdam, was held early in August, and neither the ARA nor the CAAO could complain about the organisation in 1928. Although it was possible to row only two crews abreast, there was, for the first time, a limited *repêchage* system, whereby losing crews in the first round were given a second chance to qualify. There was even a radio commentary. The *Almanack*, British to the last, said, 'The course was perfectly fair on every day except one when what we should call a "Bushes Wind" gave a great advantage to everyone on the "Bucks" side.' British spectators were again amazed at the high standard of 'foreign' rowing.

Charles Morrell of Thames, who spoke fluent Dutch, was a great success as manager to the British team. However, the British officials had again got their homework wrong, Jack Beresford reporting later:

> Once again British chances were jeopardised by the situation of the hotel, miles from the course; consequently a hair-raising motor coach or taxi run had to be undertaken four times a day. Travelling a distance under the best of conditions is to be deprecated, and on the existing, winding narrow *pavé* roads, it had to be experienced to be appreciated.

The Thames eight drew Italy in the first round, winning by only ½ length. As the reigning European champions, the Italians could have been expected to be fast, but British oarsmen were still assessing the international standards by those of Henley, and Thames underestimated the Italians' pace. When the latter went off the mark at 52 and rowed the rest of the course at 44, Thames fully expected them to 'blow up', but they did not, and, finishing at 50, they made Thames go flat out to beat them. Thames then beat Poland by 6 lengths, to meet Germany in the semi-final, this being the first time since the war that the Germans had been allowed to compete. Jamie Hamilton remembered this as the most dramatic heat of the regatta: 'They led us near the finish and when we spurted and drew level they cracked and did not finish the course.'

The other finalists, the United States crew from the University of California, averaged 13 stone, an advantage of ¾ stone a man over Thames. They had beaten every other American crew of note, breaking every record they went for. At Amsterdam they had made the same mistake that Thames had, underestimating the Canadians, represented by the Toronto Argonauts. California took things too easily and the Canadians never let them go. There was never daylight between the crews and when the Canadians made their final effort, the Americans had to go into top gear to win by ½ length. The *Almanack* records:

> The final brought together two of the finest crews in the rowing world of 1928. The spectators looked forward to a thrilling encounter and were in no wise disappointed. Both crews went off at a very high rate, putting in 22 in the first half minute, Hamilton completing 42 to the Americans' 44 in the full minute. The boats hung together, and not until a quarter of the course had been completed did the Americans show half a length ahead. At half-way they held a length, though Thames were gaining on them. From the 1,000 metre mark the Americans spurted no less than four times. Four times their coxswain rattled imperatively with the side-plates against the hull, for the last ounce to be put in; but in spite of all the efforts his men put forth, Thames came up on them. The last 500 yards saw both crews beginning a desperate final burst, Hamilton putting in 40 to his opponent's 42, and it seemed as though the Englishmen might just snatch victory on the post. They only just failed, after a long and splendid spurt. The excitement was overpowering, but the Americans kept it going and shot home a bare half-length to the good in 6min 3sec against 6min 5sec. The race came last on the programme and was a fitting wind-up to as fine an Olympic regatta as has ever been witnessed.

As Nisbet and O'Brien came through the *repêchages* to finish only 2 seconds behind the Germans, who had been coached by Ernest Barry, in the final of the pairs, and the First Trinity four did even better by winning the coxless fours by ½ length, rowing the Americans to a standstill in another magnificent final, the Thames eight's silver medal had probably been at the expense of two golds, since at Henley, the Stewards' four had proved themselves faster than the Olympic winners and the Goblets pair had beaten Nisbet and O'Brien by 5 lengths. However, no other British eight could have done as well as Thames, and it was a highly successful regatta for Britain.

On the debit side were failures in the other events. The Nottingham four, having arrived, in ignorance of the rules, with a cox who was too light and too young, had to carry the 8½ stone Arthur Sulley instead, but they were in any case outclassed. Denis Guye and Humphrey Boardman of London, a semi-scratch double scull, were eliminated in the second round, while Collet, the only man to extend Bob Pearce, the Australian winner of the single sculls, did so in a semi-final and, though clearly the second best sculler, he was denied the silver medal, one of the unfortunate consequences of two-abreast racing, with *repêchages* confined to the first round.

While the first eight were battling away in Amsterdam, the Thames second eight, with two changes, went to Cork to take part in the Irish National Games. They had a wonderful reception during their stay, and in the Tailteann Eights they beat Glasgow University by 10 lengths before taking 17 seconds off the course record when beating Queen's University, Belfast, by 3 lengths in the final, Eric Beresford having rowed the last two minutes at 40.

Gully Nickalls, who said he had never been as fit as he had been with Thames, decided to call it a day after the Olympics, and Donald Gollan, having won four Henley medals in two years, as well as his Olympic medal, also decided to rest on his laurels. Jamie Hamilton gave up to become a famous publisher, while Jock Lane, after seven Henleys, and Harold West, after five, also decided to retire at the top.

In 1929, only Bill Killick, Felix Badcock, and Jack Beresford, who was still Captain of the Club, remained from the Olympic eight. In the circumstances, Thames could hardly expect to maintain the level of the previous two seasons. Eric Beresford, though barely 10 stone, stroked the Grand eight, with Jack, only a stone heavier, at five, where, for all his skill, he was overplaced. For once, the Club had no wins at Marlow and lost the Marlow Grand by 2½ lengths to London, who had recruited some good college oarsmen, and were stroked by Terry O'Brien.

In their heat at Henley, London, with Jumbo Edwards at five and Humphrey Boardman at six, dead-heated with the Toronto Argonauts, when the Canadians, who had given California such a scare in the Olympics, caught London on the line. However, London just had the edge in the re-row, to win by ¼ length. Not surprisingly, after this, London went down to a fresh Leander crew composed entirely of winning Cambridge Blues. Thames, underrating in a strong head-wind, reached the final for the third year running by beating Jesus, who were stroked by Philip Carpmael, later to become one of London's most distinguished oarsmen and their President. However, Thames could not match Leander's pace in the final and lost by 2 lengths.

The Thames Cup eight also reached the final for the third year running but went down to Browne and Nichols School, USA, by 1¼ lengths, though the Wyfold four, drawn from the Grand eight, came through their heats with ease to beat Jesus, who hit the booms, in the final. Killick and Jack Beresford had a rather more traumatic time in the Goblets, hitting the booms just after the Barrier in their heat against a Third Trinity pair, Carver and Sanders. The Cambridge pair led by 3 lengths at the ½ Mile but Thames had reduced this to 1½ lengths at the Mile, where Jack began a sustained spurt, coming back stroke by stroke to dead-heat, twenty minutes before London did the same thing in the Grand. Thames won the re-row by 2½ lengths and were too good for the Oxford Blues Graham and Morphett in the final, retaining the trophy by 1¾ lengths.

So, despite the odds, Thames had reached four finals again. They took away only two trophies, but London, despite their revival, came away with none. Thames's tally of Henley wins since 1920 was now twenty, in addition to which the Club had twice represented Great Britain in the Olympic eights, twice in the single sculls, and once each in the coxed and coxless pairs.

Jack Beresford's record during this period was outstanding and included one gold and two silver Olympic medals, as well as winning the Philadelphia Gold Cup, the Wingfield Sculls a record seven times, the London Cup five times, and countless other regatta wins at home and abroad. At Henley, he won the Grand and Goblets twice, in addition to his four Diamonds wins. With his brother Eric's two wins in the Thames Cup and one in the Wyfold to add to Berry's 1919 Fawley Cup win, it was a great decade for the Beresfords.

It is easy to group historical happenings into decades, which can be rather artificial divisions, but the end of the 1920s did bring to an end the greatest era in Thames rowing. Other successes were to come in the 1930s, but the beginning of that decade coincided with London's own great revival, and as far as Tideway rowing was concerned it was to be their decade rather than Thames's.

16. The 'Old Men', winners of the senior eights at Walton Regatta, 1920: J. Beresford Snr, G. H. Kelly, B. Logan, C. K. Roylance, C. A. A. Robertson (cox), A. E. Ellis, E. C. Goodall, K. Vernon, V. G. Teale

17. J. Beresford Jnr, after winning the London Cup at the Metropolitan Regatta, 1921

18. Steve Fairbairn

19. Amsterdam Regatta, 1923: the Thames winning senior fours:
J. Beresford Snr (bow), T. R. F. Barrett-Lennard, W. S. Douglas, K. Vernon (stroke)

20. The Grand eight after winning at Marlow Regatta, 1924:
left to right: C. G. Chandler, C. H. Rew, A. F. Long,
H. W. Dulley, J. Godwin (cox), H. L. Morphy,
H. C. Debenham, R. G. Bare, S. I. Fairbairn

21. Thames beating Pembroke College, Cambridge,
in the final of the Grand, 1923 (from the tower of Henley Church)

22. The start of the race between J. Beresford Jnr and W. Hoover for the Philadelphia Gold Cup at Putney, 1925, won by Beresford, the holder

23. J. Beresford Jnr beating D. H. L. Gollan in the Diamond Sculls, 1926

24. Felix Badcock and the masseur, 'Darkie' Williams, in happy mood at Henley

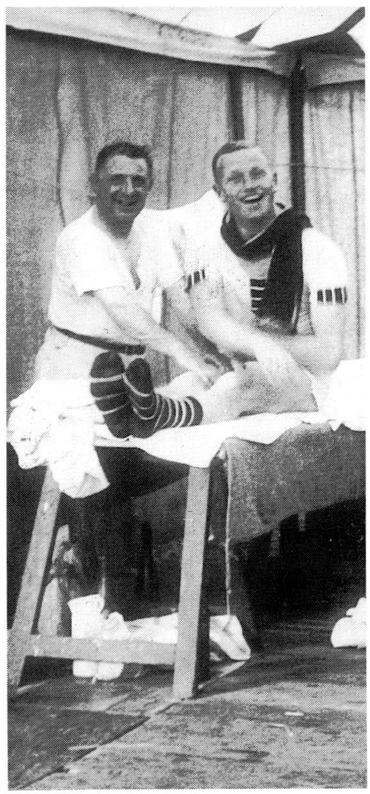

25. Thames beating London in the final of the Grand, 1927. *Top* Thames: H. E. West (bow), G. D. Smith, D. Wheeler, H. M. Lane, D. H. L. Gollan, J. C. Badcock, G. C. Killick, J. (Hamish) Hamilton (stroke), J. Godwin (cox). *Bottom* London: R. A. Nisbet (bow), C. H. Rew, W. E. E. Webb, W. A. H. Rowat, H. R. A. Edwards, J. N. Rofe, A. J. Peppercorn, T. N. O'Brien (stroke), H. D. Winkworth (cox)

26. A Thames group at Henley, 1928, the winners of the Grand, Stewards', Thames, and the Goblets. *Back row, left to right*: J. H. Hartley, A. J. Gaul, E. Everest, D. G. Newton, H. R. A. Edwards (spare man). *Third row*: W. D. Spurling, E. G. Beresford, A. P. McEldowney, H. W. Dulley, R. D. G. Barrett, J. K. Brownell, Hon C. R. Allanson-Winn. *Second row*: L. Beedell (boatman), G. C. Killick, G. O. Nickalls, J. C. Badcock, J. (Hamish) Hamilton, J. Beresford Jnr, H. E. West, D. H. L. Gollan, H. M. Lane, Darkie Williams (masseur). *Seated*: H. R. Simmonds, H. W. Burleigh, W. S. Douglas, J. Beresford Snr (coach), K. Vernon, G. B. Hicks, R. F. Reeve. *Seated foreground*: F. J. Gerring, A. L. Sulley (coxes)

27. Felix Badcock, one of the greatest of Thames strokes

28. Leander beating Thames by $\frac{1}{2}$ length in the final of the Grand, 1932. *Top* Leander: D. Haig-Thomas, K. M. Payne, T. G. Askwith, W. A. T. Sambell, C. J. S. Sergel, H. R. N. Rickett, D. H. E. McCowen, L. Luxton (stroke), J. M. Ranking (cox). *Bottom* Thames: B. E. A. Joyner (bow), T. H. Tyler, R. D. George, G. Hardwicke, J. H. M. Ward, J. C. Badcock, J. Beresford Jnr, D. C. Price (stroke), J. G. Dearlove (cox)

29. Great Britain winning the coxless fours in the 1932 Olympic Games at Long Beach, California: R. D. George (bow), J. Beresford Jnr, H. R. A. Edwards, J. C. Badcock (stroke)

30. The 1934 Thames Cup final, Thames beating London by $\frac{1}{3}$ length

31. The winning Thames Cup eight, 1934. *Standing, left to right*: R. R. E. Bradley, H. W. T. Beckett, R. C. Morris, R. H. B. Lord. *Seated*: R. W. Messom, H. E. G. Watts (stroke), J. H. Page (Captain of Thames, coach), K. A. Williams, J. A. Maclean. *Seated, front*: E. V. Pidduck (cox)

32. The Thames second eight, winners of the first North of England Head of the River Race, Chester, 1935. *Left to right* H. E. G. Watts (stroke), H. W. T. Beckett, A. E. Shave, K. A. Williams, Hon J. F. Arundell, F. C. Bunge, A. Burrough. *Out of picture* J. B. Freebairn-Smith (cox)

33. The scratch Thames scullers' eight that finished 7th in the Head of the River Race, 1935. *Left to right* E. V. Pidduck (cox), J. Beresford Snr, E. H. Beresford, J. F. Muers, T. H. Tyler, R. R. E. Bradley, J. Beresford Jnr, T. G. Askwith, L. F. Southwood

34. J. Beresford Jnr (bow), L. F. Southwood (stroke), winners of the Olympic Double Sculls in 1936, training at Putney

35. Beresford and Southwood dead-heating with Scherli and Broschi of Trieste, Italy, in the final of the Centenary Double Sculls at Henley, 1939

36. Despite an artificial lower leg, the result of his war injuries, Alan Burrough, partnered by 'Sparrow' Morris, competed in the 1947 European Championships

37. Thames (nearest to the camera) passing Temple Island in the final of the Grand against Jesus and Pembroke Colleges, Cambridge, 1948

38. The final of the Grand, 1948, with Thames beating Jesus and Pembroke by $2\frac{1}{2}$ lengths

39. The winning 1948 Grand eight. *Standing* 'Sparrow' Morris, Jerry Sangster, Urs Burkhard, Hank Rushmere, Johnny Johnson. *Seated* Tom Christie, Freddie Page (Captain of Thames, coach), Peter Kirkpatrick, Ronnie Symonds (coach), Tony Butcher. *Seated, front* Jack Dearlove (cox)

40. The Great Britain Olympic team at Henley, 1948. *Back row, left to right* W. W. Woodward, R. M. Collins, B. H. T. Bushnell, T. H. Christie, W. J. H. Leckie, A. P. Mellows, D. C. H. Garrod, P. Bradley, H. B. James, C. B. R. Barton, A. Twinn, D. G. Jamison. *Middle row* I. M. Lang, A. S. F. Butcher, M. B. Scott, A. J. R. Purssell, C. B. M. Lloyd, E. A. P. Bircher, M. C. Lapage, H. W. Rushmere, P. M. O. Massey, D. J. C. Meyrick, J. H. T. Wilson, W. G. R. M. Laurie, R. W. Phelps. *Seated* J. Beresford Jnr, J. H. Page, R. D. Burnell, H. R. N. Rickett, G. C. Richardson, E. D. Horsfall, P. C. Kirkpatrick, R. H. H. Symonds, A. D. Rowe, A. McCulloch, J. G. Dearlove. *Seated, front* J. A. D. Healey, D. S. Walker, spare cox. Over half this team were members of Thames

41. Thames winning the Stewards' fours at Marlow Regatta, 1948. This outstanding crew also won the Stewards' at Henley and represented Great Britain in the Olympic Games: Tony Butcher (bow), Tom Christie, Hank Rushmere, Peter Kirkpatrick (stroke)

42. The all-Thames final of the Silver Goblets, 1949: Tony Butcher and Tom Christie beating 'Sparrow' Morris and Alan Burrough by $2\frac{1}{2}$ lengths

43. Autumn training, 1951—the 'Lady Margaret lie-back'. *Left to right* Lawrence Guest (cox), Alastair Macleod (stroke), Peter de Giles, Paul Massey, John (R.A.F.) Macmillan, Ken Trott, Sam Hobbs, Tony Purssell, Graham Fisk (bow)

44. HRH Princess Elizabeth and Ian Fairbairn
on the launch for the Head of the River Race, 1951

45. The Thames Grand eight, 1953, in front of George Drinkwater's bronze bust of Steve Fairbairn, the trophy for the Head of the River Race. The centre trophy in front of the group is the Champions Cup. *Back row, left to right* Graham Alwin, Peter Essam, John Webb, 'Berry' (J. Beresford Snr, coach), David Whitaker, 'Sparrow' Morris (coach), Dick Phelps. *Seated* Lloyd Williams, John Pope, Joe Eldeen (stroke), Reg Swatton (Captain of Thames, coach), Reg Nicholls, Geoffrey Page, Alan Watson

46. The other side of the picture, 1953: John Macmillan, watched by Tim Wilson, 'Ham' Ward and Lionel Abel-Smith, showing proper disrespect

47. The British Empire and Commonwealth Games, 1954. The England coxed four (bronze medallists) at Vedder Canal, British Columbia. *Left to right* Arthur Sulley (coach), Geoffrey Page (bow), John Macmillan, Alistair Davidson, Maurice Legg (stroke)

48. 'The fittest, strongest, toughest eight ever to represent Thames.' The 1955 Grand eight shooting Henley Bridge during training: Maurice Legg (bow), Ken Cross, David Whitaker, Alan Watson, John Macmillan, Colin Porter, Alistair Davidson, Reg Nicholls (stroke), David Glynne-Jones (cox)

49. The first Soviet eight to appear at Henley: Krylia Sovetov, the European champions in 1953 and 1954, beat Thames by $\frac{1}{2}$ length in the semi-final of the Grand, 1954. Krylia Sovetov: E. Brago (bow), V. Rodimuskin, S. Amiragov, I. Borisov, E. Samsonov, B. Vatsberg, A. Kormarov, V. Krukov (stroke), N. Kolosovsky (cox). Thames: G. G. H. Page (bow), J. Pope, M. G. C. Savage, A. R. Watson, A. R. Davidson, R. A. F. Macmillan, M. Legg, J. N. Eldeen (stroke), D. R. Glynne-Jones (cox)

50. Thames winning the Wyfold Cup from Kettering RC by $1\frac{1}{4}$ lengths, 1955. Thames: Gordon Dear (bow), John Pope, Alex Riemer, Hugh Denning (stroke). Kettering: J. F. A. Loasby (bow), G. I. Arber, P. B. Rowe, A. G. Bates (stroke)

51. Thames beating R. A. F. Macmillan's crew by 3 feet in the Stewards', 1956. Thames: M. Legg (bow), C. F. Porter, A. R. Davidson, J. M. Beresford (stroke). R. A. F. Macmillan's crew: G. S. Dear (bow), H. G. V. Denning, D. H. McLellan, R. A. F. Macmillan (stroke)

52. The winning Steward's four, 1956. *Left to right* Michael Beresford (stroke), Alistair Davidson, Colin Porter, Maurice Legg (bow)

12 The Early Thirties

The autumn of 1929 saw a curious experiment at London Rowing Club, instigated by a well-known oarsman and coach, F.E. Hellyer. This was syncopated rowing. Hellyer reasoned that an eight loses pace between the strokes and that a constant speed could be attained if the crew were to row in pairs, with stroke and seven taking the beginning first, followed fractionally later by six and five, and so on, so that at no time would all the blades be out of the water, on the principle of a paddle steamer.

London experimented with an eight converted to hold six men, since more space was required for each pair than in conventional rowing. Berry would have nothing to do with it. Asked for his opinion by the *Manchester Guardian*, his comments were forthright and typical: 'I don't think there is anything in it. It is all tomfoolery – utter rot.' Asked what Jack's opinion was, Berry said it was the same as his.

I remember my father saying that the real problem was that the oarsmen found it difficult to keep time – or rather, to keep exactly the right amount out of time. Without the rhythm and momentum of the bodies and oars moving together, they tended to revert quickly to 'normal' rowing. Much of the joy of rowing was lost with Hellyer's method and in the end the experiment failed because London did not feel they had justified the expense of a specially built boat.

Steve Fairbairn by this time was no longer actively involved in coaching on the Tideway and was busy writing books. At Thames there was another big turnover of senior oarsmen and in the end only Henry Sporborg from the 1929 Grand eight rowed in the 1930 crew. With the exception of their one-legged cox, Jack Dearlove, the Thames Cup eight were a new crew, but among them were some men with distinguished rowing careers ahead of them, notably Roland George, who had rowed for Lincoln College from 1923 to 1925, and 'Tig' Tyler, whose rowing career had begun in the north. Others included the former London University President, K.A. Williams, and his brother.

At Henley, the Grand eight did not survive their heat against University College, Oxford, and 1930 was London's year at last. With the same crew as the previous year, in the final they cleared Leander by the top of the Island, had 2 lengths at the Barrier and came home comfortably ahead. It was London's first win in the Grand for forty years, and four of the crew also won the Stewards', in which Thames had no entry. In both crews was Jumbo Edwards, who had been forgiven for his 1926 disaster by Oxford, having rowed again in the 1930 Boat Race.

Vesta, stroked by David Baddeley, recorded their first Thames Cup win, beating Thames in the second round, but four of this Vesta eight lost the Wyfold final to a London four stroked by Terry O'Brien and containing three of their Grand eight. The Thames Wyfold four – Basil Joyner, Tig Tyler, Roland George and their German stroke, Fedor Bunge – only just failed after having led London by a length at the Barrier. They lost by 6 feet.

Jack Beresford had a last go at the Diamonds but lost in the first round to the Canadian Joe Wright, when his sportsmanship once again at least contributed to his downfall. The scullers were level at the top of the Island when Wright crabbed. Jack eased right off, but against a sculler of Wright's calibre – he had won the silver medal in the 1928 Olympic double sculls with Jack Guest, who was also competing in the Diamonds – such generosity proved fatal. Wright went past and won by $2\frac{1}{2}$ lengths. Wright was beaten by a German, G. Bötzelen, but Guest beat the German in the final.

The first British Empire Games took place in August 1930, at Hamilton, Ontario. London were chosen for the eights and coxless fours, doubling up being essential because of the cost. Jack, as one of the three selectors, could hardly select himself for the single sculls, so he went as an official and a spare man, the Pembroke sculler, Fred Bradley, who had lost by only 3 feet to Bötzelen, being chosen. Charles Morrell, now established as the ARA's Team Manager, went in that capacity.

London crowned their splendid season by winning the eights and fours, while the single sculls went to the Australian Olympic champion, Bob Pearce, but the surprise runner-up was Jack Beresford, who had persuaded the organisers to let him take part as a 'guest'. Bradley was third and Joe Wright fourth. 1930 was also the centenary of the Wingfield Sculls, which went to Denis Guye of London. He had been 4 lengths behind the holder, Collet, at one stage, but had come through to win by 10 lengths.

On his return from Canada, Jack saw a new sculler from Auriol RC and was so impressed by his form that he persuaded him to join Thames so that he could coach him. This was Dick Southwood and the start of a famous partnership.

Eric Beresford returned to stroke the Thames Grand eight in 1931, J.H.M. Ward, a winner of the Ladies' with Lady Margaret, coming in at six. There was no Stewards' four. Jack's new protégé, Southwood, went for the Diamonds, having won the junior-senior sculls at Hammersmith and senior sculls at Marlow. At the latter, London took the Grand and Marlow eights, their second crew setting a faster time than their Grand crew, to whom Thames finished second and Vesta third. London also took the senior fours.

At Henley there was not a single entry from Leander. In the Grand, Thames drew Pembroke – the same crew, with one exception, which had gone Head at Cambridge. The change was at bow, where the surprise occupant was their coach, Archie Nisbet. This was a powerful crew but Thames had two lengths at Fawley and came home comfortably $1\frac{1}{2}$ lengths ahead, to reach the final once again. Here they faced London, who had easily beaten Harvard, and then, in a very hard race, the Berliner Ruder Club. The Germans were stroked by Bötzelen and they had another fine sculler, Herbert Buhtz, at three. They led by a few feet at the Mile, and, rowing at 39, they increased this to $\frac{1}{3}$ length. London spurted at 40, making no impression, but the Germans suddenly went to pieces at the grandstand and London, all but rowed out, got home by $\frac{1}{3}$ length, the Germans drifting over the line. In the final, London were clear at Remenham but Thames then closed up and there was only $\frac{1}{2}$ length in it at the bottom of the enclosures. Both crews came in flat out, London just holding on to win by $\frac{1}{3}$ length. London also won the Stewards', and Jumbo Edwards scored a remarkable personal hat-trick when, in Christ Church colours with Lewis Clive, he also won the Goblets.

London were also successful in the Thames Cup with a crew that many considered to have been faster than their Grand eight. They were never pressed and their fastest time was only five seconds slower than the best time set by the Grand eight, who were twice stretched to the limit. In the Met later, the Thames Grand eight beat London, who had made only one change from their winning Grand crew, by 2 lengths, but two days later at Kingston, the same Thames crew were beaten by $\frac{1}{4}$ length in record time by the full London Thames Cup crew, which tended to confirm that they were the faster of the London crews.

Thames did not come away empty handed from this Henley. The Wyfold four, unchanged from the previous year, first had their revenge over London, beating them by a length on the first day, and then won their remaining races with ease. Southwood reached the semi-finals of the Diamonds but neither he nor anyone else were a match for the Olympic and Empire champion, Bob Pearce, who, at 14½ stone, was an exceptionally powerful sculler. He later turned professional and was the last professional world champion, from 1933 to 1939, retiring unbeaten on the outbreak of war.

Southwood later lost in a heat of the Wingfields to the Cambridge stroke, Tom Brocklebank. Southwood led until 300 yards from the finish, when Brocklebank put in a final spurt. Southwood, exhausted, stopped and fell in. In the final, Brocklebank was himself sculled to a standstill, leaving Guye to retain his title.

It was altogether a better year for Thames, with the highest number of regatta wins since 1926, and the Wyfold four were particularly successful, with a number of wins in the Stewards' class. At the end of the season, Dick Phelps became Waterman to the Club, succeeding Laurie Bedell, who had served Thames since 1905 but had died in July 1931.

The following year, 1932, the Olympic Games were to be held in Los Angeles and, tempted by the Olympic carrot, Jack Beresford and Felix Badcock elected to row again. Cherry Pitman was now Chairman of the ARA, whose attitude to the Olympics became more positive as a result. Bean, who was still Captain of Thames, and Berry were on the Selection Committee, which was still composed of Thames, Leander, and London men, with Pitman again Chairman. In March, they asked Brocklebank, Guye, and Southwood to use the Diamonds as the Olympic trial, and it was decided to send in addition an eight, coxless four and coxless pair.

The Cambridge crew, one of the fastest to have won the Boat Race, reformed for Henley, rowing in Leander colours. Their President was Harold Rickett, a future Chairman of Henley and of the ARA. The Thames Grand eight were stroked by Donald Price, with Jack Beresford at seven and Felix Badcock at six. 'Ham' Ward, Roland George, and Tig Tyler were also rowing and they were a fast and powerful combination. They came to Henley having won the Marlow Grand by a length from London, and the Stewards' four of Beresford, Tyler, George, and Badcock had also beaten London at Marlow, though narrowly. Dick Southwood had won the senior sculls and the junior-seniors went to Georg von Opel, a German industrialist who had joined Thames in May.

SN de la Marne were the only foreign entrants for the Grand but they were put out in the preliminary heat by London, who had five of their winning 1931 Grand eight, including Carpmael and Edwards. Leander eventually beat London by 1¼ lengths, and Thames easily beat Jesus.

The final was, in effect, an Olympic trial. The crews overlapped for the entire race, with Leander leading by ⅓ length at the Barrier, where they spurted and moved out to ½ length at Fawley. Price put in a series of spurts, but at the end of each Leander got back their ½ length. From the Mile there was a magnificent race, but Leander held on to their ½ length to the finish, to record by far the fastest time of the regatta.

That settled the problem of the Olympic eight and so Thames now had to make sure of the Stewards', in which they had drawn a bye to the final, only three crews having entered. The Berliner Ruder Club beat London by 1 length in the heat and in the final, after their gruelling race in the Grand, Thames were ½ length down to the Germans at the Barrier. Felix Badcock always preferred to row a waiting race, regarding it as a waste of energy to lead before Fawley, but with much at stake besides the Stewards' Cup, he put in a 'feeler' after the Barrier and the crews were level at the ½ Mile. Thames led by a few feet at Fawley and by ¾ length at the Mile. When Felix made his kill soon after they went right away to win by 2 lengths.

The other place at stake for Los Angeles, as far as Thames were concerned, was in the single sculls. The Berlin scullers, Bötzelen and Buhtz, were both in the Diamonds, while the British contenders, Southwood, Guye, and Brocklebank, all missed each other in the draw and in the end never met. Buhtz beat Brocklebank, who collapsed and fell out of his boat just after the Mile, and Southwood, having beaten Lewis Clive in his heat, also succumbed to Buhtz by 2 lengths in what proved to be the fastest time in the event. Guye was beaten by Bötzelen by a length in a semi-final and so Henley spectators were treated to the galling experience of watching two Germans fight it out in the final. This proved to be very one-sided, Buhtz winning as he pleased.

Buhtz and his immediate predecessor, Pearce, must still rank among the best winners of the Diamonds. Both were chosen to represent their countries at Los Angeles, but Buhtz had the misfortune to go down with flu and could not compete. After his Henley showing, Southwood was invited to go to Los Angeles but, since he had not won, only if he was willing to pay his own expenses. He was. Edwards and Clive went as the coxless pair. They had survived a dead heat with Dick and Jack Offer of Kingston in a heat of the Goblets, having hit the booms at the top of the Island. In the re-row, the Offers stopped, rowed out, at the Mile, Edwards and Clive winning the final comfortably.

The Thames Cup eight survived only one round before going down to their stable-mates, Imperial College, who failed by only 4 feet to London in the final. London again won the Wyfold Cup but after this regatta the rules were changed to prevent competitors in the Grand from competing in the Wyfold in the same year. This had been long overdue, but the change did not prevent London from winning the Cup four more times in the following six years.

The Olympic Regatta was held at Long Beach, California, against a backdrop of oil derricks. The British crews had travelled by sea to Canada, where they spent four days in Toronto as guests of the Argonaut RC before travelling on to California. Then bad luck hit the Thames four when the unfortunate Tig Tyler, like Buhtz, fell ill with influenza and could not row. 'It's a hell of a long way to go to catch flu,' commented the unhappy Tig to Dick Phelps who, in his first year with Thames, had been chosen as boatman for the Olympic team. Jumbo Edwards was brought in at three to replace him, George moving to bow, and Jack to two. There is little doubt, however, that this combination were faster than the original crew.

For Thames, and especially for Jumbo, the 1932 Olympics were a triumph. The coxless pair won their event and the four scored a resounding 2½ length victory in their final over Germany, Italy, and the USA, giving Jumbo his second gold medal in one day. It was also a personal triumph for Jack Beresford, bringing him a second Olympic gold to add to his two silvers. Tig Tyler wept unashamedly in the grandstand.

Dick Southwood also reached the final, coming up against Bob Pearce, the reigning champion, and the American and Uruguayan scullers. Pearce took the gold medal again with some ease, but Southwood's chances evaporated when he developed cramp in his arm at 1,200 metres and he could finish only fourth and last.

The eight did well to finish a bare length behind the Americans, though they, too, were fourth. Italy were 1 foot behind the winners, with Canada third. This was the Americans' fourth successive win in the eights and the second for the University of California.

R.F. Reeve ('Reevo'), Steve's old friend and a

brilliant coach of juniors, had died in June. He had been coaching the Thames novices from the beginning of the 1920s, and one of his earliest charges was Edmund Howell, who became, in the 1950s, the first editor of *Rowing* magazine. Writing in 1949 in *Blackwood's Magazine*, he drew this pen portrait of Reevo:

> He was the kindliest of men and a great sportsman, although he freely admitted that a place in an unsuccessful Thames Cup crew was the nearest he had ever got to personal distinction as an oarsman. The more profound technicalities of rig and style were beyond his ken. But whatever he lacked in personal skill and rowing erudition he more than made up for in unquenchable, infectious enthusiasm. So to Reevo, Steve Fairbairn allotted the most junior of the crews to coach. It was a shrewd decision; for we would have broken the heart of anyone except Reevo . . .
>
> We were 'Reeve's Rabbits' – and he took us to his kindly heart. Every evening he would be waiting there, down on the hard at Putney, his long nose overhanging his greying moustache, his ancient yellowing straw boater perched on the back of his head. He would be peering anxiously up towards Putney Bridge to make quite sure all his 'rabbits' were turning up that night. We always did . . .
>
> 'Reeve's Rabbits' won their Juniors. The miracle had actually occurred. The leaden skies and chill drizzle of February, the rough bluster of the high spring tides of March – snow, sleet, fog, and rain; the pitching swell of full tide at high water; the opalescent calm over the mud flats at low; we had slogged and bucketed through them all. The mile upon mile that we had rowed had all been worth while . . .
>
> But old Reevo! His hat was on the back of his head. His bright Club tie was all awry. His face was a wrinkled mask of happiness. At last he had coached a winning crew – a poor thing, but his own!

Such men as Reevo are the too often unsung heroes of clubs like Thames; yet they are the solid ground on which the foundations are laid. Reevo himself also played a large part in the administration of Thames in the 1920s, often chairing meetings. He was also the first Honorary Secretary of the Head of the River Race.

1933 proved to be disappointing season for the top end of the Club but a highly successful one for the middle section. R.C. Morris, who had rowed in the fast Imperial College crew of the previous season, came in at bow in the Grand eight, and other newcomers were Arnold Brown, who had rowed twice for St Paul's in the Ladies', and Hans Homberger, a Swiss heavyweight from Zurich, who was still very rough at this stage and did not really pull his 14 stone, but who returned later with his two brothers in Zurich crews which wrought havoc on all comers at Henley. At seven was Ronnie Symonds. From a well-known rowing family, he had rowed for Bedford School and had won the Ladies' Plate in the same Lady Margaret crew as Ham Ward. He was also a Cambridge Blue.

Ham was in the Thames Grand crew again, with Donald Price still stroking, Felix Badcock at six and Tig Tyler at two. They should have been fast, but somehow they never really got going. At Henley, they were outclassed by London, who went on to their third win in four years, beating another Berlin crew containing Bötzelen and Buhtz by ¼ length. The other Thames crews also failed, though von Opel survived two heats of the Diamonds, in which Southwood did not compete. The winner, Tom Askwith, a Peterhouse Blue who had rowed in the 1932 Olympic eight, was the last British sculler to take the Diamonds until 1950.

Dick Southwood ended Guye's three-year reign in the Wingfields, winning the final by 1 length in the record time of 21min 11sec, which bettered Ernest Barry's 21min 12⅖sec set when beating George Towns for the English professional championship in 1908, and Collet's amateur record of 21min 32sec, set in the 1929 Wingfields.

At the end of the year, Felix Badcock retired from serious rowing, having married the Olympic swimmer, Joyce Cooper, who brought two silver and two bronze medals to the family collection. From 1924 to 1933, Felix won the Stewards' four times from five attempts, the Grand twice, and the Wyfold once. He missed reaching a Henley final on only two occasions, and he also won an Olympic gold and silver medal. He was, without any doubt, one of the finest strokes of a coxless four ever to have rowed.

In 1934, my father was Captain of Thames. Eric Beresford, who had been stroking the first eight, fell ill just before the Head and did not row again that season. In the circumstances, Thames did well to finish third in the Head, London having a narrow squeak when retaining their unbeaten record by 1 second from Pembroke, who had brought in their four Blues only a week after they had rowed in the record-breaking Cambridge crew in the Boat Race.

At Henley, Arno Brown stroked the Thames Grand eight, to which a valuable addition was Tom Askwith. The Thames Cup eight were a mixture of old and new: Ray Bradley, Bob Lord, 'Sparrow' Morris, and Bill Williams filled the bow seats; Jock Maclean from Twickenham came in at five; Dick Messom, nephew of the pre-war Thames oarsman, Harold Messom, was six; 'Jum' Beckett, the son of an old Bedford friend of Berry's, Reg Beckett, was seven, and the unpredictable H.E.G. Watts stroked. They were coxed by E.V. Pidduck, another of a long line of Old Paulines who had joined Thames.

The link with St Paul's, where my father had taken charge of rowing, was encouraged by such joint expeditions as the one to Ostend Regatta in May 1934. In the school crew were Alan Burrough and Alec Forbes, both of whom were members of Thames and were later to row in winning Boat Race crews.

The Thames first eight at Ostend, on the least sheltered station, lost by ¼ length to a German eight from Godesberg after one of the Thames blades had hit the top of a wave when the crews were level. St Paul's, with a cunning belying their youth, got away before the *Partez* in the second event, but they, too, had the worst of the cross-headwind and lost to RCN de Gand. Denis Guye, another Old Pauline, was competing for London in the senior sculls but lost in the final to Georg von Opel. Guye had the best station but got entangled with a familiar hazard on the Ostend canal, a moored barge, despite warnings shouted to him by von Opel.

A week earlier, the Thames second eight, with three substitutes, had lost the senior eights at Ghent by 3 feet to the SN de la Marne, but the full crew had several pre-Henley successes, though at Marlow the only Thames winner was Southwood in the senior sculls.

Conditions at Henley were extremely fast due to a prolonged drought throughout the spring, so that there was virtually no stream. There was a light following breeze on all four days and records fell like ninepins. Leander lowered the course record in their heat of the Grand by 6 seconds, beating London by 1 length. Leander then met Thames, who had drawn a bye. The crews were level at the ¾ Mile and after a furious race home, Leander won by ½ length in 6min 44sec, which took a further second off the record. Leander went on to win the final from the only overseas entry, Princeton University, by ¾ length in 6min 45sec.

In the Thames Cup, the record was broken twice in ten minutes but Thames never got very near it. They cleared Reading University in 15 strokes, and then had to go harder to beat Yale by ½ length. They reached the final by beating one of the record-breakers, Westminster Bank, clearing them in 10 strokes when the Bank jammed a slide. Against London in the final, there was little in it most of the way. Both crews raced in at 42 but Thames came home with ⅓ length to spare. Many years later, just before my father's death, Dick Phelps said to him, 'You coached that 1934 crew, didn't you, sir? How did you coach them to race so well?'

'Well,' said Freddie, 'they were stroked by a wild sort of chap and I encouraged them to row in a wild sort of way.'

Pembroke, then near the peak of their fame, reached the final of the Stewards' when beating Thames by ½ length. In the final, London caught a crab below Fawley but Pembroke, seeing they were on target for a record, went on at full pressure and lowered it by 3 seconds.

In the Diamonds, Southwood lost to a Czech, Zavrel, but with Buhtz reappearing, the ultimate result was never in doubt. From a truly international field which included two Americans, a Brazilian, a Uruguayan, and the Czech, Buhtz stood out, and although he lowered the Fawley record in the final, despite suffering from back trouble, he won too easily to do more than equal F.S. Kelly's 1905 record for the full course, 8min 10sec. The Goblets also went to Germany.

Southwood did not defend the Wingfields and was beaten in the London Cup, and Thames had no top wins after Henley, though they again did very well at lower levels.

The most interesting event of the year was the appearance of a London eight at the Melbourne Centenary Regatta held at Henley-on-Yarra in November. This was the first time an English crew had rowed in Australia, where the controversy between Fairbairnism and Orthodoxy was in full spate, as it was in England. London won the final at Melbourne with considerable ease from a New Zealand eight from Wanganui. The regatta's President was Steve Fairbairn's brother, Sir George Fairbairn, 'Senator George'. London went on to win the State Championship by 8 lengths from Melbourne University, as orthodox as any Australian crew could be.

An Australian observer, A.N. Finlay, to whom the Fairbairn style was new territory, wrote of this London crew:

> The secret of their success is not only in what they do to get pace, but what they don't do to stop it. To begin with, the legs are the all-important driving force. They have a remarkably fast and smooth recovery. Although the hands never actually touch the body, the recovery is only a continuation of the finish, the blade being rowed out of the water and the hands carried fast and low over the knees. It is the remarkable control and poise which they get from there to the beginning which allows the boat to travel without the semblance of a check and gives them that extra pace, which is undeniable. This steadiness and ability to pose also enables them to be in a perfect position to take the catch. Their boat is still running and is perfectly under control, so that when they spring from their stretchers the blades hit the water and are rowed through with amazing speed, and the stroke is finished and the hands over the knees almost before the critic knows what has happened.

This excellent description of a good Tideway Fairbairn crew of the 1930s brings to mind Rudie Lehmann's description in *The Complete Oarsman* of the earlier Belgian style:

> They had mastered to perfection and applied with consummate ability the great theory which inculcates extreme steadiness and good balance of the body-movement forward, and of the sliding that accompanies it. To lead up to this they were very quick and springy with their hands off the chest. Then they moved forward very slowly, so slowly towards the last part that their bodies seemed to hang over the water . . . they took their beginnings firm and clean and with a hearty good will . . . No awkward plunging rush checked the even speed of the ship. She kept travelling beautifully.

Plus ça change, plus c'est la même chose!

London's victories certainly did not harm Steve's cause and gave the Australians plenty to think about. The controversy continued unabated in the English press. Articles such as 'Is Orthodox Rowing Style Doomed?', 'Something Wrong With Our Rowing' (Gully Nickalls), 'Some of my More

Printable Opinions on Style' (this by Steve, of course), and so on appeared year after year in the 1930s.

Extreme stances were taken, and often members of Thames were at loggerheads. A letter from Jimmy Heath, who had rowed for Thames in the Thames Cup from 1892–1902, the period when Steve's message had been lost, asserted that 'talking about the subconscious is piffle'. In another letter he wrote, 'The orthodox will always beat the unorthodox when the men and coaching are equal' and deprecated allowing men to look at their oars and shoot their slides. Arnold Brown firmly disagreed with him: 'Having rowed orthodox when at school' – in pre-Freddie Page days at St Paul's – 'I can assure Mr Heath that I found it the most unpleasant and fatiguing method of progression and a thing only past-masters were keen about.' Duggie Stuart, in a letter to *The Times* wrote:

> Orthodox crews were nearly always drawn from the Universities, and this gave them a greater choice in numbers and physique, and a series of victories at Henley made people hastily conclude that the way these crews rowed was and is the only way to row. At that time opposition was almost nil. From the very fact of greater choice orthodoxy should have more than held its own, not only in first-class contests but in all others. If opinion and coercion could have kept out the new style it would have done so, but, thanks to Mr Fairbairn's pertinacity, it is having a greater vogue than ever. Thanks to it metropolitan rowing has been revived, and it is to be hoped that it will resist all attempts to make it return to the old style.

This sort of correspondence continued right up to the outbreak of war in 1939 and although the controversy continued in somewhat less contentious form after the war, it was generally the pre–war generation that prolonged it. The post–war generation began to find new ways to go, though the principles that underlay Steve's coaching remain as valid today as they were fifty years ago.

13 Gathering Clouds

Beyond the confines of rowing and its enjoyable internal squabbles, the world outside was beginning to fall apart. Mussolini might have got the Italian railways running on time but Fascism was a cloud rapidly growing in size and obscuring even the threat of Bolshevism. With Hitler's rise to power, and the testing-ground for Fascist military strength in Spain, the foundations of the League of Nations had finally crumbled.

In rowing in the mid–1930s, however, the main threat was coming from the increasing strength of the invasion of foreign crews at Henley. The ARA was still not affiliated to FISA, the international rowing federation, because the FISA definition of an amateur conflicted with that of the ARA, though not with that of the NARA. Olympic regulations did not require competitors to be affiliated to the international federation, and rowing in Britain continued to be organised by these two bodies.

Apart from Henley, the Olympic Games provided the only chance for British oarsmen to compete against top-class foreign crews, and even at Henley the best European crews only rarely appeared. The Olympic regattas in the 1920s had still been very much club affairs, crews competing with oars painted in club colours. With the Berlin Olympics in 1936 and the fanatical nationalism preached by Hitler, the stress of nationalism in sport suddenly increased. It was to change the face of international sport.

In 1935, some oarsmen in Britain, notably Jack Beresford, actually began to prepare for the Olympics a year ahead, but generally it was business as usual. In the Head, London recorded their tenth successive victory, the Thames second eight finishing third, 1 second ahead of the first eight. The crews had dead–heated in practice but the second eight subsequently won the new North of England Head at Chester, which probably just gave them the edge in the Tideway event, in which the Thames fourth eight also created interest. They were based on scullers and included Jack Beresford, Tom Askwith, Dick Southwood and Tig Tyler. Eric Beresford, after a year off because of illness, stroked and at bow was Berry, aged 67. They had only two outings together but finished seventh, only 15 seconds behind the best Thames crew. It was an indication of things to come.

Despite successes before Henley up to Thames Cup level, the Club was up against it once again at Henley. Zurich, with Hans Homberger and his two brothers, had entered for the Grand, but they were not the force they were to become the following year. In their heat they rowed level with Jesus from the Barrier to the enclosures, where a final burst by Edward Szilagyi, the Jesus stroke, gained the college a 3-foot victory. Only one man in the Jesus crew was over 12 stone, while the Swiss had four men over 13 stone. It was the stuff with which to warm Steve's ageing heart.

Thames lost a hard race by ¾ length to Leander, who included Tom Askwith, but Leander lost the final to Pembroke, who had beaten Jesus. This was Pembroke's first, and so far only, win in the Grand.

In the Stewards', the Swiss were in a different class. They were 3 lengths ahead of Thames at Fawley and won in a paddle. The final was almost as easy, Zurich leading London by 2 lengths at the Barrier, and winning by 3 lengths. It was an indication of their class that, in a year when no one else, with one exception, got close to a record, they took no less than 10 seconds off Pembroke's record set the previous year when conditions had been exceptionally fast.

The Swiss had a very fast sculler in Rufli, who also rowed in their eight. The previous year he had beaten Buhtz and he showed that this was no fluke when he won the Diamonds from Zavrel in a time only 5 seconds outside the record.

The success of the Swiss four was hailed by both the Orthodox and Fairbairn camps as a triumph for their respective methods. They were, by all accounts, a beautiful crew to watch but, like all great crews, they displayed no extremes of style. In 1933 their coach, Arthur Dreyfus, had seen the Pembroke four beat the best continental fours at Mainz Regatta. This had been his first experience of Fairbairn rowing, Swiss rowing then being based on the orthodox Grasshopper Club style. Dreyfus wrote to Fairbairn for advice and in 1934 Zurich won five Swiss championship titles, the following year the winning Stewards' four going on to win the European title.

In 1935, the Thames second eight, in which Alan Burrough rowed, lost to London by ½ length in the semi-final of the Thames Cup. In the previous round Thames had beaten Oriel College. Stroked by George Moody, Oriel were the first Head crew from either Oxford or Cambridge not to go for the Grand, but Thames beat them, easing up, by ¾ length. London won the final narrowly from the Pembroke second eight.

The Thames Wyfold four, stroked by Fedor Bunge, and with George Parlby, a future President of Sydney RC, at three, reached their final, where they lost to Reading RC, who had a powerful man, Hank Rushmere, at three. A Goblets pair, B.S. Fidler and D.G. Newton, also lost in the final.

After Henley, Tig Tyler failed in the Wingfields, and as the season gathered dust eyes began to turn towards Berlin and the 1936 Olympics. In the autumn, Jack Beresford and Dick Southwood decided to try for the double sculls, even though there was no race in Britain for this class of boat, and Jack was then 36. Dick had the power, Jack the experience; both had the motivation. It was a recipe for success. In ten months of continuous training, they covered 2,000 miles.

The Olympic selectors included Charles Rew and my father, the latter Captain of Thames for a third year. It was decided to pick crews on Henley form, which posed a problem as far as the double were concerned. The selectors decided to wait and see how things developed.

In 1936, Szilagyi, another Old Pauline Blue, who later changed his name to Seely, which was easier to pronounce than his Hungarian name, stroked the Thames first eight, which included Alan Burrough and his elder brother, John, as well as Arno Brown, Jock Maclean, 'Camel' Hutton-Squire, and 'Sparrow' Morris. They at last won the Head, with London in second place. The Thames third eight, another crew of scullers which included Beresford and Southwood, had no practice outings but finished fourth.

John Burrough dropped out after the Head, Roger Harman replacing him in the eight for Henley, where they arrived having suffered a shock defeat at Marlow by the Tokyo Imperial University, who struck astronomically high rates, and who had come over for the Olympics. At Henley, to the astonishment of spectators, they spurted to 56 to beat Quintin, who were making their first entry in the Grand, but the Swiss sorted them out the next day. Striking 56 in the first minute, the Japanese, who averaged just over 10 stone, could not hold Zurich at 43, the Swiss winning in a paddle.

As an Olympic trial, the draw worked out well, Pembroke, with five of their 1935 crew, facing Thames, the winner to meet the Union Boat Club, Boston; London drew Leander, who were led by the Cambridge stroke, Ran Laurie, with Tom Askwith at four and the outstanding Oxford oarsman of the decade, Con Cherry, at five.

Pembroke proved just too good for Thames, winning by ¾ length after the crews had been level at the Mile. London's fast start got them a length ahead of Leander at the Barrier, but Leander came through to win by ½ length. The American crew turned out to be quite fast and they beat Pembroke by 1¼ lengths, but they were themselves beaten by Leander, who had something to spare. Zurich had run away from Jesus, so Leander lined up against the Swiss in the final as undoubtedly the fastest English crew. It was not enough. Zurich had ¾ length at the first signal and were clear at the ¾ Mile, to win, easing up, by 1¼ lengths.

Zurich again won the Stewards', defeating first London, who actually led them at the Mile, and then, in the final, Leander, who had beaten Thames. The Swiss cleared Leander by the top of the Island and had 2 lengths at the Barrier, which they maintained to the finish, crossing the line with something in hand. Rufli gave the Swiss their third win, retaining the Diamonds when beating Tig Tyler by a comfortable 3 lengths in the final. Rufli's hardest race, however, had been against Humphrey Warren of Trinity Hall, the scullers having been level at Fawley when Warren hit the booms.

Although they had nothing to go for, Beresford and Southwood trained at Henley during the regatta fortnight, pacing anyone who asked for it. After Henley, Cherry Pitman asked Jack whether the double was any good, having been told that they were not. 'Send us and see,' said Jack. That was good enough for Cherry, and the double, coached for the final month by Eric Phelps, developed real pace as the Olympics approached. Later, of course, the final of that Olympic Regatta would pass into legend.

The rest of the Olympic team were the slightly rearranged Leander eight, the London Stewards' four, with the Oxford Blue Jan Sturrock, replacing Edgar Howitt, who could not make the trip, and the Jesus pair, Tom Cree and David Burnford, the 1935 Goblets winners. Warren was the single sculler, and Dick Phelps was again boatman to the team.

The Germans had made enormous efforts to prepare their team for the Olympics, which were used by Hitler as a massive propaganda exercise. Tom Sullivan, the professional sculler, had for some years coached the Berliner Ruder Club, and an English professional, Dan Cordery, was coaching the German scullers. Needless to say, the Germans put up a tremendous performance, taking five of the seven gold medals. The single sculls went to 'Gummi' Schäfer, with Rufli only fifth, Warren having failed to reach the final. In the coxless fours, London did well to finish second to the Germans and ahead of the Swiss, to whom they had lost in a heat. The Swiss made the mistake of entering some of their men in three events and in the end they won nothing. The British pair were outclassed and the eight could again finish only fourth. This was one of the events the Germans missed, though only by a whisker. The United States maintained their run of successes in this event, though the Washington crew were only 1½ seconds ahead of Italy, who had lost by only 2 feet in 1932. The Germans were third by a few feet. Leander, a further length behind, at least beat the 1935 European champions, Hungary.

The achievement of the regatta was, by general consent, that of Beresford and Southwood. They had lost their heat to the German European champions after being washed by the Germans, the umpire being too far behind to do anything about it. In order to score a psychological point, the Thames double went flat out in their *repêchage* before paddling in well ahead. In the final, they were determined that the Germans would not get away, but even so they were 1½ lengths down at 1,000 metres, with Poland, France, Australia, and the United States trailing. In his *History of Rowing*, Hylton Cleaver remembered this race:

> At half-way our men really began laying it on. They were belting every stroke as hard and as long as they could, and I can see them now as they approached the enclosures, where I was standing on tip-toe scarcely able to shout for the lump in my throat.
>
> From 1,000 metres it took them 800 more before, by their utmost efforts, they got level at last, and at this point Tom Sullivan, with field glasses clapped to his eyes, snatched off the cap of the Berliner Ruder Club, which he wore, to flourish it high in the air and to bellow above the roars of the crowd, as if his heart were bursting: 'The Englishmen have got them! The Englishmen to win, for 1,000 marks!'

With 100 metres to go the crews were still level, sculling stroke for stroke, and they were so close that the blades nearly touched. Then, right in front of Hitler's own box, the Germans cracked. Southwood continued to build it in, knowing that if he let up they too would stop.

Of all Jack's successes, this was his greatest and most dramatic. It gave him his third gold medal and a remarkable record of never having failed to take silver or gold from each of his five Olympic appearances. It was, he said, the sweetest race he had ever rowed in.

In 1936, the ARA and the NARA at last got together to see whether some compromise could not be reached over the vexed question of what constituted an amateur. The matter had been brought to a head when the Australian Olympic eight had their Grand entry refused because, as policemen, they were not recognised by Henley as amateurs. The Australians at Berlin left the British oarsmen in no doubt about their views on this and public indignation in Britain resulted in a meeting between the ARA and the NARA early in 1937. The former admitted that their definition of an amateur was archaic and indefensible and, in June 1937, both the ARA and Henley agreed to withdraw all controversial phrases which debarred NARA crews from competing at ARA regattas, the vital deletion being the reference to manual labour. This was a major breakthrough for the sport, although, because of the outbreak of war, the two bodies did not merge for another fifteen years.

Contrasted with the previous year, 1937 was rather pedestrian. Oxford won the Boat Race after thirteen consecutive defeats; Alan Burrough, rowing seven for Cambridge as a Jesus freshman, was unlucky to have arrived in time for this defeat. The Head was not held because the only suitable tide was on a Sunday and the ARA disapproved of Sunday racing.

It was not a vintage year for Thames. The Stewards' four won at Marlow, where the Grand eight lost to Kingston, who were one of ten entries for the Henley Grand, for which the Swiss did not enter, the foreign opposition being the Olympic bronze medallists, Wiking from Berlin. Thames went out in the first round, Jesus, with Alan Burrough at five, being the last British hope to challenge the Germans in the final. As usual, Jesus put up a tremendous fight, with the crews at 38 to 40 most of the way. They were level at the Mile but the Germans won finally by ½ length.

Thames beat London in the only Stewards' heat but Leander were too strong in the final, though the crews overlapped all the way and the winning margin was only 1 length. The Thames Cup eight, stroked for the second year running by George Moody and reinforced at six by Peter Kirkpatrick, who was still up at Queens' College, Cambridge, lost by 6 feet in the second round to the Jesus second eight, but the ultimate winners were Tabor Academy, USA, whose stroke weighed only 9st 3lb. In the Diamonds, the Austrian Olympic silver medallist, Hasenohrl, was in a class of his own.

The Wingfields were won in Thames colours by Ralph Hope, the Oxford President who had dropped himself from the subsequently victorious Boat Race crew, and he rowed in some winning Thames crews at the later regattas.

It had not been a good season generally for the

Club but 1938 was an even leaner one. The year began with the Empire Games, which were held on the Nepean River in Australia in February. Jack Beresford raised a composite eight drawn from Leander, London, Thames, and Kingston, and Berry went as their coach. John Burrough was Captain, but Roger Harman was dropped when Tim Turner came in to stroke. Turner excelled in a great race, and England took the gold medal by ¾ length from Australia, with New Zealand third. England did not compete in the coxed fours or single sculls, both going to Australia.

In March, the Head attracted entries for the first time from Goldie and Isis, the former winning from the latter by 3 seconds, with Thames third and London fourth.

The year's rowing, from Thames' point of view, does not need dwelling on. The Club had the smallest number of regatta wins since the war and at Henley the Grand eight were comfortably beaten by London. There were no foreign crews and no Leander eight, and London went on to beat Jesus by 3 feet and then won the final from Trinity Hall. Thames beat Kingston in the Stewards' but got no further. There were again no foreign entries and Leander won the final. Tig Tyler beat Ralph Hope in the Diamonds but was then easily beaten by the sensation of the regatta, Joe Burk, of Penn Athletic Club, USA. Burk had a very individual style and struck remarkably high rates, and in the final against the Reading sculler, Len Habbitts, he was never below 39. Despite being many lengths ahead, Burk took 8 seconds off Kelly's 1905 record.

This was a sadder year for the death of Steve Fairbairn in May at the age of 75. He had been in failing health for some years but his presence had continued to be felt by Thames and London, and particularly by his old college, Jesus. Today, the affection or hostility he aroused, depending on which side of the rowing fence one stood, has faded into history. As far as Thames and London were concerned, his contribution was incalculable. A memorial to him acts as the Milepost on the Boat Race course, but his greatest memorial outside Cambridge is the annual race for the Headship of the Thames. In his memorial address, Dr Brittain of Jesus said:

> No picture of Steve would be complete if it failed to include his most intimate friend, 'Old Hutch', whose death took place a few months earlier. It is not saying too much to assert that Steve venerated Hutch, whom he often described as one of the best Christians in the world. Each of the two friends was the complement of the other. Hutch's slim figure formed a strong contrast to Steve's massive frame, and he was as taciturn as Steve was loquacious. When the two were together, Hutch seldom spoke unless Steve addressed him first, and then he answered in the fewest possible words. Steve, for his part, seldom ventured on an assertion without afterwards appealing to Hutch for his opinion before he considered the matter closed. It was worth going a long way to see the two together at Henley, with Steve enthroned in a chair facing the river and Hutch standing by him as a sort of Lord Chamberlain.

The following year, 1939, was to see the death at 91 of the last of the giants of the old generation of Thames men, Piggy Eyre, still hale and hearty almost to the end, if very deaf. Legends of Piggy abound and a typical tale of his later days, which Bill Williams was fond of recounting, concerned a Thames annual dinner in the 1930s which was attended by the Club's Patron, the Duke of Gloucester. As the company rose in silence for the Loyal Toast, Piggy, oblivious of what was going on around him, could be heard booming across the room as he ended one of his many stories of past exploits, '. . . and we rowed like lions and won by 20 lengths!' to the vast amusement of all present.

With the inexorable expansion of the Nazi war machine, 1939 began with the knowledge that war was imminent and that it could well be the last season of rowing for some years to come, if not forever for the unlucky ones.

The Club records are very sketchy for this year. John Burrough had become Captain, and his brother Alan was President at Cambridge and won the Boat Race after two defeats. One of his coaches was my father, who had coached the winning Oxford crew the year before, an unusual double, though not unique. London won the Head from a record entry of 145. Thames do not seem to have had any more success at open regattas than in 1938, though they had popular wins in the senior fours and eights at Ostend when they beat German crews. Feelings were running high on the Continent and German defeats outside Germany were loudly cheered. In the *Thames Journal* of 1949 Charles Morrell recalled this visit:

> In that year at Ostend the defeat of a German eight by a Thames crew stroked by B.N. Brooke was particularly gratifying. . . . The Germans led by nearly two lengths from the start, but Thames wore them down . . . Brooke made a magnificent effort near the finish and Thames won by a canvas. Our four, stroked by John Burrough, led from the start and beat the Germans comparatively easily, the rest of the field tailing away in the distance . . . No wins could have been more popular and our crews were fêted right royally. Other pre-war wins by Thames at Dinant and Ghent were invariably loudly applauded.

The tension that was developing at this time was also recorded in Richard Hillary's *The Last Enemy*, possibly the best book to come out of the war. An Oxford trial cap, Hillary recounts how he went with a Trinity crew to Germany in 1938. They were spat on from a bridge during a race. This was a tactical error and the crew, rowing as though they were pursued by all the hounds in hell, rowed past five German boats to win by ⅖ second for a most unpopular victory. A member of this crew was John Garton, the 1939 Oxford President and later Chairman of Henley and the ARA. Hillary, alas, did not survive the war.

This was Henley's centenary and the Stewards put on a special race for double sculls. The Grand attracted entries from Sydney RC, the Toronto Argonauts, and Harvard, and of the five home crews, only Jesus reached the semi-finals. Thames had John Burrough, Peter Kirkpatrick, James O'Mara and Sparrow Morris in the crew, and Brooke, a member of the famous family of white Rajahs of Sarawak and who had stroked so well at Ostend, was at two. They were on the light side but gave the heavyweight Toronto crew a good race before going down by ½ length.

Thames lost to London in the Stewards' but the Swiss had reappeared and they beat Oriel in the final. With no successes from the other Thames crews, it was once again the old warriors Beresford, now 39, and Southwood in the double sculls who excelled. There were eight entries, including those from Italy, Uruguay, and Belgium. The Italians defeated the Uruguayans and Thames accounted for Andersen and Piessens from Antwerp, which put them against the Italians, Scherli and Broschi from Trieste, in the final. There was a strong headwind and Thames were giving away a substantial amount of weight and years. Thames took ½ length in 20 seconds but as they came out from the shelter of the Island they lost most of their lead. The Italians were just in front at Fawley and spurted to increase their lead to ⅓ length at the ¾ Mile, but when the Italians dropped their rate again, Thames came up and went ahead by a few feet. Once more their opponents put in a dramatic spurt to gain ½ length by the Mile, and once again Thames came back, only for the Italians to make yet another effort and draw ahead. At the last signal, it looked all over. However, Southwood worked the rate up and up, and stroke by stroke Thames closed up to catch the Italians on the line for a dead heat. The Italian bowman was very distressed and it was decided not to re-row the race. It was a fitting climax to Jack's distinguished career.

PART III

1940–1990

14 The War and After

The outbreak of war in September 1939 did not result in such a complete break in activities as had occurred in 1914. There were unofficial Oxford and Cambridge Boat Races at Henley in 1940 and 1943–4–5. Colleges combined to hold internal races and the Reading University Head continued in a desultory fashion until 1942.

John Burrough remained as Captain of Thames until he joined the RAF in the autumn of 1941. After he went, Bill Williams, as Chairman, Duggie Douglas and the Honorary Secretary, Aub Turner, ran the Club. London's premises had been requisitioned by the Civil Defence authorities, so their members were invited to use Thames's facilities.

There were, inevitably, casualties among Thames members. Alan Burrough almost lost his life, his right foot being blown off in the Libyan desert when his tank was destroyed. When he recovered, he began to scull with an artificial foot. He went out in a pair with his brother at Putney in the spring of 1944, but, sadly, John was killed soon afterwards while serving with Coastal Command.

An unlucky death was that of Donald Price, who had been captured at Dunkirk at the same time as Ronnie Symonds. These two were interned in the same camp and as the Allied forces approached near the end of the war, they were being transferred to another camp when they were shot up by mistake by an American plane. Ronnie escaped but Price was hit and died in Ronnie's arms. Ralph Hope, John Arundell (by then Lord Arundell of Wardour), Fedor Bunge, Basil Drakeford and Hugh Dulley were among others to die on active service. Other losses among rowing men included Tim Turner and Desmond Kingsford from the 1938 Empire Games eight, Conrad Cherry, and another Oxford Blue, Melvin Young, who was lost on the famous Dam Busters raid. There were many others.

The pieces were quickly picked up at the end of hostilities and, though there was severe rationing of food, fuel, and clothing, nothing much changed in the rowing world. A one-day Peace Regatta was held at Henley in 1945, the crews rowing three abreast over a shortened course starting at the Barrier. There were three events only: an open eights race for the Danesfield Cup, the Hedsor Cup for schools, and the Barrier Cup for sculls. The winners of the Danesfield Cup were Imperial College, who had built their own boathouse next to Thames shortly before the war and had managed a fair amount of rowing during the war. Radley won the schools race in the fastest time of the regatta.

By 1946, to all outward appearances, rowing was back to normal, though the clock seemed to have been turned back when Oxford won the first post-war Boat Race with an orthodox crew on fixed pins. Imperial College, stroked by Joe Eldeen, won the Head, and in the autumn, St Paul's were the first winners of the new Schools' Head. Alan Burrough was Captain of Thames.

At Henley, the Double Sculls, introduced as an experiment in 1939, were retained, and a schools race for the Princess Elizabeth Cup was introduced over a short course from the Barrier, though the following year they rowed the full distance. There was a pre-war look about the Grand with an entry once again from Zurich. Thames were stroked by the former Reading oarsman and Wyfold winner, Hank Rushmere, whose first Henley appearance had been in 1932. At seven, Ham Ward could beat this by some years, having rowed for St Paul's in the Ladies' in 1926, while 'Sparrow' Morris's Henley record went back to 1931. He rowed bow. An outstanding newcomer, Guy Richardson, rowed six. Thames drew London, who included P.N. Carpmael, T.B. Langton, and J.L.L. Savill, all pre-war Cambridge Blues; their stroke, John Pinches, had won the Grand with Carpmael. However, Thames had cleared them by Fawley and won by 1¼ lengths. Zurich beat Thames in the semi-final but lost the final by ¾ length to Leander, who included Hugh Mason from the 1936 Olympic eight, the brothers Pat and Jack Bradley, and the 1939 Oxford Blue, Richard Burnell. It was an encouraging result for British oarsmen.

Leander also won the Stewards' but Thames reached the Wyfold final, where they lost to their stablemates, King's College, London, while Thames's neighbours, Imperial College, added to their successes by taking the Thames Cup from an all-British entry. Only the sculling events went overseas, the double sculls to Argentina and the Diamonds to Jean Séphériades of Basse-Seine, who had been coached by the mentor of the pre-war Zurich crews, Arthur Dreyfus.

Alan Burrough was again Captain in 1947, and in March my father returned from service with the RAF in India and resumed coaching. Guy Richardson stroked Cambridge to a 10-length win in the Boat Race, both crews rowing on fixed pins. Three weeks earlier, Thames and London had staged their own Boat Race over the reverse course, a trophy for an annual race having been presented by Guy Boustead, whose father had rowed for Oxford in the dead heat of 1877. London, stroked by 'Farn' Carpmael, won this inaugural meeting by 3 lengths, but in the Head they finished second to Jesus, Cambridge.

The Thames second eight won some senior events in early regattas, but after winning the Grand at Reading they were broken up to reinforce the first eight. This caused a minor revolution, and three of those promoted, Peter Kirkpatrick, John Wilmot, and John Dizer, together with Hank Rushmere, formed an 'umbrage' four. Despite opposition, they were entered for the Stewards', but only on condition that their training did not interfere with the Grand eight, and that if the eight won their heat, the four would scratch.

The changes came too late to help the first eight and weakened the second eight; both failed at Henley. A Delft crew beat the Grand eight but lost the final to a very fine Jesus crew, who had beaten a Zurich crew containing Rufli in the previous round. Despite the college's many appearances in Grand finals, this was only their third win.

Thames reached both the Stewards' and Wyfold finals, losing the latter to Quintin, whose first Henley win this was, if Wally Horwood's win in the single sculls in the Peace Regatta is discounted. The Stewards' four, however, were on winning form. Stroked by Kirkpatrick, with Rushmere at three, a great partnership was being formed. They beat a Czech four, then Leander, whose stern pair were Guy Richardson and that year's Cambridge seven, Tony Butcher. Thames won by 2 lengths and went on to beat London easily in the final. Wilmot, at 10 st 5 lb was the lightest man to win the Stewards' since Berry's 1911 victory at 10 st 3 lb. Nobody as light has won the trophy since.

The Henley performance that drew most praise, however, though a losing one, was that of Sparrow Morris and Alan Burrough in the Goblets. After beating Reg Swatton and Tod Hollom, both Thames men but representing Walton, Morris and Burrough rowed a desperate race with John Pinches and Edward Sturges of London. The maximum distance between the pairs was ½ length to London at Fawley. There was little in it at the Mile but London just got home by 6 feet. They won the final easily.

To the delight of both John B. Kelly and Jack Beresford, who were watching, Kelly's son Jack won the Diamonds, from which Kelly senior had been barred in 1920.

Gully Nickall was now Honorary Secretary of the ARA, which began to develop more interest in international rowing as a result. In 1947 the ARA, with the Olympic Regatta to be held at Henley the following year, at last affiliated to FISA, a move which had far-reaching implications for British rowing. The Thames four and pair were invited to row in the European Championships at Lucerne, becoming the first British crews to participate. These were the first Championships since 1938 and neither the Germans nor the Russians, who were to become such powerful forces in the next decade, were competing. Both the Thames crews finished fifth, which the ARA considered satisfactory.

My father took on the Captaincy again at the end of 1947 and shared the coaching with Ronnie Symonds and Berry, now in his eightieth year, a combination which brought a fine flowering of all that was best in Tideway rowing, with no unnecessary embellishments. Ham Ward was in charge of juniors, at which level the Club was to produce two winning eights in each of the next five years.

In 1948, Guy Richardson produced a record-breaking Cambridge crew which combined the qualities of the Jesus stroke, Chris Barton, with fixed pins and orthodox coaching. Despite a bad crab early in the race, Cambridge became the first crew to win the Boat Race in under 18 minutes. Peter Haig-Thomas, the most famous of the old orthodox coaches still active, set a precedent by coaching both crews for a spell.

On the Tideway, the professional Bert Barry was training a NARA eight, drawn from the Lea and the Thames, with an eye on the Olympics, and they were permitted to row at Henley as Leatham. A powerful Thames eight, stroked by a Swiss, Urs Burkhard, won both the Boustead Cup and the Head. Because Burkhard was not eligible to row for Britain, he was later moved to a less critical position at four, being replaced at stroke by Kirkpatrick. At seven was the Cambridge Blue, Tony Butcher, and six was Tom Christie, who had won the Wyfold with King's College. Another of the King's four, J.R. Johnson, was at two. With Rushmere at five and an ex-Emmanuel College man, Jerry Sangster, at three, they were, at 12 st 12 lb, the heaviest eight at that date to have represented the Club, though the lightweight Sparrow Morris once again filled the bow seat.

The Cambridge crew split after the Boat Race, Barton opting to row with Jesus, while six of the crew and the spare man, Paul Massey, went into the Leander eight. With no foreign entries, the Grand was a perfect Olympic trial, the only fault being a not uncommon one: the best men were scattered among several crews.

Thames arrived at Henley having had convincing wins in the Marlow Grand and Stewards' and they opened their account at Henley by paddling in at 28 comfortably ahead of London. Leatham were no match for Kingston, who were in turn well beaten by Barton's Jesus eight, who included one Pembroke man. Thames had a hard race with Leander, who led by ⅓ length from the Barrier to the Mile, at which point Kirkpatrick took over, Thames, at 37, drawing ahead to win by ½ length.

The final against the Jesus-Pembroke combination was an anticlimax, with Thames taking an immediate lead. They had 1½ lengths at Fawley and, going to 38 at the Mile, ran right away to win by 2½ lengths, the Club's first Grand win since 1928.

The Seeclub, Zurich, were the only foreign entry in the Stewards'. They drew Thames, who, with the same stern pair as the previous year, were an even better combination than the eight. Christie was two and Butcher bow. They also had weight on their side, averaging 13 st 4 lb. They scrambled off the start against the much steadier Swiss and were a length behind at the first signal, but once Thames found a stride they began to close up, taking the lead just after the Mile, after which they went right away, to win by $2\frac{1}{4}$ lengths. Leander also led them to Fawley, but Thames had $1\frac{1}{4}$ lengths at the Mile and paddled in at 26. In the final, against Isis and Granta, Thames had a length at the second signal, where they were down to 28. Soon after this, their opponents hit the booms and Thames drew right away to achieve a notable double.

The Thames Cup eight went out in the third round to Kent School, USA, while the Wyfold four lost to the ultimate winners, Victoria Lake, South Africa, in their heat. Wilmot and Dizer lost in the second round of the Goblets, which went to the 1938 winners, Ran Laurie and Jack Wilson, who had not rowed together since then. They had both been in the Sudan, where Wilson had almost lost his life when speared by a crazed woman. Coming home in 1948, they decided to have another go in the pair, and crowned their career by winning the Olympic title with a faultless exhibition.

The Thames four were chosen for the Olympics, while Leander, under the captaincy of Guy Richardson, took Barton back on board to stroke the Olympic eight, and the Thames cox, Jack Dearlove, steered. Dick Phelps was Olympic boatman for the third time.

Thames had another surprise Olympic crew when two of the second eight, Mark Scott and Bakie James, steered by a Westminster schoolboy, David Secker Walker, won the coxed pair trials. In his account of the Olympic Regatta in the *Rowing Almanack*, the old Thames oarsman, Tyke Richardson, wrote:

> The fame of the Thames RC . . . was enhanced by the almost frenzied training of their coxed pair. Two men, not by World or British standards considered great oarsmen, placed into one of these strange craft, a kind of glorified tub, trained with such conscientious determination that they were beaten only by a crew accustomed to this type of oarsmanship since childhood.

An exaggeration, perhaps, but it was an achievement for these two second-eight men to gain selection at all. Their mentor in this experiment was my father. The Stewards' four, coached by Ronnie Symonds, had been much fancied for the Olympics but were ultimately a bitter disappointment to themselves and their supporters.

The crew had no break after Henley and there was a heatwave just before the Olympic Regatta, also at Henley. They passed their peak, and to make matters worse, Kirkpatrick's seat broke at the start of the first heat against the Czechs, Thames having to come from behind to beat them. In the semi-final against Denmark, they were well below their best. They finally destroyed their chances when they hit a buoy and shipwrecked. The Danes went on to take the silver medal behind Italy.

Despite the eight losing their final by 10 seconds to the University of California, whose third Olympic eights win this was, Britain took the silver medal. To add to the coxless pair's gold medal, the double sculls were won by Bert Bushnell and Richard Burnell, the latter creating a remarkable family record. His father, whom Steve Fairbairn thought the finest oar he had ever seen, had won a gold medal in the eight in the 1908 Olympics, which had also been rowed at Henley.

The single sculls went to Mervyn Wood, who had rowed in the 1936 Australian Olympic eight whose entry had been refused by Henley. The British sculler, Tony Rowe, an Oxford Blue and a member of Thames who sculled in the Diamonds for Leander, was beaten in a semi-final after a remarkable race with Jack Kelly and a Uruguayan, Edouardo Risso. Kelly and Rowe fought it out for the lead with Risso trailing, but Rowe was beaten at 1,500 metres. However, Risso, with a series of remarkable spurts in a torrential downpour, caught Kelly on the line, to win by a few feet. He eventually took the silver medal.

After the Olympics, the Club held a reception for the competitors and officials, with a dinner and dance at the clubhouse. It is hard to realise now the extent of the austerity and shortages still being endured by the nation at that time, and a deeply appreciated gesture was that of the Mercantile RC, Melbourne, who took it upon themselves to send food parcels to the Thames first eight to supplement the severe food rationing.

An innovation in 1948 was the *Journal of the Thames Rowing Club*. A lively and informative publication, edited by Reg Swatton, it was produced annually for over twenty years until rising costs forced it to be discontinued.

In 1949 there were several Thames members in each crew in the Boat Race, which Cambridge won by ¼ length, the closest since the dead heat of 1877. At Thames, Hank Rushmere had retired, though there were many seniors from 1948 still rowing. However, the first eight made a poor start to the season, losing the Boustead by ½ length and finishing 10 seconds behind London in the Head. The eight had a narrow win over Antwerp at Ostend and the four lost by 3 feet to another Antwerp club, but both were beaten by London at Marlow. However, Butcher and Christie won the senior pairs, beating Morris and Burrough in the final, and it was decided to release them from the four to give them a better chance in the Goblets.

The eight improved at Henley, beating Clare, Cambridge, who were stroked by the Cambridge stroke, David Jennens, and then beat the Cottage Club of Princeton by 2½ lengths in 6min 49sec, coming in comfortably at 32. Leander, however, had equalled the record of 6min 44sec in their semi-final. Stroked by the only non-Blue in the crew, Pat Bradley, and with Burnell at six, they slipped the inconsistent Thames eight at the start and went on to win by 1 length.

Both Thames pairs reached the final of the Goblets, the younger, more powerful pair of Butcher and Christie again beating the veterans Morris and Burrough in a fast time. A lively Thames Cup eight, stroked by Joe Eldeen and rowing in a Stampfli boat bought from the Swiss at Henley in 1946, lost in the third round when a bad lurch in the tricky boat led to a half-crab, which let Lady Margaret away to win. The times to Fawley and the finish were new records for this event, but the ultimate winners were the Princeton lightweights. The Lady Margaret first eight set a new record for the course, 6min 43sec, beating the old Grand record by 1 second, in a heat of the Ladies', which they won.

The season as a whole turned out quite well for Thames in the end, both Henley eights and the Wyfold four winning at the Met, the Club recording 38 wins for the season. The second eight, including an Australian Oxford Blue, Graham Fisk, had had a popular win at Dinant. This was the last of many overseas trips to be managed by Charles Morrell, who had also been team manager on many occasions for the ARA. He died in December, two days after attending the Thames dinner. In the First World War, he had been shot down while serving with the RFC and was interned in Holland, which led to his long association with the Netherlands and her Far Eastern colonies. During the Second World War he had broadcast to Europe for the BBC, and on the Dinant trip, during an argument with railway officials in Belgium over reserved seats, his voice was recognised. The seats were emptied of usurpers and the Thames party were given VIP treatment. They laid a wreath on the memorial to the King of the Belgians, and after their win, the eight were garlanded with flowers. Two months before his death, Morrell, for being the voice of hope and resistance during the dark years of German occupation, had been made an Officer in the Order of Oranje Nassau by Queen Juliana of the Netherlands.

The same year Jack Beresford was awarded the

Olympic Diploma of Merit in recognition of his outstanding Olympic record.

In the autumn, Burnell was asked by the ARA to form a composite eight, based on Leander and Thames, to represent England in the Empire Games, as they were still called, to be held in New Zealand the following February. From Thames, Kirkpatrick, Butcher, and Rushmere (for whom the New Zealand carrot had proved irresistible) were selected, together with Jack Dearlove, who was recognised as the outstanding cox of the period. Jack Beresford was team manager.

It was, however, an ill-fated start to 1950. When the crew arrived in New Zealand, their riggers failed to turn up. They were using the archaic fixed pins on which Leander had won the Grand in 1949 (they were the last crew to do so), but they had to borrow riggers with an obsolete type of swivel, as well as shorter, whippy oars, changing back to their own equipment just before the racing started. It was a disaster. They were left standing after 500 metres by Australia and New Zealand. With England 4 lengths behind, Australia finished at 40, to win by a foot. In the single sculls, Tony Rowe took the silver medal behind Merv Wood, who also won the doubles with Murray Riley, the English double, Ken Tinegate and Boris Brown, being outclassed.

With Kirkpatrick now Captain, Thames won the Boustead but were only fifth in the Head. With only Kirkpatrick and Sangster from the 1948 crew, the Grand eight were unequal in weight, size and experience, Kirkpatrick at stroke weighing 14 stone, and Tim Wilson at bow, 9 st 7 lb. At Henley, they went out in the first round to London. Lady Margaret, with the extreme lie-back and low rates they had been cultivating, were approaching the peak of their success and had been expected to win, but they were rowed down by Harvard in their heat. In the final, Harvard beat a Dutch student crew, Njord, Leiden, to record their third Grand success. The Thames second eight, a better balanced crew than the Grand eight, reached their final, only to be outpaced by another outstanding Kent School crew.

It was a chastening regatta for British rowing, the Stewards' and Double Sculls going to Denmark and the Goblets to the Belgians Rosa and van Antwerpen. The one bright spot was Tony Rowe's victory in the Diamonds, the first by an English sculler since Askwith's win in 1933. In the final, Rowe beat a Dutchman, Rob van Mesdag, who was representing Trinity College, Dublin.

After Henley, Thames and London were put firmly in their places by an exceptional St Paul's School eight. At a time when British rowing was bemused by the Lady Margaret style, they were coached by my father in a way that owed something to the American style. They won the Princess Elizabeth Cup and crowned the school's best ever season by defeating both Thames and London in the Molesey Grand. The boys' success was the cause of some heart-searching among their elders.

That year a Goldie eight, based on the Lady Margaret crew, went to Italy for the European Championships, but they were well beaten by the Italians and narrowly by the Danes, with Austria a canvas behind and Portugal overlapping. Goldie's bronze medal was the first to be won by Britain in the European Championships.

In 1951 Cambridge, with five Lady Margaret men, won the Boat Race in a re-row after Oxford had sunk soon after the start, and then went on an all-conquering trip to the United States, beating several top university crews there, though what was conveniently overlooked in the euphoria of these successes was that the Americans were still at a very early stage in their training.

The season, which was to be an outstanding one for British rowing, was also a very good one for Thames, where there was a sudden influx of strong oarsmen just down from the universities, with a host of experienced coaches on hand. The

Journal mentions my father, Sparrow Morris, Alan Burrough, Arthur Sulley, Charles Allanson-Winn, Felix Badcock, 'Swat' Swatton, Jack Dearlove, and the perennial Berry, as all being available at some stage.

Nevertheless, Thames lost the Boustead, which resulted in four members, including Tony Rowe, of what was to have been a scratch eight of 'casuals' for the Head, being suddenly combined with four members of the Boustead crew. In the Club *Journal*, Rowe wrote of the Head:

> Offered a seat in Thames RC's 5th VIII in March 1951, I was delighted to accept an alternative to the hell of early training for the Diamonds – a series of lonely journeys through the raging torrent of chemicals, corpses, logs and oil-drums which, with the addition of fast tugs, tempestuous winds and an endless succession of rain, hail and snow, signify spring on the Tideway. The eight, stroked by Peter Kirkpatrick . . . were horrified (on their first outing) by instructions to take the 1st VIII over the course . . . However, we somehow held our own throughout a ramshackle row, which was enlivened by the intermittent clashing of oars and the piglet-like squeals of our cox as he tried, time and again, to sink the enemy.
>
> Next day brought news of a reconstituted eight . . . Our one and only outing took place after dark on the Wednesday before the race . . . and we hardly hoped to do more than save a place in the first division for Thames. Ultimately, the feeling that there was nothing to lose nearly enabled us to gain everything.
>
> Of the first three minutes I remember nothing, except that it was perfect. The boat ran as steady as a Leviathan, the rhythm was sublime, the wind was following and we were supremely together . . . As far as Hammersmith there was still no break in the perfection, but there the wind became head, we became tired, and for a few strokes the beginnings became ragged. But a shout from cox that we were closing on Lady Margaret inspired us to fresh efforts . . . At Beverley Brook, by some miracle, the rating rose spontaneously; opposite Thames, by no miracle, it rose astronomically, and we finished like eight windmills just astern of Lady Margaret.
>
> I have never enjoyed a row more, nor ever shall, nor have ever rowed in a better (though perhaps a fitter) crew or behind a better stroke.

The crew missed winning the Head by 1 second to Jesus, with London third, 3 seconds behind. They could not be kept together, of course, but morale had been restored. The race was watched by Princess Elizabeth, who was entertained at the Club afterwards.

Rowe went off to scull, and Graham Fisk and Tom Christie, together with Johnny Johnson, went to Leander, who were hoping to produce an Olympic eight a year in advance on composite lines. This imaginative scheme had the support of Thames. It did not in the end succeed, and the loss of three excellent men to the crew weakened Thames. However, Tony Pursssell, the Oxford stroke from 1946 to 1948, who had won the Grand with Leander, came into the Thames squad, together with two strong Durham University oarsmen, Maurice Legg and Sam Hobbs.

Another newcomer was R.A.F. Macmillan, possibly the best Oxford oarsman never to win a Blue. He had won the Ladies' Plate in 1950 with New College, the first Oxford college to do so since 1923. John Dizer also reappeared, having come down from Oxford, where he had gained a trial cap, and with Kirkpatrick to stroke and Rushmere sufficiently encouraged to continue, a crew of considerable potential was likely.

At Henley, Arthur Sulley was finishing coach for the eight and Felix Badcock for the Stewards' four. At a time when the Lady Margaret style with its extreme lie-back was even being caricatured by Leander, these two men from the vintage pre-war years put their faith in what they saw as true Tideway rowing in the Steve–Berry tradition, cultivating stride and the art of letting the boat run during a long, lazy-looking forward swing, which had been the hallmarks of the best Thames crews of the past.

It did not quite come off for the eight. Having paddled in at 28 in their heat against a Kingston crew who had entered the Grand only for purposes of prestige, they were beaten by 1⅓ lengths by the fast Lady Margaret crew, who then beat Leander, and then went on to record their club's first Grand win when beating Laga, Delft, in the final.

However, the Thames Stewards' four, by the time Felix had finished with them, were a very fine combination. Their heat against Lady Margaret was a most extraordinary race. Thames were nervous and not at their best and despite overrating LMBC from the start, they led by only a canvas at the first signal. With LMBC at 27 to 33 by Thames, the crews were level at Fawley. LMBC had raised their rate to 30 by the Mile, where they led by ½ length, with Thames at 35. However, when Kirkpatrick took the rate to 36 it soon became evident that Lady Margaret could not respond. At something like 6 strokes a minute lower than Thames, they lost by 2 feet. After this, Thames found their true form, comfortably beating New College and Gusar, Jugoslavia, on their way to the final, where they defeated Leander, who were the 1950 Clare College Stewards' four, stroked by David Jennens, by 1½ lengths, to give Kirkpatrick and Rushmere their third Stewards' win, and Dizer his second. The fourth member of the crew was Tony Purssell.

After Henley, some of Thames's prodigal sons returned to the fold. At the Met, the Club won the Champion Eights and the senior fours, Rushmere and Kirkpatrick recording their third win when taking the senior pairs.

One of the attractions of the Festival of Britain in 1951 was a sprint regatta on the Serpentine sponsored by the *Evening News*. Despite heavy rain, this was a popular success, Thames carrying off the senior eights, fours, and pairs, a fine end to a good domestic season.

Further afield, Goldie, with five of the winning Boat Race crew and their cox, John Hinde, won a first European Championship gold medal for Britain. Led by the Cambridge stroke, David Jennens, they won by the narrowest of margins from Denmark. In the single sculls, however, Tony Fox could not get his rate up sufficiently to beat Larsen of Denmark, and he had to settle for the silver medal. A Pembroke man, he had scored one of six Cambridge wins at Henley that year, almost an echo of 1887. It was certainly Cambridge's year.

Ronnie Symonds took on the Captaincy of Thames for 1952, feeling that Thames might produce a better base than Leander on which to build an Olympic challenge. Ronnie was the Lady Margaret finishing coach, and the Lady Margaret Blue, Alastair MacLeod, became Ronnie's Deputy Captain. It was a team calculated to draw good Cambridge oarsmen to the Club, and with the Cambridge Blues Paul Massey, who had won an Olympic silver medal with the 1948 eight, Peter de Giles, and MacLeod, and the Oxford Blue, Graham Fisk, all from the 1951 Leander crew, as well as Tony Butcher, who had resumed rowing, after a break to pursue his medical studies, Kirkpatrick, Hobbs, and Legg, the competition for places was so strong that such fine oarsmen as 'John' Macmillan, Johnny Johnson, and Joe Eldeen were relegated to the second eight for the Head.

But all was not right. Adopting the excessive Lady Margaret lie-back, the first eight paddled impressively, if ponderously, but they regularly feathered under water, with the result that by March the boat was not really moving. It was a serious blow when in the Head they dropped from the second place won by the 1951 scratch eight to third behind Jesus and London, while the second eight rose to finish tenth. Soon afterwards, MacLeod resigned as Deputy Captain and at Henley he rowed for Leander.

If Thames had not mastered the Lady Margaret style, the 1952 Cambridge crew produced a travesty of it, losing in a blizzard to an unfancied Oxford crew stroked by Christopher Davidge. Oxford's cox, David Glynne-Jones, outwitted the experienced John Hinde and Oxford won by a canvas, an even closer race than in 1949, when Davidge had been the losing stroke. That morning Thames, with John Macmillan replacing MacLeod, had won the Boustead Cup by ¾ length.

Oxford's win certainly upset the applecart as far as Olympic selection was concerned, but in April the ARA selectors asked Brian Lloyd to form an Olympic eight for Helsinki based on Leander. An Australian Lady Margaret Blue, Lloyd was the outstanding Cambridge oarsman of the period and had won a silver medal with the 1948 Olympic eight. At the same time, the selectors let it be known that Thames was regarded as the most likely source from which a four or fours would come.

Trials were to be held on the Saturday before Henley, except for the nominated eight and Tony Fox, who had been selected after winning the Wingfields in April. The Thames Grand eight had won at Marlow but the Stewards' four had lost and were beaten subsequently in the trials by Leander, who were stroked by the Cambridge Blue, Adrian Cadbury. The Thames coxed four, in effect the second four, stroked by Graham Fisk, won their trial from another Leander four, though not very decisively, the verdict being ¾ length. The crew – Hobbs, Legg, Macmillan, and Fisk, coxed by the youthful Lawrence Guest – were nominated, together with Massey and de Giles from the coxless four.

Ronnie Symonds then made a controversial decision. With only a few days left before Henley began, he made up a new Stewards' four consisting of de Giles, Fisk, Macmillan, and Massey. In the Stewards', this crew met the same four that Thames had beaten in the coxed four trial, though they rowed at Henley in Goldie colours. Thames had 1½ lengths over them at Fawley and paddled in at 26. They had another easy win in the final, leading London by 2 lengths at the Mile, where they were down to 29, and they won by this distance. This was Thames's fourth win in the Stewards' in six years and Ronnie felt he had been justified. It was hardly surprising that, when this became the Olympic coxed four, Legg and Hobbs were indignant.

Meanwhile, the Grand eight were well beaten by the Australian Olympic eight, Sydney RC, who lost a hard tussle with Leander in the final by ½ length. In a howling tailwind, the course record was lowered 5 seconds to 6min 38sec. The Goblets record, set in 1911 in the dead heat between the Thames pairs and the oldest Henley record still standing, also fell. Tom Christie and Chris Bywater, rowing for Westminster Hospital, took 3 seconds off the time, to Berry's chagrin. Butcher and Kirkpatrick had lost in a heat.

A young Thames newcomer to the Diamonds was Sidney Rand, then 18. At Henley, he was helped by Jack Beresford and Merv Wood, the latter, back at Henley on his way to the Helsinki Olympics, proving too strong for Fox in the final. Rand survived two rounds before losing to the veteran Australian, but he established himself as an exciting prospect with seven sculling wins during the season.

In the Thames Cup, Thames had a fast and experienced crew which had won twice before Henley, though they had lost narrowly in the final of the Marlow Eights to Lady Margaret. Stroked by Joe Eldeen, they were unlucky to draw the University of London, who had lost the final of the Marlow Grand by ¾ length to the Thames first eight. At Henley, the crews were level at the last signal, but Thames faltered and UL won by ⅓ length. After Henley, these crews had several close races, each beating the other at various times. This rivalry led to several UL men coming to Thames the following year. Among them were Alan Watson, who had rowed previously for Thames in the Grand, Stewards', and Thames

Cup, Don Elliott, John Rayne, myself, and their cox Derek Fawcett. Thames men had a considerable influence on UL at that time, their President being Ian Fairbairn, while all their coaches were Thames men: Andrew McEldowney, my father, Bean Vernon, and George Vasilesco.

Thames also had a large representation at Helsinki. Of the twenty-nine oarsmen and officials in the rowing team, fifteen were members of the Club, but the Olympic Regatta provided an anticlimax for the British contingent, five of the six British entries reaching the finals, only for all of them to finish fourth. It was the first time that Britain had come away from the Olympics without a rowing medal. The Thames coxed four were second in their heat and third in their semi-final, where they were leading at 500 metres before the pace told on them.

A feature of this regatta was the emergence of the Soviet Union as a major force, their sculler, Tukalov, beating Wood for the gold medal. Their eight were second to the US Naval Academy, who maintained the United States' dominance in this event. Navy remained unbeaten in twenty-nine races from 1952 to 1954. Leander had also been in the hunt only for 500 metres and the Sydney crew they had beaten at Henley passed them in the last 500 metres to take the bronze medal.

Germany, rowing as such since FISA did not recognise a distinction between East and West until the mid-1960s, also appeared for the first time since the war, taking a second and fifth place. Their emergence, together with that of the USSR, Czechoslovakia and Jugoslavia, was the prelude to a marked increase in the standard of international rowing. Writing in the Club *Journal*, Paul Massey made these comments:

> The standard of these Games had risen considerably since 1948, and, though Great Britain had improved too, as was shown by the times of our athletes, there were always two or three competitors a little better. Where we are backward is in the lack of interest this country shows in sport on the whole, yet the public are the first to blame our efforts for the lack of medals. To compete in the Games one has to sign a declaration of amateur status, but under the present ruling this has long been a farce. One is competing against the amateur–professionalism of most other countries . . . The gold medallist in the sculling event, a Russian student . . . stated that he had been selected eighteen months before the Games started and from that time had been maintained by his Government 'as doubtless your government keeps your athletes', he remarked.
>
> This is not a lament, for I enjoy sport for its own sake and would hate to be kept to do nothing else but train, but it is as well that the public realise what our athletes were up against.

In 1952 it was a new experience to come up against so many examples of state-backed 'amateurs', and rowing in Britain, still the most amateur of all sports, was about to have to face a challenge for which it was to have no immediate answer.

15 A Changing World and New Standards

The story of Thames now begins to take on a more personal flavour. Having been a member of Thames from the age of eight weeks, and having rowed in post-Henley Thames crews during my days at St Paul's and at college, it was natural for me to row with Thames when I finished at London University. Thames's influence at the universities was very strong at this time. Thames coaches were very active: at Oxford, George Vasilesco (New College and Queen's), my father (Oriel and Jesus), George Moody (Oriel), and Karl Vernon (wherever he was asked), and at Cambridge, Bill Williams (Queens'), Ronnie Symonds (Lady Margaret), and Andrew McEldowney (Selwyn) were some among many. But from these colleges alone, and from London University and five public schools where Thames had particular connections – St Paul's, Bedford, Oundle, Westminster, and UCS – came fifty-five oarsmen and coxes who represented Thames at Henley, twenty-four of whom became internationals, in the ten years from 1953 to 1962. It was this intake that gave stability to Thames rowing during the 1950s and 1960s.

In July 1952, Sir Harcourt Gold died. Harold Rickett had already succeeded him as Chairman of Henley and he was succeeded as Chairman of the ARA by Gully Nickalls, my father becoming Honorary Secretary. These two at once set out to bring about an amalgamation between the ARA and the NARA so that rowing in Britain could at last speak with one voice, though it was only in 1956 that this finally materialised.

1953 was Coronation Year and a happy one for the Club in every way. A Coronation Ball in the clubhouse, which went on all night and included breakfast, is memorable for me because it was the only occasion I went out in a pair with my father – a tub pair, as dawn broke, with both of us in full evening dress!

For Dick Phelps, 1953 brought his appointment as a Queen's Waterman, and in his honour a new eight the following year was named *Queen's Waterman*.

Swatton was now Captain. Nearly all the Club's senior oarsmen had retired at the end of 1952 and the 1953 first eight was partly an amalgam of men from the 1952 Thames Cup eight, Joe Eldeen and Lloyd Williams, an Australian Oxford Trialist, and Alan Watson and myself from the UL crew. Maurice Legg rowed until the Head but then went into a pair with Graham Fisk. However, John Pope, who had rowed in the 1950 Grand eight, reappeared, and there was also Reg Nicholls, an Old Pauline who had rowed in the Thames Wyfold four in 1949 and had subsequently stroked a winning Corpus Christi, Cambridge, Wyfold four. In the Head, with Eldeen stroking, and aware that we were succeeding a crew of distinguished oarsmen, we were mainly concerned with trying not to drop too far, but we caught London opposite the Clubhouse and, to our own and everyone else's surprise, we finished Head, with the second and third eights fifth and eighth respectively.

In May, the pair and Wyfold four lost at Liège and a week later the pair and the first eight competed in the Centenary Regatta of the Rowing Club of Paris. My memory of this is of a terrible row in a borrowed boat that did not suit us on water chopped up by launches and bouncing off the vertical walls on each side of the Seine under the shadow of the Eiffel Tower. We finished fourth to the Paris Metro crew that later rowed in the Grand. The pair had finished third to the reigning European Champions, Baetens and Knuysen from Antwerp, and a talented Leander four, stroked by Jennens, also finished third. Tony Fox finally saved British prestige by winning the Championship of the Seine by 1 second from a Swiss sculler.

After losing to Lady Margaret at Marlow, the eight were shuffled but were beaten by a fast Leander crew in the Grand. Stroked by Adrian Cadbury, they had earlier beaten Lady Margaret, equalling the Barrier record and finishing only 3 seconds outside the course record. They won the final from the Paris Metro crew by ¾ length. Four of the Leander eight also won the Stewards' by the same margin from First and Third Trinity, who had beaten Thames by ½ length in the semi-final.

The Thames Cup was won by a tough RAF crew, who, inspired by the former UL stroke Colin Porter, had trained on American lines, using a film of a Princeton eight as a model. In the semi-final, they beat Princeton by ⅓ length, and then beat Imperial College by ½ length in the final. This was the first win by a British eight in this event since 1935. Four of the RAF eight also won the Wyfold, in which Thames gave them their hardest race. The Goblets went to Baetens and Knuysen, who had again beaten Fisk and Legg in a heat, but Fox scored another success in the Diamonds, Rand having lost in the second round to the Ostend sculler, Henri Steenacker.

After Henley, the Club had a highly successful run, winning many trophies at all levels. The Grand eight and the Stewards' four in their Henley order were unbeaten after Henley. Thames won five events at Molesey and the Met, and a four stroked by Maurice Legg won the ARA coxed four championship which had been introduced that year. The season ended with a Coronation Regatta on the Serpentine, at which Thames won the Grand eights, Stewards' coxed fours, and senior pairs. The regatta was such a success that the sponsors, the *News of the World*, decided to make the regatta an annual one.

In the European Championships in Copenhagen, the RAF won a bronze medal in the coxless fours. Leander could not keep their eight together and Fox was the only other British entry, but he failed in a *repêchage*. Soviet crews won the eights and coxless pairs, and also took two silver medals and a bronze.

The Boustead race had been moved to December, when, after having been nearly two lengths behind at one point, Thames, paced by a visiting porpoise, came through to win by 2½ lengths.

In 1954, the 100th Boat Race was won by Oxford. In the Head, which started at Putney because of a lack of suitable tides, the Thames first eight were by no means ready to race and could finish only sixth behind the RAF. A new award this year was the Vernon Trophy, a statuette of Jack Beresford made from the silver of the Bean's trophies and presented by him for the fastest Tideway crew in the Head. London were the first winners.

The first eight were rearranged after the Head, and, with Eldeen stroking, won at Dunkirk, breaking the course record, and Ostend. These races took place on successive days and at Ostend, following a magnificent banquet in Dunkirk, we were not at our best. We had to come from behind to beat Basse-Seine, whom we had beaten comfortably at Dunkirk. However, Eldeen put in a sustained spurt which took us from a length down to ½ length up in the last 250 metres, with the other crews trailing. We won the Marlow Grand and the Stewards' fours, but the other four from the eight lost in the ARA coxed four championship, it being Marlow's turn to stage that event.

Our target for the year was the British Empire and Commonwealth Games, as they were now called, and selection was to be on Henley form. The character of Henley was transformed that year by the appearance for the first time of Soviet crews. In 1953, the Soviet eight, with only one change from the 1952 Olympic silver medal crew, had won the European title. The Krylia Sovetov eight at Henley in 1954 were the same crew with one further change. The Danish crew, Kvik, in the Grand were the crew that had won the silver medal in 1953. The Russians also had two fours in the Stewards', and their pair in the Goblets were the 1953 European champions.

Tukalov, in the Diamonds, was the Olympic champion, though he had finished only fifth in Copenhagen. The Swiss double were also 1953 European champions, who had broken the record when winning at Henley. With other strong overseas entries, it was the strongest entry ever seen at Henley and a truly formidable prospect for home competitors.

The style of the Russian crews made it hard to assess their true pace. At that time, their rhythm was very exaggerated, with a noticeable slowing down, almost a check, of the hands as they passed the thighs on the way forward, followed by a swoop up the slide and a lightning catch. They did not row a long stroke and sat very upright at the finish. They used pre-war equipment 'borrowed' from the Germans.

The Danes drew the Russians in the Grand, but in the Stewards' we drew Krylia Sovetov, who, like the other six overseas crews in the Stewards', were not doubling up. The Russians cleared us just before the second signal but soon after I heard the distinctive clunk of a blade hitting a boom. I called out to the crew and rather excitedly put in a few 'thick 'uns', with the result that, in passing them, we also shot over in front. Meanwhile, the Russians set off in pursuit at what looked like 45 and rapidly closed up behind us, to the consternation of Harold Rickett, the umpire. Faced with an international incident, he called on us feverishly to give way. Fortunately, we managed to do so just in time. We were still only ½ length behind at the Mile and this encouraged us to hang on, though they beat us in the end by 1¼ lengths.

After this, the Russians did not seem quite so invincible, and we did not have to race in the Grand until the next day. We now had Maurice Legg at seven, John Macmillan, Captain of the Club, at six and a tall former Bedford School oarsman, Alastair Davidson, at five. These three were also in the Stewards' four. The cox was David Glynne-Jones, the hero of the 1952 Boat Race when he out-steered his experienced Cambridge rival. We drew London and led by 2½ lengths at the Mile, paddling in at 30 to win by that distance. The Russians beat Kvik by 3 lengths, and nobody gave us much chance against them in the semi-final, but Joe Eldeen thought otherwise. Going off at 42 to the Russians' 40, we led by ½ length at the first signal, maintaining this until after the Barrier, when the Russians crept back. The crews were level at Fawley but the Russians slowly pulled away to lead by ¾ length at the last signal, where Eldeen mounted another great attack and we began to gain at once, but with both crews finishing at 38, Krylia Sovetov won by ½ length. No other crew got within a length of this Russia eight in 1953 or 1954.

Leander had been specially chosen with the Commonwealth Games in mind. With six Olympic oarsmen, they were based on their 1953 winning Grand eight, six of whom were in the 1954 crew. Their bowman, Ted Pain, an Oxford Blue, had won a gold medal in the Australian 1950 eight. So confident were the ARA that they would go to Vancouver that boats had already been dispatched to Canada for their use. They beat Lady Margaret on their way to the final but were overwhelmed by Krylia Sovetov after Fawley, the Russians coming in at 35 to win by 2½ lengths.

The Russians also won the Stewards' after a hard race in a headwind in the final with the RAF four, who were stroked by Eric Beresford's son, Michael, winning by 1¼ lengths. The Henley records state that the standard was lower than usual, an astonishing observation since the Krylia Sovetov four, with Tukalov at bow, won the coxed fours in the European Championships that year, and the RAF won the silver medal in the coxless fours.

The Russians also won the Goblets but the Diamonds went to the 1953 European Champion, Vlasic of Jugoslavia, who won a controversial final by 6 feet after washing the Swiss sculler, Colomb, all the way up the enclosures. Under FISA rules, Vlasic would have been disqualified, but Henley had not yet introduced a rule banning interference and since the sculls never touched Vlasic got away with it, which was not appreciated by Colomb. The Swiss double, however, won again. Six of the seven open events went abroad. Though Thames won nothing, the second eight reached the semi-finals of the Thames Cup.

Following the Henley results, the selectors changed their minds about selection for Vancouver and Thames replaced Leander as the eight and coxed four. However, it was not really practicable for the same crews to compete at Vancouver and in Amsterdam for the European Championships, which came later, though Sid Rand did so, and it was no surprise when he came nowhere in Amsterdam. Thames did not even consider Amsterdam.

Of the Commonwealth Games party, only Nick Clack, in the coxless pairs with Tom Christie, representing the Royal Navy, was not a member of Thames. Arthur Sulley coached, Dick Phelps was again boatman, and Gully Nickalls was team manager. The eight were never comfortable in the Leander boat and we never rowed to our Henley form. On top of this, the temporary dam to hold up the stream of the Vedder Canal collapsed and the races were rowed against a strong stream which gave a tremendous advantage to the stations near the bank. There were, however, only two eights, the Canadian eight from the University of British Columbia drawing lane 1, while Thames in lane 2 were against the full force of the stream. We never had a chance, though in conditions similar to rowing against the stream on the Tideway we led by nearly a length before being overhauled. We were eventually beaten by 2½ lengths and the time of 6min 59sec for the 2,000-metre course gives some idea of the strength of the current.

The coxed four, always subservient to the eight, were the Stewards' four with Glynne-Jones steering. Unlike the eight, we liked our boat and easily beat Canada in our heat. In the final, rowed after the eight's race, although again in the middle station, we were only a length behind the Australians, with Merv Wood at three, with a few strokes to go, when a sudden lurch allowed New Zealand to get past and we missed the silver medal by 1/10 second. Rand finished second to Don Rowlands of New Zealand; and New Zealand, in the best finish of the day, took the gold medal from Clack and Christie, who were also on the worst lane, by 1/5 second. Wood won a second gold medal in the double sculls, and it was a frustrating regatta for the English contingent. After it was all over, I looked up the course from a road below the start with Joe Eldeen and Merv Wood. 'It's a ruddy graveyard,' said Merv, which just about summed up this bleak course.

In the European Championships, the Russians carried off all five gold medals in the inaugural women's championships. In the men's events, the Krylia Sovetov eight retained their title, finishing 7½ seconds ahead of Kvik, who again took the silver medal. In addition to the RAF's silver medal in the coxless fours, Christopher Davidge and David Macklin, who had been in the Leander eight at Henley, won the bronze medal in the coxless pairs. With Rand in the single sculls and the Royal Engineers, coached by Bill Williams, in the coxed fours, the only men in the British team who were not members of Thames were the Sappers' cox, the London double, Fox and Marsden, and Christopher Davidge. In all, twenty Thames men represented either England or Great Britain that summer, a remarkable tally.

Thames had another outstanding post-Henley season. The first eight, before leaving for Vancouver, won the Champion Eights in the Met, where the Club won five events again, and the Molesey Grand.

Colin Porter came to the Club in the autumn of 1954. With him came another member of the RAF eight, Ken Cross, and some other powerful men. Porter also brought with him strong ideas about fitness and training, which he attempted to impose on the Club. Right through the winter, endless arguments ensued as the Club's senior oarsmen tried reconcile 'Porterism' with Thames 'Fairbairnism', while Sparrow Morris, the Club Captain, a charming and likeable man but also a rather indecisive one, found that decisions were being taken out of his hands. In the 1955 Thames *Journal*, Arthur Sulley wrote:

> As a result of general agreement in the Club that a Grand eight, to be successful, must get together in the winter and devote itself to reaching a high degree of fitness by Easter, the crew . . . embarked on a most vigorous programme of winter training with a fierce determination which aroused general admiration. Every weekend saw them covering prodigious mileage in long stretches – Richmond and back, rowing home from Mortlake, was a routine outing – with training at the Clubhouse during the week. As soon as it became light in the evenings they tore up and down the river in the twilight. By the end of April, they were the leanest, fittest, toughest and fastest crew seen on the Thames for many years, and from then on until Marlow no other crew could give them a race or even pace them for more than a minute or two.

In fact, the crew did not wait for the longer days, but rowed in the dark throughout the winter months.

Some indication of the potential of this crew came in the Boustead, which again took place in December. The crew at that time were G.G.H. Page (bow), K.S. Cross, A.R. Watson, R.A.F. Macmillan, A.R. Davidson, C.F. Porter, M. Legg, R.H. Nicholls (stroke) and D.R. Glynne-Jones (cox). On a fast stream, but with the tide well down, Thames led London from the first stroke and won easily in the fastest time ever recorded at that time from Mortlake to Putney, 17min 27sec. This was not bettered for ten years.

I went down with bronchitis immediately after this race and lost my place, though as the lightest man in a crew which put a premium on weight and strength this was probably inevitable. David Whitaker, a 14-stone man who had won the Ladies' with Lady Margaret in 1954, came into the crew. This eight won the Reading Head by 21 seconds and the Tideway Head by 9 seconds, with the RAF second in both. At Ostend, they won the senior eights and the 400-metre sprint; and a four from the eight also won. They took the Grand at Reading and Marlow, where the four won the senior fours, though the eight had resolved not to double up at Henley. In his *Journal* report, Arthur Sulley continued:

> If mileage alone could make champions this crew would have swept the board this year. But during the winter the primary object was physical fitness, with technical problems being hotly debated after the outings, rarely resolved, and usually left in an agreement to differ, no doubt in the hope that they would be smoothed out by further mileage. Strength and fitness confused the issue . . . None of the crew had ever rowed before in such a powerful eight and it should have been an exhilarating experience; yet it is doubtful whether any of them ever really enjoyed their outings. Certainly they never got out of their rowing the equivalent of the effort they put into it.

The truth is that slogging had turned the crew into a one-pace machine, incapable of increasing their speed where it mattered. They rowed without rhythm and never relaxed, and rowing in the second eight, a good but less powerful crew, was far more exhilarating.

At Henley, the Grand attracted entries from the University of Pennsylvania, the University of British Columbia (with six of their winning Commonwealth Games crew and rowing as Vancouver RC), and a new Russian eight, Krasnoe Znamia. Thames had a bye and met Penn in the second round. Penn had beaten London by 1⅓ lengths after being 1½ lengths ahead at Fawley. Against Thames, on previous form a much faster crew than London, Penn led by 1¼ lengths at Fawley, Thames having lacked the pace to hold them in the crucial second minute. Although their fitness and determination prevented the Americans from getting away, there was still clear water between the crews at the last signal and Thames eventually lost by ⅔ length.

It was a bitter pill to swallow, and it was also the end of British hopes in the Grand, in which Leander were not represented. Vancouver rowed the Russians down, cracking them along the enclosures. In the final, they almost succeeded in doing the same to Penn, being only a canvas behind at the last signal, but their cox let them down, swerving all over the place in the row in, to lose by ⅓ length.

The Thames second eight had won twelve races in a row before losing in the final of the Marlow Eights to Queens', Cambridge, who won the Ladies' at Henley, but Thames lost to the RAF in the second round at Henley. The RAF dead-heated with the Penn lightweights, winning the re-row by 3 feet, but lost in the final to the Massachusetts Institute of Technology by ⅔ length.

However, Thames had an unexpected win in the Wyfold with a four that had been plagued by illness. John Pope, who had not been rowing that season, came in at a late stage, and the crew came through to beat Kettering in the final. It was a particularly sweet success for Alex Riemer at three. He had rowed at Henley for five seasons without winning a heat. At his sixth attempt, he won a Henley medal.

Sid Rand, in RAF colours, lost in the final of the Diamonds to Theo Kocerka of Poland, and the Russians retained the Stewards' with the same Krylia Sovetov four that had won the previous year. They also won the Goblets and the Double Sculls, in the latter winning by ½ length from the future President of FISA, Thomi Keller, who was stroking the Grasshopper double from Zurich.

The Thames Grand eight were selected for the European Championships, but their Henley failure led to them looking for ways to strengthen the crew, always a gamble at such a late stage. Michael Beresford and Bill Rand, Sid's brother, stroke and six respectively in the RAF eight at Henley, were brought in, the unfortunate scapegoats being Cross and Whitaker. Beresford went to stroke and Rand to four, but the problems were too deeply rooted to be solved merely by changes of personnel. Ronnie Symonds tried to instil some stride and relaxation but he was hardly the man to get through to this particular group, and he failed badly. They won in the new order at Molesey, Bedford, and the Met, but then, with a hopelessly rushed row, suffered the indignity of a 4-foot defeat by London in the sprint regatta on the Serpentine – hardly an ideal way to tune up for the Championships in Ghent.

Matters were not helped at Ghent when Porter went sick the day before racing started. Although he rowed, a sick man at six was the final straw. The eight came last in their heat, and though Rand changed places with Porter for the *repêchage*, they failed again, being eliminated by Denmark. The Danes were last in the final, in which Krylia Sovetov, with one more change in the crew, were again successful.

For Thames, and particularly for Porter, it was a sad failure at the end of a long, hard road. The other British entries fared no better, none reaching a final.

In 1956, there was a complication with the Olympics being held in Melbourne in the autumn,

1. The start at Henley—the Stewards' Cup, 1891

Key: 1. Miss Clarke, 2. Miss Landale, *Trinity Hall Four*: 3. J. C. Garrick (bow), 4. E. M. Lord, 5. W. Landale, 6. C. T. Fogg Elliot (stroke), 7. J. H. D. Goldie (Umpire), 8. F. Willan (Umpire), 9. Master Goldie, 10. J. C. Tinné, 11. R. H. Labat, *Thames Four*: 12. B. W. Looker (box), 13. P. Landale, 14. F. E. C. Clark, 15. J. C. Gardner (stroke).

2. View of the Thames, near Putney, early 19th century

3. Henley—after a race, 1893, showing the London and Thames houseboats

4. *top left*
Bill Forster

5. *top right*
Hamish Hamilton

6. *left* 'Berry'
(J. Beresford Snr),
1952, aged 85

7. Dick Phelps in Doggett's Coat and Badge, 1953

8. Freddie Page, 1956

9. Ronnie Symonds,
a posthumous portrait,
1957

10. Prizegiving at Ostend Regatta in the 1960s. This painting was presented by the artist in 1971 to KRSN Ostend in memory of the regatta secretary, Charles Heuzel, who had been a good friend of Thames for many years

11. The Thames first eight winning the sprint at Ostend, 1985

12. National Champions in women's coxed fours, 1980: Bernadette Casey (stroke), Sally Bloomfield, Alexa Forbes, Caroline Casey (bow), Susie Hall (cox)

13. Receiving the winners' medals for senior A international eights at Ostend, 1985. *Left to right*: Gary Herbert (cox), Lee Brown (stroke), Mike Cowie, Chris Jones, Dan Badcock, John Robson, Mark Kerridge, Gavin Reddin, Steve Jones (bow)

14. The Thames first eight, Ostend, 1986. *Left to right*: Chris Bourne, James Stewart, Dan Badcock, Mike Urry, J. Lawrence (cox), Ross Thain, Luke Slemeck, John Robson, Steve Jones, Gavin Reddin

15. The Great Britain Women's Lightweight coxless four, World Championship silver medallists, 1989: Kate Brownlow (TRC, stroke), Joanna Toch, Rachel Hirst, Susan Key (TRC, bow)

while the European Championships were at Bled in Jugoslavia at the end of August, which meant a long and difficult season for European crews. Olympic selection was again to be based on Henley form.

At Thames, Colin Porter selected his own four, separate from the Club 'system'. This private army consisted of Legg (bow), Porter, Davidson, and Beresford (stroke). They got together early in the autumn of 1955 and boated almost every day or night, and when the water was bad at Putney, they took their boat to Wallingford, Molesey, Walton, or Henley. However, the crew had not learnt from the previous year's mistakes. They were once again a slogging crew, lacking in real skill and finesse, which was even more serious in a four than in an eight.

A new first eight, with the former IC and Sappers oarsman, David McLellan, at seven, Alan Watson at six, and stroked by the winning Wyfold four's stroke, Hugh Denning, won the Reading Head but the Tideway Head was won by Porter's four plus Gavin Sorrell, an Old Pauline Oxford Blue, and Ted Field, both of whom had rowed in the winning RAF crews, and the Rand brothers, to make up their numbers. As Thames third eight, they beat London second eight, a scullers crew, by 10 seconds, with Thames first eight third, a further 15 seconds behind.

Reorganised after this, with John Macmillan now at six, the first eight were well beaten by the French Army crew at Ostend, though two fours from the eight won. Nicholls then had to drop out, so I took his place. The eight then won at Walton, Reading, and Marlow, but the crew never felt right and was seated in an impossible order as far as physique was concerned. One of the winning Ostend fours were beaten by Porter's four by 2½ lengths at Reading but they were determined to have a crack at Porter's four, who were the Club's 'official' Stewards' four, at Henley. Because it was an Olympic year, the Henley Stewards had decided to allow oarsmen who were members of a recognised club to enter in any guise, but in allowing Thames to put in a second Stewards' four they insisted it should be entered privately and would not use the Club colours. Accordingly, the crew (Gordon Dear, Denning, McLellan, and Macmillan) duly raced as R.A.F. Macmillan's crew, with a white band across the blades and riggers painted white.

A strong, blustery and erratic 'bushes' wind played havoc with the first heat of the Grand. While we were waiting to start in the second heat, we saw Queens' suddenly blown right off the course as they cleared the Island. They went straight into the booms, breaking two blades, leaving London to paddle in. Against the powerful French Army crew in these conditions, our rather makeshift crew had little chance. On the Bucks station, the wind hit us like a charging buffalo at the top of the Island. The French shot ahead and all we could do was plug along in their wake for the rest of the race. Jesus, with one Blue, beat Leander, with seven, including Davidge and Leadley, by ½ length, and then they were presented with a lead of 2½ lengths when the stroke of the French Army crew came off his seat on the second stroke, but the French caught Jesus soon after Fawley and eventually won by clear water. In the final, the French led all the way from the Swedish national composite eight, Three Towns, with one change, the silver medallists at Ghent.

As luck would have it, Macmillan's crew drew Porter's in the Stewards', for which there were no foreign entries. Macmillan's had rowed earlier in the gruelling Grand heat, but with nothing to lose, they were far more relaxed than their opponents. At first, it looked very one-sided, Beresford, at a high rate, taking the lead at once. He had 1½ lengths by the first signal and increased this to 2 lengths before the Barrier, but Macmillan's then began to wear Beresford down. There was only a length in it at Fawley, with Beresford at 38.

Macmillan, spurred on by tumultuous cheering at Remenham and from the enclosures – many of the crowd were well aware of the personal issues at stake – inched back stroke by stroke. Beresford finished at 40 to Macmillan's 36 and just held on to win by 3 feet.

Having survived this needle race, Thames never rowed as badly again. They beat Leander and London comfortably, Beresford becoming the third generation of his family to win the Stewards'. There is little doubt, though, that when European and Olympic selection was being considered, their performance against Macmillan's crew weighed against them, since none of them was selected for either, which was underestimating the tremendous performance put up by Macmillan's crew. Macmillan, however, was selected for Bled.

The Thames Wyfold four lost in their semi-final to Brockville, Canada, who lost the final by 4 feet to the Royal Engineers. Coached by George Moody, the Sappers included Kerry Hennessy, from the Thames 1955 second eight, and a future Thames oarsman and Club Secretary, Peter Thomson. The Rands, still in RAF colours, won the double sculls.

Since no outstanding British crews had emerged at Henley, the selectors decided to try a composite eight for Bled, to be coached by my father. The Rands were selected for the double sculls and Fox for the single. The eight never had much of a chance to develop and, at Bled, they failed to survive their *repêchage*, the Czechs winning the gold medal with the French Army second and the Russians only fifth. The Cambridge crew had been racing in Brazil, and on their return some of them were put into a new eight for Melbourne. Macmillan had to drop out for business reasons, but Alan Watson found a place in the crew, which Davidge stroked. My father went as team manager.

None of the three British entries reached a final at Melbourne, another unfortunate first for Britain. A young Russian, Vyacheslav Ivanov, who at 18 had won the single sculls at Bled, took the Olympic title as well, beating Australia's 19-year-old Stuart Mackenzie into second place. Yale won the eights for the USA again, with the Canadians, from the University of British Columbia, taking the silver medal. Of the European eights, only Sweden reached the final. Italy won the coxed fours with the new tandem rig – two and three rowing on the same side. Germany were second in the coxed pairs with their cox lying in the bows, another innovation. But the sensational performance was that of the Canadian coxless four, originally the UBC spare men, not one of whom had touched an oar before the previous February. Last at 500 metres, they rowed through the field to win by 4 lengths.

Much heartsearching followed these Olympics, the shortcomings of the selection policy being fully exposed. Memoranda were exchanged and an enquiry into what was wrong with British rowing was launched by the ARA. The truth was that new methods which were being introduced abroad were not being adopted, while archaic ideas were not being rejected. To oarsmen at the time, it seemed that the only hope in the long term lay in combining the best talent into composite crews which would train together for months rather than weeks, and it was this role that the recently formed Barn Cottage Boat Club was to fulfil for the next few years.

A loss to the Club in 1956 and to rowing generally was that of Ronnie Symonds. He had been on good form at Marlow and was expected at Henley, but instead he went to the Channel Islands and swam out to sea and drowned. A complex and private person, he was only 46, but in recent years his private life had become confused, and he also felt he had lost his touch as a coach, though with Roy Meldrum, who had died a year earlier, and Harold Rickett, he had done much for Cambridge rowing. He had also been a magnificent finishing coach for Thames. Somehow, though, one could never see Ronnie as an old man.

16 A New Generation

In the autumn of 1956, I went to Vancouver for a year and spent some time watching UBC training for the Melbourne Olympics and later rowing with some of them, which I found illuminating.

Meanwhile, at Thames, Porter's four disbanded and disappeared, Porter going to coach National Provincial Bank. A new generation filled five of the places in the 1957 Grand eight: Felix Badcock's son, another Felix, who had learnt to row at Thames and had been in the 1956 Thames Cup eight; Tony Hancox, from St Catherine's, Oxford; a Radley first eight oarsman, Brian Tanner, the son of an old Thames member, Lewis Tanner; and two Old Pauline winners of the Princess Elizabeth Cup, Kit Nisbet and Ian Wilson. Another Old Pauline, Ray Penney, coxed. They joined Don Elliot, Bill Griffith and David McLellan from the 1956 eight. This crew were put together after the first eight had dropped to seventh in the Head. They then won at Ostend, beating London and Encouragement from Paris, and they also won the sprint by 6 feet from London. Later, they added the Reading and Marlow Grands to their tally.

At Henley, Yale had four of their winning Olympic eight, and with Cornell and Krasnoe Znamia guaranteed a high standard in the Grand. With almost no stream and a very light breeze, conditions were fast. There was again no Leander eight, and Thames, London, and the Oxford Head crew, Queen's, were outclassed. The Russians quickly had a length off Thames in their heat and won by 4 lengths. Cornell then cracked the Russians along the enclosures, winning by 1 length and setting a new course record of 6min 30sec. In the final, they beat Yale by ½ length, but with a slight headwind the new record was not in danger.

A separate Thames Stewards' four, stroked by Alan Watson, lost to London, who were outclassed in the final by a new Krylia Sovetov four. Other Thames crews fared no better, but Porter's Bank crews reached the final of the Thames Cup and the Wyfold, winning the latter.

British rowing was not entirely demolished, however, Leadley and Davidge winning the Goblets, rowing a Russian pair to a standstill half way up the enclosures and then winning the final narrowly from the European coxed pair bronze medallists from Austria. Mackenzie had his revenge over Ivanov, winning the Diamonds controversially in a manner similar to Vlasic's in the 1954 final. Mackenzie steered into the centre of the course and was warned several times before winning by 4 feet.

After Henley, the Thames eight beat Molesey in the ARA trials, but against a losing Thames Cup crew, the 3½ length win was rather meaningless. A coxed four from the eight lost their trial by a canvas to London and in the end the only crews to represent Britain at Duisburg were the Goblets pair and the National Provincial Bank coxless four, the latter doing well to reach the final, though they finished last. However, Leadley and Davidge excelled in winning the coxless pairs in record time, beating the Austrians once again by the narrowest of margins. Mackenzie also set a new record time when he won the single sculls from an unknown German, Klaus von Fersen from Ratzeburg, with Ivanov third. The Italian Moto Guzzi eight, again innovators in rigging matters, won with three pairs rowing in tandem.

At home, Thames won the Champion Eights but it was not a good year for the Club, and when Tony Hancox took over as Captain, he wrote in the *Journal*:

> British rowing was, in 1957, made to look very poor . . . we shall continue to be made to look poor in the international field until what we do in preparation for our races approximates to what the best of the rest are doing . . . We have forgotten how to row, how to work and how to train, properly. We have . . . to re-learn the best of English rowing; . . . recognise that we must then add . . . the better qualities of today's successful international rowing; and then work as our top athletes work.

As a start, Thames stepped up the land training and work in the boat, and emphasis was put on competitive racing between the Club crews. The main snag was the lack of experienced men: Porter and Beresford had decided that their way to top honours was in composite crews and had teamed up with two strong London men, Simon Crosse and John Vigurs, all four rowing in Barn Cottage colours.

However, there was a new strong and keen squad which included Michael Long, from the 1957 Thames Cup eight, who had won the Princess Elizabeth Cup with St Paul's, as had two newcomers, John Stephenson and Dick Workman. There were also Malcolm Atkins, also from the 1957 Thames Cup eight, and Peter Thomson, who had rowed with Atkins in the winning Sappers Wyfold four, Robin Anderson from King's School, Chester, and Tony Wober from Bryanston.

I returned from Vancouver in the autumn of 1957 and began to coach in the following spring. David Glynne-Jones was in charge of the Grand eight, whose target was the Commonwealth Games, and I took the Thames Cup crew.

For the previous two years, the Boustead had been won by London with crews of scullers. In 1958, the race reverted to a March date, when Thames comfortably beat the London first eight. I had to sub at seven in the Reading Head when Dennis Mount crashed his scooter, so fifth was fair enough in the circumstances, but the full crew finished only twelfth in the Tideway Head, which Barn Cottage won for the first time. The second eight did even worse, finishing twenty-ninth.

However, the hard work began to pay off and at Ostend the first eight won from stronger opponents than usual, the Marne crew that finished second containing Robert Detweiler from the legendary 1952 Navy Olympic crew. The following week in Amsterdam, Thames finished third in a borrowed boat to strong crews, and a four from the Thames eight were second in the coxed fours.

These regattas on consecutive weekends left the eight tired, and in the Walton Grand the following weekend they lost narrowly to Molesey. Glynne-Jones was faced with a dilemma: the crew needed a rest but with the Commonwealth Games trials the next week, there was no time and, believing that at least part of the tiredness was psychological, I encouraged him to take a calculated risk and set the crew to race the second eight over seven minutes on the Monday after Walton on the principle of kill or cure. It worked. The second eight were not much slower than the first but I knew that they would be rowing a sub at seven on the Monday, and this was sufficient to enable the first eight to get home first by ¾ length.

Their morale rose at once and their tiredness suddenly vanished. At Henley the following Thursday, they beat RAF, Cardington by 2½ lengths, and on Friday, Lady Margaret by 1¼ lengths. In the final on Saturday they had a desperately close race with First and Third Trinity, who had beaten Jesus and Molesey. Trinity kept slightly ahead for most of the race through repeated spurts but Thames's racing experience over 2,000 metres paid off and they found just enough at the right moment to win by a canvas and secure their selection. A coxed four from the eight also reached their final but were no match for Porter's Barn Cottage four.

After the trials, the eight took a much needed rest and did not compete at Marlow, where the second eight won the Marlow Eights, the Club's first victory in this event for 21 years.

At Henley, the Grand eight drew the Australian Commonwealth Games eight, Leichhardt RC, in their heat. Thames led by a few feet at Fawley, but the Australians passed them to lead by ½ length at the Mile, going on to win by ¾ length. London were the only other home entry now that it had dawned on Oxbridge colleges that to be Head on the Cam or the Isis or to make a lot of bumps was not enough for the standard the Grand had then reached. A fast Russian eight, Trud, easily beat London and then the Australians by 2½ lengths in the final.

The Thames Cup eight, stroked by Malcolm Atkins, reached their final. At seven was Alan Routley, a strong New Zealander with whom I had rowed briefly in Vancouver, but who was not eligible for the first eight with their Commonwealth Games aspirations. In the crew also were an Australian, Graham Crocket, and an American, Mike Harris, who had rowed in one of the Harvard lower boats. So unnerved was Mike at finding himself against his former *alma mater* in the final that he turned his blade over on the sixth stroke and Harvard led by ⅔ length at the first signal. Thames gradually pegged them back to ¼ length at Remenham but in the end Harvard won by ¾ length. The stern pair of this Harvard lightweight eight were two future Cambridge Blues, Mark Hoffman and Mark Christian. Barn Cottage won the Stewards' from National Provincial Bank, who were the coxless four for the Games and had beaten the Trud four.

The Commonwealth Games were held on Lake Padarn in Wales. It was not an ideal venue for the first four-lane 2,000-metre regatta to be held in Britain, and the finals were marred by a roaring tailwind that produced very rough water that all but sank the floating Judges' Box, though conditions for the heats had been good.

The Thames eight were beaten by Canada, the UBC crew again, with Northern Ireland third, but they qualified in their *repêchage* for the final by beating a Scottish composite eight, with the Irish again third. In the final, Canada beat Australia by 1 second, but Thames, though 15 seconds behind, took the bronze medal. Both the English fours won to round off a happy season for Colin Porter, and a young Marlow double, Baker and Spracklen, beat Mervyn Wood and Stuart Mackenzie, the latter winning the single sculls. He had not been born when Wood competed in his first Olympics.

Meanwhile, the Thames Cup eight were soldiering on, the crew changing every week as men had to drop out. Nevertheless, they took three Thames Cup events and the senior eights at Bedford, where the full London first eight and a reshuffled University of British Columbia eight also competed. At one period in the season, they were beaten only in the Henley final while winning twenty-one other races, a tribute to the spirit of the thirteen oarsmen and two coxes who made up the crew at various times.

Several Commonwealth Games crews competed in the European Championships in Poznan, Poland, though there was no British eight. Unfortunately, most of the British team were laid low by stomach upsets, which also afflicted some other teams, notably the Russians. The Barn Cottage four and the Marlow double failed to reach their finals and the National Provincial Bank coxless four came fifth. Leadley and Davidge, who had been selected in preference to the Isis pair that had rowed at Padarn, escaped the bug but managed only fourth place. Moto Guzzi, still on their tandem rig, won the eights again, and Mackenzie retained his single sculls title, with Ivanov and von Fersen again second and third.

The Soviet Union won only one title, but Germany was beginning to emerge, taking both four-oared events and the coxed pairs. The first of Karl Adam's Ratzeburg eights to reach international level finished fifth. Adam, who never rowed himself, also trained von Fersen and the coxless four. It was a foretaste of things to come.

In 1958, Thames was still weak at lower levels and for the first time since 1922 no junior eight won. The policy of having one coach in charge for each of the senior crews, introduced that year, with occasional coaches for a week or two, seemed to be paying off, and when I became Captain that autumn, we decided to extend this to the juniors, my father undertaking to coach the first junior eight through the winter. At David Glynne-Jones's request, he and I changed crews and we began to think in terms of a two-year programme with the 1960 Olympics in mind, so we set out to provide the British eight for the 1959 European Championships.

In February, Thames won the Boustead easily by 8 lengths, while the first junior eight beat the London second eight by 9 lengths. All the Thames eights went up at Reading, where the first eight tied with Crowland for second place behind Isis. Though the first eight came only seventh in the Tideway Head, over half a minute behind Barn Cottage, the second and third eights rose to tenth and fifteenth respectively, which was an encouraging trend. Oxford won the Boat Race, their President, Ronnie Howard, having successfully quelled a mutiny led by an American from Yale, Reed Rubin.

The Thames Grand eight in 1959 were an amalgam of the previous two years' Grand and Thames Cup eights, Griffith, Tanner, and Nisbet having returned after a year's absence, which resulted in two of the 1958 Grand eight losing their places. When the two top eights won at Walton, it was clear that both were above average, though both had earlier lost to the unexpectedly strong opposition of a crew from Adam's stable, Ditmarsia Kiel, the second eight at Dunkirk and the first eight at Ostend. At Marlow, the first eight won the Grand, beating Leander by 2 lengths in the final, and the second eight retained the Marlow Eights, also by 2 lengths, the first time the Club had achieved this particular double since 1927.

The Grand eight, with Malcolm Atkins stroking and Felix Badcock at six, met Leander again in the first round at Henley. Leander included the Oxford rebel, Rubin, and another American, Charlie Grimes, from the winning Yale 1956 Olympic eight. Tony Leadley was at six. They tried to shake Thames out of their stride, going off very fast but they led by only ¼ length at the ½ Mile. Thames passed them by Fawley, had ½ length at the Mile and dropped the rate to come in comfortably 1¼ lengths ahead.

This put Thames in the final for the first time since 1949, but their opponents were a formidable Harvard eight who had beaten London and Isis, the latter based on that year's winning Boat Race crew. In the final, they took Thames by surprise by slipping ahead at the top of the Island. This unsettled Thames, who lost their stride and never found it again. Harvard had a length at the Barrier and won comfortably.

The Grand eight did not double up and there was no Stewards' four. The Thames Cup eight survived a fierce opening heat against Phillips Academy, USA, winning by 3 feet, but went out in the third round to the Jesus first eight by ⅓ length. Once again Joe Brown's Harvard lightweights won, to score a notable double.

The Grand eight had expected to have to row a trial for the European Championships in Macon, but with Isis committed to a trip to Japan, Thames were selected immediately after Henley, the fourth time in six years that the Club had produced a representative eight. A combined St Edmund Hall and Lincoln four who had won the Stewards' were also selected. They had been helped at Henley when a Moto Guzzi four, all from their gold medal eight, committed suicide by twice hitting the booms and breaking a blade before the second signal. Molesey were chosen as the coxed four after winning a trial. The coxless pair, Norton and Scurfield of Hertford College, had beaten Beresford and Porter in the Goblets final, while the double scullers, Justicz and Birkmyre, had lost to Davidge and Mackenzie at Henley, but Mackenzie had also won the Diamonds again, and represented Australia in the single sculls at Macon, where Sid Rand was the British sculler. David Cazes, the team manager, was also a Thames member.

Before setting off for Macon, the Thames eight won the Grand at Molesey, breaking the course record in both heat and final, and they also won the Champion eights, beating London by nearly 3 lengths.

In FISA Championships at that time, there was only one *repêchage* system, so it was possible to calculate whom one might meet in finishing second, third, or fourth. Thus, if it were not possible to win the heat, it might not be in the crew's best interest to finish second either. At Macon Thames drew Italy, the holders, who had made only one change from their 1958 eight. In the other heat, the Ratzeburg eight met the Russians, and whoever came second or fourth in Thames's heat would meet either the Germans or the Russians in the *repêchage*.

It was soon clear that Jugoslavia and Poland, in Thames's heat, had also realised this. When, predictably, the Italians gradually drew ahead, the other three crews began to look for third place, and an extraordinary race developed. At 1,500 metres, Thames were third but there was only ⅓ length between second and fourth, with the Italians a length ahead. The fun started with 200 metres to go but Thames's lack of experience in this sort of tactical race showed up, the Jugoslavs suddenly dropping back and the Poles spurting, while Thames, believing themselves to be in the right position, were caught napping. Henley racing does not prepare one for this kind of thing and Thames lost the tactical battle. Jugoslavia came second, 1 second ahead of Poland, with Britain ½ second behind the Poles, the Italians winning by 1½ lengths.

This put Britain and Jugoslavia against France and the USSR, the latter having eased off after being 1 second down on the Germans at 1,000 metres. Thames gambled on a faster start but it did not pay off, the crew never getting down to their intended rate of 37 and scrambling over the course at 38. The Russians won, with Jugoslavia, France, and Britain overlapping each other in that order, but only the Russians went through to the final. The importance of the tactical battle in the heat was underlined when Poland beat Switzerland, Romania, and Spain, to qualify from the other *repêchage*. In the final, the Germans, who were never below 40, beat the Czechs, who had won their heat and had a young oarsman called Bohumil Janousek at three, into second place, with Russia, Italy, and Poland finishing in that order behind them.

The standard was higher than ever and I will never forget the sight of Adam's young Ratzeburg eight winning the gold medal some 10 seconds ahead of the field. With long oars and the short, wide blades which later became known as the 'Macon' blades, high rates of striking and a short swing with a powerful leg-drive, their performance suddenly opened up new horizons and put the rowing scene into a totally new perspective. Nothing that has occurred since has had anything like the impact of the sudden explosion of Ratzeburg into the rowing world, and it was very much a question of 'back to the drawing board' when we returned to England. The Germans won four of the seven events and were second in two others, only their double failing to reach the finals.

Mackenzie, who had had an operation for

a stomach ulcer and should not have been racing at all, lost his title to Ivanov and finished fourth. He was never to beat Ivanov again.

Of the British team, only Norton and Scurfield, despite capsizing in their heat, reached the finals, finishing fourth, over 20 seconds behind the gold medallists, Kruse and Kliefoth of Ratzeburg. They were the spare men for the German eight, being on the light side, and Adam had thought so little of their chances that he made them drive the boat trailer to Macon. They were 19 years old.

17 The Centenary and New Problems

In September 1959, Berry, who had seemed likely to go on for ever, died at the age of 91. He had continued to go out in a double scull with Dick Phelps during the Henley fortnight to within a few years of his death, and had frequently coached Thames, Lensbury, and the dockers' club, Argosies, among others, until failing eyesight proved too much of a handicap.

He was a marvellous coach, especially of a coxless four, and I regard myself as particularly fortunate to have been coached by him. He had a distinctive turn of phrase. In Vancouver, I found some duplicated rowing notes scattered about the changing room. The first page was missing and the last unsigned, but there was no doubting the authorship:

> The trick of taking the strain that makes the firm, hard leg-drive chump against a solid blade full of water is acquired by various methods. Everybody knows that this beginning is essential for a comfortable stroke. If one tries to get a grip on the water at a later part of the stroke it will become a frantic effort, upsetting the balance of the boat and resulting in one or another of the 'faults' bellowed through the megaphone of the coach.
>
> I pause to disassociate myself from coaches who bellow 'faults' without seeing how they arise. A man who fails to tune his mind and body to the beginning will fail to catch up with the water as it flies past; his blade will rise to the surface in the middle of the stroke with a mountain of water instead of a clean swirl. A coach who says 'Don't' does not help a man who is doing all he knows how . . .
>
> At the instantaneous beginning, the legs and back take the strain to convey the drive from the stretcher to the water . . . A slow-motion picture would show that every good oarsman does this, whatever may be his creed as to the style which he follows. But to get this result, coaches and their cat-calls have made differences in method which have caused rowing men to form into opposite camps . . .
>
> Snick the blade squarely and cleanly into the water at the instant when the power comes on. The blade must be moving against the water at the moment it goes in . . .
>
> Anybody knows that. Yes. But can you do it? Can you get the blade to cut in cleanly, like a hot knife cutting butter? And can you get that solid hump of water in front of the blade at the very beginning of the stroke? There is no need to turn your head to see. You can feel it and hear it, knowing where it should be so that it can hook on, well behind the rigger.

This is unmistakably Berry speaking, encouraging oarsmen to hear and feel rowing. Like Steve, he made his oarsmen 'hear the boat sing'. Words like 'snick', 'chump', 'swirl', 'feel it', 'hook on', and 'cleanly' were the basis of his coaching, which Frank Read was passing on to his UBC oarsmen in these notes.

There was something familiar about them, and when I came back to England I found them. Entitled *Metropolitan Rowing*, Berry had had them printed privately in 1938. The missing opening sentences were:

> I do not want anyone to think that I am laying down the law about rowing or that I intend to be the founder of a 'style' or new religion that is to be adopted by the whole rowing world . . . There are certain notions at the base of every good oarsman's mind which would be common to every style if only they could be expressed, but the manner in which these notions present themselves to a man's mind is peculiar to the man himself and depends on the process whereby he has discovered them. The path of experiences whereby each man arrives at the ultimate goal of being good company in a first-class crew is a matter of

> chance; it depends upon the conditions in which he began to row, the company in which he rowed, the difficulties which arose, and the misleading or well-directed remarks of his coach – or series of coaches. Consequently, each man is inclined to think that his path is the true road and that another man's path must necessarily be the wrong road. In the result, we have advocates of 'style' who become unpleasantly assertive in the changing room or the bar of the Club.

Berry was closer to Steve in his philosophy than he would ever admit. He also showed that in the modern rowing world there was still a place for the old standards.

He died just before the Club's centenary in 1960, but in celebrating its first hundred years the Club was about to face a very difficult decade. It had been becoming increasingly clear that to compete at international level, some sort of composite scheme, run under the direction of the ARA, would have to be evolved, which would leave a question mark over the role of club rowing.

Meanwhile, for Thames's centenary it seemed appropriate to try to get an eight to the Rome Olympics, and to row two fours from the eight as insurance against the eight failing. Soon after the eight returned from Macon, the senior oarsmen decided to train six days a week from the outset and to do supervised weight training at the Spur Gym at Blackfriars since the Club at that time had no gymnasium of its own; and there would be various other training activities. I had already begun to experiment with rigging and longer oars of the Macon type, and Thames became the first club in the country to adopt these.

Due to a lack of suitable tides, the Boustead was not held and the first eight, in a very experimental stage, did not compete in any Head races. Such was the competition for places, with the 1957 stroke, Ian Wilson, returning and another Old Pauline, Stuart Miskin, who had rowed twice for Oxford, coming in, together with a tall Old Bedfordian, Peter Laws, that for the second year running some of the previous year's Grand eight lost their places. It says much for the Club spirit at the time that these men continued to row in the second eight. A newcomer to the latter crew was Fred Lambert, formerly of Crowland. With this talent available, we hoped to produce fours outside the first eight that might be good enough for the Olympic trials.

It was clear that the route to Olympic selection would be a hard one. Germania Dusseldorf, then at the peak of their success, having won the coxed fours at Macon, won the eights at Ghent, where Thames beat the French national eight but were beaten into third place by Oxford's winning Boat Race crew, who also had Olympic aspirations. The Germans also won both the coxed and coxless fours with Thames taking second and third places.

At Ostend a week later, Germania Dusseldorf again won the eights. Molesey, the other main British Olympic hopes, were in second place. They were a composite crew based on Porter's Barn Cottage four. The Polish national eight were third and Thames fourth, but less than 2 lengths separated the crews, all of whom were using long oars and various types of spade blades. It was a tough baptism.

Shortly afterwards, Thames had a serious setback when the Club launch *Thelma* accidentally cut off the stern of a four when turning, the crew finishing up in the river. Ian Wilson, who was stroking, swallowed some river water, then more polluted than it is now, and the resulting infection led to his being out of action for two weeks at a vital stage. Nevertheless, the eight had a good win at Marlow, where, for the first time, the second eight also competed in the Grand, losing by ¼ length to the London first eight in their heat. The Stewards' four, stroked by the recovered Wilson, also won, beating in a heat the St Edmund Hall/Lincoln four that had rowed at Macon.

In the Grand at Henley, Thames met Oxford, who led by a canvas at the Barrier and ⅓ length at Fawley. They then spurted, to lead by ¾ length at Remenham, but Thames pulled this back to ½ length at the Mile. However, Oxford drew away along the enclosures to win by 1⅓ lengths in 6min 39sec. Five minutes later, Molesey, stroked by Christopher Davidge, were 15 seconds slower when beating London. Molesey went on to beat Lady Margaret to reach the final, where they met Oxford, who had beaten Yale. Oxford had been consistently faster than Molesey in their heats, but Davidge hustled them from the start and they never got into their stride, though Molesey won by only ⅓ length in 6min 35sec.

Once again, Thames had to pin their hopes on the Stewards' four, who had come on exceptionally well in training. They drew the Macon gold medallists, Belvoir RC, Zurich, stroked by a famous Swiss oarsman, Gopf Kottmann. Thames had a magnificent start, and were leading by ¾ length at the top of the Island and striding beautifully when they were brought to an abrupt halt as both bowside blades hit a pile, the blades breaking clean off at the necks, and that was that, a sad end to a fine piece of rowing. Barn Cottage, four of the Molesey eight, put the Swiss out in the semi-final and went on to win the event.

The Thames second eight lost in the semi-final of the Thames Cup to Detroit Boat Club, USA, but Harvard won the final for the third year running, Mark Christian having rowed in all three crews. In their semi-final, Harvard had beaten the recently formed Tideway Scullers School, whose founder, Alastair Provan, was a Thames man.

Henley had not worked out correctly so far as the selectors were concerned, so Oxford and Molesey did a deal with them. The Oxford eight were nominated on condition that the Molesey fours both won their trials, which they did. The Thames coxed and coxless fours both went down by 1¼ lengths, the latter never recapturing their Henley form. The second eight held their own trials to find a coxed pair, and eventually Wober and Lambert, with a diminutive cox from University College School, took part, albeit briefly, in the ARA trials, their hopes coming to a premature end when Fred Lambert caught a crab and fell in!

The team for Rome consisted of two Henley winners – the Molesey coxed four who had won the Stewards' as Barn Cottage, and the double scullers, Justicz and Birkmyre – and four crews and a sculler (Rand) who had either lost at Henley or, in the case of the London University coxed pair, had not existed until the trials: hardly the standard required to win Olympic medals, and only the Molesey coxless four reached the finals, finishing fifth. The Ratzeburg eight finally ended the United States' long run of victories in the eights, with Frank Read's Canadian crew from UBC taking the silver medal once again just over a length behind the Germans. The Americans managed only fifth place and the Russians did not even make the final. Germany won three gold medals, the Russians two, and Czechoslovakia and the USA one each. Ivanov won the single sculls again.

At home, the Thames Grand eight after Henley won almost everything they went for in eights and fours, beating London by 4½ lengths in the Champion Eights, and breaking the course record at Bedford. The eight's only defeats came on the Serpentine, where they all but beat Oxford, who were training for the Olympics, losing by 3 feet in their heat. In the final as the fastest heat losers, they again pushed Oxford until the last few strokes, *The Times* describing the Thames eight as 'formidable'. The Stewards' four broke the course record, and the Thames Cup eight also won on the Serpentine as well as at the Met and Staines, where they won the Grand.

Two junior eights and a novice eight won during the year, the Club winning in all classes of eights, and in fours, pairs, and sculls. By the end of the Club's centenary season, the collection of silverware went some way towards compensating for the earlier disappointments.

The Centenary Dinner was a magnificent affair, held in the Grocers' Hall in the presence of the Club's Patron, the Duke of Gloucester, and with the President, the Earl of Iveagh, in the Chair. The Club's guests included Viscount Simon, Chairman of the Port of London Authority, Viscount Bruce of Melbourne, Lord Cottesloe, Gully Nickalls, Chairman of the ARA, and the Lord Mayor of London, Sir Bernard Waley-Cohen, and the Sheriffs, who were in full court dress, having earlier attended a royal function.

The Club had launched a Centenary appeal to finance the building of a new eight-oared tank and a gymnasium, and to help with the refurbishing of the clubhouse. Ian Fairbairn made a considerable donation towards the new tank, which was to be named the Steve Fairbairn Tank in memory of his father.

An honour during the year was the award of the CBE to Jack Beresford for his services to rowing, while another centenary was that of the Phelps family, the first member of the family to win Doggett's Coat and Badge having done so in 1860. He was H.J.M. Phelps, the son of 'Honest John', immortalised for his Boat Race verdict in 1877 of 'dead heat for Oxford by five yards'. Ten members of the family had won Doggett's by 1960 and a celebration dinner at the Half Moon, Putney, was attended by representatives of the ARA, the Fishmongers' and the Watermen's and Lightermen's Companies, as well as the Captains of the senior rowing clubs.

From modest beginnings at the turn of the century, women's rowing had achieved international recognition with the introduction of the Women's European Championships in 1954. In 1960 these were held on the Welsh Harp in London, Penny Chuter, aged 17, finishing fourth in the single sculls. In the British eight, which also finished fourth, was Pauline Baillie-Reynolds, better known later by her married name, Churcher, as Honorary Secretary of the Head of the River Race.

The end of the 1960 season was inevitably followed by the departure of a number of good oarsmen, but 1961 turned out to be another successful season, even though at Henley only three former Grand oarsmen, 'Puppy' Miskin, John Stephenson, and Felix Badcock, and one Thames Cup oarsman, Fred Lambert, were still rowing. At one time in the late winter I had to row in the eight for six weeks when we were particularly short of suitable men. The personnel were settled by February, however, and remained unchanged throughout the season. Newcomers included Doug Culpan, a New Zealander, and Michael Woolner, who had rowed for Oundle but still had novice status.

The crew looked rough and unpolished by comparison with the 1960 eight but turned out to be faster. They were second in the Reading Head and then won the Boustead comfortably. In the Head, despite breaking part of John Stephenson's blade on a marshal's boat just before the start, they finished second behind Barn Cottage, winning the Vernon Trophy.

At Ostend, the eight and two fours from it, all in borrowed boats as usual, finished second to Nassovia Hochst, who included Jordan and Neuss, later winners of the Goblets and European coxed pair champions. The eight lost by only ½ length with the Belgian composite eight a poor third. In the sprint, Thames lost narrowly to Nassovia Hochst and Germania Dusseldorf, with Molesey fourth and Spartak, Prague, fifth. Both Thames fours beat the Czechs, whose coxless four later competed in the European Championships, and the standard at Ostend that year was probably as high as it had ever been. That weekend, the second eight won at Dunkirk before coming over to Ostend to support the first eight, and morale was high.

The Grand eight and coxed and coxless fours all won at Reading, and at Marlow the Grand and Stewards' fours came to the Club for the third year in succession. The press brought out their best pens and we basked in the rare sunshine. 'Thames were the outstanding crew' (*The Times*), 'A thoroughly sound crew' (*Daily Telegraph*), 'Thames have a field day at Reading' and 'A most attractive four of real class' (*Sunday Telegraph*). Thinking back to the cold, wet, windy days of winter, it was hard to believe that we had reached even this level of success.

By Henley, Thames had beaten the Head crews of the Isis and the Cam, and at Marlow the future winners of the Thames Cup (University of London) and the Wyfold (National Provincial Bank). But Henley was, as usual, a step up in class, the USSR Navy Club, the powerful Molesey eight, and Leander, all recent Oxford Blues, including four from the Olympic eight, providing strong opposition in the Grand.

Molesey, stroked by Davidge with Porter at six, were beaten by Leander by 1 length and Thames, with a bye, met Leander on the Friday, when Leander led by ½ length at Fawley. Miskin, stroking Thames, put in a typical burn at Remenham, reducing the lead to ¼ length at the Mile. Mike Davis, the Leander stroke, replied. Leander were still only ⅓ length ahead at the last signal, but, as in 1960, Thames could not hold Leander along the enclosures, and lost by 1 length. Leander lost the final by the same margin to the Russians.

The Stewards' four – Woolner, Lambert, Stephenson, and Badcock – went straight into the final when Leander scratched, to meet the Trud Club, USSR. As in 1960, Thames had a superb start to lead by ⅔ length at the ¼ Mile. The Russians then began to close and had their bows in front at Fawley, gradually pulling away as Thames's steering became erratic, Trud winning by 2 lengths.

Neither the Thames Cup eight nor the Wyfold four survived the first round, but the latter had a remarkable season. Their stroke, Michael Lohnberg, whose father, Herbert, had rowed for Thames before the war, and Richard Willett at two had both started the season as juniors and the crew were put together after a memorable 'Lawns Committee' at Twickenham Regatta, when we changed all the Thames crews round after I had suddenly realised they were all in the wrong combinations. The Wyfold four did not win a final until after Henley, but then were victorious at the Met, Molesey, and Staines, and when put into a Thames Cup eight, they won three times.

The week after Henley, the Grand eight rowed a trial with Molesey, but in a strong headwind they could not hold their heavier opponents in the last stages of the race, though, says the *Almanack*, Thames continued to press them with a series of courageous spurts.

Yet again, we had to concentrate on the fours, the trials for which were held in the first week of August. The coxed four, stroked by Miskin, lost their final to the University of London, who were drawn from their Thames Cup eight that had recorded UL's first Henley win. However, the coxless four beat National Provincial Bank, and were then selected for the European Championships in Prague, Miskin being chosen as spare man for the British team. This was the Club's third representative crew in four seasons, and its sixth in ten years.

The eight raced at two more regattas, despite having only two outings in a fortnight, and won at Kingston and Bedford, where they set a new course record once again. The coxless four also won at both regattas and equalled the Bedford record. In all, the Grand eight recorded fifteen wins in eights, fours, and pairs, Mike Woolner featuring in all but one and gaining an international vest in his first season as a senior.

Three of the coaches at Prague – Alan Watson (London University), Colin Porter (Molesey) and myself – were Thames members but we had occupied the stern seats in the 1951 UL eight. Porter, through injury, had dropped out of the Molesey eight since the trials, and Mackenzie, who had won the Diamonds for the fifth successive year, took his place. Raymond Owen, the team manager, was also a Thames member.

The four had a difficult opening heat against the Olympic silver medallists, Italy, as well as Germany and Holland. For once, Thames had a bad start and never got going properly, finishing a close fourth. In the *repêchage*, Thames had to face Germany again, as well as the USA and Poland. The Poles set far too fast a pace, but Thames were second at 500 metres with only ½ length between all four crews. The Poles blew up eventually, finishing last, and Germany won by about 1½ lengths, Thames just failing to catch the Americans on the line, missing second place by ⅓ length.

Justicz and Birkmyre excelled in finishing second in the double sculls, while Molesey reached the final of the eights but finished last. The other crews failed to qualify. The official report in the *Almanack* said that, apart from the double, 'a study of results . . . will show that the coxless four came nearest the standard needed' and British rowing emerged from these championships with rather more credit than they had at Macon and Rome.

Timothy Shaw, who had coxed the Grand eight that year, took over the Captaincy for 1962 though I continued to coach. Two members of the UL four at Prague, John James and David Gramolt, came down to Thames, and Robin Anderson returned. Because of a congenital back condition, only Mike Woolner did not continue from the Thames four, and Puppy Miskin also carried on. The Grand eight were coxed by Roger Weston, who had come to Thames to learn to cox before going up to Selwyn and winning his Blue.

The eight had a series of troubles in the winter and were ultimately disappointing, though they tied for the first place with London University in the Reading Head, and the following week won the Golden Oar in Antwerp in record time. Even fourth place in the Tideway Head was a good performance, and the disappointment felt at the time reflected the high standard the Club was now setting itself.

The Boustead was held after the Head, Thames winning easily, and at Ostend, the eight, still in a borrowed boat as the Club had not yet got round to buying a trailer, took the senior eights for the first time since 1958 with a convincing win over a Dusseldorf crew. Leander, second to a Polish eight at Ghent a week earlier, finished fifth. Thames also won the sprint, while the fours from the eight both finished second to Nassovia Hochst.

Something was lacking in the crew, however, and they lost in the final at Reading. The following weekend at Amsterdam, where they went in preference to Marlow, and in a borrowed boat that was too small for them, they came second in their heats on both days but failed to reach the finals, Ratzeburg setting a new unofficial world record time in their heat and lowering it again in the final.

In the Grand at Henley, they had a beautiful start against Pennsylvania University, a high rating crew. Thames leapt into the lead to have clear water at the first signal, but Penn had drawn level at Fawley. Both crews were at 39 from the ¾ Mile and the pace was blistering, with Penn beginning to forge ahead. In the last 20 strokes, Thames were totally exhausted and Penn rowed right away. The standard in the Grand was very high, however, and Penn went out to Moto Guzzi, who had four gold medallists in their crew, though the Italians were themselves beaten in the final by the Soviet Navy Club by ½ length. The Stewards' final was fought out between two unchanged Prague finalists, Trud, the silver medallists, and the Dutch four from Nereus, who had beaten Thames in Prague. They beat Thames again in the Stewards', rowing at 38 the whole way and drawing away after Fawley to win by 2 lengths, but Trud beat them by 1½ lengths in the final.

The Thames Cup eight reached the final for the first time since 1958, 'Donkey' Long rowing two on both occasions, but they went down by 3 lengths to National Provincial Bank.

In the trials for the first World Championships in Lucerne, the Grand eight lost to Molesey again and both fours also lost. The Molesey eight were sent to Lucerne, and London University provided the coxless four and pair. None of these crews reached the main finals, but *petites finales*, to settle the order from 7 to 12, were introduced at Lucerne, the eight finishing ninth, the coxless four tenth and the coxless pair seventh. Justicz and Birkmyre came fifth. Mackenzie, who represented Britain in the single sculls after winning the Diamonds for a record sixth time in yet another controversial final, had to be content with the silver medal behind Ivanov. The Germans had a field day, taking five gold medals, Ratzeburg, who had rowed in small boats in 1961, taking the eights again.

Later in the year, at the Commonwealth Games in Australia, Molesey (coxless fours), Farquharson and Lee-Nicholson (coxless pairs), and Justicz and Birkmyre (double sculls), all won gold medals, the Molesey eight and coxed four won bronze, and Bill Barry took the silver medal in the single sculls, in which Mackenzie was not competing as he would not go back to Australia for trials. Rowing was not included in the Games again until 1986.

Thames did have a modest representative role when the Thames Cup eight rowed for England in the Home Countries Match which was staged as part of the Serpentine Regatta. Coached by Felix Badcock Jnr, after Henley, they had had a string of successes, and on the Serpentine they won the eights for England.

Felix took over the Captaincy for the 1963 season, firmly intending not to row, while I had resolved to take a break from coaching, rowing in the winter in the second eight, but things did not work out as planned. The shortage of good men was acute, John James, David Gramolt and Fred Lambert having gone off to form a four which rowed in the Skiff Club colours. At Henley in 1963, only one member of the Grand eight had rowed throughout from October. Three started rowing in January and three did not start training until after the Head. All through the season the crew suffered from having men in various stages of fitness and the vital autumn period of training and coaching had been lost. The coldest January and February for many years did not help and when the first eight came only eighth at Reading and tenth in the Tideway Head, it was clear that they needed strengthening.

As a result, Felix was persuaded to row, Ray Penney took over the coxing, and I was put in charge of coaching. Things began to look rosier when, at Chiswick, what was to become the Stewards' four beat a London University four containing their internationals, but the crews were not quite ready for Ostend, though the eight reached the final, to lose to Nassovia Hochst once again, while the coxless four came third behind the French World Championship silver medallists and Germania Dusseldorf.

The Grand eight arrived at Henley having won no important races, and they faced a Herculean task, although they improved rapidly. Felix Badcock was back at six, Stephenson at five, and a promising Salopian, Adrian Mill, rowed seven. Sadly, he was killed in a car crash two years later while up at Cambridge.

That year, the Henley Stewards had introduced the Prince Philip Cup for the coxed four equivalent of the Stewards' Cup, so the eight were at

53. Thames members of the England team for the 1958 Commonwealth games at Padarn, Wales. *Left to right* David Badcock (spare man), Peter Thomson, Tony Hancox (Captain of Thames), John Stephenson, Ray Penney, Dick Workman, Felix Badcock, Dennis Mount. *Kneeling* Gordon Dear (spare man), Don Elliott, Tony Wober

54. Thames beating Leander by 1¼ lengths in the semi-final of the Grand, 1959. Thames: D. R. Mount (bow), W. M. Nisbet, B. S. Tanner, J. A. Stephenson, R. D. F. Anderson, J. F. C. Badcock, W. J. Griffith, M. S. Atkins (stroke), R. L. Penney (cox). Leander: C. K. Smith (bow), B. S. Mawer, H. E. Fitzgibbon, R. Rubin, C. L. Grimes, D. A. T. Leadley, R. A. J. Southgate, I. F. C. S. Clayre (stroke), S. G. B. Underwood (cox)

55. The Thames Grand eight which represented Great Britain in the European Championships at Macon, 1959. *Standing, left to right* Bill Griffith, John Stephenson, Ray Penney (cox), Kit Nisbet, Dennis Mount. *Seated* Robin Anderson, Felix Badcock, Geoffrey Page (Captain of Thames, coach), Malcolm Atkins (stroke), Brian Tanner

56. The Earl of Iveagh, the Thames President, receiving the Duke of Gloucester, Patron of the Club, at the Centenary dinner at the Grocers' Hall, 1960. Watching are, *left*, Sir Bernard Waley-Cohen, Lord Mayor of London, and Sherriffs Studholme and Kirk

57. The Centenary dinner

58. The Great Britain coxless four at Prague for the European Championships, 1961. Michael Woolner, Fred Lambert, John Stephenson, Felix Badcock (stroke)

59. The first eight winning the Senior Eights at Bedford Regatta, 1961. *Left to right* Timothy Shaw (cox), Stuart Miskin (stroke), Michael Woolner, Fred Lambert, John Stephenson, John Palmer, Scott Kennedy, Doug Culpan, Felix Badcock (bow)

60. The semi-final of the Stewards', 1963. Thames beat the Skiff Club by 1 length. Thames: A. C. W. Mill (bow), M. J. Lohnberg, J. A. Stephenson, J. F. C. Badcock (stroke). Skiff Club: J. J. James (bow), F. J. Lambert, R. Hughes, D. W. Gramolt (stroke)

61. The semi-final of the Prince Philip Cup, 1965. Thames beat Melbourne University, Australia, by 4 feet. Thames: J. E. Taylor (bow), C. R. Barker, C. J. F. S. Rowley, S. F. A. Miskin (stroke), J. R. Winner (cox). Melbourne: J. A. Goodsall (bow), R. A. Jones, P. A. V. Roff, J. M. Jelbart (stroke), C. McCall (cox)

62. Thames beating Keble College, Oxford, by ¼ length in a heat of the Grand, 1963. Thames: C. J. F. S. Rowley (bow), S. F. A. Miskin, J. E. Taylor, C. R. Barker, J. A. Stephenson, J. F. C. Badcock, A. C. W. Mill, M. J. Lohnberg (stroke), R. L. Penney (cox). Keble: N. D. Tinné (bow), A. W. Pengelly, R. C. T. Mead, G. V. Cooper, R. A. Morton-Maskell, D. S. D. Skailes, J. Leigh-Wood, N. C. Bonsor (stroke), P. C. Cherry (cox)

63. Ostend, 1965. Brian Hanham and Chris Barker, bow and two in the coxed four

64. The University College school coxed four at the inaugural FISA Junior Regatta, Ratzeburg, 1967. In Thames colours, they were the Club's first representative junior crew: B. R. Watson (bow), R. C. Fowler, N. M. L. Aitchison, C. J. Rodrigues (stroke), J. P. Hunt (cox)

65. The National Champions in women's coxed fours, 1981, who represented Great Britain in the World Championships at Munich: Caroline Casey (bow), Sarah Hunter-Jones, Jane Cross, Bernadette Casey (stroke), Sue Brown (cox)

66. Penny Haslam (stroke) and Jean Rankine (bow), Thames's most prolific medal winners at the National Championships, after receiving silver medals in the double sculls, 1977

67. The Women's quadruple scullers, 1983, the silver medallists in the National Championships: Jean Rankine (bow), Penny Haslam, Pauline Rayner, Stephanie Price (stroke), Christine Letch (cox)

68. The Thames quad winning the women's division of the Head of the River Fours, 1985: Pauline Rayner (bow), Nina Streeter, Priscella Plummer, Heather Brown (stroke)

69. Thames A, the Thames Cup finalists in 1988: T. G. Hockley (bow), J. Ferraro, N. Roullier, N. B. Copley, A. S. E. Johnson, A. J. R. Inglis, J. Woodiss-Field, S. P. Austin (stroke), T. Lohmann (cox)

70. The Thames women's first eight competing in the first Women's Henley Regatta, 1988: Julie-Anne Baines (bow), Pat Harkness, Caroline Christie, Helen Layng, Lesley Baguely, Sarah Bolton, Miriam Batten, Elizabeth Banks (stroke), Tim Lohmann (cox)

71. David Gower confusing his sports during a sponsorship visit to the Club in 1986

72. HRH Prince Michael, the Patron of Thames Rowing Club, Alan Burrough, the President, and Alan Reddin, the Chairman, at Henley, 1987

73. The Thames Clubhouse on Boat Race Day, 1990

last able to row in two fours as well.

In the Grand, Thames drew Keble, Head of the River at Oxford and loaded with Blues. The press thought highly of them, giving Thames no chance, but a magnificent race ensued, with never more than 15 feet between the crews. Thames made a vital last effort and crossed the line ¼ length ahead. However, in the semi-final they were no match for London University, containing their Commonwealth gold medal pair, Farquharson and Lee-Nicholson. In the final, UL beat Cornell, who had put out Nassovia Hochst, by ¾ length.

The Thames Stewards' four, stroked by Felix Badcock, faced a needle match with the Skiff Club. They judged the race beautifully, Felix taking a leaf from his father's book by rowing through the Skiff Club at the Mile after being led by ¾ length in the early stages, to win by a length. The coxed four, stroked by Puppy Miskin, raced Melbourne University, who had beaten another Australian crew, Sydney RC, in their heat. Thames led by a length at Fawley, only to be steadily pegged back, but Miskin held Melbourne off with a final burst at 40, Thames winning by 4 feet.

So, despite everything, and with a little bit of luck, Thames were in two finals. The Stewards' four raced Molesey, who were stroked by John Russell. He struck 37 to Badcock's 36 for most of the race. Molesey led by ¾ length at the Barrier but could get no more, while Thames could not close up. Russell took Molesey clear briefly at the Mile, but Badcock replied and closed up again. However, Molesey's steering was better than Thames' along the enclosures and they eventually won by ⅔ length. The coxed four were never in the hunt against Auckland RC, New Zealand, who had two of their Commonwealth Games silver medal eight rowing, but there was a general feeling of relief in the Club that something had been salvaged from the wreckage of the winter.

The Thames Cup eight got through two rounds before losing to London by a length, and the Wyfold four also lost to London.

The Stewards' four beat the Skiff Club again at Kingston and Molesey, though by only 3 feet each time. Both these fours were invited to the trials, but both lost to the winners of the Wyfold, Nottingham and Union. The coxed four also failed in the trials and no coxed four was sent to the European Championships in Copenhagen, where the best British results were fifth places for the UL eight and Davidge and Mackenzie in the coxless pairs. Once again, the standard seemed to be slipping out of reach. The Germans took another four gold medals; the Russians, despite reaching five finals, took none.

The Thames first eight got together again for the Serpentine, winning the Grand, and the Stewards' four again beat the Skiff Club. The Thames *Journal* (the style is unmistakably Ray Penney's) reported an 'unprecedented and unquestionably unrepeatable' entry in junior clinker eights, the crew consisting entirely of coxes, among whom were Ray Penney, Tim Shaw, Roger Weston, and Richard Matthiae:

> Formed late in the season and with very little time for training by mutual agreement, the crew progressed remarkably in practice, brought up as they were variously in the traditional homes of the 'lay-back', the orthodox, and the short jab. Perhaps the high level of improvisation achieved in so short a time can be laid at the door of experience, for this crew, with its average weight of 9st 2½ lb, featured among its number a Cambridge Blue, a former Captain of the Club, and successful competitors at Henley and in the East London Licensed Victuallers Invitation coxed fours.
>
> On the day of the race the crew took to the water in an atmosphere of incredulity and progressed to the start spurred to greater endeavour by the beer tent activities of one Honest Glynne-Jones (a regrettably suspended member of the Coxswains' Union) who was accepting side bets as to whether the course

would be completed at odds which paid absolute disregard to the form book.

A slight side wind prevailing at the start provoked some delay (damn fool cox) but perhaps at this juncture the editor would permit an expression of surprise at being addressed by a formerly respected elder member of the Club in the terms 'Come along, you Trippers, get sorted out!'

Matthiae took the opposition and the crew by complete surprise by setting off at a lively 36 in the quarter which the bow four had managed to steady to 32 by the Island and at the boat enclosure the crew, emitting a low hiss, had settled into a rhythm which enabled them to increase the distance from the other competitors with consummate ease . . .

In concluding, one can only sum up the performance . . . by suggesting that it is surely encouraging, to say the least, that in the first year of their office the national coach and training director will have such talent available with which to combat the Teutonic challenge.

18 A New Broom

The lighthearted remarks quoted at the end of the previous chapter drew attention to fundamental changes that were taking place in British rowing. These came about mainly through two memoranda submitted to the ARA, one in the name of several clubs but principally the work of Peter Coni of London, and the other from the International Oarsmen's Union, which had been been formed in 1963 to provide a forum for British rowing internationals, and was the result of a meeting convened at Thames by Felix Badcock, Alan Watson, and myself.

The proposals in the two memoranda were far-reaching and were put into effect immediately by the ARA. The selection board was restructured to the IOU plan, which enlarged it and gave it a wider sphere of influence; the formation of composite crews by the ARA was agreed in principle; a Director of Training, Jim Railton, was appointed from outside the sport (he was a sprinter) to develop land training; three of the IOU committee (Colin Porter, Doug Melvin, and myself) were drafted onto the selection board; the ARA reformed itself into a council; the Women's ARA ceased to exist and became a council within the ARA; the *ARA News* was launched to publicise the Association's activities; and my father, on his retirement from St Paul's School, became the first full-time paid Secretary of the ARA. His office had been a room in his own house, but one was now found in Park Crescent.

A technical committee was formed to study technical aspects of the sport, and there was an instructional committee, a regattas committee, and so on, and a lot of valuable information was disseminated over the next few years at coaching conferences, and through visits all over the country by the selectors.

All these developments were to have a decisive effect on the sport by the end of the 1960s. The thorny question, as ever, was that of composite crews. There was no Karl Adam and no coach who could command the support of all factions. In the end, Jumbo Edwards, Oxford's highly successful chief coach, took the job on at a hiding to nothing, running the abortive Nautilus scheme which was started in the autumn of 1964. It was regarded with deep suspicion and received scant support from those who could easily have made it successful, not least the Tideway Scullers, who had taken over from Barn Cottage and Molesey as the top base for composite crews, as well as Thames, London, and Leander.

There was not time, however, to plan a composite ARA squad for the 1964 Olympics in Tokyo, and the 1964 domestic season was very like those that had immediately preceeded it.

At the end of 1963, Miskin took over as Captain of Thames and had some good material available. Gramolt returned to stroke the eight, in which three members of the 1963 winning St Paul's PE eight, Chris Barrett, Peter Lacey, and Tony Hewlett, found places. Badcock was at two and Lohnberg was bow. A talented RAF and Broxbourne oarsman, Mike Wise, was at seven for what was, alas, to be his last season; he was killed in a car crash in the spring of 1965. The crew also had an experienced cox in Richard Matthiae. A fourth member of the St Paul's crew, 'Pop' Allen, together with Chris Barker, John Stephenson, and Mike Woolner, now recovered from a major back operation, rowed in a separate Stewards' four. In 1964, the eight were second at Reading and fourth in the Tideway Head, the Tideway Scullers winning the latter in a new record time of 17min 24sec.

The Club had at last bought itself a boat trailer and the eight and four went to several continental regattas with their own boats. Against strong opponents, neither crew could finish better than third at Ostend or Ghent, while at Duisburg the eight were only fourth, behind two German eights and the Italian army crew, Sabaudia, but ahead of London University.

For the four, Duisburg was a disaster. Racing at three continental regattas in close succession was asking a lot and they succumbed to a type of staleness associated with interval training, Addison's Syndrome. Their legs looked as though they were made of marshmallow and they came last in their heat. It is not possible to recover quickly from this sort of staleness and this regatta was only ten days before Henley, where they lost their Stewards' heat to a moderate Molesey four who went out in the next round.

The Grand eight, however, came to Henley in excellent form. They drew Leander, with four of the Oxford 1960 Olympic eight, including Mike Davis at stroke, and three other Oxford Blues, one of whom, Duncan Spencer, was a powerful Yale oarsman. Thames were at their very best, although Leander led by 1¼ lengths at Fawley where Thames began to close the gap. Leander were still leading by ¾ length at the Mile but when Gramolt put on the pressure here, it was at once obvious that Leander were vulnerable. Striking 42 along the enclosures, with Leander at 39, Thames were only ¼ length behind at the last signal, where Leander suddenly cracked. Thames went past to cross the line ⅔ length ahead for a memorable victory.

Fine effort thought this was, Thames were outclassed by a very fast eight from Lithuania, Zalgiris Vilnius who took a second off the Fawley record. Finishing at 39, Vilnius shattered Cornell's 1957 record by 7 seconds, winning by 20 seconds in 6min 23sec. It was a thought-provoking performance. In the final, the Lithuanians also overwhelmed the University of London, winning by 18 seconds, lowering the Barrier and Fawley records again, but they were 2 seconds outside their own record at the finish. They just failed later to win the European Championships where, after rowing neck and neck all over the course against Ratzeburg, a small lurch let the Germans snatch the gold medal by 1/50 second – to all intents and purposes a dead heat – on the last stroke.

At Henley, the Thames second eight reached the semi-final but were beaten by London by ⅔ length. The Grand eight had won at Reading and a mixed crew containing the recovered coxed four won the Grand on the Serpentine at the end of the season.

No British eight was sent to the European Championships in Amsterdam or to the Tokyo Olympics later in the year. A Thames coxless four lost their heat in trials. The Tideway Scullers, with John James at bow, had won the Stewards', and were selected for the European Championships, which were used as trials for the Olympics. The four finished only ninth in Amsterdam and they were then strengthened by the inclusion of the single sculler, Bill Barry, whose father, Lou, was their coach and a selector, and the reserve, Hugh Wardell-Yerburgh; John Russell was at stroke and James at bow. They were sent to Tokyo, as were Farquharson and Lee-Nicholson in the coxless pairs, who had got together again after Henley and had come only ninth at Amsterdam.

The selectors came in for some criticism for these selections, but the four lost the gold medal by less than a length and the pair were a close fourth. The double scullers, Cooke and Webb, who won a silver medal in Amsterdam with some assistance from the notoriously unequal lanes on the Bosbaan, were only seventh in Tokyo, but the course there was also palpably unfair and led to the defeat of Ratzeburg by the American eight from Vesper. Only in the single and double sculls did the European champions win in Tokyo, Ivanov winning his third Olympic gold medal.

Meanwhile, the Nautilus scheme had got under way, though no oarsmen of established reputation joined the squad, and with the success of the Scullers' four in Tokyo, Lou Barry, who was originally one of the national coaches, decided he could do it better himself, which virtually guaranteed that the scheme would fail.

Most of the Thames seniors were available again in 1965, only Pop Allen opting for Nautilus, but in the Head they finished sixth, with the relatively inexperienced Nautilus crews, starting low down as new entries, finishing fifth, eight, and twelfth. The death of Mike Wise shortly afterwards, together with three others in the crew dropping out, left morale low. It was decided to concentrate on a strong four for Henley and a new Stampfli coxed four was ordered and taken to Trier, where the crew won from two German crews, which helped to restore morale.

At Ostend, with a lighter cox, Peter Bailey, they lost to a Leander four comprised of the four powerful Americans who had filled the stern seats in that year's winning Oxford crew, but Thames finished ahead of Germania Dusseldorf and Nautilus. The same Thames four, in a coxless boat, were only fourth, and the following week were beaten comfortably by Nautilus at Reading. In the coxed boat, they again did better, though losing to the Tideway Scullers by a canvas. Nautilus beat Thames in the Stewards' final at Marlow, but once again Thames did better in the coxed event, dead-heating with Leander's Americans in the final, to lose the re-row by 3 feet in record time.

As a result, at Henley Thames settled on the Prince Philip. Another four, stroked by Fred Lambert, went for the Stewards', but their main function was to make up an eight as a token entry for the Grand. The coxed four – Brian Hanham, Chris Barker, Chris Barrett, and David Gramolt, and their cox, 'Pinhead' Bailey – were the other half of the eight.

Of all years, this was not the one for entering scratch crews for the Grand. None of the four English crews had a chance, the scene being set for a revenge meeting between Ratzeburg and Vesper. Any crew in their way were simply cannon fodder, the draw having put Vesper and Ratzeburg in different halves.

Thames met Nautilus, the winners facing the doubtful privilege of meeting the winners of the Vesper–Harvard race. Nautilus had 2 lengths at Fawley and eased off to win by 1⅔ lengths. Vesper beat Harvard and Nautilus, while Ratzeburg beat the University of London, to set the stage for a classic final. The record went at every point, Ratzeburg never dropping below 39 to Vesper's 37–38. There was ⅓ length in the Germans' favour at the Mile, where they raised their rate to 40. They led by ¾ length at the last signal and won a magnificent race by ½ length, taking 7 seconds off the year-old record with a time of 6min 16sec. In two years, the Grand record had been reduced by 14 seconds, which represents about 3¾ lengths.

Quintin, with three of the Tokyo Olympic four and coached by Lou Barry, beat Thames in a heat and Nautilus in the final of the Stewards', becoming the first four to break 7 minutes for the course. The Prince Philip records tumbled in almost every race, Thames breaking the intermediate and full course records before losing to Leander by 1¾ lengths in the semi-final, Leander equalling the record set by the Tideway Scullers the previous day. In the final, Leander reduced this time by another 13 seconds to 7min 3sec, beating the Scullers by ½ length.

With the Leander Americans out of contention, Thames won the coxed four trials, beating the Scullers with unexpected ease. They beat Derby in the final by 5½ seconds but were not selected for Duisburg. In this they were unfortunate, being at least as good as several other recent British representative fours, but the selectors had decided to set higher targets for selection. As a selector myself, it was embarrassing for me, and in the Club *Journal* that year, I wrote:

> The present selection board feels that the ARA can no longer afford to send crews to championships unless they stand a reasonable chance of reaching the final. Instead, it feels that the ARA's money should be put into an official composite team open to any oarsman prepared to put in the time and effort required and to train this team up over a number of years until it reaches the requisite standard. Such a team has the advantage that it can call on financial support from the Government . . .
>
> What will be the effect of this on the clubs? Obviously, the fear of the big clubs is that without the carrot of international selection, many of their best oarsmen will stop rowing . . .
>
> The time has come for some objective thinking from our senior oarsmen. In the international sphere the clubs face tremendous problems which could be overcome by pooling financial resources, equipment, coaching and oarsmen into Nautilus. Club interests are not best served by a parochial attitude, nor are national interests. Without adequate support, Nautilus could fail, but can the clubs really find another answer?

In the end, through lack of support, Nautilus did fail. It was not until the beginning of the next decade that the ARA insisted on the squad system, and in the interim the clubs did not succeed in finding an alternative. The 1965 European Championships underlined the problem, and for the umpteenth time demonstrated the difference between Henley's two-abreast, knock-out racing and the high-standard multi-lane racing of the championships. Hugh Wardell-Yerburgh, who had pushed the American Don Spero to ¾ length in a record-breaking Diamonds final at Henley, reached the final at Duisburg, only to adopt, against all advice, ridiculous tactics to finish a poor fifth. In the coxless fours, Quintin finished sixth and last in their final, which was won by four of the Vilnius eight.

As far as Thames was concerned, the point was made in the coxed fours, when the Leander Americans, representing the USA, despite having been well beaten in the American trials by the stern four of the Vesper eight, finished only eleventh at Duisburg. An over-confident Vesper eight also came unstuck when they finished third behind Ratzeburg and a new Soviet eight.

Despite the coxed four's efforts, it was not one of Thames' better years, though the Thames Cup eight had three wins, and at this difficult juncture in the Club's history, John Stephenson took over as Captain. Deciding that the coxed four should be allowed another crack at international honours in 1966, he kept them separate from the eight and found that in doing so, he did not have enough experienced men to form a good Grand eight. As it turned out, this was somewhat academic, since East Germany, now recognised by FISA as an independant state, sent a powerful eight to Henley in 1966.

The coxed four combined with Vesta for the Head but finished seventh behind two Tideway Scullers crews and Nautilus, though ahead of Thames first eight, who were only eleventh. However, a potential Grand eight won at Ghent from moderate French, Belgian and Polish crews, but the coxed four were third behind two Polish fours, though they redeemed themselves with a win at Ostend over Antwerp, Germania Dusseldorf, and Nautilus. At Walton, the Grand eight were well beaten by the Nautilus eight made up from two fours who rowed as an eight only once a week, and at Reading they lost to Oxford. At Henley, they drew TSC, Berlin, and were never in the race, the East Germans paddling in at 29.

The four did rather better in the run-up to Henley, winning at Walton, Reading (by ¼ length from Nautilus), the Met, which was now held before Henley, and Marlow, where they beat Nautilus, who had already rowed twice to win the Grand, by a length. Any hopes for a Henley win were quickly dashed, however, when they also drew an outstanding East German four from Dynamo, Potsdam. Potsdam had a length at the ¾ Mile but then went ahead fast to lead by 2½ lengths at the Mile and won easily, a bitter blow for the Thames four. Potsdam easily beat Kobenhavns Roklub, Denmark, in the final and later became world champions at Bled. The Danish 1964 Olympic gold medallists, Kvik, won the Stewards', beating a different Potsdam four in the semi-final by ¼ length.

Gramolt went into a four with three Vesta men for the trials, but although they beat Nautilus in the final it was clear that no coxed four would be good enough for Bled, where the experienced Tideway Scullers eight were the only British entry to reach a final, taking a creditable fourth place behind West Germany, USSR and East Germany, who had a different crew from the one that had won the Grand. The East Germans, on their first championship appearance in their own right, took three gold medals and two bronze. Their worst position was fourth and once again the standard was being lifted to a new level.

Dick Phelps, the Club's waterman, retired in 1966. He had served Thames for thirty-five years and he had become well known throughout the rowing world. As well as his trips with international teams, he went to many Continental regattas, including fifteen visits to Ostend. As a boatman, he was unsurpassed, a fact acknowledged far and wide. On his retirement, he was made an honorary life member of Thames. His son and grandson both rowed for Thames, the latter, another Richard, winning a World Championship bronze medal in 1989 as a member of the national squad.

Dick was guest of honour at the 1966 annual dinner, at which Ian Fairbairn took the chair, and which was attended by over 150 members. He was succeeded as the Club's waterman by Norman McIver, but could frequently be seen at the Club until his death at the age of 92 in 1989.

A very poor season followed for the Club in 1967 and does not need dwelling on. For only the second time Thames did not enter a Grand eight. The increase in both the numbers and quality of foreign entries, and the emergence of what were in effect composite crews in various guises, had made it certain that clubs like London and Thames would find it increasingly difficult to put on Grand crews that were serious contenders. The 1967 first eight had sunk to a lowly thirty-second in the Head, and Thames third eight, with several men who were not rowing regularly, had finished eight places ahead of them.

This situation precipitated the decision not to try for the Grand, and London's performance in the Grand that year, when they were trounced by a French national composite crew, underlined the correctness of the difficult, and to some older members unpopular, decision that the Captain, Gordon Dear, had had to make. The following year, London followed suit.

Some shuffling after the Head resulted in a Wyfold four, stroked by Brian Hanham, with a London University Purple, Tom Bakiewicz, and two lightweights, Vic Temple and David Pedraza, behind him. This was the Club's best crew and they finished second in the elite fours at Ghent. At Marlow, they were beaten in the final of the Town Cup by Quintin, whom they drew at Henley, when fate took a hand. Thames were ½ length ahead after 20 strokes when Hanham's blade was shattered by some half-submerged object. Hanham continued with what little was left of his blade but Quintin won and went on to the final, where they lost by ½ length to a Tideway Scullers crew containing one of their 1966 world championship eight, Mike Muir-Smith, and Mike Sweeney, who was to win an international vest that year. After Henley, Thames beat Quintin by 3½ lengths in the final of the Wyfold fours at Molesey.

The only other Thames entry, a Thames Cup eight, had two strong recruits in David Cruttenden, at 15 stone the heaviest man to have represented the Club at Henley, and David Warbrick-Smith, who had rowed for two years in the Bedford School eight, but they lost by a canvas to the Severn Scullers in the second round. The East Germans won four events and the Swiss sculler, Martin Studach, became the first man to win both the Diamonds and the Double Sculls, and Britain won no top event.

Thames did at least find one representative crew from an unexpected source when a University College School coxed four won the youth championships, representing the Club in exchange for the loan of the Club's Stampfli. Stroked by Christopher Rodrigues, the four represented Britain at the first FISA junior regatta at Ratzeburg, and narrowly failed to reach the final. They won their little final, finishing seventh overall. 'junior' was now an age category, the old junior status having become senior C, and the junior championships were eventually given world status.

At senior international level, Britain had a depressing year. The best place obtained in the North American Championships, which had been graced with this title in 1967 by FISA, was fourth by the Tideway Scullers coxed four, and at Vichy in the European Championships no British crews reached a main final for the first time in eleven years.

In September, the Earl of Iveagh died at the age of 93. He had been President of Thames since 1911 and his last appearance at the Club had been at the opening of the Fairbairn Tank in 1962. He was said to have been one of the strongest boys ever to have gone to Eton, with 'legs like a tree', which speaks well for the Guinness family brew! He was succeeded as President by Ian Fairbairn.

In the autumn of 1967, I became Captain again and tried to outline the problems in the Club *Journal*:

> Most clubs nowadays seem to feel that top-class rowing is beyond them. Too many have been aiming for second-class events from the outset, believing that second-class wins are better than failure at the top.
>
> In my experience, the attitude invariably leads to failure in the lesser events as well, and it would be difficult to deny that the standard of even the best crews in this country has been depressingly low . . .
>
> I wrote in the 1959 *Journal*: 'I am sure that many races are lost simply because the odds appear to be formidable . . . but there is a great deal of truth in the saying that much more would be done if people believed less was impossible.'
>
> I think this needs to be said again. There has been too much defeatism and lack of determination to win and even to learn to row well. These qualities of determination and willingness to learn used to be the hallmarks of this Club, and they need to be re-asserted if we are to rise above the mediocre standards that surround us. Nobody pretends there is a simple way; but if you really intend to win and not merely compete, this realism will in the end produce crews which are physically and mentally tough. If there is real determination to trounce every crew we come up against, we shall eventually do so. But it must be real determination, not just wishful thinking. Two of the real dangers to any club are apathy and lack of dedication . . .
>
> Earlier, I wrote of international honours. For a top-class oarsmen this must nowadays be the ultimate goal, but this is not the be-all and end-all of club rowing. A club's immediate aim ought to be to win at regattas up and down the river in all classes of events. If it succeeds in doing this, the top honours will come in due course. What really matters is that rowing must become exciting and enjoyable, and this, in the end, is the greatest victory.

I believe these words still apply today. Looking back, I can see that I was trying to re-establish those values that I have always associated with the qualities that made Thames a great club and which, I felt in 1967, were becoming lost. We were forgetting the lessons of Micky Slater, Piggy Eyre, and Jimmy Hastie, and of Steve and Berry.

The real problem with which Thames was faced in 1968 was that many oarsmen of the type that had been attracted to Thames in the 1950s and early 1960s were now going to the Tideway Scullers or Leander, or were simply not rowing at all because of the rival attractions of an affluent society. The simple truth was that we did not have the material to challenge top crews. Nevertheless, by the end of the season the Club had won thirty-two trophies, thirteen in senior events, though no top honours came our way. Starting with individual and team wins in the rapidly proliferating sculling Heads in the autumn, by the following summer thirty oarsmen had shared in wins at various levels, though we had been unable to race a serious eight. It seemed to me that we were at least moving in the right direction.

The main concern at Henley was whether to row a Stewards' four or to go for the new Henley Prize, a lower event for coxed fours introduced that year, and which was renamed the Britannia Cup the following year. There was also a Wyfold four. Both fours had early successes and eventually had six wins apiece, as well as wins in other boats.

At Ghent, two ex-Kensington oarsmen, another John Stephenson and David Hanham, whose brother, Brian, had also rowed for Kensington before moving to Thames, won the senior coxless pairs. With two lightweights, Bob Hackford and Vic Temple, they made up the Wyfold four. At Wallingford, this four beat both halves of the Oxford eight. Oxford had won the elite eights and fours at Ghent, and when Thames beat the fours, Jumbo Edwards was so demoralised that he scrapped the fours and concentrated on the eight for the Grand.

A storm of exceptional severity hit the Thames Valley on the evening of the first day of Henley. Millions of gallons of water poured into the Thames from the hills, and by Friday morning, the boat rafts were submerged and one of them was swept off its piles. The result was that the stations became manifestly unfair, the discrepancy increasing as the regatta progressed. Much of the racing was a travesty and Thames were only one of those to be deprived of an almost certain win by the conditions.

The coxed four – Tom Bakiewicz, Pop Allen (back with Thames now that Nautilus had folded), David Gramolt and Brian Hanham, with Pinhead Bailey coxing – were on the favoured Berks station until the final, where they ran out of luck, being on Bucks against Crowland, whom they had twice beaten before Henley. Crowland, staying close to the bank, led by ¾ length at the Barrier, but at Fawley Thames had less stream to battle against and closed up. However, when the stream hit them again approaching the Mile, they faltered, and Crowland drew away to win by 2 lengths in 9min 32sec, a time which indicates the strength of the stream. After the first day, no crew in the Henley Prize won on Bucks.

The Wyfold four, on the Bucks station on the second day, led Quintin by ½ length at Fawley but once again, after Remenham the stream was too great a handicap, Quintin going away to win by 2 lengths. No Wyfold crew won on Bucks that day.

In the final of the Grand, London University, on Berks, actually offered to let Oxford row a few strokes before they themselves started. Oxford declined and were well beaten. All but one of the finals were won on Berks, the exception being in the Princess Elizabeth Cup, when a fast American school crew beat Eton by a canvas. Fortunately, because the Olympic Games were to be rowed in very different conditions in Mexico, overseas crews were absent and did not witness the unfairness of the course, or Henley might have lost its overseas entries for ever.

Britain sent only the London University eight and Ken Dwan in the single sculls to Mexico. This again caused much criticism and even led to questions being asked in the House of Commons, but with the problems involved in rowing at altitude at Mexico, and the lack of a real international standard in British crews, it was realistic. London University came tenth out of twelve, and Dwan, a young apprentice waterman, did well to finish sixth. Many oarsmen collapsed because of the thin air, though much of this was hidden from television viewers; Martin Studach nearly died when somebody gave him an oxygen mask attached to an empty cylinder. The West Germans, who had undergone intensive altitude training prior to the Olympics, regained the eights title, and the Americans won no gold medals.

Ian Fairbairn died towards the end of the year aged 71, having been President of Thames for only one year. He was succeeded by the 'Little Moke', Harold Greenwood.

Ian had great affection and respect for his father. Rowing friends who dined with him at his Chelsea home would drink to Steve's memory, facing the portrait on the wall behind their host. As a coach, he helped whoever asked him, and in particular the less privileged and less fortunate clubs. For some years, he ran and largely financed the Fairbairn Boys' Club at Hammersmith, to provide rowing for boys who would not otherwise have been able take part, coaching and rowing with them. A Henley Steward, he served on the Committee of Management, but one of his main interests to the end of his life was the Head of the River Race. He also shared, with Harold Rickett, the reputation of being the best Chairman of a meeting you could wish for.

Harold Rickett himself was to die early the following year, at the age of 59. The first President of the ARA and an honorary member of Thames, he would always wear his Thames tie on the Thursday before Henley, when he sought out the Thames crews and coaches to chat with them.

Ian continued to correspond about rowing matters to the end of his life, and the week he died, he wrote to the Club Captain:

> My thoughts often turn to the Thames Rowing Club, and the immense pleasure which I have derived, from time to time, from being connected with its activities . . . All I can say is that the way [to Olympic medals] is by devoting all one's energies to the job. 'Show me a first-class oarsman and I will show you a first-class lunatic,' my father used to say. It means, of course, that you have got to forsake all other pleasures in a way which seems mentally deficient to the normally minded. But I believe the joy to be derived therefrom surpasses anything the normally minded have ever experienced.

The Captain to whom Ian wrote was A.M. St L. Ramsay-Murray, who had taken the job on after some merciless bullying by me in the Club bar one evening when I was looking for someone to take over from me in 1969. It was one of the best evening's work I ever did for Thames, as he proved to be an outstanding Captain, going everywhere with the crews and competing himself in many long distance sculling races in the veteran class.

David Cruttenden had gone up to Cambridge and David Warbrick-Smith to London University and big men were once again in short supply, but six of the two fours were still available to form the nucleus of an eight, and a promising stroke, Tony Stocking, who was still a junior, arrived from Latymer Upper School, where Alan Watson was in charge of rowing. They did better than recent crews in the Heads, coming fourth at Reading and seventh in the Tideway Head, in which they beat London by 18 seconds to take the Boustead Cup, which was decided that year on the Head results.

After an easy win at Thames Ditton, they went

to Ostend, only for Stocking to fall ill and the crew had to scratch on the first day after qualifying for the final. They won the sprint, however. They reached the final on the second day as well, and in the circumstances third behind the Tideway Scullers and the Dutch Army crew, Dudok van Heel, was not unreasonable. A second eight at Ostend finished second and third in the two second events.

The first eight had three wins before Marlow, twice beating the London first eight, but a week before Marlow we took a calculated risk by bringing in Chris Rodrigues to stroke, Stocking moving back to three. Rodrigues had stroked the Goldie crew and as spare man for Cambridge, who were in the Grand, he was without a Henley row. In this order, they were beaten in the final of the Marlow eights, but the day before Henley began, Bob Hackford's back went, and Derek Pollard, the victim of the recent shuffle, came back in at two.

On the second day, Thames met the giant Penn freshmen, who had arrived at Henley undefeated. Averaging 13 st 9 lb, they were 17 lb a man heavier than Thames, despite Rodrigues's 13 stone. Penn were ahead at Fawley but two determined bursts by Rodrigues brought Thames back and at the Mile Penn's lead was down to ¼ length. Penn's greater weight told in the end, however, and they got home by ¾ length. They went down in the final to the fast Leander cadets, who were coached by Derek Drury, a Thames member and rowing coach at Emanuel School.

The Wyfold four lost to the South African squad crew, Trident, in the second round, and the Britannia four went out to London. An unlikely double, because of differences in physique and technique, David Pedraza and David Gramolt, were beaten comfortably by the eventual winners, Denis Oswald, a future President of FISA, and Mel Burgin from Zurich. The Thames double were encouraged by the selectors to compete at Amsterdam after Henley but they were outclassed, which ended any hopes for a trial.

The Thames first eight had four wins after Henley and the club finished the season top of *Rowing* magazine's table of regatta winners, with over fifty trophies or pennants, the highest in the Club's history. Though seldom in the top events, the spread was right across the board, which was a healthy sign. It was a poor weekend when only one trophy was brought back to the Club: three was accepted as a reasonable tally, and Thames crews reached four or five finals on one day on several occasions.

Tony Stocking was chosen as spare man for the FISA junior championships, having finished second in the coxed pairs in Thames colours in the ARA youth championships with a UCS boy, Tim Cooper-Jones.

In the European Championships at Klagenfurt, Dwan finished fourth in the single sculls. The only other British finalists, the Tideway Scullers eight, finished fifth.

The *Rowing Almanack* review of 1969 ended with these words:

> The sixties – in which Great Britain collected only four silver medals in 43 international appearances – faded out on a more encouraging note for greater success abroad in the seventies, with work in progress on the Holme Pierrepont 2,000-metre six-lane rowing course outside Nottingham and the appearance of Bohumil Janousek, a 32-year-old Czech, as ARA National Coach. At the same time however we bid farewell to Jim Railton, our Director of Training since 1964 . . .

The wind of change was beginning to blow across Britain's rowing scene, and the Brave New World promised in the developments begun in 1963 was at last moving into view.

19 A Difficult Decade

The role of Thames Rowing Club had changed significantly by the end of the 1960s. Though the Club had produced several fast crews during the decade, and had reached five Henley finals, no Henley trophies had come to the Club. The standard of the lesser events had risen, many oarsmen who would previously have gone for the major events having been forced by the standard of foreign opposition to move down to the minor ones, which at that time the regulations still allowed.

The 1970s were going to make life even more difficult for the major clubs with the introduction of national squads and a system which meant that unless an oarsman or woman was a member of one of the squads, there would be no chance of selection for international championships, which depleted the already weaker intake even further. While most clubs accepted that the squad system was the only realistic way to compete on fair terms with the top foreign squads, it was at a heavy price as far as domestic rowing was concerned and standards fell alarmingly.

Thames made a good start in 1970, finishing second in the Reading and Kingston Heads, but then fell to twelfth in the Tideway Head. The eight and two fours from it raced in early regattas, recording several wins. The fours took part in a training weekend at Boston under the direction of Bob Janousek, the ARA's new national coach, but this was too disorganised to be of much significance.

After the eight were defeated by Leander at Reading, the Captain, Alan Reddin, decided that the stern four should concentrate on the Britannia and a new eight were put together for Henley. At Henley, the Thames Cup eight, stroked by a lightweight, Tony Bingham, went through two rounds before going down to Quintin, the Britannia four went out in the second round to the Nottingham and Union four they had beaten twice previously, and the Wyfold four also survived only one round before coming up against the ultimate winners, Trident, South Africa, who were almost two stone a man heavier. The Club had entered a second Wyfold four in Eyre Club colours, but they failed to qualify. The Eyre Club had been formed that year to make it possible to put in second entries in events which barred more than one crew from a club. The Metropolitan RC was London's equivalent. Theoretically Eyre and Thames were separate clubs, but Bill Williams was secretary and mentor of Eyre until his death in 1982.

Henley had decided to admit composite crews made up from different clubs in the Grand, Stewards', and Prince Philip, but no British crews that year took advantage of this long overdue innovation, and the Grand went to East Germany for the fourth time in five years. They had not competed in 1968. The Ladies' had been opened to foreign crews in 1967 and went to a Dutch student crew for the second year running, and the only eight-oared event to stay at home was the Thames Cup, in which the Leander cadets scored their third successive win. It was a similar story in the fours, Potsdam winning the Stewards' and the massive West German 'Bulls of Konstanz', the reigning European champions, the Prince Philip. The Bulls, who became world champions in 1970, averaged 15 st 7 lb, while the East Germans in the Grand, at 14 st 10 lb, were the heaviest crew to have won the trophy. All the other top events went overseas and it was a rout for British rowing.

Internationally as well, Britain had a disastrous season. A full team went to the 1970 World Championships in St Catharine's, Ontario, no British entry reaching a main final, and Britain's performance was the worst ever. At junior level, in the intense heat at Ioannina in Northern Greece, Britain did not even rank in the first twelve of the fifteen competing nations, the East Germans winning all seven events.

At home, Thames hauled in some silverware after Henley, for a total of thirty-eight wins for the season, but once again the Club had to content itself with minor honours.

It was a sad year for the Club, with the loss of several well-known older members, notably Harold Greenwood, aged 90, who had been President for barely a year. His first appearance as a cox for Thames was in 1899, and he steered the Grand eight from 1903 to 1913. According to Jack Beresford, who succeeded him as President, Moke steered largely by intimidation. He was feared by other coxes because of his forceful personality and great flow of invective, but he was a very skilful cox as well. He was a well-known character on the floor of the Stock Exchange, and was for many years chairman of Kempton Park racecourse, while Remenham Club prospered during his years as President. A Huguenot by descent, he was at the time of his death Governor of the French School at Rochester.

Another loss, at the age of 84, was Tyke Richardson. Apart from his rowing successes in the years before the First World War, he was a boxing Blue and, with his wife, Wag, an Olympic figure skater. He was made an OBE in 1955 for his services to skating. Each year, he was to be found with his wife at Henley during training, outspoken in criticism of poor crews and encouraging Thames crews and those of his old College, Trinity Hall.

A premature loss in 1970 was that of Sparrow Morris, who died suddenly. A Vice-President and former Captain, he was a superb bow and steersman of fours and pairs. His rowing career has been recorded in these pages, but he was also a successful coach for Thames, Imperial College, and Portora Royal School.

Another to die that year was A. St G. Lyster, whose only appearance for Thames was in the 1910 Wyfold four. He spent much of his life in India and when he retired he became one of the Club's principal supporters at home and abroad. His visits to Ostend were always memorable, and I recall the occasion in a seedy bar with some of the more experienced Thames tourists, when he persuaded some extremely rough looking youths to play a Viennese waltz for him on the jukebox. They even came back to ask if there was anything else they could put on for him, recognising, no doubt, the authority of someone who had made a career out of running the Raj!

There was another occasion when Lyster, Tagg (the Club Steward), Dick Phelps, Ray Penney, my wife Paddy and myself were sitting outside an Ostend café on a particularly cold, blustery day, Lyster insisting that on the Continent everyone sat outside cafés. Needless to say, everyone else was warm and snug inside. The waiter opened the door to take our order, letting out a burst of light and warmth. 'Will you please shut that door?' said Tagg. 'There's a hell of a draught out here!'

David Cruttenden came down from Cambridge in 1970 and promptly took on the Captaincy of Thames, but with his exception, the material was even lighter than usual. In 1971 there were few successes and the eight arrived at Henley with no wins. Stroked again by Tony Bingham, with Nigel Read at seven and Hank Rushmere's son, Paul, at two, they survived two rounds in the Thames Cup before losing to the Harvard lightweights. Harvard won the final from the 13-stone Kingston eight, who had earlier ended Leander's run of successes.

The Wyfold four, with Cruttenden at three, reached the semi-finals, where a Marlow four containing Mike Spracklen beat them, though Harvard scored a second win in the final.

There were only three overseas entries for the regatta, apart from the usual American quota, and a sub-standard Grand with three entries was won by the Tideway Scullers. At two was David Gramolt, who finally received his reward for perseverance in a career that had contained many disappointments. He had been winning veteran sculling pennants for Thames earlier in the year.

For the second year running, no British crew reached a main final in the European Championships. The DDR took four golds and three silvers. Bob Janousek told the British team that they were still 'playing at rowing'.

The ARA changed the rules governing status and introduced new laws and rules for regattas because of the imminent introduction of the new six-lane 2,000-metre Holme Pierrepont course. The main difference was that junior became an age category in line with the FISA definition. Anyone over the age of 18 became a senior; senior C represented the old junior status; senior B, junior–senior; and so on, up to elite.

Eric Beresford and Donald Gollan died in 1971. Eric might have been more successful had not his brother Jack been rowing at the same time. Jack, the dominant one, disliked rowing behind Eric, who, though very light, was a brilliant stroke. It was really a clash of temperaments that led to Eric often failing to find a place in crews he should have stroked. He eventually retired to Spain, where he died.

In 1972, Thames won the Boustead but the summer was disastrous, only seven trophies coming to the Club. No Thames crew survived a heat at Henley, the Britannia four failing even to qualify, but if it was a dismal Henley for Thames, it was not much better for British crews generally. All the eight-oared trophies went abroad, the Stewards' attracted no British entries, and the Prince Philip and Goblets went abroad again. Only the Double Sculls were kept at home by Pat Delafield and Laurie Tann's grandson, Tim Crooks.

The year saw the Holme Pierrepont course in action for the first time, National Championships being held there at the end of July, as a new chapter in British rowing began. It was an exciting moment for those of us who had been waiting so long for such a course. Ninety-four clubs, including Scottish ones, entered and the weather was ideal. Several prospective Olympic crews took part. Thames had nothing to offer, but in the Tideway Scullers eight who became the first national champions were David Gramolt and Christopher Rodrigues, the latter, in 1971, as President, having stroked Cambridge to a 10-length Boat Race victory.

Janousek had begun to get his national squad together, and at the Munich Olympics in 1972 Britain was represented in every event except the eights. The results were only marginally better than in recent FISA Championships, though Delafield and Crooks finished fifth, but the national squad was still in its infancy and the general opinion was that judgement should be reserved.

Jumbo Edwards and Charles Rew both died in 1972. Jumbo had become a highly successful coach with Oxford in the 1950s and 1960s, and he did much to bring methods, rigging, and equipment up to date in Britain during this period, while preserving some remarkably traditional ideas on rowing technique. Never afraid of experimenting, he naturally had his failures, for which he was sometimes ridiculed, but he produced some fast crews.

John Levy became Captain of Thames in 1972 at the lowest point in the Club's fortunes, and Freddie Page, having retired that year as Secretary of the ARA after twenty years, became Deputy Captain to take charge of the general administration. Levy records:

The Club had three senior oarsmen, one of whom went immediately to Kingston, the House Steward had resigned, the boatman left for another job, the launch sank at her moorings. The boats were by no means new or of the latest type, and the tank was in disrepair.

Freddie suggested we started with juniors and novices. We invited all the junior members to a dinner in the Club and organised a coaching week for them during the Easter and summer vacations. Schools were encouraged to send juniors to row at the Club and for two or three years the Club had a number of successes at the National Championships, including a gold medal in the junior single sculls for Gordon Jack, who represented Britain in the FISA junior championships in Montreal in 1975, and silver and bronze medals in the eights. One of the bronze medallists, Malcolm McGowan, together with one of a junior Under-16 four that won a bronze, John Pritchard, went on to win silver medals with the British eight at the Moscow Olympics in 1980 and the World Championships in 1981. These two also won the Grand in 1982 and 1984. In 1984, they were again in the Olympic eight, though they finished only 5th. Pritchard rowed three times for Cambridge and in 1986 stroked them to end Oxford's ten-year run of Boat Race victories.

Within six months of our joining forces to revivify Thames, Freddie asked me if I had any objection to Thames housing the boats of the United Universities Women's Boat Club, and since there was nothing in the rules to prevent women becoming members of the Club, we decided to sound out members on the matter.

Freddie masterminded the whole operation in his inimitable way. Without any overt argument or discussion, the matter was left to the AGM in March, 1973. Under 'any other business', an innocent question was asked by a married member whose wife under the then by-laws was not allowed in the bar. Surely, he said, it was time this law was altered. This was given general approval. Another member then asked whether, if women were to be allowed to use the bar, there was anything in the rules to prevent them joining the Club . . . There was no dissent and the Committee were asked to consider opening membership to women.

In this way, the Club took into membership all members of the UUs, which included the President (my mother), Chairman, and Vice-Presidents of the Women's Amateur Rowing Council, most of the Committee, and the national selectors, becoming at a stroke a major force in women's rowing.

Thanks to the activities of the juniors and the new women members, the Club provided the biggest entry at the National Championships of 1973–4–5, with several successes, including the Victor Ludorum for women.

Jean Rankine, the UU's Captain, became the first woman Deputy Captain of Thames, a post she held for two years. Since Thames opened its doors to women, it has established itself as the most successful Club in British women's rowing today.

The men still faced major problems, however, and so short was the senior material that for the first time since 1871 no Thames eight competed at Henley in 1973. Only the Wyfold four, averaging 10 st 12 lb, survived a heat, to lose in the second round. The Club's bleakest ever record produced only one win in a junior four and five wins in sculling events. What was even more galling was that in this year and previously, London had been recording an enormous number of victories. Levy has commented that Steve's efforts to revive London for the greater good of Tideway rowing in the 1920s was paralleled by the two Captains of London during his own two years in office, 1973–74, who said they would not see the Club go down and would do anything they could to help.

However, the tide was at last beginning to turn for British rowing generally, aided by sponsorship for the national squads until the 1976 Olympics. FISA had decided that after 1973 World Championships would be held every year and at the last European Championships at Moscow in 1973, two former Cambridge Blues, Mike Hart and Chris Baillieu, emerged as formidable double scullers, taking the bronze medal. Also in these Championships was Tony Stocking, who was rowing in the coxless fours with the University of London four that had won the Stewards', but who finished only tenth at Moscow.

Jean Rankine made an auspicious debut in her new colours at the 1973 National Championships, winning gold medals in the double sculls with Liz Lorrimer and, also with Lorrimer, in the quadruple sculls, as well as taking the single sculls silver.

Two of the Club's Vice-Presidents, Duggie Douglas, aged 85, and Karl Vernon, 'The Bean', aged 92, died in 1973. Both had put an enormous amount of time into helping the Club in all sorts of ways. The Bean, an architect, was also an etcher of some ability and his etchings were given as prizes for the Club pairs and at Putney Town Regatta. He was well-known among rowing enthusiasts, as was his wife, Dorothy, who died before him. Like Duggie, he was an unaffected, kindly, and charming man. Both could be seen on the river at an advanced age, and Bean was a much sought after coach. His enthusiasm was infectious and he would frequently make up scratch crews of veterans and novices, bringing on many beginners in this way.

In the autumn of 1973, with the object of freeing the Captain from some of the administrative chores, the office of Chairman was introduced. Freddie, now 73, declined to take this on, so Bill Williams became the Club's first Chairman.

In 1974, Oxford won a memorable Boat Race victory after six successive defeats, taking 15 seconds off the record with a time of 17min 35sec. The Tideway Scullers recorded their tenth win in eleven years in the Head, in which the national squad eight, starting low down as a new entry, finished second.

The Club managed twenty victories and produced some better Henley crews. Henley finals were held on Sunday for the first time, though it remained a four-day regatta. The Thames Cup eight, which included John Levy's sons, Martin at five and Tim coxing, and a UCS 1972 junior international, Paul Budd, at four lost to a good Quintin eight in the second round of the Thames Cup, which was won by an Antwerp crew, for whom David Pedraza was rowing.

The Thames Wyfold four, however, was a very good crew. Bingham, at bow, and Read, at two, joint Deputy Captains that year, having stuck with the Club through its leanest period, had been joined by two of the winning UL Stewards' four who had rowed at Moscow, Chris George and Tony Stocking. All were lightweights, the crew averaging under 11 stone. They won two rounds and then met the far heavier Porcellian Club, USA. The official records state:

> On Friday the American four had one of the best races of the regatta, against Thames Rowing Club, who were probably the second fastest crew in this event . . . The crews raced almost level to Fawley, where Thames, at 35½, had ½ length over Porcellian, at 31½. Thames increased their lead to ¾ length at the ¾ Mile, but Porcellian drew level again at the Mile. Though Thames went to 38, Porcellian, at 32, had ¼ length at the final signal, and won a magnificent race by ¾ length.

Porcellian later won the final, leading Nottingham and Union all the way.

Bob Janousek's squad eight lost the final of the Grand by ½ length to Trud. Stroked by Tim Crooks, the British eight took the silver medal in the World Championships at Lucerne using special carbon fibre oars that Jerry Sutton and I had developed at Richmond. The Russian eight finished only fifth. It was Britain's best international season for years, and, with Hart and Baillieu taking another bronze, Britain finished fourth in the medals table.

At Nottingham International Regatta, which had been instituted in 1973, though the East Germans and Russians dominated the top events, Britain were second in the points table.

The next few years saw little change in Thames's fortunes, with minor successes from time to time, though the women continued to score frequent wins. The ever-faithful Nigel Read went off to try his hand with the new lightweight squad. FISA had introduced lightweight championships in 1974, and though these were, in effect, World Championships, they were not officially given this status until 1985, so the lightweight squad did not get full financial support from the ARA. As a result, they rowed, somewhat controversially, under the flag of convenience of London RC. Read became a key man in the British eight, with whom he won three gold medals, one silver, and one bronze. He also won the Thames Cup twice, well-earned rewards after all his efforts.

In 1975, the year Gordon Jack was selected for the FISA junior championships, an Ealing High School four were also selected. The winners of the Visitors', they rowed from Thames, two of them, John Beattie and Ian McNuff, having won a bronze medal in a combined Ealing/Thames junior eight at the previous year's National Championships. They won a silver medal at the FISA Championships but were lost to Thames in the autumn when the Club declined to provide them with a new boat so that they could continue at senior level. This short-sighted decision led to the boys and their coach, David Tanner, moving to London, who were only too happy to oblige, the crew going on to win an Olympic bronze and two World Championship bronze medals. The stroke of this crew, Martin Cross, later won an Olympic gold medal as bow of the British coxed four in 1984, and failed by centimetres to win the coxless pairs in the World Championships in 1985.

The ARA squad eight won the Head for the first time in 1975, their winning time of 17min 17.34sec. beating the 1964 record by 6 seconds. Thames produced a record of a different kind when the first eight finished only 105th, though a crew of veterans finished forty-first. The Captain, Bill Needham, resigned shortly afterwards, Jock Mackerrell taking over. At Henley, the Club was represented only by an eight, which lost to Leander in the third round.

The World Championships were held at Holme Pierrepont this year. Hart and Baillieu won their third bronze medal but the ARA squad, despite the eight's performance at Henley, where they had won the Grand, concentrated on fours instead and missed medals when both finished fourth. Thames were represented in the women's events by Helen McFie, who stroked the composite eight, but British women's rowing was still not up to international standard and the eight finished tenth and last. Once again, the East Germans took the lion's share of the men's and women's heavyweight events, though they did not recognise lightweight rowing, where Britain took a silver and a bronze.

Thames's main hopes at Henley in 1976 were a heavyweight Britannia four stroked by John Pritchard, with Gordon Jack at three, but they fell in the second round to the juniors from Wallingford School. The women continued on their winning ways, two doubles winning the elite event on different days at Nottingham International Regatta, and Jean Rankine, who was in one of them, was in the winning quad again at the National Championships.

In the Olympic Games in Montreal, the British eight excelled in taking the silver medal behind the East Germans, who won five of what had become, with the introduction of quadruple sculls in 1975, eight events. Hart and Baillieu improved their placing with a silver medal behind the world champions, the Norwegian Hansen brothers, but none of the other British men reached a main final. Women's events were included for the first time, Britain's two entries finishing well down. The East

Germans and Bulgarians shared the gold medals between them.

Earlier in the summer, Felix Badcock Snr had collapsed at a dinner for Henley winners at Thames, dying the next day. The Club minutes record:

> Felix will always be remembered as one of the greatest strokes of a four of his generation. His kindness in teaching juniors and everyone who would learn was an example to all. And many will long remember his great hospitality at Hedsor Wharf in the years after the war, where his ground encompassed the only privately owned half-mile stretch of the river below Oxford.

His widow, Joyce, remarked to my mother immediately after his death that there could have been no better way for Felix to go than among his many Thames friends.

That autumn, Bob Janousek resigned as the ARA's national coach, disillusioned by the hit-and-miss attitude he found among all sportsmen in England. He went into boatbuilding, eventually setting up his own successful business.

Thames's Captain in 1977, Tony Bingham, still had an uphill task ahead of him, though there were welcome early successes when the first eight won the sprint and elite eights at Ostend, but after defeating Williams College, USA, by 1¾ lengths in the second round of the Thames Cup at Henley, they went out to Kingston, and two fours failed to survive the first round.

The ARA eight lost the Grand to the University of Washington but Tim Crooks won the Diamonds, while Hart and Baillieu scored their third successive win in the Double Sculls. They went on to take the gold medal at last in the World Championships in Amsterdam, their old adversaries the Hansens having temporarily retired. The lightweights also struck gold for the first time when the eight won by the narrowest of margins. Ray Penney, who had coxed Thames in the 1958 Commonwealth Games and the 1959 European Championships, had been coaxed out of retirement and had steered the lightweights to win the Thames Cup, but he could not lose the vital few pounds at Amsterdam, and he gave way to Pat Sweeney, the 1976 Olympic cox, who was coaching at Amsterdam. Penney was the first to greet the crew at the landing stage after their victory.

Three prominent Thames members died in 1977: the President, Jack Beresford, and two Vice-Presidents, Tig Tyler and my father, Freddie Page. Jack had attended the Club dinner the evening before his death and died suddenly while walking in his garden at Shiplake, and my father, who had been ill for some time, died three weeks later. Tig had collapsed in the boathouse after a sculling outing earlier in the year, but lived on for a further six months. Alan Burrough became the Club's new President the following March.

John Stephenson, now Chairman of Thames, was a strong advocate of an Under-23 squad at Thames for 1978 but this was not a success. Three successful Leander coaches had been drafted into the Club to help but their hearts were not in it. They had drifted away by the spring, and the scheme petered out.

Rather more successful was a junior women's squad. In the National Championships the previous year, when the women had had another good haul of medals, taking the Victor Ludorum again, the women's junior single sculls had been won by Bernadette Casey. She and her sister Caroline were the daughters of a successful Vesta oarsman and coach, Noel Casey. Both girls were highly successful from the start, and in the autumn of 1977, Noel formed a women's junior squad based on Thames. The senior women won the Women's Head in 1978, while the juniors won their division. Bernadette Casey, still a junior, won the elite sculls at Nottingham International and two other regattas. She sculled by invitation in the

Three Nations match held as part of Ratzeburg Regatta and with her sister she won the Women's Rowing Council double sculls.

After the demise of the Under-23 scheme, the performances of the Thames men were much as usual, winning the odd heat at Henley but being well short of winning standard. The occasional elite trophy came their way but Pritchard and McGowan had now moved to Leander, where their undoubted talent would have a better chance to emerge. McGowan, having been persuaded by Thames to give up dangerous attempts to keep his weight down in the hope of getting into the lightweight squad, rowed at Henley that summer at 13 st 5 lb!

In the World Championships in New Zealand, Jim Clark and John Roberts took the coxless pairs silver medal for the second year running, having been coached by the ARA's new senior national coach, Penny Chuter. The return of the Hansens put Hart and Baillieu back in second place, while the former Ealing four, now rowing in London colours, were considerably strengthened by the London University Olympic oarsman, David Townsend, and took their first bronze medal.

In 1979, there was a turbulent Head of the River Race, for which the entry had reached 400 for the first time. Fifteen crews sank in the rough conditions and Thames dropped to 116th. The Tideway Scullers, waterlogged, came 212th. In the summer, regatta wins for the Thames men remained spasmodic and, to the dismay of the older members, no Thames eight appeared at Henley for the second time in the decade, and a Wyfold four lost in the first round.

The success of the women, however, continued unabated. Stephanie Price, Bernadette Casey, and a cox, Nicky Mason, the daughter of the 1957 Oxford stroke, Keith Mason, were chosen for the World Championships in Bled, though they had no more success than usual against the powerful Eastern bloc countries. Caroline Casey and Katie Ball won the junior double sculls at the National Championships and were selected for the FISA Junior Championships in Moscow. This was the first time that events for girls had been included, but unfortunately Katie Ball fell ill in Moscow and had to be replaced by Alexa Forbes from Nottingham. Not surprisingly, they could finish only ninth.

In the World Championships in Bled, the lightweight coxless four won a gold medal but Baillieu, with his new partner, Jim Clark, finished out of the medals for the first time in seven years.

At the end of the most difficult decade in Thames's history, the women maintained their record as the most successful women's club in the country, but the men had become also-rans. Revival in the 1980s had become an urgent problem, but how this was to be achieved was not immediately clear.

20 Climbing Back

The Club's response to the questions posed at the end of 1979 was to look once again towards the younger oarsmen, but with so many juniors being catered for by schools or junior squads, the answer seemed to lie in a school leavers' group, the 18-to-21-year-olds. This is the age group where over 50 per cent of school leavers give up active sport, and Thames set out to attract as many as possible from rowing schools in the London area. A letter was sent to the rowing masters of all the major schools, drawing a sympathetic response. By the autumn of 1979 recent leavers from St Paul's, UCS, Emanuel, Latymer and elsewhere had begun to join the Club. I had not coached at Thames for a few years but undertook to organise the scheme. However, I should have known better: with the chronic shortage of coaches, I found myself having to coach the resulting senior B eight as well. At the same time, Noel Casey undertook to run a lightweight squad. This also attracted outsiders and soon Thames began to take on a healthier look.

The Club was fortunate to have found an excellent Captain in Richard Willett, and his sustained direction of the Club's affairs engendered a new enthusiasm. Though the lightweights, rowing as the first eight, lost the Boustead in February 1980, the Cubs, as the Under-21s had become known, easily beat the London second eight, and the novices and veterans also beat their London counterparts. The Club was now boating four regular eights, as well as a veteran eight, for the first time for very many years. London, however, had been unable to raise a senior C eight to race Thames.

The old problem of lack of weight remained: the newcomers were mostly very light, several being under 11 stone, and eventually one or two slightly older, stronger men of the same status were brought in. The Cubs rowed as Thames first eight in the Head, rising from the previous year's lowly 116th place to a slightly more respectable thirty-ninth, and with the lightweights having disappointed and disbanded after the Head, the Cubs became the first eight. They won at two early regattas and at Ostend they won the senior A eights. This new FISA status was the Over-23 age group, senior B being Under-23.

At Henley, however, they simply lacked the power to cope with the College Boat Club of Pennsylvania, to whom they conceded 32 lb a man, though the Americans were beaten by ¼ length by the London lightweights, who themselves succumbed in the final to the 13 st 10 lb London University eight.

Tony Ross, a former Radley first eight oarsman, rowed for a time in the Cubs eight but he was also a good sculler, winning senior A sculls at Chiswick, Reading, and Marlow. He thus elected to go for the Diamonds, where he proceeded to upset form by beating a selected Norwegian sculler, Gilje, before losing by ½ length to an American, Brad Lewis. Lewis was to win a gold medal in the 1984 Olympic double sculls, though at Henley in 1980 he went out to another Norwegian, Rolf Thorsen, who became double sculls world champion with Alf Hansen in 1982. Even Thorsen failed in the Diamonds, however, the winner being the experienced Argentinian, Ricardo Ibarra. Ross was in good company.

The two Thames fours at Henley disappointed, the Britannia four failing to qualify and the Wyfold four going out in the first round.

The regatta was notable in that no British

crew rowed in the Grand, a situation that had previously occurred only in 1973. It was won by what had been intended to be the American Olympic eight, rowing as the Charles River Rowing Association, who also took the Prince Philip and Stewards' with other Olympic nominees. The United States were foremost among many countries that boycotted the 1980 Olympic Games in Moscow as a somewhat futile protest against the Soviet invasion of Afghanistan. Other boycotting nations included Canada, New Zealand, Holland, and Argentina, which resulted in an unusually strong overseas entry for Henley, the frustrated Olympic competitors seeking some compensation for their disappointment. The ARA elected to send crews, but because of the closeness of the date of the Olympic Regatta, none of them competed at Henley, nor did any other Olympic competitors.

In the absence of some top rowing nations, Britain ranked fifth in Moscow. John Pritchard had joined Malcolm McGowan in the British eight, which put up a spectacular performance in the final, despite the rudderlines breaking. The cox, Colin Moynihan, a former Oxford cox and boxing Blue, who later became Minister for Sport, took hold of the t-bar behind his back and Britain took the silver medal close behind the East Germans. The Tanner four won a third bronze, and Wiggins and Carmichael also took a bronze in the coxless pairs. In the women's events, Beryl Mitchell did well to finish fifth in the single sculls.

Britain did well elsewhere, the lightweight eight again winning the gold medal, while in the Junior Championships, Adam Clift and Steve Redgrave produced an outstanding performance when winning the silver medal in the double sculls less than a second behind the East Germans. Thames had a girl in the junior women's eight, Clare Carpenter, but they were outclassed.

In the National Championships, Thames won the women's coxed fours with a crew containing the two Caseys, and Stephanie Price won the single sculls, the Victor Ludorum again coming to the Club.

In 1981, a diminutive brunette at Oxford attracted the attention of the press not normally expected to show an interest in rowing. She was Sue Brown, who made history and countless front pages by becoming the first woman to compete in the Boat Race, steering Oxford to their sixth consecutive victory.

Thames were at last able to boat some heavier crews, the Thames Cup eight containing three men in the region of 14 stone. They won two heats, coming from behind to beat Trinity College, Hartford, USA, by 4 feet. Leander then beat them but they in turn fell to a massive Charles River crew, averaging 15 stone. As a squad crew with the 1984 Olympics in mind, the Americans ought not to have been in this event. Their winning time was only 1 second slower than that of the ARA crew in winning the Grand. It illustrated the escalation of the difficulties faced by British clubs.

Thames beat old friends, Argonaut RC, Toronto, in the Wyfold, but got no further. A Canadian squad crew, Hanlan BC, stroked by Pat Turner, who was to win an Olympic gold medal in 1984, won the final.

As an experiment, invitation events for women's coxed fours and double sculls were introduced at Henley in 1981. A Thames/Upper Thames combination were one of the four crews invited for the fours, but they lost to an American crew. The experiment was tried again in 1982 but was then discontinued.

Noel Casey produced an exceptional women's coxed four in 1981. Consisting of Sarah Hunter-Jones, Caroline Casey, Bernadette Carroll (née Casey), and stroked by Jane Cross, the daughter of the former RAF and Thames oarsman from the 1950s, Ken Cross, and with Sue Brown coxing, they won the elite fours at the NIR and the

National Championships. They became the first Thames women's crew to compete in the World Championships, finishing seventh at Munich. The women's team produced one outstanding result when Beryl Mitchell took the silver medal in the single sculls. This was the first medal to be won by a British woman in the World Championships, and the first in any international championship since Penny Chuter's 1962 European Championships silver.

The men also brought home some medals: silver by the eight and bronze by London University's coxed pair, Tom Cadoux-Hudson and Richard Budgett, coxed by Adrian Ellison. The Tanner four at last failed, finishing only tenth. The lightweights came home empty handed.

The ARA's centenary fell in 1982 and the most spectacular of the various celebrations was a Centenary Pageant in September when over 600 men and women, many in period costume or fancy dress of various sorts (one women's eight had dyed their hair green) rowed or sculled down to Greenwich.

Earlier in the year, the Head of the River Race celebrated its fiftieth race, which was won by an ARA eight. Thames were still down the field in the 30s though they were able to enter two eights for the Thames Cup, the rules having been changed to allow this, but the B crew failed to qualify and the A crew had the misfortune to draw another massive Charles River crew, for whom they were again no match. The Americans beat Goldie, who were almost the complete Cambridge Boat Race crew, in the final.

The University of London had an outstanding Henley. They won the Ladies' and, with combined UL/Tyrian crews (Tyrian are former UL students), the Prince Philip, and reached the final of the Stewards' and the Grand, losing the former to the Swiss four that later won the World title, and the latter narrowly to the ARA squad eight. Chris Baillieu won the Diamonds for the second time, with verdicts of 'Easily' in every race, and the junior silver medallists, Clift and Redgrave, won the Double Sculls, and, as part of the ARA quad, the Queen Mother Cup for quadruple sculls which had been introduced in 1981. Beryl Mitchell, in women's single sculls, and Rosie Clugston (later Mayglothling) and Astrid Ayling in the double sculls became the first, and so far only, British competitors, other than coxes, to win at the Royal Regatta.

After those good performances, the World Championships in Lucerne provided some rude shocks for British competitors. The London University/Tyrian coxed four had the best result when finishing fifth. Baillieu and the quad were sixth and the biggest disappointment were the eight in ninth place. Beryl Mitchell, who had lost several months' training following injury to her head in a winter tobogganning accident, narrowly missed a bronze medal, the gold going to Stephanie Foster of New Zealand, whom Beryl had beaten at Henley.

For Thames, it was another average season. The Wyfold four had reached the third round before going out to the London squad lightweight four by 1½ lengths, and at the NIR the eight had won the ARA Centenary 500-metre sprint, while a junior double won a bronze in the National Championships. It was still all rather humble stuff.

During the year, the Club's former Captain and Chairman, as well as a Vice-President, Bill Williams, died aged 79 after a short illness. He was Chairman of the Thames Amateur Rowing Council and President of Remenham Club and had devoted innumerable hours of his spare time to rowing administration and coaching. He had been one of the recipients of the Queen's Silver Jubilee medal awarded for services to rowing.

Thames at last began to emerge from the doldrums in 1983 and the Club had its best season for many years, though the forty-seven regatta wins were not in the top flight. The Wyfold four won at Reading and at Marlow took the notoriously difficult Town Cup from an entry of nineteen, though at Henley they lost to Leander in the first round. Two different senior A coxed fours had wins, and the Britannia four, with Dan Badcock, the third generation of his family to row for Thames, at two, though they also lost in the first round at Henley, later won at Bedford, Molesey and Staines. Two Thames Cup eights competed at Henley, the A crew beating London B before going down to a good Ghent crew that reached the final, where they lost to a heavyweight UL crew. The B crew had started the season as a senior C eight but Tony Ross was recruited to stroke them at Henley. They came through the qualifying round and lost by only ¾ length to Twickenham.

Ross was doubling up in the Diamonds and reached the semi-final, where he lost to Tim Crooks. The ultimate winner, however, was the young rising star, Steve Redgrave, who collected his fourth Henley trophy in three years with this victory. London University had a share in the Grand, and wins in the Thames Cup and Visitors', while a Tyrian pair won the Goblets. UL also reached the final of the Britannia, where they lost to the newly formed Lea RC, an amalgamation of the old River Lea clubs. Lea also won the Wyfold with another crew.

The winning Grand eight were an ARA composite, but they competed in the World Championships at Duisburg in two fours, and a new young eight were put together for the Championships, only to finish eleventh and last. The championships proved even more disastrous for Britain than in the previous year, with only the coxed four reaching a main final, finishing sixth. The coxless four were tenth, and Redgrave was unplaced in the single sculls, in which the West German, Peter-Michael Kolbe, won his third gold medal. But the saddest sight was that of Chris Baillieu, with a new young partner, Joff Spencer-Jones, trailing in last in heat and *repêchage* of the double sculls in what turned out to be his last international appearance. There were no British finalists in the women's championships.

At domestic regattas, Tony Ross continued to win senior A events for Thames and represented England in the Home Countries International on the new Scottish 2,000m course at Strathclyde Park, winning the single sculls. Jean Rankine and her perennial partner, Penny Haslam, were still winning medals at the National Championships, and with Pauline Rayner and Stephanie Price, took another gold in the quadruple sculls.

Thames rowing was reviving, but in 1983 the best men had been scattered among different crews. At Henley, there had been three men over 14 stone and seven over 13 but at the end of the season, the new Captain, Tim Levy, felt that they had not been trained hard enough in the winter, so he formed a squad of men, which included most of the heavyweights, who were prepared to train hard for 1984.

A strong, tough eight began to take shape and in addition to undertaking a punishing programme of land training they covered many miles on the water, with a second, younger and lighter crew as company in the early stages. The first eight easily won the Boustead, and sixth in the Reading Head and twelfth in the Tideway Head, despite having been decimated by flu in the preceding week, were the Club's best placings for over ten years.

The 1984 Boat Race produced some excitement, not to say consternation, when the Cambridge cox ran his crew into a moored barge on the way to the stakeboats. The bows broke and the crew, with John Pritchard at six, just made it to the bank. The race was postponed to the following day. This was the first time the race had been held on a Sunday, and Oxford recorded their ninth successive win, to equal their best-ever run.

The Thames eight had eight wins during the season, and, at Reading, they won their first elite eights for several years. A four from the eight also won two elite events. At Henley, the eight beat

Stourport in their opening heat of the Thames Cup, their time of 6min 34sec, aided by a minimal stream as a result of a very dry, hot summer, and despite a comfortable win, being surprisingly the fastest recorded by any Thames eight in a Henley race. They then came up against the South African national squad eight, rowing under the flag of convenience of Cantabrigian RC, since an entry under their own name of Trident would undoubtedly have led to trouble, the climate of opinion being strongly against South African entries. Although the Thames crew averaged over 13 stone, they still had to concede 9 lbs a man to the South Africans. This might not have been too much of a handicap had not the crew added another by having a very rushed first minute, which allowed the South Africans to lead by a length at the Barrier. They did not get away, however, and spirited rowing by Thames held them to 1¼ lengths at the finish.

Thames were one of the best crews in the event and the South Africans went on to win the Thames Cup, having set a new record time of 6min 16sec in their semi-final against Vesta. This was only 6 seconds slower than the ARA eight's winning time in the Grand, which was a new course record. In the Ladies', theoretically a better event than the Thames Cup, the winners, Brown University, USA, also set a new event record of 6min 23sec, some 7 seconds slower than the new Thames Cup record. This anomaly finally led to the Henley Stewards taking a hard look at the regulations in the autumn.

There was a notable upset in the Goblets when Ewan Pearson, a Cambridge Blue that year, and David Riches of Molesey defeated the already selected Olympic pair of Beattie and Stanhope, rowing them down at the last signal, the ARA pair stopping at the bottom of the Stewards' Enclosure. The selected coxless four, based on the Nottinghamshire County Rowing Association squad, scraped home a canvas ahead of the non-squad UL/Tyrian four. These performances did not augur well for the Olympics, but there was never any doubt that the best squad crew, the coxed four, would easily defeat Njord, Holland, the only other entry for the Prince Philip. Steve Redgrave, at stroke, took his fifth Henley medal and his first in a rowing event.

In the Diamonds, Tony Ross, after being asked to qualify and becoming one of only four of the seventeen contenders to do so, produced another of his giant-killing acts, this time accounting for Tim Crooks in his heat, and then defeating another selected sculler, Brad Cooper from New Zealand. This put him in the semi-final again but he could not hold the 1983 world lightweight champion, Bjarne Eltang, in the later stages, though he fought hard all the way before going down by 1¾ lengths. Baillieu beat the Dane in the final to become the first English sculler to take the Diamonds for a third time since Jack Beresford. He was not selected for his third Olympics, however, and retired from serious competition at the end of the season.

After Henley, the Thames eight lost their six, the Henley based Lee Brown, a former international and Grand winner, and their five, Mike Urry. A reconstituted eight nevertheless won elite eights at Bedford, and the four from the eight won the elite coxless fours. Thames had five finalists at this regatta, winning three when the second eight took the senior A event. This crew later won twice more, and it was the first time since the 1960s that the Club had produced two winning eights in senior events.

However, the new first eight were not strong enough at the National Championships, where the standard was higher than usual and they could finish only fourth in the final, two lengths behind the winners, Leander.

Tony Ross won the single sculls gold medal and represented England in the Home Countries International for the second year running but was beaten into second place by the Irish sculler, John Armstrong, at Blessington. After two more senior A wins, Ross finally won elite sculls at Maidenhead.

In a season which brought the Club its highest number of wins at that date (sixty-six), the most successful oarsman was Mike Cowie, a Cambridge Blue who had rowed for the Club in 1983 without much to show for it. In 1984, he took fourteen trophies, several in the elite class, in the eights or fours. He also rowed in the Thames eight, stroked by Tim Levy, which won the Boston Marathon in record time in September.

The Thames women accounted for twenty-one of the Club's wins, as well as sharing two others in composite crews. They took the silver medal in the quad sculls in the National Championships, the bronze in the coxed fours, and the Victor Ludorum. Three members represented Britain in composite crews in the Olympics: Tessa Millar (coxed four), Sarah Hunter-Jones (eight) and Sally Bloomfield (double sculls). Sadly, Sally was killed in the first week of 1985 in a car crash in France, in which the Cambridge and squad coach, Graeme Hall, who had coached the British men's eight in 1980 and 1984, also died.

In the spring of 1984, the Russians pulled out of the forthcoming Olympic Games. Denying that this was tit-for-tat for the American-led boycott of the Moscow Olympics, Soviet officials claimed that the reason was fear for the safety of their athletes in Los Angeles, and accused the Americans of organising an anti-Russian campaign and of violating the Olympic Charter. Most of the Eastern bloc followed the Russian example, though a notable exception was Romania, whose team received sustained applause from the predominantly American crowd as they marched round the stadium at the opening ceremony. Women's rowing was seriously affected by the boycott, but the men's less so, since in the 1983 World Championships Western countries had taken five of the eight men's gold medals, and eight of the sixteen minor medals. Nevertheless, the Games were inevitably devalued.

The British squad coxed four, coached by Mike Spracklen, had at least beaten the East Germans at Lucerne and the Soviet four at Grunau, and at Lake Casitas won Britain's first Olympic rowing gold medal since 1948, Redgrave mounting a sustained attack over the last 500 metres to take his crew past the Americans for a ½ length victory. Martin Cross, at bow, became the first Briton to win medals at two Olympics since Jack Beresford had won his fifth medal in 1936.

Unfortunately, the rest of the British team did not perform so well, the eight finishing fifth behind the Canadian winners, while none of the other men's crews reached the main finals. The gold medals were shared between eight different countries, and Pertti Karppinen, the Finnish sculler, emulated Vyacheslav Ivanov in winning the single sculls for the third time.

The Romanians took five of the six women's gold medals, the American eight taking the other. The British women, despite the absence of many of the top nations in women's rowing, had little chance, but the eight, coached by Noel Casey, did well, finishing only 4.7 seconds behind the gold medallists, missing the bronze medal by ½ length.

In December, the Henley Stewards decided on major changes in the qualifications for the Ladies' Plate and Thames Cup. The former was opened to club crews and ceased to be simply a collegiate event, while the latter was closed to foreign crews, other than school crews, and club crews could not include more than four oarsmen of senior A or higher status. The intention was to restore the Ladies' to its traditional place as the second eights event after the Grand by forcing the best of the old Thames Cup crews into the Ladies', and by lowering the Thames Cup standard to give the smaller clubs and Oxbridge colleges a better chance of surviving a round or two, at the same time producing some closer races. However, the Stewards had created some new problems for the clubs. On the day the changes were announced, I suggested to Peter Coni, the Chairman of Henley's Committee of Management, that he had made a gift of the Thames Cup to Ridley College, the highly successful Canadian school who had already had a number of wins in the Princess Elizabeth Cup. 'Oh, do you think so?' he said. 'I don't think it will work out like that. We shall have to wait and see.' Ridley won the event for the next two years.

Thames went into 1985 with Tim Levy still Captain and an even tougher and more dedicated senior squad, supported by a growing number of intermediate and novice oarsmen, and the problem now was how best to deploy the Club's resources to fit in with the new Henley regulations.

Oxford won the Boat Race to record their best-ever run of ten successive victories, three short of Cambridge's record of thirteen straight wins, and Bruce Philp made history by becoming the first man to have rowed for both universities, having twice lost with Cambridge before winning with Oxford.

Earlier, Thames had won the Boustead easily, when the second, third, and novice eights also won. Head results were marginally better: second in the Trent Head, where the second eight were fifth, fifth and tenth at Reading, and twelfth and thirty-sixth in the Tideway Head.

Stroked by Lee Brown, with Mike Cowie at seven, the first eight won both the 2,000m and the sprint eights at Ostend. At Ghent, having just failed to qualify from their heat on the Saturday, they produced an inspired row in the final on the Sunday. In the last race of the regatta, accompanied by a violent thunderstorm, Thames faced London University, the Tideway Scullers, Vesta, and an Antwerp crew. Thames set the pace from the start and were just ahead at 1,500m, but the powerful UL crew forced their way past to win by ½ length, with Vesta third and the Scullers fourth.

At Marlow, Thames lost the final of the Grand to Vesta by a canvas, due entirely to some poor steering, which also led to their disqualification in the sprint. It was not their day.

Meanwhile, the effects of the new Henley regulations became only too clear when the second eight chalked up four senior A wins before Henley as well as taking the elite eights at Twickenham, for the best pre-Henley run by Thames eights for many years, but the result was that the second eight became ineligible for the Thames Cup, and in the end the Club had to enter two crews for the Ladies', one of the less acceptable consequences of the changes.

Nevertheless, the second eight were made to qualify, becoming one of only five crews to do so. They were then unlucky to draw Nautilus, the ARA lightweights, losing by 1⅔ lengths in the second fastest time of the day. The fastest time was set by the Norwegian eight from Ormsund, whose stern four were all Olympic or world gold medallists, two of them being the Hansen brothers. The first eight drew Njord (Leiden University), beating them by 1 length, but lost to Vesta again in the next round by ½ length after a fiercely fought race, again in the second fastest Ladies' time that day. Ormsund beat Nautilus narrowly but they were not fully fit and lost by ½ length to Garda Siochana, who in turn fell to Leander in the final by a canvas. If it was close racing the Stewards had been after, they had certainly succeeded.

The new rules had produced an enormous entry of seventy-three for the Thames Cup, for which Thames put on a semi-scratch crew that had rowed together for only three weeks. Stroked by that year's winning Isis stroke, Chris Bourne, they turned out to be quite fast but drew one of the favourites, University College, Dublin, to whom they lost by ¾ length. UCD reached the final, losing to Ridley in a time that was only 8 seconds slower than Leander's winning time in the Ladies'.

There was no ARA crew in the Grand, in which there was an all-American final, and it is an indication of the high standard of the Ladies' that Harvard's winning time in the Grand against Princeton was 1 second slower than Leander's.

The Thames men fared better than usual in the National Championships, the first eight taking the bronze medal behind London University and the ARA lightweights, and Tony Ross also took the bronze medal in the single sculls, which were won by Redgrave. The women had two crews in the coxed fours final, finishing second and third to the ARA squad four, in which Sarah Hunter-Jones was rowing, which meant that eleven Thames women won medals in this event. The women's eight were third behind the ARA eight, which included Tessa Millar, and Cambridge University, while the quad took the bronze medal, behind the ARA quad, which included Stephanie Price. This was the best combined haul of medals to date by Thames men and women at the National Championships. The men also won the sprint eights and the women the sprint fours, which were not championship events. The following weekend at Holme Pierrepont, the men's eight, the women's coxed four, and Tony Ross represented England in the Home Countries International, where the eight finished second to the Garda Siochana, and both Ross and the women's four were third.

In the whole season, the Club had a record seventy-four wins, sixteen of them in eights.

Redgrave pulled a back muscle in the World Championships at Hazewinkel in Belgium, finishing only twelfth in the single sculls, but another member of the Olympic coxed four, Martin Cross, very nearly won another gold medal in the coxless pairs with Redgrave's former junior double sculling partner, Adam Clift. The British pair were a length behind the 1981 world champions, the Soviet Pimenov twins, at 1,750m, but an astonishing burst of power failed by only centimetres to get the British pair home first. Yuri Pimenov collapsed and had to be taken to hospital, but he soon recovered.

None of the other British men, lightweights or heavyweights, or the heavyweight women, made the main finals, but the experienced duo of Lin Clark and Beryl Crockford (formerly Mitchell), who first appeared together in the coxless pairs in the 1976 World Championships, took the first gold medal to be won by British women in any major championship, winning the lightweight double sculls, lightweight events for women having been introduced that year.

In the junior championships at Brandenburg, East Germany, the gold medals were spread between four countries to confirm that other countries were beginning to catch up on the East Germans. A composite British coxless four won a silver medal.

Towards the end of the year, the most successful of the Thames women, Heather Brown, a former winning Cambridge Blue who scored fourteen victories in 1985, was tragically killed when driving back from Henley after a training session with the ARA squad. Charming and dedicated, she was only 23 and her death was a sad loss to the Club and to British rowing. The following year, a new Club eight was named in her memory.

To mark the Club's 125th anniversary, Prince Michael of Kent, who had rowed for Sandhurst in 1961, winning the maiden fours at Bedford on a day when Thames had been particularly successful there, was invited to become Patron of the Club and he accepted with enthusiasm.

Early in 1986, the ARA appointed Penny

Chuter Director of International Rowing with complete control over the forming and selection of representative international crews, a bold decision not without its critics. This was a difficult year for Chuter to begin her development of the prospective 1988 Olympic squad since rowing had been re-introduced for the Commonwealth Games in Scotland. This involved forming both a Great Britain team for the World Championships in Nottingham and an England team for Strathclyde.

That year also, racing at Henley was extended to five days because of the increasingly large entry, something for which many had been clamouring, but there was still no room for women's events. New regatta headquarters by Henley Bridge were opened by the Queen in April.

The Thames first eight, though second again in the Trent Head and fourth at Reading, lost a few places in the Tideway Head, but later they won the 2,000m event on both days at Ostend and also won the sprint. Gavin Reddin, now Club Captain, finished second in the 2,000 single sculls and the sprint. At Ghent, the eight took the silver medal behind the West German Under-23 crew, and they had three other wins at home before Henley. Stroked by the 1985 winning Isis stroke, Chris Bourne, with a 1984 Oxford Blue, Jim Stewart, at seven, Dan Badcock at six and the powerful heavyweight Mike Urry at five, they were the heaviest eight ever to have represented the Club, averaging 13 st 9 lb, but faults persisted and they never realised their full potential.

In the Ladies' Plate at Henley, they demolished a sub-standard American entry from Leverett House, being 4 lengths ahead at the Barrier and paddling in along the enclosures at 24, but the next day they succumbed by 2¼ lengths to the 14½ stone University of London eight, the winners of the Marlow Grand. However, it was to be Ireland's year and UL went out to the Dublin club, Neptune, by ½ length in the next round. Neptune then beat their Islandbridge neighbours, Garda Siochana, by the same distance, going on to win the final by ⅔ length from the previously unbeaten Harvard Freshmen, who had beaten their own Junior Varsity eight in their semi-final. Only two British crews reached the last eight and none the last four in the Ladies'.

The Grand was won by the ARA squad eight rowing as Nautilus. They beat Pennsylvania in the final and this time the winners were 11 seconds faster than the winners of the Ladies', who were in turn 6 seconds faster than Ridley, again winners of the Thames Cup. In a semi-final in the morning, though, Imperial College, the losing finalists, stroked by Donkey Long's son, Christopher, a former Oxford Blue, produced a time only 2 seconds slower than Neptune's winning time, which must have given the Henley Stewards more food for thought. Even the standard of the Princess Elizabeth Cup was remarkably high, Hampton winning for the second year running with a time only 2 seconds slower than Ridley's.

The Stewards' record went when the Canadian squad four, Ridley BC – not the college, but also coached by Neil Campbell – recorded 6min 41sec. They were all from the winning 1984 Olympic eight and Tyrian were also inside the old record when going down by only ½ length.

Steve Redgrave, doubling up in the Diamonds and the Goblets, made a hash of the former. He completely misjudged his pace, going right away from the Danish lightweight, Bjarne Eltang, only to be pulled back and sculled to a standstill at the ¾ mile, to his considerable embarrassment. However, with Andy Holmes, he made amends later when winning the Goblets easily. Holmes had earlier won the Grand as a last minute substitute in the ARA eight.

Thames had two eights in the Thames Cup, the B crew drawing a bye into the second round, when their race against Oriel College lasted only

18 strokes, the Thames stroke breaking his swivel, leaving Oriel to paddle in alone. The A crew easily beat the Gunnery School, another sub-standard American entry, but went out in the second round to Imperial College. The Wyfold four, drawn from the A eight, won a heat but were well beaten by Nottingham County, who were themselves overwhelmed in the final by Charles River, the American squad lightweights.

The Match des Seniors, the unofficial Under-23 championship which had been in existence for eleven years, was at last being taken seriously in several countries. Trials for British hopefuls were held at Henley under Chuter's supervision, and at Hamburg in 1986 British crews took two gold medals and a bronze in the men's events. Kingston won the coxed fours and Imperial College dead-heated with France in the quad sculls, the FISA President, Thomi Keller, who was present, deciding that both crews should be awarded gold medals. This was the first time that this had been done. Both the British gold medal crews competed in the World Championships later in the year.

The Commonwealth Games at the end of July were no longer accessible to club crews, Chuter having decreed that all candidates for the team had to be registered with the national squad. For the first time, women and lightweights were included, the programme being arranged to allow for doubling up.

The regatta was a triumph for Redgrave, who became the first Englishman to win the single sculls. He also won the coxed fours and coxless pairs, becoming the first of any nationality to win three gold medals at a single Games regatta. The Canadian Stewards' winners took the coxless fours, while an impressive Australian eight beat England into second place. Guy Thomas, who had rowed in the Thames second eight in 1985, had the doubtful distinction of being the first man in the Games to have jumped out of a boat, which he did after crabbing and losing his blade when bowman in the Welsh eight. A first-ever rowing medal for Scotland, a bronze, went to Pearson and Riches in the coxless pairs.

The World Championships at Holme Pierrepont looked likely to provide Britain with a world heavyweight gold medal at last. At Mannheim early in the season, Holmes and Redgrave had put up an astonishing performance in the coxless pairs, beating the 1985 world silver medallists, Clift and Cross, by several lengths in a time that made them faster than all but one of the coxed and two of the coxless fours that day. This had settled the Commonwealth Games selection, but Holmes and Redgrave had their eyes set on the coxed pairs in the World Championships. At Lucerne, where Clift and Cross won the coxless pairs, Holmes and Redgrave not only trounced the Italian Abbagnale brothers, the Olympic and world champions, but also took 5 seconds off the world record and 9 off the Rotsee record. By this time, the pair were the talk of Europe.

In the World Championships, with Pat Sweeney coxing, they had a sterner battle in the final, though it was an East German pair that led for much of the way, but once again Redgrave's storming finish carried the day, powering the pair through to win the gold medal, the Italians overtaking the exhausted Germans to steal the silver medal just over a length behind the British pair. Clift and Cross could finish only a disappointing fourth behind the Pimenovs in the coxless pairs but another popular gold medal came to Britain through the Nottingham lightweight double scullers, Carl Smith and Allan Whitwell. The Nottingham lightweight four, the women's lightweight four and double, Gill Bond and Carrie Wood, the latter from Bill Mason's IC stable, all took silver.

The success of the lightweight crews was especially praiseworthy because of their almost complete lack of financial support, but their performances, and that of the coxed pair, could not conceal deficiencies in the heavyweight squads. Of the six heavyweight men's entries, four failed to make the main finals, the eight finishing twelfth and last.

Australia put up a magnificent performance in the eights, finishing clear of the Russians, with the United States third. The Western countries continued to erode the superiority of the Eastern bloc, fourteen of the twenty-four available men's heavyweight medals, including five of the eight golds, going to Western countries.

At Roudnice, Czechoslovakia, the British boys collected two more silver medals in the junior World Championships, as they were now officially designated, though none of the three girls' entries reached the main finals.

At home, Thames ended the season with eighty-one wins, improving on the Club's previous best tally for the third year running. In the Women's Head, rowed over the full Mortlake to Putney course for the first time, the women's first eight finished second to the ARA squad eight, winning the Club Pennant, other Thames eights taking the senior B and C Pennants. The women again took the Victor Ludorum at the National Championships, the coxed four winning the gold medal, the eight and the double scullers taking silver medals, and the lightweight four a bronze. The double, who had earlier won at Ghent, combined in the National Championships with two Oxford University girls to take the gold medal in the quads. Altogether, the Club's men and women won twenty-three eights and twenty-seven quad or fours events between them. At last, the Club's revival seemed to be getting into full swing.

21 Moving with the Times

The start of 1987 brought a protracted and much publicised mutiny in the Oxford crew, fostered by five Americans but backed by some of the British members, who questioned the selection methods of Oxford's most successful coach ever, Daniel Topolski, the architect of all the Dark Blues' recent victories. The President, Don Macdonald, the son of a former Thames oarsman, Ian Macdonald, supported Topolski, and the Americans dropped out. Despite the loss of these top oarsmen, and last minute shuffles, which put the tallest and heaviest man to have competed in the race at that time, the 6ft 8in, 16½ stone Gavin Stewart, at stroke, Oxford triumphed on the day. The race was, appropriately, preceded by a dramatic thunderstorm and Macdonald, winning the toss, wisely chose the Middlesex station. In very rough conditions, Oxford made straight for the Fulham wall while Cambridge, uncertain about what to do, floundered along in the middle until they, too, made for shelter. It was too late: Oxford were a length up by Craven Cottage and Cambridge never found a stride.

This was also a good year for Thames, although without quite as many regatta wins as in the previous three years, but the Club at last provided another representative British men's crew after a gap of twenty years, albeit in the relatively humble Match des Seniors.

Bourne and Stewart had retired and Dan Badcock departed to try his luck with Leander. The first eight dropped to eighth at Reading, where the women won the elite and senior A Pennants, and to twentieth in the Tideway Head, which was held on the same day as the Boat Race. The standard of the Ladies' Plate had now reached a level which made the Club decide to concentrate its best men in a Britannia Cup four in the summer. They were stroked by a former junior international, Xavier Calamita, with Mike Urry at three. They did not compete at Ostend, where Gavin Reddin won the senior A sculls. But at Ghent, where the Thames women won the women's fours, they beat one of their main home rivals, Lea, when finishing third on the second day, Lea having beaten them on the previous day. It was the beginning of an intense rivalry.

In May, a two-day regatta over 1,500m on the Royal Albert Dock was inaugurated and despite heavy rain and having been hastily organised to demonstrate to the London Docklands Development Corporation the need for a watersport centre in the redundant docks, the regatta was a success. The Thames four, taking delivery of a new boat, did not compete, but the women took three events and the men two.

Both the men's and women's fours won the second senior event at Nottingham International, Lea finishing a length down in the men's event. The men then went on to finish third at the Ratzeburg Regatta on the Saturday, and second to a Polish squad crew on the Sunday, which augured well for Henley.

At Henley, the standard was exceptionally high, although, with the exception of Holmes and Redgrave, the ARA squad did not compete, Penny Chuter stating that to do so would damage prospects for the following week's regatta at Lucerne. After weeks of dismal weather, summer suddenly arrived and there were again enormous crowds. No British crew entered for the Grand, in which Ridley BC beat Harvard and then lost to the Soviet Army Club in the final. The winners equalled the Barrier record and lowered the Fawley record by 1 second but just missed the full course record.

The highlight of the regatta was the eagerly awaited meeting between Holmes and Redgrave and the Pimenovs. The British pair had once again set tongues wagging at Mannheim Centenary Regatta by winning the coxless event on both days and then taking the coxed pairs as well on the second day only ninety minutes after the coxless pairs final. The Pimenovs did not compete there and Henley provided the first opportunity for the pairs to meet. They were both in a different class from the rest, winning all their races easily on the way to the final. Despite this, the Russians equalled the full course record in the first round, only for the British pair to lower it by 12 seconds the next day.

The final was dramatic from the start and reminiscent of races that had been only too familiar in the previous century. The trouble began approaching the Barrier, when two girls in a canoe strayed onto the course in front of Holmes and Redgrave, who had a narrow lead at the time. In the ensuing collision, the canoe capsized and the race was stopped, Holmes punching a hole in the canoe with his fist, which he fortunately did not damage. The pair's boat was also undamaged, so the crews returned immediately to the start. After a false start by the Russians, the race finally got under way again, the Pimenovs going flat out for the lead. Their Fawley time equalled Holmes' and Redgrave's record, and the Russians were still a length ahead at the Mile, when, having made an unsuccessful push to shake off their opponents, they suddenly stopped, leaving Holmes and Redgrave to paddle in alone.

However, the Russian contingent, induced by financial assistance from the Stewards to return to Henley for the first time since 1974, were rewarded with wins in four other events, though in the Diamonds the West German world champion, Peter-Michael Kolbe, beat the Russian sculler, Jakusha, in the final, and the Canadian 1985 world champion quad broke the record when beating the Russian quad by ½ length.

London University won the Ladies', equalling the record, while the Irish had a field day in the Thames Cup, providing three of the four semi-finalists. Ridley did not enter and the ultimate winners were University College, Galway, who beat Neptune in the final. Both Thames entries went out to Durham University, who lost to Neptune in a semi-final.

In the Britannia, the Thames four, one of the favourites, were a selected crew, together with Lea, Vesta, Tideway Scullers, and the Garda Siochana. Thames met Lea in a semi-final, having previously disposed of Nottingham BC and the Scullers. It was an unexpected disaster for Thames, Lea producing one of the upsets of the regatta. Hitting their best form at the right moment, they slipped away from Thames with surprising ease to win by 2½ lengths, going on to win the final from the unseeded Kingston crew by 1¾ lengths.

Following the success of the rearranged programme for the 1986 Commonwealth Games, FISA had decided to split the finals in the World Championships over two days and the same pattern was adopted at Lucerne, where Holmes and Redgrave went for both pair-oared events, winning the coxless pairs after beating the Pimenovs in the heat, the Russians again giving up well before the finish, but they lost the coxed pairs final to the Abbagnales by just over a length.

After Henley, Thames brought in a Hampton schoolboy to replace Urry in the coxed four so that they could be eligible for the Match des Seniors; and in the new order, they lost by only a length to Lea at the National Championships, with Kingston third. At these Championships, Thames also took a bronze medal in the coxed pairs, and the women took a silver medal in the coxed fours.

Thames won selection for the Match des Seniors, the first British representative crew at any level from the Club since the junior coxed four in 1967. Without Urry, Thames lacked power and just missed the bronze medal, being passed in the closing stages. Leander won the eights, with the West Germans taking the silver medal.

In the junior World Championships in Cologne, the British boys excelled in two events, the coxless four passing the Russians in the last few strokes, with the East Germans third, to take Britain's first junior world gold medal. The eight were only ¾ length behind the United States, whose first gold medal this was also, yet failed by 0.17 seconds to snatch the bronze medal from the Russians. It was the beginning of a series of outstanding championship performances by the junior men.

The senior World Championships at Copenhagen were marred by the extreme unfairness of the lanes on the Bagsvaerd course, caused by a diagonal wind, which was at its worst for the first day finals. Conditions were fairer on the last day but several gold medals were lost simply by the stations. On the Saturday, though racing was postponed for three hours, conditions were such that nobody on lanes 1 or 2 stood a chance, competitors on lane 1 finishing last in every race and on lane 2, fifth, except for one fourth place. On the Sunday all the gold medals came from lanes 4 to 6, but the stations had been redrawn, the fastest qualifiers being placed on lane 6 and the slowest on lane 1.

Among those to suffer were the British coxed four. Stroked by Martin Cross, they had set a new world record of 6min 1.91sec in their heat, but drawing lane 2 in the final on the Saturday, they could finish only fifth, Cross giving up the struggle before the finish. 'The conditions were a joke,' he said. 'You train all year to end up in this, a form of lottery.'

The men's lightweight four from Nottingham drew lane 6 but their stroke, Stuart Forbes, had been suffering from gastroenteritis and they had to settle for the silver medal for the second year running. The lightweight double also suffered from the same problem and lost their title, but still took the bronze on an unfavoured lane.

Holmes and Redgrave, who had qualified for both pairs finals, were fortunate to draw lane 6 in the coxless pairs on the Saturday and won the gold medal, though under some pressure from the Romanians. The next day, on lane 5, they let the Italians get too far away in the early stages, eventually failing to win a second gold medal by about a length, but this was still a fine performance.

At home, the Thames women won the coxed fours for England in the Home Countries International, and there was one more international event that season when the Serpentine Regatta was revived in October after a long lapse. Sprint racing had been becoming increasingly popular and in May, Leyland DAF, who were sponsors for Holmes and Redgrave, and Channel 4 TV had set up the Leyland DAF Power Sprints for men's eights and single sculls, and women's coxed fours. There were regional heats and finals at Bristol, with substantial cash and equipment prizes for winning clubs in heats and finals, but the Thames women's four lost their final. The Serpentine event included an invitation international match but the regatta nearly failed to take place at all when the great hurricane in the early hours of Friday 16 October destroyed several boats in Hyde Park, including some lent to foreign crews by Thames, and blew away all the tents. The Saturday racing had to be abandoned but Herculean efforts by the organisers restored facilities sufficiently for a modified programme to be carried out on the Sunday.

Italy, France, the Soviet Union, and Britain contested the international events and once again Steve Redgrave was Britain's hero, winning the single sculls, coxless pairs, and the eights, the pair recording yet another win over the Pimenovs, who had taken the bronze medal in Copenhagen.

In the domestic events, Thames's only win came

in the women's double sculls, but in other post-Henley regattas, the Thames men had a number of elite wins, though for once the overall tally for the season dropped slightly.

In November, Alan Burrough held a reception at the Club in honour of Dick Phelps's 90th birthday, a happy event attended by many of the Club's oarsmen from the past, among them the seven surviving members of the winning 1948 Grand eight.

Alan's generosity that year also extended to Henley Royal Regatta when he and his wife Rosemary donated £500,000 to the regatta for the purchase of Temple Island, so helping to safeguard this famous landmark.

1988 saw the introduction of individual registration of oarsmen and women by the ARA, and there was yet another change in status regulations, based on the total of points scored in competition by individuals. Elite events were renamed open; senior A, B, and C becoming senior 1, 2, and 3. The Henley Stewards changed the Thames Cup qualifications to senior 1 status, overseas crews of the same status being admitted. School crews were exempted from the status qualification, while anyone who, in the three years prior to the regatta, had competed in the Olympic Games or World Championships, or was intending to compete that year in either of these, was barred, as were previous Henley winners other than in the school events.

At Thames, among other departing members, all the previous year's Britannia four left and their cox, Gary Herbert, went into the national squad. The result was that the first eight not only lost the Boustead Cup to the London lightweights but, after finishing twelfth at Reading, they dropped to thirtieth in the Tideway Head, the Club's lowest position for six years. With the number of squad crews of various sorts rowing in the event, however – in 1988, five national squad eights finished in the first eleven places, as well as one from the Italian squad and another from the Nottingham squad – it was becoming increasingly difficult for any club crews to get near the top.

With one of the American rebels at Oxford, Chris Penny, now President, Mike Spracklen took over from Dan Topolski as the Dark Blues' chief coach. Oxford comfortably won the Boat Race for their thirteenth win in fifteen years.

In April, Steve Redgrave bettered Dick Southwood's 1933 record by 10 seconds when retaining the Wingfield Sculls with an easy win over Philip Kittermaster of Barclay's Bank.

Thames reversed the previous year's policy for the summer, concentrating the best men in an eight. Results soon justified this, and the first eight won open eights at Reading and, for the first time for many years, the Marlow Grand, though not against top-class opponents.

There still being no women's events at Henley, a special women's regatta over the reverse Henley course to just below the Barrier was inaugurated in 1988 on the same day as Marlow. Despite the lack of overseas crews, it was a success, but Thames came away empty handed, losing their semi-final of the open eights by a length to the ARA squad eight, who beat all their other opponents easily.

In the Ladies' Plate at the Royal Regatta, the Thames eight went down by 2 lengths in the second round to the University of London. UL lost a magnificent race the next day by 2 feet to the ultimate winners, Mercantile RC, Melbourne. Mercantile's coach, Marty Aitken, became UL's chief coach the following autumn.

However, the A crew in the Thames Cup went from strength to strength as racing progressed. A second crew had also qualified, disposing of the Oxford University lightweights before losing in the second round by ¼ length to Lady Margaret. The A crew were stroked by an experienced former Emanuel School lightweight, Steve Austin, who had first competed in the Thames Cup with Thames as a cox in 1976 and had first rowed for the Club at Henley as stroke of the Wyfold four in 1982. They beat Bedford, Lea, Trinity College, Dublin, and London before meeting University College, Galway, in a semi-final. UCG were leading by ¾ length at the bottom of the enclosures when, as in previous rounds, Austin mounted a tremendous final burst. Thames began to pull the Irish back, but the UCG cox came across and the blades clashed. UCG crossed the line first but there was some delay before Thames were awarded the race, the umpire having asked UCG to confirm that the blades had touched, which, sportingly, they did. This put Thames in the final for the first time since 1962 but the powerful Tideway Scullers proved too strong, winning by 1½ lengths.

Ian Pritchard, who had won the open sculls at Chester for the Championship of the Dee, also won at Reading, where he also won the double sculls with Gavin Reddin, but at Henley these two went out to Scrivener and Henderson of Lea, ultimately the losing finalists, in the second round. However, it was a better than average Henley for Thames.

Henley that year was one of the wettest for several years, with people sloshing about in the mud in the enclosures, but the final of the Grand was probably the finest ever witnessed. I wrote at the time that it was unlikely that there would be a better race at Henley, a view I still hold. This was an Olympic year and the Australians had sent their potential Olympic eight to Henley. In the final they met the British Olympic eight designate. The Princess Royal followed the race, and I count myself fortunate to have been in the launch as well.

The Australians at 40 led the British at 39 by ¼ length at the first signal. Rowing with great precision, they had stretched this to ⅔ length at the Barrier. At Fawley, the ARA crew had dropped their rate to 36 and looked ragged, but the Australians, still at 39, were beginning to come back. The Australians tried a push but this was expensive and at the Mile, with Nick Burfitt, the ARA stroke, taking the rate to 38, the difference was only ½ length. However, at the last signal it looked as though the Australians would hold on to their lead. By now the crowd in the enclosures were on their feet and the noise was deafening. Burfitt made a last big effort and suddenly the Australians were struggling. From the launch it was impossible to see who had won, but the British crew's reaction and the roar of the crowd told us the result: Britain had won by 1 foot. Despite the conditions, the Australians had been only 3 seconds outside the Barrier record. This was probably too fast, and at Fawley and the finish the times were 7 seconds outside. Nevertheless, these were remarkable times, but even more remarkable was Mercantile's time for the Ladies' Plate of 6min 23sec, a new record and only 6 seconds slower than the Grand time, despite having had to row two rounds on the last day, but conditions had eased when they rowed. The Thames Cup time was 18 seconds slower than Mercantile's.

Britain's best hopes for the Seoul Olympics, Holmes and Redgrave, had been plagued by a rib injury to Holmes and they had to withdraw from the Goblets after two rounds, and also could not compete at Lucerne, where, though the men's heavyweight coxless four were a good second, the only two British winners were the men's and women's lightweight fours. The latter, a squad crew, were stroked by Kate Brownlow of Thames, with another Thames girl, Susan Key, at bow. They were selected for the World Lightweight Championships to be held in Milan in conjunction with the junior World Championships. Unfortunately they were below form in the final and could finish only fifth, China winning their first gold medal.

At the Junior Championships, Tim Foster and Matthew Pinsent won the coxless pairs in impressive style and the coxless four took the bronze medal.

Seoul might have been a problem for political

reasons, but it was the scandal of the disqualification of the Canadian 100-metres sprinter, Ben Johnson, for taking anabolic steroids that ultimately cast a shadow over the Games. Holmes, now fully recovered, and Redgrave tried again to win both the pair-oared events, but again it proved to be too tall an order. They won the coxless pairs, to add to the gold medal they had won in the coxed fours in 1984, but had had too many races by the time they faced the Abbagnales in the coxed pairs final. The Italians again got too far ahead and a new East German pair forced the British pair into third place. If this was a disappointment for the pair, it was still another distinguished Olympics for them.

Both men's fours and the eight finished fourth, the Australian eight finishing fifth, and the best women's performance was sixth in the coxed fours, the last occasion on which this event was to be held, being replaced by coxless fours in 1989. Thames had a representative at Seoul, Sally Andreae. With Alison Gill, she was originally a reserve, but these two were allowed to compete in the double sculls, where they predictably came nowhere and their selection aroused the wrath of Gillian Bond and Caroline Lucas, world lightweight bronze medallists at Milan, who had never been considered for Seoul but who were undoubtedly faster.

At home, the Thames women won the eights silver medal in the National Championships, and they also won the open eights in the Serpentine Regatta, where Redgrave was again the hero in the international match. He won the single sculls and stroked the eight to win the decisive event by thirty-four hundredths of a second. Earlier, the Olympic champions suffered an unexpected reverse in the coxless pairs when Redgrave's rowing pin slipped and they skidded to an ignominious halt. Nobody realised at the time that this anticlimax was to be the last appearance of this distinguished duo. The following year, Holmes became a paid consultant to the French Rowing Federation.

1989 was marred by some acrimonious moments on the domestic front, starting with a controversial Boat Race. For the first time both universities had women coxing, Oxford's Alison Norrish, who had steered the women's Olympic four, being more experienced than Cambridge's American, Leigh Weiss. These two were clashing 25 strokes after the start, but Norrish got the better of a whole series of subsequent clashes and Oxford came home 2½ lengths ahead. Toby Backhouse, the Cambridge five, was at 16 st 11 lb the heaviest man to have rowed in the race. No crew with such a massive weight advantage as Cambridge's – nearly 11 lb a man – had ever previously lost the Boat Race. Norrish was later elected as the first woman President of the OUBC but she had to resign later in the year for academic reasons.

In April, in ideal conditions, Steve Redgrave lowered the Wingfields record he had set the previous year by a further 45 seconds with a time of 20min 16sec, to win the title for the fifth year running. Rorie Henderson, in second place, also beat the 1988 record.

Thames first eight dropped six places in the Head, to finish a lowly thirty-sixth, although they had beaten London by 15 lengths in the Boustead. Sean Bowden, who was receiving a modest stipend to coach, decided to concentrate again on a Britannia four and a Ladies' Plate eight, but neither crew were very fast. The four raced at Ghent and Ratzeburg without success, and recorded only one regatta win.

Henley was celebrating its 150th anniversary and the permitted entry for the Visitors', Britannia and Diamonds had been increased in anticipation of a large entry, which turned out to be a record 480 crews and scullers, nearly a hundred more than the previous best. Of these, 126 were from abroad, forty-one more that the 1980 record. The standard was exceptionally high, and the finest summer for many years had resulted in there being a very slack stream, all the records going except in the Prince Philip, which was equalled. The Hansa Dortmund eight, with only one of their Olympic gold medallists, became the first crew to cover the course in under 6 minutes, recording 5min 58sec when beating Dinamo, USSR, by 3 lengths in the final. A serious mutiny by the ARA heavyweight men's squad, who were unhappy with the organisation of the squad, had led to several men withdrawing. They were later persuaded back into the fold but the eight that rowed in the Grand was a rather hastily assembled crew in Leander colours. Even so, they beat the Hungarian eight and lost a hard semi-final to the West Germans by only ½ length.

Steve Redgrave had found a new partner in Simon Berrisford and this new combination duly won the Goblets, having beaten the perennial Pimenovs by 2½ lengths in the semi-final after being a length down at the Barrier.

The Thames Ladies' Plate eight were stroked again by Steve Austin but he had only two of the previous year's Thames Cup finalists behind him. In the first round they met an experienced but recently formed London eight containing the former Oxford 'mutiny' President, Don Macdonald, and the former UL World bronze medallist and Oxford Blue, Tom Cadoux-Hudson. The evergreen Dan Topolski was at bow. London led by ½ length at the Barrier but Thames had whittled this down to 3 feet by the ¾ Mile. There was still only a canvas in it at the last signal but London's greater experience carried the day and they won a great race by ½ length. London lost to Penn in the next round but the final was fought out by the Nottingham County lightweights and the full Harvard University eight, with sensational results.

Nottingham demolished Harvard, to whom they were conceding 30 lb a man, by 5 lengths and took 10 seconds off the record. They had already unrigged their boat when they were told that Harvard had protested, backed by the FISA President, Thomi Keller, claiming they had been handicapped by a piece of wood jammed in their rudder, and the race was to be re-rowed. This controversial decision was accepted by Nottingham who, two hours later, and to the tumultuous applause of a huge crowd that had stayed on to watch, not only beat Harvard again, this time by ⅔ length, but also took a further 2 seconds off the record.

In the Britannia, the Thames four easily beat an American crew from Baltimore but then lost by 2¾ lengths to a selected crew, Lea, who eventually lost the final to Leander.

Thames had formed a Thames Cup eight late but they beat the Queen's University, Belfast, comfortably in the first round. They were unlucky to meet the ultimate winners, the University of London, the next day. UL broke the Barrier record and equalled the Fawley record, going on to win by 2¾ lengths.

Thames had a strong sculling squad in 1989, and four of them were entered for the Diamonds. Ian Pritchard had retained his Championship of the Dee at Chester, Gavin Reddin had won open events at the Met, Reading and Hereford, and Bill Baker, twenty-fifth in the Scullers Head, had won two senior 2 and a senior 1 event before Henley. These three survived the qualifying round, in which the fourth sculler, Dominic MacDonald, failed. They were unlucky in the draw, however, Reddin going out to the Dutch heavyweight Hans Kelderman, who was to win a World gold medal with the Dutch quad later that year, while Pritchard on the first day, and Baker, who had drawn a bye, on the second, both went down to Bruce Ford, a former winner of the Double Sculls and a bronze medallist with the Canadian 1984 Olympic quad. Kelderman went out in a semi-final to a rising young Czech sculler, Vaclav Chalupa, and Ford to the Polish Olympic finalist, Kajetan Broniewski. The Czech won the final, lowering Sean Drea's 1975 record by 17 seconds.

At Lucerne, Berrisford and Redgrave decided to go only for the coxed pairs but came fourth in a blanket finish in which .08 of a second separated the first four, the Abbagnales finishing third. In the eights, the Leander eight were third and a new coxless pair, John Garrett and Salih Hassan, second. The men's and women's lightweight fours both won again, but the Nottingham eight, embroiled in a selection row with Penny Chuter and tired after their Henley efforts, finished only fifth.

The scandal of the selection for the World Championships was that the Nottingham eight were not selected. They had refused to submit to what they considered unjustified changes and so disqualified themselves, though it was generally felt that the Henley crew should have been sent to Bled. A new crew was hastily assembled but could finish only sixth.

Redgrave insisted on going for both the pairs again, but failed to win either, taking a silver medal in the coxless pairs behind an outstanding East German pair, but fifth place in the coxed event was a considerable disappointment. However, the British team, having overcome their earlier objections, distinguished themselves. A new young eight based on recent junior medallists produced a spirited final burst to snatch the bronze medal from the United States, while the coxed four only just failed to take a silver. The men's lightweight coxless four also won bronze, while the women's lightweight four, again stroked by Kate Brownlow with Sue Key at bow, took the silver medal after being passed by China in the closing stages.

Earlier, the juniors had continued their outstanding run in their World Championships at Szeged, Hungary, the coxless four winning the third gold medal in as many years. The eight took the bronze medal and a pair produced the best result so far from the girls' squad, narrowly missing third place.

On the domestic front, Thames women had done exceptionally well, the first eight dominating the home regattas. Two Thames eights contested the final of the Club Eights at the Women's Henley. The first eight won at Ghent on both days and took the gold medal in the National Championships, where Lucy Baird and Caroline Christie won the coxless pairs, and Baird, with Lesley Baguely replacing the injured Christie, easily won the Home Countries International pairs. The women's double won a silver at the National Championships, and once again the Victor Ludorum came to the Club. The first eight finished the season with a win on the Serpentine, and the women's intermediate group had seven wins, progressing from senior 3 to open eights by the end of the season.

The rowing world was shocked by the unexpected death, soon after the World Championships, of Thomi Keller, the outstanding and popular President of FISA. He had been intending to resign at the end of the following year, and his successor, Denis Oswald, had already been elected to take over.

In December, Dick Phelps died at the age of 92. The funeral cortège of this much loved riverside character passed the boathouses at Putney, led by the Bargemasters of the Watermen's and Fishmongers' Companies, and flanked by past Doggett's winners in their scarlet livery. Alan Burrough, the Club President, together with other members of the Club and neighbouring clubs, followed the cortège to the church by Putney Bridge, which was filled to capacity. Dick had lived to see his grandson win a bronze medal, of which he was very proud, in the eight in the World Championships at Bled.

There was a change in the ARA's international rowing structure in 1990. A new office of international performance director, assisted by an international manager, replaced Penny Chuter's old post. Chuter was not appointed to either of the new posts, Bruce Grainger, after a highly successful period in charge of the junior squads, taking over as performance director, the manager's job going to Brian Armstrong, who had already managed several international teams. Chuter remained with the ARA as its principal national coach.

This year it was Oxford's turn to produce a massive crew for the Boat Race, with 17st 5lb Christopher Heathcote becoming the heaviest man in the history of the race. For the first time the two crews met before the race, Oxford beating Cambridge by 16 seconds to win the Reading Head, where the Oxford reserves also finished in front of Cambridge. Cambridge later rowed in the Tideway Head, finishing eighth. Oxford duly won the Boat Race once again, but their over-confidence led to a bad row as Cambridge harried them all the way and the Dark Blues looked the more exhausted at the finish.

Rorie Henderson won the Scullers Head and followed this up by ending a surprisingly listless Redgrave's five-year reign in the Wingfields.

Thames had a good season, the men recording their best total of regatta wins for some years. The women distinguished themselves by winning the fiftieth Women's Head in front of the ARA lightweights, and the eight won two gold medals at Ghent. The second eight, many of whom started the season as novices, won the Club Eights at the Women's Henley, though the first eight were beaten in the final of the open eights by the ARA heavyweights, which contained some Thames members.

Henley was something of an anticlimax after the previous year's special atmosphere. The rules had been changed once again and the Ladies' reverted to being a student event, although this proved a failure and the Stewards changed the Ladies' back to an open event for 1991. There was a new Henley Prize for lesser student crews and schools. The Thames Cup became primarily a club event once again and the Wyfold and Britannia became similar events for fours.

The Grand was won again by Hansa Dortmund, with four of their 1989 World medallists. They beat the young ARA eight without difficulty. The ARA squad turned out in force but in small boats, in which they had had a remarkably successful run on the Continent before Henley. Illness forced the coxed four to withdraw and once again Redgrave had to scratch from the Goblets after two rounds when an injury to Berrisford's back, sustained in the winter in head-on collision with a sculler, proved too much. The Goblets were won by the Austrian World bronze medallists, Karl Sinzinger and Hermann Bauer, who beat Martin Cross and Tim Foster by 1 foot in the final.

Under the new rules, Nottingham County were unable to defend the Ladies', Harvard easily beating the University of London in the final. Nottingham, moving into the Thames Cup, were far too good for their opponents, beating the Danish lightweights, with seven 1989 World silver medallists, by 2½ lengths in a semi-final and the junior Harvard crew by 2 lengths in the final.

Thames again entered two Thames Cup eights, the B crew, more experienced than fit, being well beaten by Vesta on the first day, but the A crew survived a hard race with Royal Chester before succumbing to the Thames Tradesmen. The Wyfold four also survived only one heat, but the main Thames hopes lay with the Britannia four, a selected crew. They also beat a Royal Chester crew but then went out to University College, Galway who, though not a selected crew, went on to beat Cappoquin in an all-Irish final.

Gavin Reddin, who was also in the Thames Cup A crew, and Ian Pritchard both failed to qualify for the Diamonds and it was altogether a less successful Henley for the Club.

The Thames four went to Lucerne but were well below this class of rowing. The ARA put their best men, including Redgrave, into an eight and won the event narrowly from Canada and East Germany, the West Germans being absent. The women's lightweight four, still with the two Thames girls, won their event again, but the Nottingham eight, having their seventh race in ten days, had to concede first place to the Italians.

Once again, the Under-23s in the Match des Seniors and the juniors pulled in the medals. A Nottingham lightweight four and the women's double scullers, Suzanne Kirk and Adrienne Grimsditch, were easy winners in the Match in Austria, and the London University eight and coxless four won bronze medals. The junior men's coxless four won another gold medal, a second one for Gregory Searle, whose brother Jonathan had also won this event in 1987. Gregory Searle later made the record books by being the first oarsman to be selected for the senior team while still a junior. He joined his brother in the eight for the World Championships in Tasmania. The juniors also took a silver medal in the eights and a bronze in the coxed fours. A Thames junior, Domenyk Honey, sculled in the quad which won the small final to take seventh place.

In the National Championships, the Thames women took the silver medal in the coxed fours and some individuals also won medals in squad or composite crews, but an encouraging success was a gold medal for the junior men in the coxed pairs. Nottingham crews and scullers equalled their 1989 record, taking seven titles, and the Nottingham County lightweight eight, unfortunate not to have been selected for the World Championships in 1989, were finally selected for the 1990 Championships in Tasmania.

The World Championships team was large but uneven in quality. The Thames men at last had a representative, Bill Baker being selected for the lightweight quad. Besides Kate Brownlow and Sue Key in the women's lightweight four, Miriam Batten was chosen for the women's openweight coxless four. However, the regatta at Lake Barrington proved disappointing for Britain after the previous year's good results at Bled. Redgrave was forced to take another partner in the coxless pairs when Berrisford's injury did not clear up, and though Matthew Pinsent was certainly a strong replacement, Redgrave was not at his best and the new combination could take only a bronze medal. The pair did not double up and the only other medal for Britain, also a bronze, came to the Nottingham lightweight eight. Whereas in 1989 Britain had narrowly made several medal places, in 1990 they missed several equally narrowly, the men's coxless four finishing fourth for the fourth year in succession. They were squeezed out in the last few strokes, as were the women's lightweight four, who missed the bronze by centimetres. The men's coxed four and the eight also took close fourth places in a frustrating championship for Britain. A major cause for concern was the total failure of the British scullers.

Following the unification of the two Germanies a few weeks earlier, this was the last regatta in which the East Germans competed as a separate federation and after the final of the men's eights, in which they finished third, they and the West Germans, who retained their title, mixed their crews and paddled away together as a symbolic gesture to a new era.

Thames also entered a new era by electing a woman Captain of the Club for the first time. Pauline Rayner, who had been the Women's Captain a few years earlier, was accorded this honour in the autumn. With plenty of keen and enthusiastic men and women available to row, it is not unreasonable to end this history on an optimistic note. If these pages can help to inspire future generations of Thames men and women by recalling the spirit of the giants of earlier years, they will have served their purpose.

Postscript

Comparing the restricted world within which the Victorian oarsmen competed, and its limited horizons and simple ideals, with the neo-professional, internationally orientated arena in which today's top rowing men and women find themselves, it is not difficult to lament the loss of some of the old values.

Club rowing in recent years has changed out of all recognition. Despite a few forays abroad in the 19th century by such stalwarts as Woodgate, and London's unhappy excursion to the Philadelphia Centennial, as well as private matches like the Thames race with Hillsdale, international rowing had little impact on the pattern of English rowing until the beginning of this century. It was not until the Belgians threw down the gauntlet at Henley in the early 1900s that English oarsmen began to realise that there was a world beyond theirs about which they knew next to nothing. The success of the home crews in the 1908 Olympic Regatta at Henley no doubt encouraged rowing enthusiasts in this country to believe that all was well in the cradle of rowing, but from then on it began to dawn on them that standards abroad were often higher than those in England.

Organised rowing, with a few exceptions, began and developed earlier in Britain than on the continent. In the early days it centred on a few fixed points such as the public schools, Oxford and Cambridge, the Boat Race, and Henley, with a secondary focus on the clubs and certain regattas. These were the perimeters of the sport in Piggy Eyre's days and they remained so for the vast majority of British oarsmen until after the Second World War. For Piggy's contemporaries, the main topics of interest were such vexed questions as the amateur-professional definition, fixed pins versus swivels; later, Orthodoxy versus Fairbairnism and similar subjects that were aired at length in the sporting journals of the time, such as *The Field* and *Bell's Life*. It was a comfortable world in which the gentlemen amateurs could compete within a code of conduct which they had themselves set up and which they all understood. They asked for nothing more.

Despite an increasing awareness of a bigger world after the First World War, the British season remained primarily a domestic one until well after the Second World War. Even as late as the 1950s, when I was rowing, the season for top crews was closer to that of the Victorian era than it is to today's. True, we trained through the winter and took part in Head of the River races which were unknown to the Victorians. We made forays to minor Continental regattas such as Ostend, but for a Thames first eight in my day the programme was the Grand, often with a Stewards' four doubling up, at Reading, Marlow, and Henley, then a post-Henley circuit which included the Met, Bedford and Molesey. Most of the best crews would appear at Marlow, and the Met was still an important Tideway event.

The Olympic Games and the Empire Games, the latter transforming themselves into the Commonwealth Games in keeping with the country's reduced circumstances from 1945, were an occasional international target for club crews, often successfully reached, and by the 1950s, before the influx of Eastern bloc crews onto the international scene, club crews were still being selected for the European championships and the Olympics.

All that began to change in the 1960s, which was probably one of the most critical decades in the history of rowing. The Henley Grand was put out of reach for club crews with the appearance of national squad crews from the USSR and East

Germany. The British answer, the mushroom-like growth of more and more national squads in the 1970s, and the consequent loss to the clubs of many top oarsmen, though an effective force to resist the foreign challenge, left the clubs even further out of touch. Finally, the closing of international selection to all but registered squad members took away one of the main incentives for clubs to aim higher.

Rowing in Britain became two-tiered, with squad crews racing mainly in international regattas abroad and the clubs battling among themselves at domestic regattas of an inevitably reduced standard. The top British crews are now seldom seen at home and on some occasions they do not even compete at Henley. If the latter pages of this history are concerned more with international rowing than with the domestic scene, it is because that is the way the sport has moved.

There can be no return to the old days, nor should there be. Of course, there is still an active domestic programme in which Thames and other well-established old clubs such as London, Kingston and Molesey are prominent, but there can be no denying that the larger clubs have suffered more from the demands of the national squads than have the smaller ones and this has led to a general levelling out of standards.

However, Thames continues to thrive with up to a hundred oarsmen and women now active each season. Whatever the disadvantages of rowing on the Tideway may be, they are more than outweighed by the advantages. The long reaches of the river to Richmond and Teddington and down to Westminster have helped to form the character of Thames crews from the Club's earliest days, and if, when the river is at its worst, with sleet or rain and gales, together with driftwood and flotsam at high tide, one sometimes feels like the madman who hit his head against the wall because it was so nice when he stopped, it is memories of long paddles and rows on calm autumn or spring days that remain with me. This is when the oarsman truly hears the boat sing.

One of my favourite paintings by Paul Gauguin is entitled *Where do we come from? What are we? Where are we going?* I hope these pages will, in the context of Thames Rowing Club, have answered the first two questions. The third can be answered only by the present generation of Thames men and women. They are the custodians of 130 years of tradition, and it is upon them that the Club's future depends.

Maps

The maps on the following pages depict the changes that have occurred both at Henley and on the Championship course from Putney to Mortlake.

The maps of the Tideway course show the landmarks in the second half of the 19th century, many of which have given way to later developments. For example, the Soap Works were on the present site of Harrods Wharf, and while the Crabtree Inn still exists, Dorset Villa has long since disappeared. Craven Cottage is still remembered in the name of the Fulham football ground. The Thames RC boathouse had not been built at the time of the earlier map and is now immediately up river of the Putney boathouses. Chiswick bridge was not completed until the 1930s.

The Henley map shows the 'Old' course, in use until 1885 and the 'New' course in use until 1922. A shorter course, beginning near the top of Temple Island but with the start switched to the Berks side, was used in 1923. The present course, starting at the bottom of the Island, has been in use since 1924.

Map A

Map of the Championship course on the Tideway from Putney to Mortlake in 1870.

Map B

Map of the Championship course today.

Map C

Map showing the 'Old' and 'New' courses at Henley Royal Regatta. The present course is not shown.

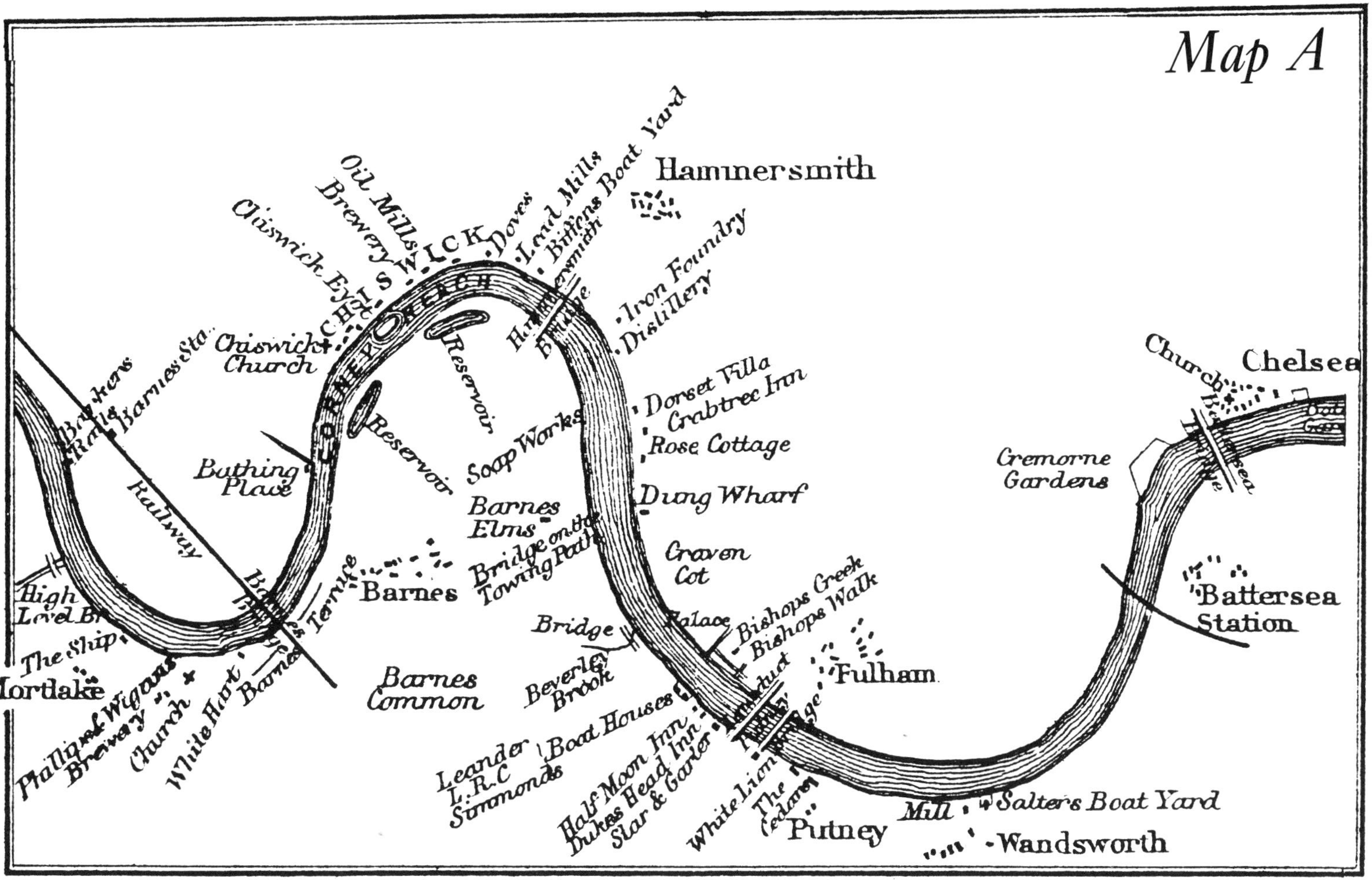
Map A
Hammersmith
Chelsea
Church
Cremorne Gardens
Battersea Station
Fulham
Putney
Wandsworth
Mill
Salters Boat Yard
Oil Mills
Brewery
Chiswick Eyot
CHISWICK
CORNEY REACH
Chiswick Church
Doves
Lead Mills
Biffens Boat Yard
Iron Foundry
Distillery
Dorset Villa
Crabtree Inn
Rose Cottage
Dung Wharf
Craven Cot
Soap Works
Reservoir
Reservoir
Bathing Place
Barnes Elms
Bridge on the Towing Path
Barnes
Barnes Common
Barnes Terrace
Railway
Barnes Sta.
Bridge
Beverley Brook
Palace
Bishops Creek
Bishops Walk
Boat Houses
Leander
L.R.C
Simmonds
Half Moon Inn
Dukes Head Inn
Star & Garter
White Lion
The Cedars
High Level Br.
The Ship
Mortlake
Phillips Brewery
Church
White Hart

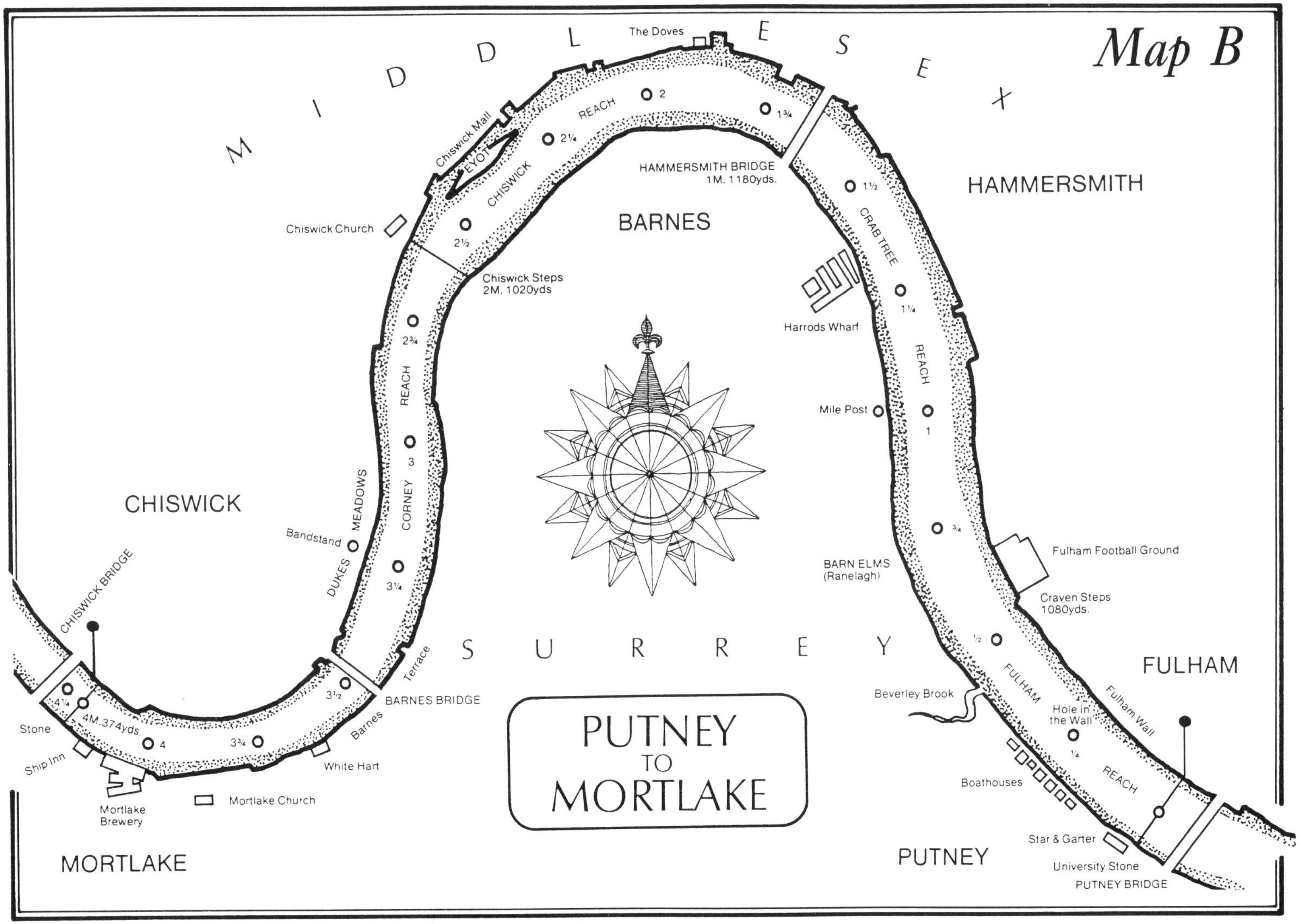

Map B
MIDDLESEX
SURREY
PUTNEY TO MORTLAKE
HAMMERSMITH
BARNES
CHISWICK
FULHAM
PUTNEY
MORTLAKE
The Doves
Chiswick Mall
EYOT
CHISWICK REACH
Chiswick Church
Chiswick Steps
2M. 1020yds
HAMMERSMITH BRIDGE
1M. 1180yds.
CRAB TREE REACH
Harrods Wharf
Mile Post
BARN ELMS
(Ranelagh)
Fulham Football Ground
Craven Steps
1080yds.
FULHAM REACH
Fulham Wall
Hole in the Wall
Beverley Brook
Boathouses
Star & Garter
University Stone
PUTNEY BRIDGE
CORNEY REACH
DUKES MEADOWS
Bandstand
Terrace
BARNES BRIDGE
Barnes
White Hart
Mortlake Church
Mortlake Brewery
CHISWICK BRIDGE
4M. 374yds.
Stone
Ship Inn
¼
½
¾
1
1¼
1½
1¾
2
2¼
2½
2¾
3
3¼
3½
3¾
4
4¼

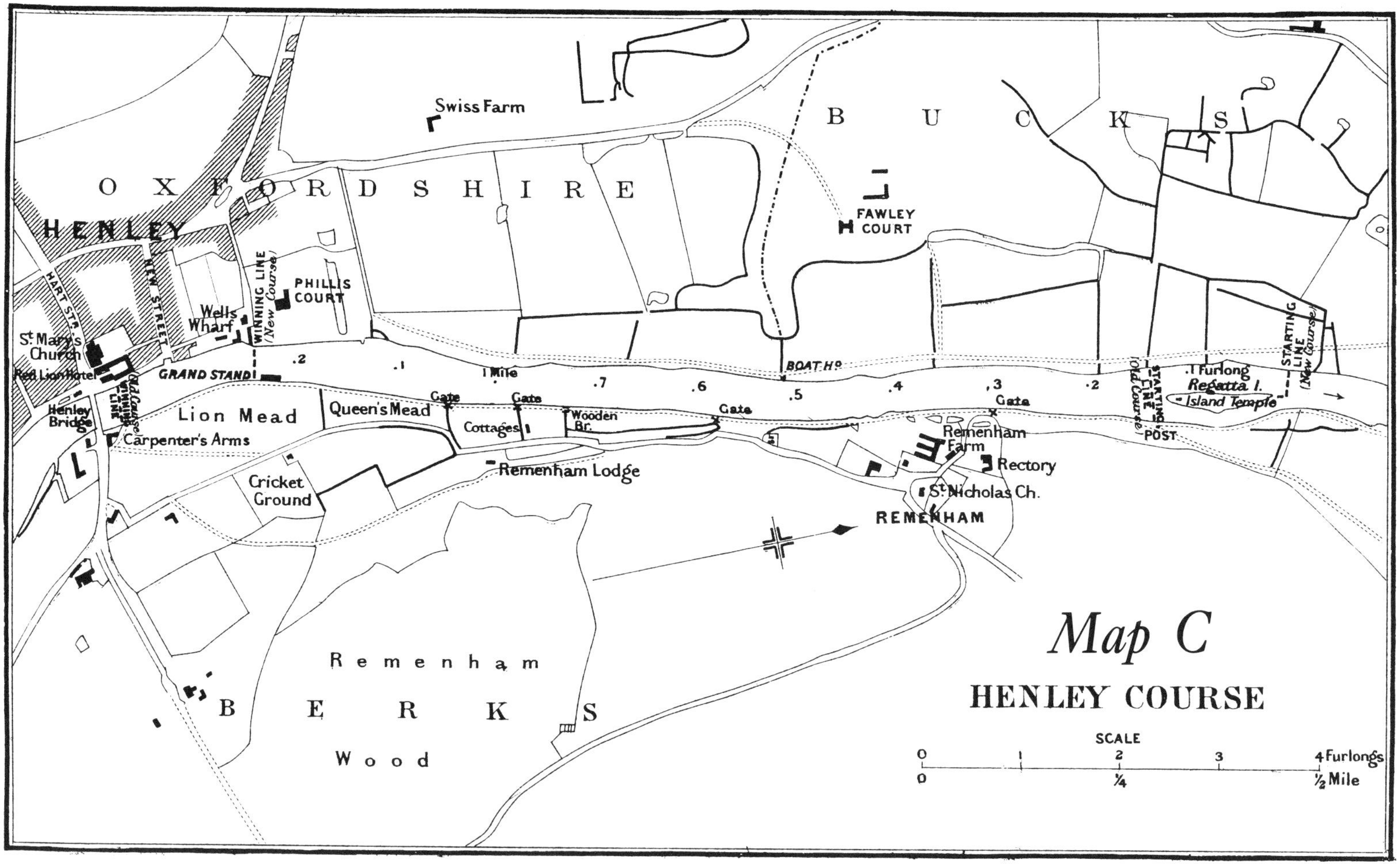
Map C
HENLEY COURSE
SCALE
0 1 2 3 4 Furlongs
0 ¼ ½ Mile
O X F O R D S H I R E
B U C K S
B E R K S
HENLEY
Swiss Farm
FAWLEY COURT
PHILLIS COURT
Wells Wharf
WINNING LINE (New Course)
HART STR.
NEW STREET
St. Mary's Church
Red Lion Hotel
GRAND STAND
(Old Course) WINNING LINE
Henley Bridge
Lion Mead
Queen's Mead
Carpenter's Arms
Cottages
Wooden Br.
Gate
1 Mile
BOAT Ho
Cricket Ground
Remenham Lodge
Remenham Farm
Rectory
St. Nicholas Ch.
REMENHAM
Remenham Wood
STARTING LINE (Old Course)
POST
1 Furlong
Regatta I.
Island Temple
STARTING LINE (New Course)
.2
.1
.7
.6
.5
.4
.3
.2

PART FOUR

Thames Rowing Club Facts and Figures

Appendix 1 Presidents, Vice-Presidents, Chairmen, Captains: 1860–1991

Presidents

1870–71	Colonel Beresford, MP
1911–67	The Earl of Iveagh, KG, CB, CMG, DL, FRS
1968–69	S. Ian Fairbairn
1969–70	H.E. Greenwood
1970–77	J. Beresford Jnr, CBE
1978–	A. Burrough, CBE

Vice-Presidents

1911–12	W.H. Eyre
1929–39	W.H. Eyre
1911–14	G.H. Vize
1911–15	F.G. Naumann
1913–33	S.D. Muttlebury
1914–34	S.H. Gollan
1921–35	J.C. Gardner
1922–59	J. Beresford Snr
1925–38	S. Fairbairn
1927–68	S. Ian Fairbairn
1936–76	J.C. Badcock
1936–77	J. Beresford Jnr, CBE
1937–69	H.E. Greenwood
1943–62	G.C. Killick
1943–73	K. Vernon, MM
1949–77	J.H. Page, OBE
1961–72	W.S. Douglas
1911–22	R.H. Forster
1963–73	H.M. Lane
1964–	J.H.M. Ward
1962–82	K.A. Williams
1969–78	A. Burrough, CBE
1969–	P.C. Kirkpatrick
1969–71	R.C. Morris
1971–84	J.L. Tann
1973–77	T.H. Tyler
1975–	R.S. Hollom
1976–	Lord Headley
1976–	H.W. Rushmere
1976–	R.A.F. Macmillan
1978–	G.G.H. Page
1978–	A.M.St L. Ramsay-Murray
1982–	J.F. Levy
1982–	J.A. Stephenson

Chairmen

1973–76	K.A. Williams
1977	J.A. Stephenson
1978–81	A.R. Reddin
1982–83	M.J. Walker
1984	W.L. Ross
1985–	A.R. Reddin

Captains

1860–63	F.W. Catty
1864–66	T. Oswin
1867–68	T.G. Radmall
1869–70	J.E. Catty
1871	W.H. Eyre
1872–74	J.E. Catty
1875–81	J. Hastie
1882	F. Canton
1883–86	E.C. Otter
1887	J.A. Drake-Smith
1888	A.M. Hutchinson
1889	J.A. Drake-Smith
1890	B.W. Looker
1891	A.M. Hutchinson
1892–93	F.E.C. Clark
1894–95	S.D. Muttlebury
1896–97	R.H. Forster
1898	T. Young
1899	R.H. Forster
1900–02	A.F. Johnstone
1903–07	R.H. Forster
1908	R.H. Forster & S.C. Smith
1909	R.H. Forster & H. Messom
1910	R.H. Forster
1911	H.C. Irwin
1912–13	H.E. Greenwood
1914	J. Beresford Snr
1919–26	S. Fairbairn
1926–27	J. Beresford Snr
1928–29	J. Beresford Jnr
1930–32	K. Vernon
1933	S. Ian Fairbairn
1934–36	J.H. Page
1937–38	Hon C.R. Allanson-Winn
1939–40	J.H. Burrough
1946–47	A. Burrough
1948–49	J.H. Page
1950	P.C. Kirkpatrick
1951	H.W. Rushmere
1952	R.H.H. Symonds
1953	R.R. Swatton
1954	R.A.F. Macmillan
1955–56	R.C. Morris
1957	K.A. Williams
1958	A.C. Hancox
1959–61	G.G.H. Page
1962	J.T. Shaw
1963	J.F.C. Badcock
1964–65	S.F.A. Miskin
1966	J.A. Stephenson
1967	G.S. Dear
1968	G.G.H. Page
1969	A.M.St L. Ramsay-Murray
1970	A.R. Reddin
1971	D.L. Cruttenden
1972	A. Hawes
1973–74	J.F. Levy
1975	W.H. Needham & J. Mackerrell
1976	A.G. Bingham
1977	D.G. Shove & R.V. O'Farrell
1978–79	R.V. O'Farrell
1980	R.H. Willett
1981	W.L. Ross
1982	M.J. Walker
1983	A. Hill
1984–85	T.J.S. Levy
1986	G.P.R. Reddin
1987	G.J. Elkington
1988–89	S.L. Jones
1990	S.R. Crump
1991	Mrs P. Rayner

Appendix 2 Representative Crews

1912 Olympic Games, Stockholm
Coxed Fours – silver medal
J. Beresford Snr (bow); K. Vernon;
C.G. Rought; H.B. Logan (stroke);
G. Carr (cox)

1920 Olympic Games, Antwerp
Single Sculls – silver medal
J. Beresford Jnr

1924 Olympic Games, Paris
Single Sculls – gold medal
J. Beresford Jnr

Eights – 4th
G.C. Chandler (bow); R.G. Bare;
H.W. Dulley; H.L. Morphy; H.C. Debenham;
C.H. Rew; A.F. Long; S.I. Fairbairn (stroke);
J.S. Godwin (cox)

1928 Olympic Games, Amsterdam
Eights – silver medal
H.E. West (bow); J. Beresford Jnr;
G.C. Killick; H.M. Lane; D.H.L. Gollan;
J.C. Badcock; G.O. Nickalls; J. Hamilton
(stroke); A.L. Sulley (cox)

1930 British Empire Games, Ontario
Single Sculls – silver medal
J. Beresford Jnr

1932 Olympic Games, Los Angeles
Coxless Fours – gold medal
R.D. George (bow); J. Beresford Jnr;
H.R.A. Edwards; J.C. Badcock (stroke)

Single Sculls – 4th
L.F. Southwood

1936 Olympic Games, Berlin
Double Sculls – gold medal
J. Beresford Jnr (bow); L.F. Southwood
(stroke)

1947 European Championships, Lucerne
Coxless Fours – 5th
J.P. Dizer (bow); J.A. Wilmot;
H.W. Rushmere; P.C. Kirkpatrick (stroke)

Coxless Pairs – 5th
R.C. Morris (bow); A. Burrough (stroke)

1948 Olympic Games, Henley
Coxless Fours
A.S.F. Butcher (bow); T.H. Christie;
H.W. Rushmere; P.C. Kirkpatrick (stroke)

Coxed Pairs
H.B. James (bow); M.B. Scott (stroke);
D.S. Walker (cox)

1952 Olympic Games, Helsinki
Coxed Fours – 4th
P.A. de Giles (bow); G.C. Fisk;
R.A.F. Macmillan; P.M.O. Massey (stroke);
L.K. Guest (cox)

1954 British Empire and Commonwealth Games, Vancouver
Eights – silver medal
G.G.H. Page (bow); J. Pope; M.G.C. Savage;
A.R. Watson; A.R. Davidson;
R.A.F. Macmillan; M. Legg; J.N. Eldeen
(stroke); D.R. Glynne-Jones (cox)

Coxed Fours – bronze medal
G.G.H. Page (bow); R.A.F. Macmillan;
A.R. Davidson; M. Legg (stroke);
D.R. Glynne-Jones (cox)

1955 European Championships, Ghent
Eights
M. Legg (bow); R.H. Nicholls; A.R. Watson;
C.F. Porter; R.A.F. Macmillan; W.H. Rand;
A.R. Davidson; J.M. Beresford (stroke);
D.R. Glynne-Jones (cox)

1958 British Empire and Commonwealth Games, Padarn
Eights – bronze medal
R.J. Workman (bow); J.P.M. Thomson; J.A. Stephenson; H.A. Wober; A.C. Hancox; J.F. Badcock; D.R. Mount; D.S.S. Elliott (stroke); R.L. Penney (cox)

1959 European Championships, Macon
Eights
D.R. Mount (bow); W.M. Nisbet; B.S. Tanner; J.A. Stephenson; R.D.F. Anderson; J.F.C. Badcock; W.J. Griffith; M.S. Atkins (stroke); R.L. Penney (cox)

1961 European Championships, Prague
Coxless fours
M.R. Woolner (bow); F.J. Lambert; J.A. Stephenson; J.F.C. Badcock (stroke)

1981 World Championships, Munich
Women's Coxed Fours
S.L. Hunter–Jones (bow); C.F. Casey; B.R. Carroll; J.M. Cross (stroke); S. Brown (cox)

Appendix 3 International Medal Winners

This includes those who won medals when not rowing for the Club
but who rowed regularly with the Club at some stage in their rowing careers

OG = Olympic Games
CG = Commonwealth Games or Empire Games
EC = European Championships
WC = World Championships
8+ = Eights
4+ = Coxed Fours
4− = Coxless Fours
2− = Coxless Pairs
2× = Double Sculls
1× = Single Sculls
Lwt = Lightweight
W = Women

MEN

St G. Ashe	1900 OG 1×: bronze
J.C. Badcock	1928 OG 8+: silver
	1932 OG 4−: gold
J.F.C. Badcock	1958 CG 8+: bronze
J. Beresford Snr	1912 OG 4+: silver
J. Beresford Jnr	1920 OG 1×: silver
	1924 OG 1×: gold
	1928 OG 8+: silver
	1930 CG 1×: silver
	1932 OG 4−: gold
	1936 OG 2×: gold
J.M. Beresford	1954 EC 4−: silver
	1958 CG 4+: gold
J.H. Burrough	1938 CG 8+: gold
G. Carr	1912 OG 4+: silver
T.H. Christie	1954 CG 2−: silver
A.R. Davidson	1954 CG 8+: silver
J.G. Dearlove	1948 OG 8+: silver
	1950 CG 8+: bronze
J.N. Eldeen	1954 CG 8+: silver
D.S.S. Elliott	1958 CG 8+: bronze
R.D. George	1932 OG 4−: gold
P.A. de Giles	1950 CG 8+: bronze
D.R. Glynne-Jones	1954 CG 8+: silver
	1954 CG 4+: bronze
D.H.L. Gollan	1928 OG 8+: silver
J. Hamilton	1928 OG 8+: silver
A.C. Hancox	1958 CG 8+: bronze
J.J. James	1964 OG 4−: silver
G.C. Killick	1928 OG 8+: silver
P.C. Kirkpatrick	1950 CG 8+: bronze
H.M. Lane	1928 OG 8+: silver
M. Legg	1954 CG 8+: silver
	1954 CG 4+: bronze
H.B. Logan	1912 OG 4+: silver
R.A.F. Macmillan	1954 CG 8+: silver
	1954 CG 4+: bronze
P.M.O. Massey	1948 OG 8+: silver
M.R. McGowan	1980 OG 8+: silver
	1981 WC 8+: silver
D.R. Mount	1958 CG 8+: bronze
G.O. Nickalls	1928 OG 8+: silver
G.G.H. Page	1954 CG 8+: silver
	1954 CG 4+: bronze
R.C. Phelps	1989 WC 8+: bronze
J. Pope	1954 CG 8+: silver
C.F. Porter	1953 EC 4−: bronze
	1954 EC 4−: silver
	1958 CG 4+: gold
	1962 CG 8+: bronze
	1962 CG 4+: bronze
J.M. Pritchard	1980 OG 8+: silver
	1981 WC 8+: silver
S.C. Rand	1954 CG 1×: silver

W.H. Rand	1954 EC 4−: silver	L.F. Southwood	1936 OG 2×: gold
N.S. Read	1975 WC Lwt8+: bronze	J.A. Stephenson	1958 CG 8+: bronze
	1976 WC Lwt8+: silver	A.J.H. Stocking	1975 WC Lwt8+: bronze
	1977 WC Lwt8+: gold	A.L. Sulley	1928 OG 8+: silver
	1978 WC Lwt8+: gold	J.P.M. Thomson	1958 CG 8+: bronze
	1980 WC Lwt8+: gold	K. Vernon	1912 OG 4+: silver
G.C. Richardson	1948 OG 8+: silver	A.R. Watson	1954 CG 8+: silver
C.G. Rought	1912 OG 4+: silver	H.E. West	1928 OG 8+: silver
H.W. Rushmere	1950 CG 8+: bronze	H.A. Wober	1958 CG 8+: bronze
M.G.C. Savage	1954 CG 8+: silver	R.J. Workman	1958 CG 8+: bronze

WOMEN

K.D. Brownlow	1989 WC WLwt4−: silver	S.R. Key	1989 WC WLwt4−: silver

Appendix 4 Henley Crews: 1870–1990

GRAND CHALLENGE CUP

1874 J. Howell 10.8 (bow); A.C. Radmall 10.5; J. Maycock 10.12; C. Russell 10.9; J. Hastie 11.6; W. Page 11.6; W.H. Eyre 10.7; W.L. Slater 11.5 (stroke); E.A. Safford 7.7 (cox). Av: 10.12½
Heat: 1 TRC 2 Jesus College, Cambridge. ½ length, 8m 41s
Final: 1 London RC, 2 Eton College, 3 TRC. ⅔ length, 7m 41s

1875 J. Howell 10.13 (bow); A.C. Radmall 10.5; G.C. Gordon 11.5; C.C. Cream 11.10; W. Page 11.6; W.H. Eyre 11.0; J. Hastie 11.7 (stroke); E.A. Safford 8.0 (cox). Av: 11.3¼
Heat: 1 Leander Club (winners) 2 TRC 3 London RC. 1 length, 7m 30s

1876 R.H. Labat 10.4 (bow); J. Howell 10.11; G.C. Gordon 11.4; C.C. Cream 11.11; W.L. Slater 12.3; J.A.M. Robertson 11.5; W.H. Eyre 10.12; J. Hastie 11.5 (stroke); E.A. Safford 8.0 (cox). Av: 11.3¼
Heat: 1 TRC 2 London RC. Easily, 7m 20s
Final: 1 TRC 2 Jesus College, Cambridge 3 University and Brasenose Colleges, Oxford. 1 length, 7m 26s

1877 W.B. Giles 10.7 (bow); F. Canton 10.11; J. Howell 11.2; W. Page 11.7; W.L. Slater 11.8; J.A.M. Robertson 11.2; W.H. Eyre 10.12; J. Hastie 11.3 (stroke); E.A. Safford 8.0 (cox). Av: 11.1¼
Heat: 1 TRC 2 1st Btn, Grenadier Guards. 1½ lengths, 8m 2½s
Final: 1 London RC 2 TRC. 1¼ lengths, 8m 2½s

1878 J.C. Sutherland 10.7 (bow); J.G. Jones 10.5; E.C. Otter 11.0; B.J. Angle 11.3; C.H. Scales 11.9; W. Nottebohm 10.7; W.H. Eyre 11.0; J. Hastie 11.8 (stroke); E.A. Safford 7.7 (cox). Av: 10.13½
Heat: 1 TRC 2 Kingston RC. 1½ lengths, 7m 38s
Final: 1 TRC 2 Jesus College, Cambridge. 2 lengths, 7m 42s

1879 J.C. Sutherland 10.6 (bow); J.G. Jones 10.5; E.C. Otter 10.12; W. Nottebohm 10.12; W.A. Jenkin 11.7; F. Canton 11.0; W.H. Eyre 10.11; J. Hastie 11.7 (stroke); E.A. Safford 7.12 (cox). Av: 10.12½
Heat: 1 Kingston RC 2 TRC. 2 lengths, 8m 39s

1880 J.C. Sutherland 12.7 (bow); F. Fenner 10.10; W.H. Eyre 11.0; W. Nottebohm 10.11; W.A. Jenkin 11.11; D.E. Brown 12.0; F. Canton 11.0; J. Hastie 11.8 (stroke); E.A. Safford 8.0 (cox). Av: 11.2¼
Heat: 1 Leander Club (winners) 2 TRC 3 Jesus College, Cambridge. 2 lengths, 7m 6s

1881 J.C. Sutherland 10.10 (bow); W. Nottebohm 11.0; W.H. Eyre 10.7; E.D. Johnson 11.5; W.A. Jenkin 11.9; H.J. Rust 12.0; F. Canton 11.0; J. Hastie 11.6 (stroke); E.A. Safford 8.0 (cox). Av: 11.2¾
Heat: 1 London RC (winners) 2 TRC 3 Kingston RC. 1½ lengths, 7m 49s

1882 J.C. Sutherland 10.10 (bow); W. Nottebohm 11.0; H.B. Tween 10.4; F. Canton 10.10; H.J. Rust 12.0; G. Smith 11.9; D.E. Brown 12.6; J. Hastie 11.13 (stroke); E.A. Safford 8.2 (cox). Av: 11.4¾
Heat: TRC rowed over.
Final: 1 Exeter College, Oxford 2 TRC. 5 lengths, 8m 11s

Grand Challenge Cup

1883 C. Dangerfield 10.2 (bow); J.A. Drake-Smith 10.5; H.J. Rust 12.2; W. Liddle 11.13; E.C. Otter 12.4; W. Nottebohm 11.5; H.B. Tween 10.5; J. Hastie 11.9 (stroke); E.A. Safford 8.0 (cox). Av: 11.3¾
Heat: 1 Exeter College, Oxford 2 TRC 3 Kingston RC. 3 lengths, 8m 14s

1884 B.E. Cole 10.10 (bow); G.H. Eyre 11.1; G. Smith 11.6; A.M. Hutchinson 11.7; S. Fairbairn 13.4; J. Hastie 11.11; H.J. Rust 11.13; J.A. Drake-Smith 10.5 (stroke); E.A. Safford 8.1 (cox). Av: 11.7¼
Heat: 1 London RC (winners) 2 TRC 3 Royal Chester RC. 1 length, 7m 20s

1885 B.W. Looker 10.6 (bow); B.E. Cole 10.10; W. Nottebohm 11.9; P.S.G. Propert 11.9; W. Liddle 12.6; J. Hastie 12.3; H.J. Rust 12.3; J.A. Drake-Smith 10.8 (stroke); E.A. Safford 8.1 (cox). Av: 11.6¾
Heat: 1 Jesus College, Cambridge (winners) 2 TRC 3 Kingston RC. 2 lengths, 7m 24s

1886 B.W. Looker 11.0 (bow); B.E. Cole 10.10; H.B. Tween 10.9; P.S.G. Propert 12.0; H.J. Rust 12.10; A.M. Hutchinson 11.10; R.H. Coke 12.3; J.A. Drake-Smith 10.8 (stroke); E.A. Safford 8.1 (cox). Av: 11.7¼
Heat: 1 Trinity Hall, Cambridge (winners) 2 TRC. 1 length, 7m 3s

1887 C.W. Hughes 9.13 (bow); S.M. Cooke 11.1; B.W. Looker 10.13; A.S. Falconer 11.13; F.E.C. Clark 12.4; A.M. Hutchinson 12.2; S. Fairbairn 13.7; J.A. Drake-Smith 10.6 (stroke); E.A. Safford 8.1 (cox). Av: 11.7¼
Heat: 1 TRC 2 Oxford Etonian Club. ⅓ length, 6m 56s
Final: 1 Trinity Hall, Cambridge 2 TRC. 4 feet, 6m 56s

1888 B.W. Looker 11.0 (bow); J.W. Fogg-Elliot 11.1; P.S.G. Propert 12.0; A.S. Falconer 12.6; W. Broughton 12.4; A.M. Hutchinson 11.13; F.E.C. Clark 12.20; J.A. Drake-Smith 10.6 (stroke); E.A. Safford 8.4 (cox). Av: 11.10¼
Heat: 1 TRC 2 Kingston RC. 1½ lengths, 7m 58s
Final: 1 TRC 2 Leander Club. ¾ length, 7m 1s

1889 B.W. Looker 11.2 (bow); B.E. Cole 11.4; P.S.G. Propert 11.10; A.S. Falconer 12.3; W. Broughton 11.12; A.M. Hutchinson 11.12; F.E.C. Clark 12.11; J.A. Drake-Smith 10.6 (stroke); E.A. Safford 8.0 (cox). Av: 11.8½
Heat: 1 TRC 2 London RC. ¾ length, 7m 1s
Semi-final: 1 TRC 2 Leander Club. 1¾ lengths, 7m 1s
Final: 1 TRC 2 New College, Oxford. 1 length, 7m 4s

1890 B.W. Looker 11.1 (bow); B.E. Cole 11.4; P.S.G. Propert 12.4; A.S. Falconer 12.7; W. Broughton 12.11; P. Landale 12.4; F.E.C. Clark 13.2; J.A. Drake-Smith 10.12 (stroke); E.A. Safford 8.0 (cox). Av: 12.0½
Heat: 1 London RC (winners) 2 TRC. 2 lengths, 7m 24½s

1891 B.W. Looker 11.2 (bow); J.A. Drake-Smith 10.10; P. Landale 12.6; A.M. Hutchinson 12.3; W. Broughton 12.9; S.D. Muttlebury 13.12; F.E.C. Clark 12.12; J.C. Gardner 11.11 (stroke); E.A. Safford 8.0 (cox). Av: 12.2¾
Heat: Leander Club, TRC; dead heat, 7m 38s
Re-row: 1 Leander Club (winners) 2 TRC. 2 lengths, 7m 7s

1892 E.A. Staines 10.8 (bow); G. Hering 11.7; A. Allport 12.5; T. Young 13.6; W. Broughton 12.9; S.D. Muttlebury 13.7; F.E.C. Clark 13.1; J.A. Drake-Smith 10.12 (stroke); E.A. Safford 8.0 (cox). Av: 12.3½
Heat: 1 TRC 2 London RC. 1 length, 7m 58s
Final: 1 Leander Club 2 TRC. 3 lengths, 7m 48½s

1893 E.A. Staines 10.1 (bow); A. Bogle 11.9; H.C. Arthur 12.3; T.H. Burrows 12.4; F.E.C. Clark 12.10; S.D. Muttlebury 13.7; W. Broughton 12.9; L.H.K. Bushe-Fox 10.11 (stroke); E.A. Safford 8.0 (cox). Av: 11.12
Heat: 1 TRC 2 SN de la Basse-Seine, France. ¾ length, 6m 59s
Semi-Final: 1 London RC 2 TRC. 2 lengths, 7m 1s

1894 G.G. Taylor 11.5 (bow); A.Bogle 11.4; H.C. Arthur 11.13; J.R. Orford 12.8; F.E.C. Clark 13.0; W. Broughton 12.12; S.D. Muttlebury 13.5; J.C. Gardner 11.9 (stroke); E.A. Safford 8.0 (cox). Av: 12.3½
Heat: 1 TRC 2 Trinity Hall, Cambridge. ¼ length, 7m 14s
Final: 1 Leander Club 2 TRC. ½ length, 7m 22s

1895 G.G. Taylor 11.2 (bow); G. Hering 11.9; G.E. Gill 12.4; R.O. Atcherley 12.10; W. Broughton 12.13; S.D. Muttlebury 13.9; G. McHenry 11.9; A. Bogle 11.5 (stroke); E.A. Safford 8.0 (cox). Av: 12.2¼
Heat: 1 Eton College 2 TRC. 1¼ lengths, 7m 34½s

1896 E. Campbell-Muir 11.1 (bow); W.G. Ross 10.11; G.E. Gill 12.7; G. Hering 11.8; W. Broughton 12.7; A. Bogle 11.10; E. Green 10.11; G.G. Taylor 11.3 (stroke); E.A. Safford 8.0 (cox). Av: 11.7¼
Heat: 1 TRC 2 First Trinity, Cambridge. 1 length, 7m 29s
Final: 1 Leander Club 2 TRC. 2¼ lengths, 7m 43s

1897 E. Campbell-Muir 11.1 (bow); W.G. Ross 10.13; C.H. Allin 11.10; G.E. Gill 12.3; A.F. Johnstone 12.8; J.A. Rennie 12.3; G. Rixon 11.8; G. Hering 11.10 (stroke); E.A. Safford 8.0 (cox). Av: 11.11¾
Heat: 1 Leander Club 2 TRC. 1¾ lengths, 7m 21s

1898 F. Collinson 10.0 (bow); G. Rixon 11.11; S.C. Smith 11.9; G. Hering 11.9; W.A. Bieber 12.4; W. Broughton 12.12; A. Bogle 11.5; W.J. Fernie 12.0 (stroke); E.A. Safford 8.0 (cox). Av: 11.9¾
Heat: 1 New College, Oxford 2 TRC. ⅓ length, 7m 23s

1899 E.O. Capon 10.6 (bow); A.C. Scoular 10.11; P.H. Devitt 11.5; F.H. Harrison 11.5; S.C. Smith 11.13; G. Rixon 11.10; F.W. Chambers 11.7; A.F. Johnstone 12.6 (stroke); E.A. Safford 8.1 (cox). Av: 11.6
Heat: 1 London RC 2 TRC. 1¾ lengths, 7m 25s

1900 G.A. Carr 10.9 (bow); W.H. Godfrey 9.10; G. Rixon 11.9; H.V. Maycock 11.0; J.F.S. Mellor 11.9; F.W. Chambers 12.2; W.A. Bieber 12.10; A.F. Johnstone 12.7 (stroke); H.T. Wright 8.1 (cox). Av: 11.7
Heat: 1 Trinity College, Cambridge 2 TRC. 1 length, 7m 35s

1901 H. Sanger 10.3 (bow); C.F.H. Greenwood 11.0; H.G. Finch 11.4; S.C. Smith 12.8; F.J. Francillon 13.2; A.F. Johnstone 12.9; H.S. Ferrar 12.3; A.E. Snellgrove 9.9 (stroke); E.A. Safford 8.0 (cox). Av: 11.8¼
Heat: 1 University of Pennsylvania, USA 2 TRC. Easily, 7m 22s

1902 G.F. Humphreys 9.13 (bow); C.F.H. Greenwood 11.1; H.S. Warschawski 11.7.; D.M. Haig 11.3; G.L. Jacobs 12.6; H.G. Finch 11.10; A.M.H. Scott 11.9; A.E. Snellgrove 9.13 (stroke); H.E. Greenwood 8.6 (cox). Av: 11.2½
Heat: 1 London RC 2 TRC. 1¼ lengths, 7m 58s

1903 R.A. Sparks 10.10 (bow); G.B. Hicks 11.1; G.L. Jacobs 12.7; W.S. Hallett 11.11; J.M. Lecocq 11.13; R.H. Forster 12.0; A.M. Henderson-Scott 11.7; A.E. Snellgrove 9.12 (stroke); H.E. Greenwood 8.6 (cox). Av: 11.5¾
Heat: 1 Leander Club (winners) 2 TRC. 6 lengths, 7m 40s

1904 R.F.M. Bigby 10.7 (bow); H.V. Maycock 11.4; S.O. Pugh 12.2; W.S. Hallett 12.4; S.C. Smith 12.3; H. Borrmann 12.3; G.H. Kelly 10.10; H. Messom 11.5 (stroke); H.E. Greenwood 8.12 (cox). Av: 11.8¼
Scratched after the draw

1905 G.H. Kelly 11.1 (bow); H.V. Maycock 11.2; R.A. Sparks 11.1; S.H. Jones 12.5; S.O. Pugh 12.9; R.W. Roylance 12.1; A.E. Snellgrove 9.13; H. Messom 11.8 (stroke); H.E. Greenwood 9.2 (cox). Av: 11.6¾
Heat: 1 SN de Gand, Belgium 2 TRC. 5 lengths, 7m 16s

Grand Challenge Cup

1906 G.H. Kelly 10.12 (bow); H.B. Harrison 11.5; R.W. Roylance 12.6; W.S. Hallett 12.10; S.O. Pugh 12.11; G.L. Thomson 12.3; H. Messom 11.8; C.G. Sprague 11.0 (stroke); H.E. Greenwood 8.13 (cox). Av: 11.12
Heat: 1 Argonaut RC, Toronto 2 TRC. 3 lengths, 7m 4s

1907 S. Wood 10.8 (bow); R.A. Sparks 11.3; S.O. Pugh 12.9; H. Messom 11.6; F. Trewby 12.0; W.S. Hallett 12.10; J.S. Wilkes 12.10; C.G. Sprague 10.9 (stroke); H.E. Greenwood 9.1 (cox). Av: 11.10 ¼
Heat: 1 Christ Church, Oxford 2 TRC. Easily, 8m 3s

1908 A.E. Snellgrove 9.11 (bow); W.B. Liebert 10.13; F. Trewby 11.12; K. Doulton 12.6; C.G. Rought 13.1; B. Logan 12.7; J.S. Wilkes 12.7; C.G. Sprague 10.11 (stroke); H.E. Greenwood 8.12 (cox). Av: 11.10¼
Heat: 1 TRC 2 London RC. 1½ lengths, 7m 14s
Semi-final: 1 Eton College 2 TRC. ¾ length, 7m 6s

1909 A.E. Snellgrove 10.0 (bow); H.G. Irwin 10.12; F. Trewby 11.8; A. Elms 11.6; C.G. Rought 13.0; C.M. Spielman 12.11; H. Messom 11.10; B. Logan 12.8 (stroke); H.E. Greenwood 9.6 (cox). Av: 11.10¼
Heat: 1 Magdalen College, Oxford 2 TRC. Easily, 7m 30s

1910 J. Beresford 10.5 (bow); H.G. Irwin 11.11; E.C. Goodall 11.12; W.S. Douglas 12.11; C.G. Rought 13.4; B. Logan 12.11; G.H. Kelly 11.7; T.D. Richardson 9.10(stroke); H.E. Greenwood 8.11 (cox). Av: 11.10½
Heat: 1 Jesus College, Cambridge 2 TRC. 2 feet, 7m 26s

1911 D.F. Humphreys 10.3 (bow); R.H. Thomson 10.9; G.A.L. Hatton 11.2; J.F.S. Hards 11.8; W.S. Douglas 13.1; C.M. Spielman 12.12; H.G. Irwin 11.9; G.H. Kelly 11.4 (stroke); H.E. Greenwood 8.11 (cox). Av: 11.8¾
Heat: 1 Jesus College, Cambridge 2 TRC. Easily, 7m 18s

1912 D.F. Humphreys 10.3 (bow); G.T. Wilkes 11.9; Sir G. Fetherston 11.1; H.J. Davis 12.1; E.C. Goodall 11.9; G.A.L. Hatton 11.5; M.S. Gunn 11.8; H. Messom 11.11 (stroke); H.E. Greenwood 9.6 (cox). Av: 11.5¾
Heat: 1 Leander Club 2 TRC. 1¼ lengths, 7m 25s

1913 G. East 11.8 (bow); H.M. Southwell 10.13; G.L. Thomson 11.9; K. Doulton 12.6; C.G. Rought 13.2; B. Logan 12.11; P.A. Cooper 12.7; H. Messom 12.2 (stroke); H.E. Greenwood 9.6 (cox). Av: 12.2
Heat: 1 Leander Club (winners) 2 TRC. 1¼ lengths, 7m 4s

1914 P. Beresford 9.2 (bow); V.G. Teale 10.5; I.M. Woozley 10.3; A.C. Chibnall 11.8; K. Vernon 11.4; B. Logan 13.0; E.L. Watts 12.8; J. Beresford 10.3 (stroke); H. Sunley 9.0 (cox.). Av: 10.12¾
Heat: 1 Winnipeg RC, Canada 2 TRC. Easily, 1½ lengths, 7m 55s

1920 V.G. Teale 10.10 (bow); K. Vernon 11.5; E.C. Goodall 11.10; A.E. Ellis 12.3; C.K. Roylance 12.8; B. Logan 12.13; G.H. Kelly 11.6; J. Beresford Snr 10.3 (stroke); C.A.A. Robertson 8.6 (cox). Av: 11.9
Heat: 1 Leander Club 2 TRC. 1½ lengths, 7m 58s

1921 C.M. Morrell 11.5(bow); C.H. Pickworth 11.9; J.L. Tann 11.12; G.H. Kelly 11.10; W.S. Douglas 12.8; K. Vernon 11.10; R. Teale 12.6; J. Beresford Snr 10.4 (stroke); P.S. Martin 7.7 (cox). Av: 11.9¾
Heat: 1 New College, Oxford 2 TRC. ¾ length, 7m 2s

1922 C.G. Chandler 11.9 (bow); V.G. Teale 10.9; R.G. Bare 11.0; C.H. Rew 11.4; A.F. Long 11.4; C.T. Southgate 12.2; H.L. Holman 10.6; S.I. Fairbairn 12.0 (stroke); J. Godwin 7.7 (cox). Av: 11.4¼
Heat: 1 TRC 2 Grasshopper Club, Zurich. Easily, 7m 50s
Semi-final: 1 TRC 2 Christiania Roklub, Norway. ¾ length, 7m 48s
Final: 1 Leander Club 2 TRC. 1 length, 7m 36s

1923 C.G. Chandler 11.0 (bow); R.G. Bare 11.6; J. Beresford Jnr 11.6; C.H. Rew 11. 4; A.F. Long 11.7; K.C. Wilson 11.12; H.L. Holman 9.11; S.I. Fairbairn 12.0 (stroke); J. Godwin 8.0 (cox). Av: 11.4¼
Heat: 1 TRC 2 Christ Church, Oxford. 1¼ lengths, 7m 4s (shortened course)
Semi-final: 1 TRC 2 Brasenose College, Oxford. ½ length, 6m 58s
Final: 1 TRC 2 Pembroke College, Cambridge. ⅓ length, 6m 45s

1924 C.G. Chandler 11.1 (bow); R.G. Bare 11.9; H.W. Dulley 11.0; H.L. Morphy 10.10; H.C. Debenham 12.12; C.H. Rew 11.4; A.F. Long 11.9; S.I. Fairbairn 12.0 (stroke); J. Godwin 8.5 (cox). Av: 11.7¼
Heat: 1 Leander Club (winners) 2 TRC. ½ length, 8m 1s

1925 C.G. Chandler 11.3 (bow); K. Vernon 11.5; G.C. Killick 12.4; H.M. Lane 13.1; H.C. Debenham 12.4; J.C. Badcock 12.4; A.F. Long 11.13; C.H. Rew 11.7 (stroke); J. Godwin 8.9 (cox). Av: 11.13¾
Heat: 1 TRC 2 Jesus College, Cambridge. ½ length, 7m 4s
Semi-final: 1 TRC 2 Christ Church, Oxford. ¾ length, 6m 58s
Final: 1 Leander Club 2 TRC. ¾ length, 6m 53s

1926 H.E. West 10.8 (bow); G.D. Smith 11.6; G.C. Killick 12.1; H.C. Debenham 12.6; H.M. Lane 13.2; J.C. Badcock 12.7; R. Teale 11.7; J. Beresford Jnr 11.6 (stroke); J. Godwin 8.9 (cox). Av: 11.12¼
Heat: 1 Leander Club 2 TRC. ½ length, 6m 59s

1927 H.E. West 11.6 (bow); G.D. Smith 11.4; D. Wheeler 12.12; H.M. Lane 13.3; D.H.L. Gollan 13.6; J.C. Badcock 12.5; G.C. Killick 12.2; J. Hamilton 10.10 (stroke); J. Godwin 8.12 (cox). Av: 12.2½
Heat: 1 TRC 2 Leander Club. 2 lengths, 7m 6s
Final: 1 TRC 2 London RC. ½ length, 7m 26s

1928 H.E. West 11.1 (bow); J. Beresford Jnr 11.4; G.C. Killick 13.2; H.M. Lane 13.0; D.H.L. Gollan 14.4; J.C. Badcock 12.5; G.O. Nickalls 12.12; J. Hamilton 10.10 (stroke); A.L. Sulley 8.9 (cox). Av: 12.4½
Heat: 1 TRC 2 London RC. 1 length, 7m 22s
Final: 1 TRC 2 First Trinity, Cambridge. 1½ lengths, 6m 56s

1929 Hon C.R. Allanson-Winn 10.7 (bow); H.W. Dulley 11.9; H.N. Sporborg 11.6; A.E. Shave 12.5; J. Beresford Jnr 11.1; J.C. Badcock 12.2; G.C. Killick 12.2; E. Beresford 10.0 (stroke); J.G. Dearlove 7.7 (cox). Av: 11.5½
Heat: 1 TRC 2 Jesus College, Cambridge. 1 length, 7m 59s
Final: 1 Leander Club 2 TRC. 2 lengths, 7m 0s

1930 C.L. Champion 11.5 (bow); R.R. Swatton 11.8; H.N. Sporborg 11.9; D. Carey 13.4; A.W. Holden 12.13; F.E.C. Cox 12.7; R. Teale 12.9; D.C. Price 11.2 (stroke); J. Godwin 8.13 (cox). Av: 12.1¾
Heat: 1 University College, Oxford 2 TRC. 1 length, 7m 57s

1931 R.R.E. Bradley 10.8 (bow); F.G. Bunge 11.9; R.D. George 12.8; T.H. Tyler 11.11; F.E.C. Cox 12.3; J.H.M. Ward 12.3; Hon C.R. Allanson-Winn 11.0; E. Beresford 9.12 (stroke); J.G. Dearlove 8.0 (cox). Av: 11.8
Heat: 1 TRC; 2 Pembroke College, Cambridge. 1½ lengths, 7m 37s
Final: 1 London RC 2 TRC. ⅓ length, 7m 33s

1932 B.E.A. Joyner 10.6 (bow); T.H. Tyler 12.0; R.D. George 12.10; G. Hardwicke 12.9; J.H.M. Ward 12.10; J.C. Badcock 12.6; J. Beresford Jnr 11.7 (stroke); J.G. Dearlove 8.3 (cox). Av: 11.13
Heat: 1 TRC 2 Jesus College, Cambridge. Easily, 7m 48s
Final: 1 Leander Club 2 TRC. ½ length, 7m 19s

Grand Challenge Cup

1933 R.C. Morris 10.8 (bow); T.H. Tyler 11.9; J.H.M. Ward 12.8; A.P. Brown 12.9; H. Homberger 13.12; J.C. Badcock 12.0; R.H.H. Symonds 11.6; D.C. Price 11.4 (stroke); J.G. Dearlove 8.3 (cox). Av: 12.0
Heat: 1 London RC (winners); 2 TRC. 1 length, 7m 2s

1934 B.P. Drakeford 12.5 (bow); T.H. Tyler 11.12; T.G. Askwith 11.12; A.E. Shave 13.0; A.J. Hutton-Squire 13.2; R.C. Harman 11.6; Hon C.R. Allanson-Winn 11.8; A.P. Brown 12.12 (stroke); J.G. Dearlove 8.7 (cox). Av: 12.3½
Heat: 1 Leander Club (winners) 2 TRC. ½ length, 6m 44s (record)

1935 R.C. Morris 10.13 (bow); R.C. Harman 11.5; A.J. Hutton-Squire 13.1; T.H. Tyler 11.8; J.A. Maclean 12.10; A.P. Brown 12.12; B.P. Drakeford 12.2; E.G. Beresford 10.1 (stroke); J.G. Dearlove 8.2 (cox). Av: 11.11¾
Heat: 1 Leander Club 2 TRC. ¾ length, 7m 17s

1936 R.C. Morris 11.3 (bow); R.C. Harman 11.12; A. Burrough 11.10; A.P. Brown 13.7; J.A. Maclean 13.0; A.J. Hutton-Squire 13.5; F.J.R. Dodd 11.4; E.A. Szilagyi 11.5 (stroke); J.G. Dearlove 8.5 (cox). Av: 12.2¼
Heat: 1 Pembroke College, Cambridge 2 TRC. ¾ length, 7m 23s

1937 J.H. Burrough 12.5 (bow); H.E.G. Watts 11.7; J.T.M. O'Mara 13.5;. H. Lohnberg 13.8; A.J. Hutton-Squire 13.6; R.C. Harman 11.8; H.W.T. Beckett 10.11; A.P. Brown 13.2 (stroke); J.G. Dearlove 8.0 (cox). Av: 12.6½
Heat: 1 Trinity Hall, Cambridge 2 TRC. 1 length, 7m 33s

1938 W.C. Wilkinson 11.5 (bow); R.C. Gussman 12.0; N.T. Taylor 11.12; H. Lohnberg 13.0; J.T.M. O'Mara 12.12; J.A. Maclean 12.3; R.C. Morris 10.13; E.G. Beresford 10.5 (stroke); J.B. Freebairn-Smith 9.3 (cox). Av: 11.11½
Heat: 1 London RC (winners) 2 TRC. 3 lengths, 7m 27s

1939 R.C. Morris, 11.1 (bow); B.N. Brooke 11.2; C.M.E. Eugster 10.10; A.G.C. Whalley 12.5; J.T.M. O'Mara 13.0; P.C. Kirkpatrick 14.1; J.H. Burrough 12.3; R.W. Brown 11.1 (stroke); G.W. Wright 8.1 (cox). Av: 11.13½
Heat: 1 Argonaut RC, Canada 2 TRC. ½ length, 7m 48s

1946 R.C. Morris 11.0 (bow); H.C. Bolton 11.2; R.W. Brown 11.7; J.H. Garson 12.13; D. Belson 12.13; G.C. Richardson 12.3; J.H.M. Ward 12.0; H.W. Rushmere 13.1 (stroke); G.W. Wright 8.5 (cox). Av: 12.1¼
Heat: 1 TRC 2 London RC. 1¼ lengths, 7m 43s
Semi-final: 1 Ruder Club, Zurich 2 TRC. 1 length, 7m 24s

1947 J.W. Wilmot 10.5 (bow); J.P. Dizer 10.12; J.H.M. Ward 12.2; W. Bull 12.12; H.W. Rushmere 13.2; P.C. Kirkpatrick 13.11; R.C. Morris 11.2; F.L.A. de Marneffe 11.1 (stroke); J.G. Dearlove 8.3 (cox). Av: 11.12¾
Heat: 1 Delftsche Sport, Holland 2 TRC. 1 length, 7m 24s

1948 R.C. Morris 11.1 (bow); J.R. Johnson 12.5; J.L. Sangster 12.11; U. Burkhard 13.5; H.W. Rushmere 13.7; T.H. Christie 13.7; A.S.F. Butcher 12.2; P.C. Kirkpatrick 14.2 (stroke); J.G. Dearlove 8.4 (cox). Av: 12.12
Heat: 1 TRC 2 London RC. 1½ lengths, 7m 1s
Semi-final: 1 TRC 2 Leander Club. ½ length, 6m 59s
Final: 1 TRC 2 Jesus and Pembroke Colleges, Cambridge. 2½ lengths, 7m 2s

1949 P.S. Pusey 11.1 (bow); A.J.G. Wood 11.9; P.R. Simnett 12.2; B.R. Worsnop 12.7; J.L. Sangster 12.10; T.H. Christie 13.3; A.S.F. Butcher 11.11; P.C. Kirkpatrick 14.3 (stroke); J.G. Dearlove 8.1 (cox). Av: 12.5¾
Heat: 1 TRC 2 Clare College, Cambridge. 1¼ lengths, 7m 15s
Semi-final: 1 TRC 2 Cottage Club of Princeton, USA. 2½ lengths, 6m 49s
Final: 1 Leander Club 2 TRC. 1 length, 6m 54s

1950 T.P. Wilson 9.7 (bow); A.J.G. Wood 11.5; J. Debenham 12.10; J. Pope 11.2; J.L. Sangster 12.13; J.B. Shaw 13.3; A.R. Watson 12.5; P.C. Kirkpatrick 14.0 (stroke); B. Graydon 8.1 (cox). Av: 12.2
Heat: 1 London RC 2 TRC. 1 length, 6m 59s.

1951 J.P. Dizer 10.13 (bow); A.J.R. Purssell 11.7; M. Legg 12.9; R.A. Strong 12.10; S. Hobbs 13.6; R.A.F. Macmillan 13.8; H.W. Rushmere 13.8; P.C. Kirkpatrick 13.13 (stroke); G.J. Alwin 9.4 (cox). Av: 12.11
Heat: 1 Lady Margaret, Cambridge (winners) 2 TRC. 1⅓ lengths, 7m 3s

1952 P.A. de Giles 11.13 (bow); G.C. Fisk 11.9; S. Hobbs 12.13; M. Legg 12.4; R.A.F. Macmillan 13.6; P.M.O. Massey 13.8; A.S.F. Butcher 13.5; P.C. Kirkpatrick 14.0 (stroke); G.J. Alwin 9.3 (cox). Av: 12.12½
Heat: 1 Sydney RC, Australia 2 TRC. 3 lengths, 6m 45s

1953 P.G. Essam 11.12 (bow); J. Pope 11.1; J.T.H. Webb 12.12; L.S. Williams 13.1; A.R. Watson 13.3; R.H. Nicholls 12.0; G.G.H. Page 11.3; J.N. Eldeen 11.13 (stroke); G.J. Alwin, 9.4 (cox). Av: 12.0½
Heat: 1 Leander Club (winners) 2 TRC. 2 lengths, 6m 44s

1954 G.G.H. Page 11.4 (bow); J. Pope 11.4; M.G.C. Savage 12.7; A.R. Watson 12.8; A.R. Davidson 12.13; R.A.F. Macmillan 13.8; M. Legg 12.11; J.N. Eldeen 12.1 (stroke); D.R. Glynne-Jones 9.1 (cox). Av: 12.5¼
Heat: 1 TRC 2 London RC. 2½ lengths, 7m 11s
Semi-final: 1 Krylia Sovetov, USSR (winners) 2 TRC. ½ length, 6m 54s

1955 M. Legg 12.11 (bow); K.S. Cross 11.3; D.H. Whitaker 13.11; A.R. Watson 12.6; R.A.F. Macmillan 13.9; C.F. Porter 13.3; A.R. Davidson 13.3; R.H. Nicholls 11.13 (stroke); D.R. Glynne-Jones 8.11 (cox). Av: 12.11
Heat: 1 University of Pennsylvania, USA (winners) 2 TRC. ⅔ length, 7m 20s

1956 G.G.H. Page 11.4 (bow); D.S.S. Elliott 12.10; W.J. Griffith 12.7; A.R. Watson 12.0; D.H. McLellan 14.13; H.G.V. Denning 12.4; G.S. Dear 11.1; R.A. Macmillan 14.1 (stroke); D.R. Glynne-Jones 8.10 (cox). Av: 12.8½
Heat: 1 Centre Sportif des Forces de l'Armée Française (winners) 2 TRC. 2½ lengths, 7m 38s

1957 W.J. Griffith 12.8 (bow), J.F.C. Badcock 12.1; A.C. Hancox 12.8; B.S. Tanner 12.5; D.H. McLellan 15.1; D.S.S. Elliott 12.6; W.M. Nisbet 11.8; I. Wilson 12.4 (stroke); R.L. Penney 8.11 (cox). Av: 12.8½
Heat: 1 Club Krasnia Znamia, USSR 2 TRC. 4 lengths, 6m 43s

1958 R.H. Workman 11.5 (bow); J.P.M. Thompson 11.13; J.A. Stephenson 13.4; H.A. Wober 12.4; A.C. Hancox 13.1; J.F.C. Badcock 12.0; D.R. Mount 13.2; D.S.S. Elliott 12.6 (stroke); R.L. Penney 8.11 (cox). Av: 12.6
Heat: 1 Leichhardt RC, Australia 2 TRC. ¾ length, 6m 57s

1959 D.R. Mount 13.1 (bow); W.M. Nisbet 12.11; B.S. Tanner 13.2; J.A Stephenson 13.4; R.D.F. Anderson 13.1; J.F.C. Badcock 12.6; W.J. Griffith 13.4; M.S. Atkins 13.3 (stroke); R.L. Penney 8.12 (cox). Av: 13.0¾
Heat: 1 TRC 2 Leander Club. 1¼ lengths, 7m 6s
Final: 1 Harvard University, USA 2 TRC. 2¾ lengths, 6m 57s

1960 S.F.A. Miskin 12.11 (bow); R.D.F. Anderson 13.7; B.S. Tanner 13.0; P. Laws 13.6; W.J Griffith 13.12; J.F.C. Badcock 12.4; D.R. Mount 13.4; I. Wilson 12.12 (stroke); R.L. Penney 9.3 (cox). Av: 12.12½
Heat: 1 Oxford University 2 TRC. 1⅓ lengths, 6m 39s

Grand Challenge Cup

1961 J.F.C. Badcock 12.0 (bow); J.D. Culpan 12.2; D.S. Kennedy 12.8; J. Palmer 12.8; J.A. Stephenson 14.0; F.J. Lambert 12.13; M.R. Woolner 12.10; S.F.A. Miskin 13.1 (stroke); J.T. Shaw 8.9 (cox). Av: 12.10½
Heat: 1 Leander Club 2 TRC. 1 length, 6m 40s

1962 S.F.A. Miskin 12.13 (bow); A.J. Hodgins 12.5; D.W. Gramolt 13.2; R.D.F. Anderson 13.4; J.A. Stephenson 13.12; F.J. Lambert 13.7; P. Laws 13.8; J.J. James 12.0 (stroke); R.T. Weston 8.6 (cox). Av: 13.1
Heat: 1 University of Pennsylvania, USA 2 TRC. 2¼ lengths, 6m 44s

1963 C.J.F.S. Rowley 12.3 (bow); S.F.A. Miskin 12.11; J.E. Taylor 12.10; C.R. Barker 13.0; J.A. Stephenson 13.13; J.F.C. Badcock 11.12; A.C.W. Mill 11.6; M.J. Lohnberg 12.5 (stroke); R.L. Penney 9.1 (cox). Av: 12.7½
Heat: 1 TRC 2 Keble College, Oxford. ¼ length, 6m 55s
Semi-final; 1 University of London (winners) 2 TRC. 3¼ lengths, 7m 17s

1964 M.J. Lohnberg 12.5 (bow); J.F.C. Badcock 11.9; A.M. Hewlett 12.7; P.D. Spatz 13.0; P.E. Lacey 13.1; C.D. Barrett 13.6; M.J. Wise 12.5; D.W. Gramolt 12.12 (stroke); R.A. Matthiae 9.3 (cox). Av: 12.9
Heat: 1 TRC 2 Leander Club. ⅔ length, 7m 8s
Semi-final: 1 Club Zalgiris, Vilnius, USSR (winners) 2 TRC. Easily, 6m 23s

1965 B.R. Hanham 12.4 (bow); P.D. Spatz 13.3; I.A. MacRae 13.1; C.R. Barker 13.8; C.D. Barrett 14.4; F.J. Lambert 14.0; J.W. Fryer 13.9; D.W. Gramolt 12.13 (stroke); R.A. Matthiae 9.8 (cox). Av: 13.5¼
Heat: 1 Nautilus Club 2 TRC. 1⅔ lengths, 6m 42s

1966 R. Hackford 11.3 (bow); S.R. Boddington 12.7; A. Rice 12.1; B.M. Barker 13.7; J.E. Taylor 12.4; T. Kirby 13.7; T.A. Bakiewicz 12.2; J.E. Lester 11.12 (stroke); R.A. Matthiae 9.7 (cox). Av: 12.5¼
Heat: 1 TSC Berlin, East Germany (winners) 2 TRC 4 lengths, 6m 56s.

LADIES' CHALLENGE PLATE

1985 A: S.L. Jones 11.4 (bow); G.P.R. Reddin 13.1; M.P. Cowie 13.8; J.E. Robson 13.13; D.J. Badcock 13.8; C.R. Jones 13.4; M.W. Kerridge 12.4; L.P. Brown 14.0 (stroke); G.G.P. Herbert 7.11 (cox). Av: 13.1
Heat: 1 TRC A 2 KSR Njord, Holland. 1 length, 6m 39s
Heat: 1 Vesta RC 2 TRC A. ½ length, 6m 39s
B: W.J. Baker 11.9 (bow); A.T. Smith 11.12; W.G. Lloyd 11.3; J.F. Lane 12.9; G.J.H. Thomas 13.13; A.M. Ward 13.8; S.P. Bowden 11.5; S.P.K. Austin 10.0 (stroke); G. Denny 8.0 (cox). Av: 11.13
Heat: 1 Nautilus Lightweights RC 2 TRC B. 1⅔ lengths, 6m 34s

1986 P.C. McConnell 12.7 (bow); J.E. Robson 13.7; A.L. Slemeck 13.0; R.H.B. Thain 14.0; M. Urry 15.2; D.J. Badcock 14.8; J.A.G.H. Stewart 14.9; C. Bourne 12.0 (stroke); G.G.P. Herbert 8.1(cox). Av: 13.9
Heat: 1 TRC 2 Leverett House, USA. Easily, 7m 10s
Heat: 1 University of London 2 TRC. 2¼ lengths, 6m 39s

1988 A: P.R. Williams 13.1 (bow); W.J. Baker 11.0; H. Worden 14.4; S. Todd 14.5; C.A. Maby 15.1; B.D. Crawford 14.7; R.S. Court 11.0; C. Slemeck 14.4 (stroke); I. Grindal 7.10 (cox). Av: 13.6
Heat: 1 TRC A 2 Elizabethan BC. 1¼ lengths, 7m 18s
Heat: 1 University of London 2 TRC. 2 lengths, 7m 7s
B: M. Wolff 12.0 (bow); B.D. Crawford 11.0; L. McLachlan 12.0; M.R. Thomas 12.0; M.J.S. Levy 13.2; J.E. Robson 15.0; S.L. Jones 11.7; R.M. Payn 13.0 (stroke); C.L. Salmon 8.0 (cox). Av: 12.6
Heat: 1 Argonaut RC, Canada 2 TRC B. Easily, 7m 10s

1989 R.S. Court 11.5 (bow); A.M. Ward 11.12; S.R. Allpass 13.0; A.J.R. Inglis 14.7; D. Gates 14.6; J. Ferraro 13.5; M. Treserden 13.1; S.P.K. Austin 10.2 (stroke); I. Grindal 8.0 (cox). Av: 12.10
Heat: 1 London RC 2 TRC. ½ length, 7m 18s

THAMES CHALLENGE CUP

1872 W.B. Giles 10.4 (bow); H.J. Smith 10.9; J. Hastie 10.12; W. Page 11.2; G.H. Vize 12.3; J.A. Cameron 11.3; W.H. Eyre 10.13; W.L. Slater 11.5 (stroke); A. Christie 8.0 (cox). Av: 11.1
Final: 1 TRC 2 London RC; 3 Ino RC. 1 length, 8m 42s

1873 J.W. Hughes 10.5 (bow); C. Russell 10.6; J. Maycock 11.0; W. Page 11.4; G.H. Vize 12.3; A.C. Radmall 10.0; J. Hastie 11.5; W.L. Slater 11.3 (stroke); H.R. Trehearne 8.0 (cox). Av: 10 13¾
Heat: 1 TRC 2 Oriel College, Oxford. Easily
Final: 1 TRC 2 London RC. 5 lengths, 8m 2s

1874 F. Canton 10.10 (bow); W. Johnson 11.3; B.J. Angle 11.1; C.C. Cream 11.2; E.T. Barrett 11.3; J.A.M. Robertson 11.3; A.O. Ward 11.6; W.B. Giles 10.8 (stroke); E.A. Safford 8.0 (cox). Av: 11.1
Heat: 1 TRC 2 West London RC. 1 length
Final: 1 TRC 2 London RC. 1 length, 8m 19s

1875 H.F. Nicholls 10.3 (bow); C.E. Jolliffe 10.0; B.J. Angle 11.1; W. Johnson 11.4; E.T. Barrett 11.11; S. Smelt 11.3; F. Canton 10.12; J.W. Hughes 10.4 (stroke); E.A. Safford 7.10 (cox). Av: 10.11¾
Heat: 1 London RC 2 TRC. 1¼ lengths, 7m 33s

1876 J.W. Hughes 10.2 (bow); A.C. Radmall 10.7; A. Hall 11.1; C. Russell 11.2; F. Young 11.12; S. Smelt 11.12; J. Maycock 10.13; W.B. Giles 11.2 (stroke); E.A. Safford 8.0 (cox). Av: 11.1
Heat: 1 West London RC (winners) 2 Grove Park RC; 3 TRC. 2 lengths, 7m 33s

1877 J.W. Hughes 10.4 (bow) C.E. Jolliffe 10.1; J.C. Sutherland 10.8; A. Gardiner 10.13; B.J. Angle 11.3; E.C. Otter 11.1; W. Nottebohm 10.5; A. Smelt 11.10 (stroke); E.A. Safford 8.0 (cox). Av: 10.10¾
Heat: 1 TRC 2 Ino RC 3 Grove Park RC. ½ length.
Final: 1 London RC 2 TRC. 1½ lengths, 8m 29s

1878 C. Dangerfield 9.9 (bow); R. Humfray 10.2; A.C. Dryden 11.1; H. Markham 10.8; H.J. Rust 11.9; C.M. Brunker 11.8; C.W. Hughes 9.10; J.W. Hughes 10.8 (stroke); E.A. Safford 7.7 (cox). Av: 10.10¼
Final: 1 London RC 2 Ino RC 3 TRC. 2 lengths, 7m 55s.

1879 C.W. Hughes 9.6 (bow); C. Dangerfield 10.0; J.W. Grieg 10.2; A.H. Bond 10.13; A.C.F. Gore 12.9; F. Whitehurst 10.13; H. Markham 10.10; G. Smith 11.2 (stroke); E.A. Safford 7.12 (cox). Av: 10.10¼
Heat: 1 London RC 2 TRC 3 Ino RC. 3 lengths, 9m 18s

1880 C.W. Mapleton 9.7 (bow); J.A. Drake-Smith 10.1; H.B. Tween 10.6; H.J. Rust 12.0; A.C.F. Gore 12.6; G. Smith 11.7; C. Dangerfield 10.0; E.D. Johnson 11.0 (stroke); E.A. Safford 8.0 (cox). Av: 11.1½
Heat: 1 Twickenham RC 2 Trinity Hall, Cambridge. Easily. TRC disqualified.

1881 R.H. Smith 10.5 (bow); E.C. Griesbach 9.0; B.W. Looker 10.6; S. Gollan 11.4; G. Baker 11.1; J.A. Drake-Smith 10.9; C. Dangerfield 10.0; C.W. Hughes 9.10 (stroke); E.A. Safford 7.13 (cox). Av: 10.5
Heat: 1 Twickenham RC 2 TRC. Easily

1882 N. Deguine 10.1 (bow); B.E. Cole 10.6; B.W. Looker 10.9; H.G. Bennett 10.10; M. Shearman 12.11; J.A. Drake-Smith 10.10; C. Dangerfield 10.1; C.W. Hughes 9.13 (stroke); E.A. Safford 8.2 (cox). Av: 10.9¼
Heat: 1 Royal Chester RC 2 West London RC 3 TRC. 2 lengths

1883 C.W. Hughes 9.12 (bow); C.F. Russell 10.2; S.M. Cooke 10.9; B.E. Cole 10.5; G.H. Eyre 10.11; E.D. Johnson 11.9; B.W. Looker 10.9; R.H. Smith 10.6 (stroke); E.A. Safford 7.13 (cox). Av: 10.7¾
Heat: 1 West London RC 2 TRC 3 East Sheen BC. 1 length, 8m 7s

1884 W.S. Warlters 9.5 (bow); F.W. Long 9.3; W. Theobald 10.5; S.M. Cooke 10.9; W. Liddle 12.6; B.W. Looker 10.3; C.W. Hughes 9.512; H. Atkinson 9.11 (stroke); E.A. Safford 8.1 (cox). Av: 10.3
Heat: 1 TRC 2 London RC 3 Albion RC. 2 lengths
Final: 1 Twickenham RC 2 TRC. Easily, 7m 48s

1885 F.W. Long 9.4 (bow); C.E. Smith 9.10; W.S. Warlters 9.12; W. Theobald, 10.10; R.J. Twyford 12.3; W. Andrew 11.8; S.M. Cooke 10.8; E. Shortt 10.13 (stroke); E.A. Safford, 8.1 (cox). Av: 10.8½
Heat: 1 TRC 2 West London RC. ½ length
Final: 1 London RC 2 TRC. Easily, 7m 36s

1886 C.E. Smith 9.13 (bow); W.M. Hopkins 10.12; A.S. Falconer 12.5; F.E.C. Clark 12.7; W. Andrew 11.8; R.E. Moore 12.0; S.M. Cooke 10.9; C.W. Hughes 9.13 (stroke); E.A. Safford 8.1 (cox). Av: 11.1½
Heat: 1 TRC 2 Ibis RC. Easily
Heat: 1 TRC 2 Twickenham RC. 1 length
Final: 1 London RC 2 TRC. ⅔ length, 7m 8½s

1887 J.E. Spagnoletti 9.7 (bow); C.B. Carpenter 10.11; M.C. Gie 10.7; W.E. Clares 11.10; R.J. Twyford 12.4; B.E. Cole 10.12; C.E. Smith 9.12; F.W. Long 9.3 (stroke); E.A. Safford 8.1 (cox). Av: 10.8¼
Heat: 1 TRC 2 Anglian BC. 1 length, 7m 30s
Final: 1 Trinity Hall, Cambridge 2 TRC. 1 length, 7m 20s

1888 C.E. Smith 9.13 (bow); C.J. Thomas 9.13; R.H. Landale 11.5; E.A. Staines 9.13; T.Young 13.6; W.H. Cumming 11.12; M.C. Gie 10.9; H. Osborne 10.2 (stroke); E.A. Safford (cox). Av: 10.12½
Heat: 1 TRC 2 Twickenham RC. 3½ lengths, 8m 26s
Final: 1 Lady Margaret, Cambridge 2 TRC. 5 lengths, 7m 19s

1889 C.E. Smith 9.8 (bow); F.W. Long 9.0; G.G. Spray 10.5; C.B. Carpenter 11.6; F.L. Otter 11.12; T. Young 13.1; J. Bransbury 11.8; E.A. Staines 10.0 (stroke); E.A. Safford 7.11 (cox). Av: 10.12
Heat: 1 London RC 2 TRC. ¾ length, 7m 9s

1890 J.E. Spagnoletti 9.8 (bow); J. Bransbury 11.6; H.C. Arthur 11.8; T.H. Burrows 12.1; T. Young 13.8; F.L. Otter 12.1; E.A. Staines 10.1; G. Hering 11.2 (stroke); H.S. Soden 8.4 (cox). Av: 11.6
Heat: 1 TRC 2 Emmanuel College, Cambridge. 1 length, 7m 3½s
Semi-final: 1 TRC 2 Balliol College, Oxford. 1 length, 7m 34s
Final: 1 TRC 2 Molesey BC. 1⅓ lengths, 7m 21½s

1891 F.A. Cumming 9.7 (bow); J. Bransbury 11.0; H.C. Arthur 12.0; L.H.K. Bushe-Fox 10.12; T. Young 13.8; T.H. Burrows 11.12; E.A. Staines 10.6; G. Hering 11.6 (stroke); H.S. Soden 8.4 (cox). Av: 11.4½
Heat: 1 TRC 2 Balliol College, Oxford. ½ length, 7m 53s
Semi-final: 1 TRC 2 Trinity College, Dublin. ½ length, 7m 31s
Final: 1 Molesey BC 2 TRC. ¼ length, 7m 18s

1892 J.M. Heath 9.2 (bow); J.T. Musgrave 11.13; R.H. Forster 10.10; W.H. Cumming 11.8; F.D. Rae 12.2; T.H. Burrows 12.0; C.N. Wood 10.0; L.H.K. Bushe-Fox 11.2 (stroke); H.S. Soden 8.4 (cox). Av: 11.1
Heat: 1 Molesey 2 TRC. ¾ length, 7m 45s

Thames Challenge Cup

1893 G.G. Taylor 10.13 (bow); W.J. Child 11.5; S. Atherton 11.0; S.H. Gollan 12.0; C.C. Luke 12.2; A. Allport 12.13; R.J.A. Morrison 11.7; J.M. Heath 9.6 (stroke); H.S. Soden 8.6 (cox). Av: 11.5¾
Heat: 1 TRC 2 Vesta RC. 2½ lengths, 7m 32s
Final: 1 TRC 2 Eton Excelsior RC. Easily, 7m 49s

1894 R.C. Whiteing 10.3 (bow); W.G. Ross 10.7; W.J. Child 11.7; C. Dixon 12.0; T.H. Burrows 12.5; G. Hering 11.7; W.H. Cumming 11.3; J.M. Heath 9.7 (stroke); H.S. Soden 8.2 (cox). Av: 11.1 ¼
Heat: 1 First Trinity, Cambridge 2 TRC. 1¼ lengths, 7m 38s

1895 R.C. Whiteing 10.1 (bow); M.T. Llewellyn 10.6; F. Stevenson 9.13; R.G. Bullock 11.4; A.F. Johnstone 12.0; W.G. Ross 10.9; E. Green 10.9; C.N. Wood 9.13 (stroke); H.S. Soden 8.6 (cox). Av: 10.8½
Heat: 1 St John's College, Oxford 2 TRC. 1½ lengths, 7m 57s

1896 F. Stevenson 10.3 (bow); M.T. Llewellyn 10.9; W.R. Manning 11.2; H. Price 12.11; S.C. Smith 11.12; W.G. Stoffell 12.2; R.C. Whiteing 10.5; J.M. Heath 9.11 (stroke); H. Pares 7.10 (cox). Av: 11.1½
Heat: 1 Molesey BC 2 TRC. ¾ length, 8m 7s.

1897 W.F. Mildren 9.6 (bow); F.W. Payn 10.13; H.B. Batt 10.12; W.L. Castleden 10.9; R.St J. Matthews 13.8; R.H. Forster 11.10; S.C. Smith 12.0; J.B. Sharpe 9.6 (stroke); E.A. Safford 8.0 (cox). Av: 11.1
Heat: 1 Delftsche SR Laga 2 TRC. 1 length, 7m 27s

1898 W.F. Mildren 9.6 (bow); R.C. Whiteing 10.8; H.M. Wood 11.0; S.M. Sharwood 11.10; E. Bousfield 13.11; A.F. Johnstone 12.9; R.H. Forster 11.12; W.G. Ross 10.9 (stroke); H.T. Wright 8.2 (cox). Av: 11.6¼
Heat: 1 TRC 2 London RC. ½ length, 7m 35s
Heat: 1 Merton College, Oxford 2 TRC. 2¾ lengths, 7m 27s

1899 H.R. Hewison 9.7(bow); C.F.H. Greenwood 10.9; H.G. Ford 10.4; A.V. Carroll 11.1; H.M. Wood 11.5; R.H. Forster 11.6; W.A.S. De Gale 11.2; H.V. Maycock 10.13 (stroke); H.E. Greenwood 7.11 (cox). Av: 10.11¾
Heat: 1 Kingston RC 2 TRC. 1 length, 7m 37s

1900 H.R. Hewison 9.9 (bow); A. Collins 10.12; J.B. Grove 10.8; E.R. How 11.7; E.H. Benjamin 12.5; R.H. Forster 11.12; E.O. Capon 10.6; G. Bullock 9.13 (stroke); H.E. Greenwood 8.3 (cox). Av: 10.12½
Heat: 1 London RC 2 TRC. 1 length, 7m 53s

1901 W.H. Godfrey 10.1 (bow); N.C. Nichols 10.2; J.B. Grove 10.10; H. Messom 11.5; E.H. Benjamin 12.5; J.F.W. James 10.10; H.W. Hesse 10.1; M.W. Ashby 10.6 (stroke); H.E. Greenwood 8.7 (cox). Av: 10.12 ½
Heat: 1 Kingston RC 2 TRC. Easily, 7m 57s

1902 J.M. Heath 10.0 (bow); A.J. Matthew 10.5; F.B. Bentley 10.12; R.F. Reeve 12.3; J.A. Halford 11.12; R.H. Forster 11.12; H.R. Hewison 9.9; G.C. Owen 10.6 (stroke); H.E. Greenwood 8.10 (cox). Av: 10.12½
Heat: 1 TRC 2 London RC. 3½ lengths, 8m 16s
Semi-final: 1 Royal School of Mines 2 TRC. ¾ length, 7m 42s

1903 H.R. Hewison 9.13 (bow); H.B. Langton 10.6; W.B. Liebert 10.9; J.G.N. Clift 10.12; L.N. Elliot 11.9; A.V. Carroll 11.9; H. Buchanan 10.1; H. Messom 11.4 (stroke); H.E. Greenwood 8.6 (cox). Av: 10.11¼
Heat: 1 Newry RC, Ireland 2 TRC. 1 length, 7m 44s

1904 M.C. Aldwright 9.9 (bow); G. Turner 9.12; F.B. Bentley 11.0; R.A. Sparks 10.8; E.R. Odell 10.1; H.B. Harrison 11.3; H.G. Irwin 10.5; H.G. Bartol 9.6 (stroke); H.E. Greenwood 8.12 (cox). Av: 10.3¾
Heat: 1 TRC 2 Kingston RC. 1¾ lengths, 8m 14s
Semi-Final: Caius College, Cambridge (winners) 2 TRC. 1¼ lengths, 8m 0s

1905 B.T. Monier-Williams 10.0 (bow) H.B. Harrison 11.6; H.C. Huxley 12.1; W.S. Hallett 12.8; F. Trewby 11.5; G.L. Thomson 12.1; H.G. Irwin 10.13; C.G. Sprague 11.0 (stroke); H.E. Greenwood

9.2 (cox). Av: 11.6
Heat: 1 TRC 2 Mersey RC. 1 length, 7m 30s
Semi-final: 1 TRC 2 Twickenham RC. ½ length, 7m 31s
Final: 1 TRC 2 Kingston RC. 1 length, 7m 28s

1906 H.A. Forrest 10.0 (bow); G.T. Wilkes 11.2; K. Vernon 10.12; K. Doulton 12.3; C.H. Huxley 13.2; B. Logan 12.3; R.A. Sparks 11.1; L.S. Waterall 11.4 (stroke); H. Hunter 8.5 (cox). Av: 11.6¾
Heat: 1 Twickenham RC 2 TRC. ½ length, 7m 20s

1907 E.B. Musson 10.7 (bow); H.B. Langton 11.5; F.R.P. Stringer 10.11; W.B. Liebert 10.13; K. Doulton 12.6; S. Harrison-Jones 12.1; A. Elms 11.1; R.F.M. Bigby 10.9 (stroke); D.V. Johnson 8.5 (cox). Av: 11.3
Heat: 1 Vesta RC 2 TRC. ⅓ length, 7m 31s

1908 H.C. Johnson 9.2 (bow); J.F.S. Hards 11.5; J. Aitcheson 10.11; H.W. Taylor 10.13; E.R. Folkes 12.13; N.A. Wright 12.0; L.P. Langton 11.4; H.G. Salmond 10.12 (stroke); H.E. Greenwood 8.12 (cox). Av: 11.2¼
Heat: 1 Clare College, Cambridge 2 TRC. 1¼ lengths, 7m 29s

1909 F. Engert 10.5 (bow); A.F. Greenwood 10.2; F.J. Stewart 11.0; L.P. Langton 11.7; N.A. Wright 12.0; J.Y. Fletcher 13.2; R.D.W. Thompson 11.4; C.G. Williams 9.11 (stroke); E.D. Rutter 9.0 (cox). Av: 11.2
Heat: 1 Royal Engineers Yacht Club 2 TRC. ¾ length, 7m 57s

1910 H.A. Forrest 10.5 (bow); G.T. Wilkes 11.6; G.T. Sherwood 12.10; C. Keuth 11.12; E.R. Folker 13.8; E.L. Watts 12.5; E.S. Rowsell 13.8; A.F. Greenwood 10.2 (stroke); H. Hunter 8.13 (cox). Av: 12.0
Heat: 1 TRC 2 Pembroke College, Oxford. ⅓ length, 7m 36s
Heat: 1 Clare College, Cambridge 2 TRC. 1¾ lengths, 7m 44s

1911 H.W. Burleigh 10.10 (bow); F.R.P. Stringer 11.1; E.S. Rowsell 11.8; F.L. Roberts 10.10; M.S. Gunn 11.6; H.J. Davies 12.3; Sir G. Fetherston 11.1; W.B. Long 9.12 (stroke); H. Sunley 8.6 (cox). Av: 11.1
Heat: 1 Clare College, Cambridge 2 TRC. 2 feet, 7m 27s

1912 H.W. Burleigh 10.11 (bow); C.W. Story 10.11; G. East 11.8; R.S. Wilshire 11.1; J.F.S. Hards 11.5; L.P. Langton 12.6; W.B. Long 10.2; S.H.M. Johns 10.7 (stroke); H. Sunley 8.7 (cox). Av: 11.1
Heat: 1 RC de Paris (winners) 2 TRC. Easily, 7m 36s

1913 D.F. Humphreys 10.3 (bow); W.B. Long 10.5; Sir G. Fetherston 11.2; L. Garson 12.0; E.G. Greville 13.3; W.S. Douglas 12.11; S.H.M. Johns 11.5; G.A.L. Hatton 11.3 (stroke); R.M. Goodman 8.13 (cox). Av: 11.7½
Heat: 1 Twickenham RC 2 TRC. ½ length, 7m 24s

1914 E.V. Colley 9.13 (bow); W.B. Long 10.6; P. Rought 11.6; W.B. Clayton 12.2; F.C. Howard 13.5; O.B. Wallis 11.10; H.C. Evans 9.13; J.K. Dunlop 11.1 (stroke); H. Sunley 9.0 (cox). Av: 11.3½
Heat: 1 TRC 2 Royal Engineers. 1½ lengths, 7m 57s
Heat: 1 St Catharine's College, Cambridge 2 TRC. 1½ lengths, 7m 59s

1920 A: C.G. Chandler 10.11 (bow); C.H. Rew 11.0; W.S. Douglas 12.6; K.C. Wilson 11.12; A.R. Ditterick 11.7; Count S. Wachtmeister 12.0; S.I. Fairbairn 12.0; R.G. Bare 10.12 (stroke); C.A.A. Robertson 8.6 (cox). Av: 11.9½
Heat: 1 TRC 2 Downing College, Cambridge. Easily, 8m 2s
Heat: 1 TRC 2 Emmanuel College, Cambridge. Easily, 8m 10s
Semi-final; 1 TRC 2 Magdalen College, Oxford. ¾ length, 7m 35s
Final: 1 TRC 2 Caius College, Cambridge. 1 length, 7m 43s
B: C.B. Maynard 8.13 (bow); A.L. Westwood 10.6; J.H. Mair 10.11; H.A.A. Howell 11.11; F.C. Howard 13.12; A.H. Turner 12.0; C.M. Morell 11.6; C.S. Burge 10.8 (stroke); C.T. Lane 8.3 (cox). Av: 11.3
Heat: 1 Trinity College, Oxford 2 TRC. 3 lengths, 8m 8s

Thames Challenge Cup

1921 E.D. Palmer 10.2 (bow); K.P.D. Thomas 11.0; E.A. Pounds 11.5; J.G. Worth 12.2; A.F. Long 11.6; C.R. Williams 11.9; T.R.F. Barrett-Lennard 11.7; A.P. Dawes 9.10 (stroke); P.S. Martin 7.7 (cox). Av: 11.1½
Heat: 1 Corpus Christi College, Oxford 2 TRC. Easily, 7m 12s

1922 A.P. Dawes 9.12 (bow); T.R.F. Barrett-Lennard 12.1; E.A. Pounds 11.8; E.H. Brown 12.0; G.C. Killick 11.4; H.M. Lane 13.0; H.E. West 10.13; J.C. Marshall 11.3 (stroke); L. Cave-Chinn 7.7 (cox). Av: 11.6¾
Heat: 1 TRC 2 Wadham College, Oxford. 2 lengths, 7m 43s
Heat: 1 Trinity Hall, Cambridge 2 TRC. ½ length, 7m 59s

1923 L. Long 9.10 (bow); F.R. Barker 11.6; W.L.G. Day 11.12; E.A. Pounds 11.11; G.C. Killick 11.13; H.M. Lane 13.2; C.T. Southgate 12.3; H.E. West 11.3 (stroke); R. Myer 8.0 (cox). Av: 11.9¼
Heat: 1 TRC 2 Oriel College, Oxford. 1¼ lengths, 7m 29s (short course)
Heat: 1 TRC 2 St Catharine's College, Cambridge. Easily, 7m 2s
Heat: 1 First Trinity, Cambridge (winners) 2 TRC. 1 length, 7m 2s

1924 L. Long 9.10 (bow); A.P. Dawes 9.13; C.N. Shawcross 12.4; C.M. Morrell 11.8; G.C. Killick 11.12; J.C. Badcock 12.3; C.T. Southgate 12.11; C.C.B. Danvers 10.7 (stroke); K. Muskett 8.7 (cox). Av: 11.5
Heat: 1 Trinity Hall, Cambridge 2 TRC. 1¼ lengths, 8m 22s

1925 L. Long 9.4 (bow); E.A. Morphy 11.11; J.A. Brownell 11.2; L. Shillito 11.10; D. Wheeler 13.1; G.D. Smith 11.2; F.H. Wigglesworth 10.3; B.A. Lansdowne 10.8 (stroke); E.H. Deane 9.5 (cox). Av: 11.1½
Heat: 1 Henley RC 2 TRC. ⅓ length, 7m 22s

1926 L. Long 9.7 (bow); A.P. Dawes 9.13; P. McMullen 10.10; E.W. Bradford 11.8; D. Wheeler 13.4; F.E.C. Cox 12.4; F.H. Wigglesworth 10.3; B.A. Lansdowne 10.7 (stroke); J.C. Hellberg 7.7 (cox). Av: 11.0
Heat: 1 TRC 2 Henley RC. Easily, 7m 30s
Heat: 1 TRC 2 Imperial College. 1 length, 7m 21s
Heat: 1 TRC 2 Queens' College, Cambridge. ½ length, 7m 19s
Semi-final: 1 Kingston RC 2 TRC. ¾ length, 7m 8s

1927 J.K. Brownell 10.3 (bow); W.H. Lyons 10.2; W.D. Spurling 11.10; E.W. Bradford 11.9; F.E.C. Cox 12.3; A.P. McEldowney 11.9; F.H. Wigglesworth 10.4; E.G. Beresford 9.10 (stroke); F.J. Gerring 8.7 (cox) Av: 10.13¼
Heat: 1 TRC 2 Kent School, USA. ¼ length, 7m 44s
Heat: 1 TRC 2 Worcester College for the Blind. Easily
Heat: 1 TRC 2 Lady Margaret, Cambridge. Easily, 7m 31s
Semi-final: 1 TRC 2 Quintin BC. 3 lengths, 7m 38s
Final: 1 TRC 2 Twickenham RC. ¼ length, 7m 34s

1928 J.K. Brownell 10.7 (bow); R.D.G. Barnett 11.3; W.D. Spurling 11.11; H.W. Dulley 11.10, H.N. Sporborg 11.9; A.P. McEldowney 11.10; Hon C.R. Allanson-Winn 10.8; E.G. Beresford 10.1 (stroke); F.J. Gerring 8.8 (cox). Av: 11.2
Heat: 1 TRC 2 Trinity College, Dublin. Easily, 7m 45s
Heat: 1 TRC 2 Peterhouse, Cambridge. ¾ length, 8m 25s
Heat: 1 TRC 2 First Trinity, Cambridge. 1¾ lengths, 7m 40s
Semi-final: 1 TRC 2 Kingston RC. 1¼ lengths, 7m 8s
Final: 1 TRC 2 Twickenham RC. ¾ length, 7m 23s

1929 J.K. Brownell 10.3 (bow); R.M. Bethell 11.9; B.S. Fidler 12.0; D. Neal 11.3; A.H. Clarkson 12.11; F.E.C. Cox 12.3; R.R. Swatton 11.9; F.E. Michaelis 11.6 (stroke); F.J. Gerring 8.4 (cox). Av: 11.9
Heat: 1 TRC 2 Henley RC. 1¼ lengths, 7m 44s
Heat: 1 TRC 2 London RC. 1⅓ lengths, 7m 34s
Heat: 1 TRC 2 National Provinicial Bank RC. Easily, 8m 37s

Semi-final: 1 TRC 2 Quintin BC. Easily, 7m 27s
Final: 1 Browne and Nichols School, USA 2 TRC. 1¼ lengths, 7m 28s

1930 B.E.A. Joyner 9.12 (bow); R.H.B. Lord 11.0; R.D. George 12.8; T.H. Tyler 11.13; R.H. Williams 12.0; K.A. Williams 12.0; R.R.E. Bradley 10.10; F.G. Bunge 11.12 (stroke); J.G. Dearlove 7.11 (cox). Av: 11.6¾
Heat: 1 TRC 2 First Trinity, Cambridge. 1¼ lengths, 7m 48s
Heat: 1 Vesta RC (winners) 2 TRC. 1 length, 7m 37s

1931 F.E. Michaelis 11.4 (bow); R.F.W. Patterson 11.12; R.H. Williams 12.2; K.A. Williams 12.2; A.W. Holden 13.0; G. Hardwicke 12.10; D.C. Price 11.0; H.E.G. Watts 10.10 (stroke); G.R. Watson 8.13 (cox). Av: 11.11¾
Heat: 1 TRC 2 St Catharine's College, Cambridge. 1¼ lengths, 7m 39s
Heat: 1 Twickenham RC 2 TRC. ¾ length, 7m 50s

1932 H.E.G. Watts 11.0 (bow); R.H. Coombe 10.6; A.E. Shave 12.11; B.P. Drakeford 11.7; R.H. Williams 12.0; K.A. Williams 12.2; F.G.C. Catling 11.6; F.G. Bunge 11.12 (stroke); D.L. Bell 8.3 (cox). Av: 11.8¾
Heat: 1 TRC 2 Westminster Bank RC. ¾ length, 7m 49s
Heat: 1 Imperial College 2 TRC. 1¼ lengths, 7m 53s

1933 A.G. Thoday 10.6 (bow); R.W. Messom 11.11; E.H.L. Wigram 12.4; J.B. Tointon 11.7; Hon J.F. Arundell 11.3; A.E. Shave 12.8; R.H.B. Lord 11.6; F.G. Bunge 11.12 (stroke); J. Agelasto 8.6 (cox). Av: 11.8¾
Heat: 1 TRC 2 Ottershaw College. Easily, 7m 28s
Heat: 1 TRC 2 Quintin BC. Canvas, 7m 12s
Heat: 1 Lensbury RC 2 TRC. 1¾ lengths, 8m 0s

1934 R.R.E. Bradley 10.9 (bow); R.H.B. Lord 11.9; R.C. Morris 10.13; K.A. Williams 12.3; J.A. Maclean 12.13; R.W. Messom 12.2; H.W.T. Beckett 10.8; H.E.G. Watts 11.5 (stroke); E.V. Pidduck 8.8 (cox). Av: 11.7¾
Heat: 1 TRC 2 Reading University. Easily, 7m 10s
Heat: 1 TRC 2 Yale University, USA. ½ length, 7m 3s
Semi-final: 1 TRC 2 Westminster Bank RC. 1 length, 7m 2s
Final: 1 TRC 2 London RC. ⅓ length, 7m 4s

1935 A. Burrough 11.6 (bow); R.W. Messom 11.11; Hon J.F. Arundell 11.3; K.A. Williams 12.4; H. Lohnberg 13.3; A.E. Shave 13.6; F.J.P. Dodd 11.3; H.E.G. Watts 11.6 (stroke); J.B. Freebairn-Smith 9.2 (cox). Av: 12.0
Heat: 1 TRC 2 Ibis RC. Easily, 7m 46s
Heat: 1 TRC 2 Molesey BC. ¾ length, 7m 40s
Heat: 1 TRC 2 Oriel College, Oxford. ¾ length, 7m 36s
Semi-final: 1 London RC (winners) 2 TRC. 1 length, 7m 12s

1936 E.J. Reed 10.3 (bow); S.R. Tubbs 11.10; R.T.R.Cowper 12.0; H. Lohnberg 13.5; T.K. Hanson 13.4; H.M. Fox 12.6; D.F. Braham 11.0; E.G.H. Moody 11.3 (stroke); R.W. Strokes 8.9 (cox). Av: 11.12½
Heat: 1 TRC 2 Reading University. ½ length, 7m 43s
Heat: 1 Browne and Nichols School, USA 2 TRC. ½ length, 7m 29s

1937 R.E. Harrison 11.2 (bow); E.W. Huggins 12.4; R.T.R. Cowper 12.1; R.W. Messom 12.4; A.E. Shave 13.8; P.C. Kirkpatrick 13.12; R.C. Morris 11.2; E.G.H. Moody 11.9 (stroke); R.W. Stokes 8.9 (cox). Av: 12.3½
Heat: 1 TRC 2 Lady Margaret, Cambridge. Easily, 7m 50s
Heat: 1 Jesus College, Cambridge 2 TRC. 6 feet, 7m 40s

1938 W. Myers 10.5 (bow); R.M. Bethell 11.7; H.C. Albery 11.10; D. Belson 12.1; J.C. Bryce 12.1; R.W. Messom 12.1; P. Gordon-Crosby 12.9; S.C. Lowe 10.1 (stroke); W.E.S. Bain 9.5 (cox). Av: 11.7¾
Heat: 1 Reading University 2 TRC. ¾ length, 7m 25s

Thames Challenge Cup

1939 C.H.W. Messer 11.3 (bow); J. March 11.2; N.T. Taylor 12.0; J.F.G. Sykes 12.6; J.A. Churchill 13.4; A.W. Holden 14.3; D. Belson 12.4; E.W. Huggins 11.13 (stroke); J.B. Freebairn-Smith 9.9 (cox). Av: 12.4¼
Heat: 1 TRC 2 Metropolitan Police. 1½ lengths, 8m 38s
Heat: 1 Tabor Academy, USA 2 TRC. Easily, 7m 39s

1946 I.S. Waller 11.10 (bow); F.P.S. Scott 12.3; J.L. Cooke 11.3; K.A.P. Liddy 11.7; S.P.B. Way 12.5; J.A. Maclean 13.9; A.F. Fox 11.8; R.C. Farnham 11.4 (stroke); J.F. Levy 9.6 (cox). Av: 11.13
Heat: 1 TRC 2 Reading University. 5 feet, 7m 48s
Heat: 1 Isis BC 2 TRC. Easily, 8m 52s

1947 K.J. Holt 10.11 (bow); R.W. Brown 11.11; H.B. James 13.0; A.C. Penley 12.6; A.R. Watson 11.11; T.H. Christie 12.13; J.R. Johnson 12.7; R.C. Farnham 11.5 (stroke); J.F. Levy 8.13 (cox). Av: 12.1
Heat: 1 Emmanuel College, Cambridge 2 TRC. ¾ length, 7m 39s

1948 P.S. Pusey 11.7 (bow); J.C.M. Currie 11.12; A.R. Watson 11.12; H.B. James 12.12; M.B. Scott 13.6; A.C. Penley 12.3; C.B.B. Bond 12.0; A.K. Stuart 12.6 (stroke); J.F. Levy 9.1 (cox). Av: 12.3¾
Heat: 1 TRC 2 University College and Hospital. 1½ lengths, 7m 31s
Heat: 1 TRC 2 Westminster Bank RC. 1 length, 7m 15s
Heat: 1 Kent School, USA 2 TRC. ¾ length, 7m 23s

1949 T.P. Wilson 9.9 (bow); A.W. Mills 10.8; I.F. Macdonald 11.0; R.H. Beaton 11.11; K.N. Woodward-Fisher 12.7; J. Pope 11.8; J.C. Hyem 11.5; J.N. Eldeen 12.0 (stroke); B. Graydon 8.5 (cox). Av: 11.4¼
Heat: 1 TRC 2 Marlow RC. 1¼ lengths, 6m 58s
Heat: 1 TRC 2 Lensbury RC. 1¼ lengths, 7m 29s
Heat: 1 Lady Margaret, Cambridge 2 TRC. 1 length, 6m 51s (record)

1950 G.S. Dear 10.11 (bow); M.F. Alexander 10.2; I.F. MacDonald 10.7; B.C. Lawrence 13.3; G.A. Napper 11.2; K.N. Woodward-Fisher 12.13; P.S. Pusey 10.9; A.F. Fox 11.8 (stroke); L.K. Guest, 7.7 (cox). Av: 11.5
Heat: 1 TRC 2 Peterhouse, Cambridge. Canvas, 7m 10s
Heat: 1 TRC 2 Magdalene College, Cambridge. ¾ length, 7m 27s
Heat: 1 TRC 2 Bedford RC. ⅔ length, 7m 28s
Semi-final: 1 TRC 2 Jesus College, Cambridge. 1½ lengths, 7m 33s
Final: 1 Kent School, USA 2 TRC. 2½ lengths, 7m 34s

1951 A.C. Riemer 12.4 (bow); G.S. Dear 11.1; J.F. Williams 12.5; F.E. Hunter 12.11; A.C. Coates 12.6; P.J.B. Stevens 11.8; P.S. Pusey 11.0; P.W.J. Simcox 10.7 (stroke); D.H.W. Thomas 9.8 (cox). Av: 12.3½
Heat: 1 University of Pennsylvania, USA 2 TRC. Easily, 7m 10s

1952 G.S. Dear 10.11 (bow); H.G.V. Denning 12.1; J.A.C. Andrews 11.10; B.C. Lawrence 13.4; A.C. Riemer 11.10; L.S. Williams 13.2; T.E.M. Douglas 11.10; J.N. Eldeen 12.7 (stroke); L.K. Guest 8.3 (cox). Av: 12.8½
Heat: 1 University of London 2 TRC. ⅓ length, 7m 35s

1953 B.T. Ramm 11.7 (bow); T.P. Wilson 10.0; R.C. Bray 11.2; M.S. Atkins 11.8; A.C. Hancox 11.10; A.R. Reddin 12.12; G.S. Dear 11.3; P.B. Rooksby 10.11 (stroke); D.B. Fawcett 8.5 (cox). Av: 11.4¾
Heat: 1 Royal Air Force (winners) 2 TRC. 1¼ lengths, 7m 5s

1954 A. Hawes 11.8 (bow); P.B. Rooksby 10.13; D.A. Dunton 12.6; J.P.M. Thomson 11.7; D.P.C. Platt 13.2; A.R. Reddin 13.2; J.P. Hindle 11.1; P. Nyffeler 10.7 (stroke); D.B. Fawcett 8.11 (cox). Av: 11.11
Heat: 1 TRC 2 Yale University, USA. 4 lengths, 7m 23s
Heat: 1 TRC 2 National Provincial Bank RC. 1/3 length, 7m 26s
Heat: 1 TRC 2 Royal Air Force. 1/4 length, 7m 18s
Semi-final: 1 Massachusetts Institute of Technology, USA (winners) 2 TRC. 1 length, 7m 37s

1955 G.G.H. Page 11.7 (bow); P.H. Swift 11.8; D.A. Dunton 12.7; A. Hawes 11.10; D.R. Mount 13.3; A.R. Reddin 13.3; J.K.M. Hennessy 11.5; P.B. Rooksby 11.3 (stroke); D.B. Fawcett 8.11 (cox). Av: 11.11
Heat: 1 TRC 2 Jesus College, Cambridge. 2 lengths, 7m 40s
Heat: 1 Royal Air Force 2 TRC. 1/2 length, 7m 29s

1956 R.C. Bray 11.2 (bow); M.J. Long 11.7; A. Hawes 11.11; J.F.C. Badcock 12.1; A.S.J. Fingland 12.9; J. Rayne 12.9; A.C. Hancox 12.12; M.M. Tanner 10.10 (stroke); R.L. Penney 8.6 (cox). Av: 11.13
Heat: 1 TRC 2 Brockville RC, Canada. 2/3 length, 7m 22s
Heat: 1 Princeton University, USA (winners) 2 TRC. 1 1/4 lengths, 7m 28s

1957 R.C. Bray 11.5 (bow); M.J. Long 11.5; R.F. Clipson 12.5; C.P. Baker 12.11; M.S. Atkins 12.2; R.C. Wright 11.1; A. Hawes 11.9; R. Neale 12.1 (stroke); J.T. Shaw 8.6 (cox). Av: 11.11 3/4
Heat: 1 Royal Air Force 2 TRC. 1/2 length, 7m 15s

1958 D. King 11.11 (bow); M.J. Long 11.8; J.N. Gladstone 13.4; G.C. Crocket 12.12; R.D.F. Anderson 13.5; P.M.G. Harris 13.12; A. Routley 13.7; M.S. Atkins 12.8 (stroke); R.A. Matthiae 8.10 (cox). Av: 12.10 1/2
Heat: 1 TRC 2 Royal Air Force, Cardington. 1/4 length, 7m 12s
Heat: 1 TRC 2 Oriel College, Oxford. 1 3/4 lengths, 7m 18s
Heat: 1 TRC 2 The Queen's University, Belfast. 2/3 length, 6m 59s
Semi-final: 1 TRC 2 Molesey BC. 1 length, 7m 5s
Final: 1 Harvard University, USA 2 TRC. 3/4 length, 6m 57s

1959 D. King 11.12 (bow); R. Neale 11.12; M.T. Carrigg 12.5; J.W. Varian 12.5; G.J. Peakin 13.13; P.M.G. Harris 13.10; J.P.M. Thomson 12.0; R.J. Workman 11.8 (stroke); R.A. Matthiae 8.9 (cox). Av: 12.9 3/4
Heat: 1 TRC 2 Phillips Academy, USA. 3 feet, 7m 16s
Heat: 1 TRC 2 Pembroke College, Cambridge. 1 1/4 lengths, 7m 31s
Heat: 1 Jesus College, Cambridge 2 TRC. 1/3 length, 7m 17s

1960 E.V. Harris 11.6 (bow); A. Sacker 11.11; D. King 11.12; J.P.M. Thomson 12.1; J.A. Stephenson 13.11; F.J. Lambert 13.0; H.A. Wober 12.1; M.S. Atkins 13.7 (stroke); R.A. Matthiae 8.11 (cox). Av: 12.10 1/4
Heat: 1 TRC 2 Nottingham University. 1 1/2 lengths, 7m 9s
Heat: 1 TRC 2 Crowland RC. 2 lengths, 7m 3s
Heat: 1 TRC 2 Thames Tradesmen's RC. 1 1/4 lengths, 7m 15s
Semi-final: 1 Detroit BC, USA 2 TRC. 1 length, 6m 51s

1961 T.J.R. Moore 10.4 (bow); P.M.G. Moore 10.9; D.R. Allen 11.13; D. King 11.10; C.J.F.S. Rowley 11.7; A.N. Boydell 10.11; B.J. Gauld 11.10; J.A. Mees 11.2 (stroke); R.T.H. Helby 8.3 (cox). Av: 11.3
Heat: 1 Poplar, Blackwall and District RC 2 TRC. 2/3 length, 7m 8s

Thames Challenge Cup

1962 C.J.F.S. Rowley 11.12 (bow); M.J. Long 12.5; B.M. Webster 12.11; J.E. Taylor 12.5; B.J. Gauld 12.4; B.D. Gibbs 13.12; W.H. Jackson 12.5; M.J. Lohnberg 12.0 (stroke); J.T. Shaw 8.10 (cox). Av: 12.10¼
Heat: 1 TRC 2 St Edmund Hall, Oxford. 2⅓ lengths, 7m 11s
Heat: 1 TRC 2 Menoetes BC. 3 lengths, 6m 51s
Heat: 1 TRC 2 London RC. Canvas, 6m 56s
Semi-final: 1 TRC 2, Nottingham University. 2½ lengths, 7m 3s
Final: 1 National Provincial Bank RC 2 TRC. 3 lengths, 6m 46s

1963 V.B.A. Temple 10.7 (bow); R.J. Workman 12.4; J.P.M. Thomson 12.0; W.H. Needham 11.10; I.A. MacRae 13.2; R.M. Telling 11.9; P.F. Crowley 12.2; D.D. Skinner 11.7 (stroke); R.A. Matthiae 9.9, (cox). Av: 12.1½
Heat: 1 TRC 2 Staines BC. 2 lengths, 7m 27s
Heat: 1 TRC 2 Imperial College. 3 lengths, 7m 20s
Heat: 1 London RC 2 TRC. 1 length, 7m 24s

1964 V.B.A. Temple 10.6 (bow); R.J. Worthington 12.4; A.A. Reader 12.5; J.E. Taylor 12.5; J.A. Tod 12.11; A.D. Warden 12.11; T.A. Bakiewicz 12.4; D.D. Skinner 11.6 (stroke); J.T. Shaw 8.10 (cox). Av: 12.4¾
Heat: 1 TRC 2 Tyrian BC. 2 lengths, 7m 0s
Heat: 1 TRC 2 Wallingford RC. 1½ lengths, 7m 11s
Heat: 1 TRC 2 Walton RC. 2 lengths, 6m 58s
Semi-final: 1 London RC 2 TRC. ⅔ length, 6m 56s

1965 V.B.A. Temple 10.10 (bow); J.E. Lester 11.10; R. Hackford 11.7; R.J. Worthington 12.9; J.E. Taylor 12.10; A.G. Flight 12.4; A.A. Reader 12.9; D.D. Skinner 11.12 (stroke); N.H. Clarke 9.2 (cox). Av: 12.3½
Heat: 1 Cornell University, USA 2 TRC. ¾ length, 6m 45s

1966 V.B.A. Temple 10.12 (bow); R. Flueler 11.0; R. Farrants 13.4; F.D.L. Wilmot 12.7; B. Murphy 12.11; P.J. Peacock 13.4; A.G. Rogers 12.11; M.W. Stone 12.2 (stroke); J. Hurst 8.10 (cox). Av: 12.8
Heat: 1 TRC 2 Bedford RC. ⅔ length, 6m 58s
Heat: 1 Nottingham and Union RC 2 TRC. 1¾ lengths, 7m 10s

1967 A.G. Rogers 12.3 (bow); A.T.G. Hooper 11.13; D.C.Pollard 12.4; N. Tebbs 12.10; J.E. Taylor 12.6; D.L. Cruttenden 15.0; D. Warbrick-Smith 13.4; M.W. Stone 12.1 (stroke); D.M.R. White 8.0 (cox). Av: 12.13¾
Heat: 1 TRC 2 Burton Leander RC. 4 lengths, 7m 21s
Heat: 1 Severn Scullers RC 2 TRC. Canvas, 7m 16s

1968 N.A. Morley 12.10 (bow); J.A. Friend 11.13; G.L. Harris 11.10; A.F. Sharp 13.10; M.W. Taylor 15.4; J.K. Mackley 11.11; N.S. Read 11.1; A.G. Bingham 10.1 (stroke); J. Nichol 8.13 (cox). Av: 12.7½
Heat: 1 Molesey BC 2 TRC. 3 lengths, 6m 51s

1969 V.B.A. Temple 10.13 (bow); D.C. Pollard 12.5; A.J.H. Stocking 12.4; T. Bakiewicz 12.11; J.S. Stephenson 12.6; D. Hanham 12.8; B.R. Hanham 12.11; C.J. Rodrigues 13.1 (stroke); P.G. Bailey 9.0 (cox). Av: 12.6
Heat: 1 University of Pennsylvania, USA 2 TRC. ¾ length, no time taken

1970 R. Hackford 11.13 (bow); V.B.A. Temple 10.10; K.F. Reid 12.2; S.J. Wise 12.13; R. Hedont 12.2; S.D. Nevin 12.12; P.M.J. Meagher 12.9; A.G. Bingham 10.11 (stroke); M.H.P. Denny 9.2 (cox). Av: 12.0
Heat: 1 TRC 2 Derby RC. 1½ lengths, 7m 13s
Heat: 1 TRC 2 Scottish Argonauts BC. 1⅓ lengths, 7m 25s
Heat: 1 Quintin BC 2 TRC. 2¼ lengths, 6m 51s

1971 N. Rudd 11.4 (bow); P.W.H. Rushmere 11.6; G.A. Hodson 11.11; S.J. Barber 12.0; R.J.B. Hedont 11.9; S.J. Wise 12.6; N.S. Read 10.13; A.G. Bingham 10.7 (stroke); M.H.P. Denny 8.12 (cox). Av: 11.7
Heat: 1 TRC 2 Nottingham BC. 4 lengths, 7m 25s
Heat: 1 TRC 2 Metroplitan RC. ½ length, 7m 8s
Heat: 1 Harvard University, USA (winners) 2 TRC. Easily, 7m 4s

1972 A.G. Taylor 11.12 (bow); P.J. Norman 11.8; P.F. Wilson 14.0; J.M. Lee 12.9; R.J.B. Hedont 12.7; R.R. Brown 13.9; N.S. Read 11.2; A.G. Bingham 10.12 (stroke); T.J.S. Levy 8.0 (cox). Av: 12.4
Heat: 1 Vesta RC 2 TRC. 1½ lengths, 7m 41s

1974 S.L. Jones 10.3 (bow); J.T. Hopkins 12.0; J.F. Knight 11.10; P.V. Budd 12.10; M.J.S. Levy 11.5; J.T. Armstrong 13.13; A.G. Taylor 11.7; R.J. Macartney 11.5 (stroke); T.J.S. Levy 8.0 (cox). Av: 11.12
Heat: 1 TRC 2 Severn Scullers RC. 1½ lengths, 7m 38s
Heat: 1 Quintin BC 2 TRC. 3½ lengths, 7m 30s

1975 D.G. Shove 11.11 (bow); J.T. Hopkins 12.3; G.D.St J. Bagnall 10.4; J.P. Kelly 14.0; M.R. McGowan 11.7; P.V. Budd 13.0; S.P.C.H. Woods 10.8; R.J. Macartney 10.8 (stroke); T.J.S. Levy 8.0 (cox). Av: 11.9
Heat: 1 TRC 2 Crowland RC. 1 length, 7m 1s
Heat: 1 TRC 2 Eton Excelsior RC. 2¼ lengths, 6m 51s
Heat: 1 Leander Club 2 TRC. 4 lengths, 6m 47s

1976 T. Stedman 11.0 (bow); R.C. Killick 11.0; G.D.St J. Bagnall 11.0; P.H. Chamberlain 12.0; J.C.S. Groves 13.5; W.G. Sandifer 11.13; T.J.S. Levy 9.4; J.T. Hopkins 11.10 (stroke); S.P.K. Austin 8.0 (cox). Av: 11.6
Heat: 1 Rollins College, USA 2 TRC. Easily, 6m 38s

1977 R.F. Kenyon 11.9 (bow); M.D. Croft 11.4; B.G.W. Smart 11.12; M.P. Kaminski 11.7; P.H. Chamberlain 12.6; K. Pattinson 11.13; P.N. Davis 11.0; J.T. Hopkins 12.6 (stroke); S.P.K. Austin 8.3 (cox). Av: 11.12
Heat: 1 TRC 2 Cambridge '99 RC. 2½ lengths, 7m 31s
Heat: 1 TRC 2 Williams College, USA. 1¾ lengths, 7m 46
Heat: 1 Kingston RC 2 TRC. 1¼ lengths, 6m 50s

1978 P.N. Davis 11.0 (bow); M. Johnson 10.8; R.C. Chapman 11.8; J.T. Hopkins 12.7; J.D.M. Scoular 12.6; W.G. Sandifer 11.7; S.J. Webb 11.5; J.P. Davis 10.10 (stroke); J. Hague 7.12 (cox). Av: 11.6¼
Heat: 1 TRC 2 Barclay's Bank RC. 2¾ lengths, 7m 34s
Heat: 1 London RC (winners) 2 TRC. Easily, 6m 46s

1980 P.D. Roberts 11.11 (bow); T.J.S. Levy 10.8; S.R. Wigfall 12.7; J.P. Davis 11.11; S.J. Crump 11.12; G. Spice 10.13; D. Wilson 10.10; M.J. Donaldson 10.9 (stroke); P. Berners-Lee 8.2 (cox). Av: 11.7
Heat: 1 College BC, Pennsylvania, USA 2 TRC. Easily, 7m 3s

1981 P.N.G. McCord 12.7 (bow); P.J.H. Whitfield 12.4; S.R. Wigfall 12.7; A. Hill 14.7; C. Waller 14.1; C.R. Jones 13.11; P.D. Roberts 12.1; G. Spice 12.1 (stroke); D. Reid 8.8 (cox). Av: 12.13½
Heat: 1 TRC 2 Worcester RC. 1 length, 7m 14s
Heat: 1 TRC 2 Trinity College, Hartford, USA. 4 feet, 6m 54s
Heat: 1 Leander Club 2 TRC. 3 lengths, 6m 56s

1982 S.J. Crump 12.7 (bow); M.R. Thomas 12.0; S.R. Wigfall 12.10; S.L. Cole 12.10; C.V. Hughes 13.0; C.R. Jones 14.0; P.D. Roberts 12.8; G. Spice 12.8 (stroke); M.G. Rowan 8.2 (cox). Av: 12.11
Heat: 1 Charles River RA, USA (winners) 2 TRC. 3 lengths, 7m 4s

Thames Challenge Cup

1983 A: S.P.K. Austin 10.3 (bow); S.R. Wigfall 12.7; S.L. Cole 12.2; T.W. Baker 13.1; M.P. Cowie 13.9; A.M. Ward 14.0; P.D. Thomas 12.9; M.R. Thomas 12.5 (stroke); M. Roome 8.7 (cox). Av: 12.2
Heat: 1 TRC A 2 London B. 2⅓ lengths, 6m 57s
Heat: 1 KR Sport Gent, Belgium 2 TRC A. 3 lengths, 7m 10s
B: K. Palethorpe 11.6 (bow); M. Muggeridge 11.13; K. Tomlinson 12.7; D. Douglas 12.10; R. Why 14.8; D. Avery 13.7; W. Stephenson 12.4; A.J. Ross 12.10 (stroke); K. O'Meara 9.0 (cox). Av: 12.10
Heat: 1 Twickenham RC 2 TRC B. ¼ length, 6m 59s

1984 S.L. Jones 11.8 (bow); J.E. Robson 13.5; M.P. Cowie 13.7; D.J. Badcock 13.2; M. Urry 14.7; L.P. Brown 14.0; T.W. Baker 13.3; D.P. McDonald 11.13 (stroke); A. Billson 7.10 (cox). Av: 13.1
Heat: 1 TRC 2 Stourport BC. 2 lengths, 6m 34s
Heat: 1 Cantabrigian RC (winners) 2 TRC. 1¼ lengths, 6m 36s

1985 G.D.St J. Bagnall 11.13 (bow); J.C.B. Sutherland 12.4; T.W. Baker 13.7; A.J. Ross 12.11; M.R. Dunstan 13.5; M.J.S. Levy 13.3; G.P. Wells 13.3; C. Bourne 13.6 (stroke); C.M.D. Jones 9.1 (cox). Av: 12.13
Heat: 1 University College, Dublin 2 TRC. ¾ length, 6m 45s

1986 A W. Dunnett 12.8 (bow); B.D. Crawford 13.8; M. Otto 12.4; S. Todd 14.0; P. Westwood 14.2; J.F. Lane 13.0; M.W. Kerridge 12.7; T.J.S. Levy 11.0 (stroke); G.M. Denny 7.7 (cox). Av: 12.13
Heat: 1 TRC A 2 The Gunnery School, USA. Easily, 7m 11s
Heat: 1 Imperial College A 2 TRC A. 3¾ lengths, 6m 53s
B: J. McConnor 10.10 (bow); D. Catmur 12.8; J.W.P. Chalmers 12.3; G.J. Elkington 12.10; A. Seddon 12.1; M. McElroy 12.9; C. Mruck 10.8; J. Gaulier 12.0 (stroke); N.S. Mason 8.1 (cox). Av: 11.13
Heat: 1 Oriel College, Oxford 2 TRC B. Not rowed out.

1987 A: B.A. Crawford 12.0 (bow); S. Gales 10.13; R.M. Payn 13.1; H.F.W. Worden 13.10; B.D. Crawford 14.1; G.J.H. Thomas 14.9; J.E. Robson 15.0; P.R. Williams 13.5 (stroke); C.L. Salmon 8.10 (cox). Av: 13.5
Heat: 1 TRC A 2 Henley RC A. ⅓ length, 6m 47s
Heat: 1 TRC A 2 Kingston RC B. ¾ length, 6m 45s
Heat: 1 Durham University 2 TRC A. ½ length, 6m 38s
B: A.J. Tyler 13.7 (bow); A.R.J. MacLeod 12.8; J.E. Heath 13.3; A.J.R. Inglis 13.13; C.A. Maby 13.12; T.A. Earnshaw 14.2; T.G. Hockley 11.6; M.C.A. MacDougall 11.8 (stroke); N.S. Mason 8.9 (cox). Av: 13.0
Heat: 1 TRC B 2 Marlow RC B. ⅓ length, 6m 55s
Heat: 1 Durham University 2 TRC B. 1¼ lengths, 6m 47s

1988 A: T.G. Hockley 11.2 (bow); J. Ferraro 13.0; N. Roullier 13.0; N.B. Copley 13.10; A.S.E. Johnson 12.8; A.J.R. Inglis 13.10; J. Woodiss-Field 13.0; S.P.K. Austin 10.7 (stroke); T. Lohmann 8.0 (cox). Av: 12.8
Heat: 1 TRC A 2 Bedford RC A. 4¾ lengths, 7m 11s
Heat: 1 TRC A 2 Lea RC. 2¾ lengths, 7m 27s
Heat: 1 TRC A 2 Trinity College, Dublin. ¾ length, 6m 59s
Semi-final: 1 TRC A 2 University College, Galway, disqualified.
Final: 1 Tideway Scullers School 2 TRC A. 1½ lengths, 6m 41s
C: A.T. Smith 11.6 (bow); A.C. Mitchell 12.8; S. Baldwin 11.8; R.J. Moon 12.6; D. Cammegh 13.7; C. Rumboll 13.12; M.R. Rawlinson 14.0; J.C. Rawlinson 12.1 (stroke); N.J. Fyfe 8.6 (cox). Av: 12.10
Heat: 1 TRC C 2 Oxford University Lightweight RC. 1¾ lengths, 7m 17s
Heat: 1 Lady Margaret, Cambridge 2 TRC C. ¾ length, 7m 1s

1989 W.H.A. Powell 11.10 (bow); J.P. Clarke 12.8; D. Winner 13.9; R.M. Payn 13.3; M.P. Clark 12.2; R.M. Storry 13.2; S.A. Kirkpatrick 11.8; G.J. Elkington 12.0 (stroke); C.L. Salmon 8.11 (cox). Av: 12.10
Heat: 1 TRC 2 The Queen's University, Belfast. 2¾ lengths, 7m 17s
Heat: 1 University of London (winners) 2 TRC. Easily, 6m 37s

1990 A: J-L. Harny, 12.5 (bow); R.J. Moon 12.10; D.B. Gates 14.4; A.J.R. Inglis 14.10; J.M. Woodiss-Field 14.0; G.P.R. Reddin 13.3; S.L. Jones 10.0; A.A. Dodd 11.11 (stroke); T. Lohman, 9.5 (cox). Av: 12.12
Heat: 1 TRC A 2 Royal Chester RC. ¾ length, 7m 28s
Heat: 1 Thames Tradesmen's B 2 TRC A. 2 lengths, 6m 57s.
B: W.H.A. Powell 12.6 (bow); G. Davy 12.6; G.J.H. Thomas 14.10; J.E. Robson 14.4; M.P. Cowie 13.4; M.P. Clark 12.11; M.W. Kerridge 13.10; J.G. Elkington 13.0 (stroke); V.M. Connolly 8.4 (cox). Av: 13.4
Heat: 1 Vesta RC 2 TRC B. Easily, 7m 15s

STEWARDS' CHALLENGE CUP

1874 W.H. Eyre 10.7 (bow); J. Maycock 10.12; J. Hastie 11.6; W.L. Slater 11.5 (stroke). Av:10.11
Heat: 1 TRC 2 Trinity College, Dublin. 1¼ lengths
Final: 1 London RC 2 TRC. 3 lengths, 9m 0s

1875 W.H. Eyre 11.0 (bow); J. Howell 10.13; J.A.M. Robertson 11.5; J. Hastie 11.7 (stroke). Av: 11.1¼
Heat: 1 Leander Club 2 TRC. Royal Chester RC disqualified. 8m 6s

1876 W.H. Eyre 10.12 (bow); J. Howell, 10.11; W.L. Slater 12.3; J. Hastie 11.5 (stroke). Av: 11.4¼
Heat: 1 TRC 2 Molesey BC 3 Dublin University BC. 2 lengths, 7m 57s
Final: 1 London RC 2 TRC. Easily, 8m 27s

1877 W.H. Eyre 10.12 (bow); J. Hastie 11.3; W.L. Slater 11.8; J. Howell 11.2 (stroke). Av: 11.2¾
Final: 1 London RC 2 TRC. Easily, 9m 7s

1879 W.H. Eyre 10.11 (bow); F. Canton 11.0; W. Jenkin 11.7; J. Hastie 11.7 (stroke). Av: 11.2¾
Heat: 1 TRC 2 London RC 3 First Trinity, Cambridge. 2 lengths, 10m 4s
Final: 1 Jesus College, Cambridge 2 Lady Margaret, Cambridge 3 TRC. 2 lengths, 9m 37s

1880 W.H. Eyre 11.0 (bow); J. Hastie 11.8; D.E. Brown 12.0; F. Canton 11.0 (stroke). Av: 11.5½
Heat: 1 TRC 2 Jesus College, Cambridge 3 London RC. 2 lengths, 7m 48s
Final: 1 TRC 2 Molesey BC. Easily, 7m 58s

1881 W.H. Eyre 10.7 (bow); J. Hastie 11.6; W.A. Jenkin 11.8; F. Canton 11.0 (stroke). Av: 11.1¾
Heat: 1 TRC 2 London RC 3 Cornell Navy BC, USA. 2 lengths, 8m 58s
Final: 1 Hertford College, Oxford 2 TRC. Not rowed out, 8m 15s

1882 H.B. Tween 10.4 (bow); J. Hastie 11.13; W.H. Eyre 10.10; F. Canton 10.10 (stroke). Av: 10.11¾
Final: 1 Hertford College, Oxford 2 TRC 3 London RC. Easily

1883 H.B. Tween 10.5 (bow); J. Hastie 11.9; H.J. Rust 12.2; J.A. Drake-Smith 10.5 (stroke). Av: 11.1¾
Heat: 1 TRC 2 Twickenham RC. Easily.
Heat: 1 TRC 2 London RC. Not rowed out.

1884 G.H. Eyre 11.1 (bow); J. Hastie 11.11; H.J. Rust 11.13; J.A. Drake-Smith 10.5 (stroke). Av: 11.4
Heat: 1 Twickenham RC 2 TRC. Not rowed out.

1885 B.W. Looker 10.6 (bow); J. Hastie 12.3; H.J. Rust 12.3; J.A. Drake-Smith 10.8 (stroke). Av: 11.5
Heat: 1 TRC 2 London RC. Easily, 8m 13s
Final: 1 Trinity Hall, Cambridge 2 Jesus College, Cambridge 3 TRC. Easily, 7m 53s

1886 B.W. Looker 11.0 (bow); A.M. Hutchinson 11.10; S. Fairbairn 13.10; J.A. Drake-Smith 10.8 (stroke). Av: 11.10½
Heat: 1 TRC 2 Berliner RC. 3 lengths.
Semi-final: 1 TRC 2 Kingston RC. Easily
Final: 1 TRC 2 Trinity Hall, Cambridge. 1 length, 7m 39s

1887 B.W. Looker 10.13 (bow); A.M. Hutchinson 12.2; S. Fairbairn 13.7; J.A. Drake-Smith 10.6 (stroke). Av: 11.10½
Heat: 1 Trinity Hall, Cambridge 2 TRC. Not rowed out, 7m 45s

1888 B.W. Looker 11.0 (bow); A.M. Hutchinson 11.13; F.E.C. Clark 12.10; J.A. Drake-Smith 10.6 (stroke). Av: 11.3
Heat: 1 Brasenose College, Oxford 2 TRC. Not rowed out, 8m 16s

1889 C.W. Hughes 10.4 (bow); A.M. Hutchinson 11.12; F.E.C. Clark 12.11; B.W. Looker 11.2 (stroke). Av: 11.7¼
Heat: 1 TRC 2 Leander Club. 4 lengths, 7m 47s
Final: 1 TRC 2 Third Trinity, Cambridge. Easily, 7m 53s

1890 C.W. Hughes 10.3 (bow); P. Landale 12.4; F.E.C. Clark 13.2; B.W. Looker 11.1 (stroke). Av: 11.9½
Heat: 1 TRC 2 London RC. ¾ length, 7m 32s
Final: 1 Brasenose College, Oxford 2 TRC. ¾ length, 7m 37s

1891 B.W. Looker 11.2 (bow); P. Landale 12.6; F.E.C. Clark 12.12; J.C. Gardner 11.11 (stroke). Av: 12.0¾
Heat: 1 TRC 2 Magdalen College, Oxford. 1¾ lengths, 8m 5s
Final: 1 TRC 2 Trinity Hall, Cambridge. 1¼ lengths, 7m 45s

1892 C.W. Hughes 10.2 (bow); W. Broughton 12.9; F.E.C. Clark 13.1; S.D. Muttlebury 13.7 (stroke). Av: 12.4¾
Heat: 1 TRC 2 London RC. 2 lengths, 8m 37s
Final: 1 Royal Chester RC 2 TRC. ¼ length, 8m 38s

1893 C.W. Hughes 10.3 (bow); W. Broughton 12.9; F.E.C. Clark 12.10; S.D. Muttlebury 13.7 (stroke). Av: 12.3¾
Heat: 1 TRC 2 Brasenose College, Oxford. Not rowed out, 8m 12s
Semi-final: 1 TRC 2 SN de la Basse-Seine. 2 lengths, 7m 42s
Final: 1 Magdalen College, Oxford 2 TRC. ¾ length, 7m 45s

1894 G. McHenry 10.12 (bow); W. Broughton 12.12; S.D. Muttlebury 13.5; J.C. Gardner 11.9 (stroke). Av: 12.1¼
Heat: 1 TRC 2 Leander Club. Not rowed out, 7m 55s.
Final: 1 TRC 2 New College, Oxford. Easily, 8m 20s

1895 G. McHenry 10.12 (bow); W. Broughton 12.13; S.D. Muttlebury 13.9; A. Bogle 11.5 (stroke). Av: 12.2¾
Heat: 1 TRC 2 Leander Club. Easily, 7m 58s
Final: 1 London RC 2 TRC. 1¼ lengths, 7m 43s

1896 E. Campbell-Muir 11.1 (bow); G. Hering 11.8; A. Bogle 11.10; G.G. Taylor 11.3 (stroke). Av: 11.5½
Heat: 1 TRC 2 Magdalen College, Oxford. 1 length, 7m 50s
Final: 1 London RC 2 TRC. 1 length, 8m 42s

1897 E. Campbell-Muir 11.1 (bow); J.A. Rennie 12.3; G. Dixon 11.8; G. Hering 11.10 (stroke). Av: 11.9
Heat: 1 London RC 2 TRC. 1 length, 7m 57s

1898 G. McHenry 11.1 (bow); A. Bogle 11.5; W.A. Bieber 12.4; W.J. Fernie 12.0 (stroke). Av: 11.9½
Heat: 1 Leander Club (winners) 2 TRC. Not rowed out, 7m 42s

1899 P.H. Devitt 11.5 (bow); G. Rixon 11.10; F.W. Chambers 11.7; A.F. Johnstone 12.6 (stroke). Av: 11.10½
Heat: 1 Balliol College, Oxford 2 TRC. 3 lengths, 8m 11s

1900 G. Rixon 11.9 (bow); F.W. Chambers 12.2; W.A. Bieber 12.10; A.F. Johnstone 12.7 (stroke). Av: 12.3½
Heat: 1 Leander Club (winners) 2 TRC. Easily, 8m 19s

1905 J. Beresford 10.2 (bow, strs); R.W. Roylance 12.1; S.O. Pugh 12.9; G.H. Kelly 11.1 (stroke). Av: 11.6¾
Heat: 1 Third Trinity, Cambridge 2 TRC. ½ length, 7m 57s

1908 J. Beresford 10.2 (bow, strs); K. Vernon 11.3; C.G. Rought 13.1; B. Logan 12.7 (stroke). Av. 11.10¼
Heat: 1 Magdalen College, Oxford (winners) 2 TRC. 1½ lengths, 7m 28s (record)

1909 J. Beresford 10.4 (bow, strs); K. Vernon 11.4; C.G. Rought 13.0; B. Logan 12.8 (stroke). Av: 11.11
Heat: 1 TRC 2 Trinity Hall, Cambridge. Easily, 8m 10s
Final: 1 TRC 2 Magdalen College, Oxford. 1½ lengths, 7m 38s

Stewards' Challenge Cup

1910 J. Beresford 10.5 (bow, strs); K. Vernon 11.6; C.G. Rought 13.4; B. Logan 12.11 (stroke). Av: 11.13½
Heat: 1 TRC 2 Leander Club. 1¼ lengths, 7m 27s
Semi-final: 1 Winnipeg RC, Canada (winners) 2 TRC. 1 length, 7m 49s

1911 J. Beresford 10.3 (bow, strs); K. Vernon 11.4; C.G. Rought 13.1; B. Logan 12.8 (stroke). Av: 11.11
Heat: 1 TRC 2 Magdalen College, Oxford. 2½ lengths, 7m 54s
Semi-final: 1 TRC 2 Third Trinity, Cambridge. 1¾ lengths, 7m 36s
Final: 1 TRC 2 Trinity Hall, Cambridge. 1¼ lengths, 7m 35s

1912 J. Beresford 10.2 (bow, strs); 2 K. Vernon 11.3; C.G. Rought 13.0; B. Logan 12.10 (stroke). Av: 11.10¾
Final: 1 New College, Oxford 2 TRC. 2¼ lengths, 7m 36s

1914 J. Beresford 10.3 (bow, strs); K. Vernon 11.4; E.L. Watts 12.8; B. Logan 13.0 (stroke). Av: 11.10¾
Heat: 1 Leander Club (winners) 2 TRC. 2 lengths, 7m 45s

1920 V.G. Teale 10.10 (bow, strs); K. Vernon 11.5; C.K. Roylance 12.8; B. Logan 12.13 (stroke). Av: 11.12½
Heat: 1 TRC 2 Leander Club. ¼ length, 8m 38s
Final: 1 Magdalen College, Oxford 2 TRC. Easily, 8m 3s

1921 C.G. Chandler 11.2 (bow, strs); S.I. Fairbairn 12.2; R. Teale 12.6; C.H. Rew 11.6 (stroke). Av: 11.11
Heat: 1 Magdalen College, Oxford (winners) 2 TRC. 2 lengths, 8m 5s

1923 A: C.H. Chandler 11.0 (bow, strs); C.H. Rew 11.4; A.F. Long 11.7; R.G. Bare 11.6 (stroke). Av: 11.7¼
B: J. Beresford Snr 10.5 (bow, strs); T.R.F. Barrett-Lennard 11.5; W.S. Douglas 12.13; K. Vernon 11.6 (stroke). Av: 11.7¼
Heat: 1 TRC A 2 TRC B. ¾ length, 7m 42s (short course)
Semi-final; 1 Third Trinity, Cambridge (winners) 2 TRC A. Easily, 7m 30s

1924 R.G. Bare, 11.9 (bow, strs); H.L. Morphy 10.10; A.F. Long 11.9; S.I. Fairbairn 12.0 (stroke). Av: 11.7
Heat: 1 Third Trinity, Cambridge (winners) 2 TRC. Easily, 8m 54s

1925 C.G. Chandler 11.3 (bow, strs); H.C. Debenham 12.4; A.F. Long 11.13; C.H. Rew 11.7 (stroke). Av: 11.10¼
Heat: 1 Third Trinity, Cambridge (winners) 2 TRC. Easily, 7m 36s

1926 H.E. West 10.8 (bow, strs); H.M. Lane 13.2; R. Teale 11.7; J.C. Badcock 12.7 (stroke). Av: 11.13
Heat: 1 TRC 2 Christ Church, Oxford. 1¼ lengths, 7m 42s
Final: 1 TRC 2 Leander Club. Easily, 7m 34s

1927 H.E. West 11.6 (bow, strs); H.M. Lane 13.3; D.H.L. Gollan 13.6; J.C. Badcock 12.5 (stroke). Av: 12.8½
Heat: 1 TRC 2 London RC. Easily, 8m 12s
Final: 1 TRC 2 Leander Club. 2 lengths, 8m 12s

1928 H.E. West 11.1 (bow, strs); G.O. Nickalls 12.12; D.H.L. Gollan 14.4; J.C. Badcock 12.5 (stroke). Av: 12.9
Heat: 1 TRC 2 Third Trinity, Cambridge. ¾ length, 8m 3s
Final: 1 TRC 2 London RC. 2 feet, 7m 43s

1932 J. Beresford Jnr 11.7 (bow, strs); T.H. Tyler 12.0; R.D. George 12.10; J.C. Badcock 12.6 (stroke). Av: 12.1
Final: 1 TRC 2 Berliner RC, Germany. 2 lengths, 8m 9s

1933 R.C. Morris 10.8 (bow, strs); T.H. Tyler 11.9; R.H.H. Symonds 11.6; J.C. Badcock 12.0 (stroke). Av: 11.5¾
Heat: 1 Leander Club 2 TRC. ⅓ length, 7m 36s

1934 Hon C.R. Allanson-Winn 11.8 (bow, strs); A.P. Brown 12.12; T.G. Askwith 11.12; R.C. Harman 11.6 (stroke). Av: 11.13
Heat: 1 Pembroke College, Cambridge (winners) 2 TRC. ½ length, 7m 31s

1935 R.C. Morris 10.13 (bow, strs); A.P. Brown 12.12; J.A. Maclean 12.10; R.C. Harman 11.5 (stroke) Av: 11.10
Heat: 1 Zurich RC, Switzerland (winners) 2 TRC. Easily, 8m 0s

1936 R.C. Morris 11.3 (bow, strs); A.P. Brown 13.7; A. Burrough 11.10; F.J.R. Dodd 11.4 (stroke). Av: 11.13
Heat: 1 Leander Club 2 TRC. 2½ lengths, 8m 1s

1937 J.H. Burrough 12.5 (bow, strs); A.P. Brown 13.2; A.J. Hutton-Squire 13.6; R.C. Harman 11.8 (stroke). Av: 12.8¾
Heat: 1 TRC 2 London RC. 1 length, 8m 26s
Final: 1 Leander Club 2 TRC. 1 length, 8m 32s

1938 R.C. Morris 10.13 (bow, strs); J.A. Maclean 12.3; J.T.M. O'Mara 12.12; E.G. Beresford 10.5 (stroke). Av: 11.8¼
Heat: 1 TRC 2 Kingston RC. 3 lengths, 8m 9s

1939 R.C. Morris 11.1 (bow, strs); B.N. Brooke 11.2; J.H. Burrough 12.3; R.W. Brown 11.1 (stroke). Av: 11.5¼
Heat: 1 London RC 2 TRC. 2 lengths, 8m 41s

1946 R.C. Morris 11.0 (bow, strs); A. Burrough 11.10; J.H.M. Ward 12.0; H.W. Rushmere 13.1 (stroke). Av: 11.13¼
Heat: 1 TRC 2 London RC. ¾ length, 8m 49s
Semi-final: 1 Leander Club (winners) 2 TRC. 2½ lengths, 7m 48s

1947 J.A. Wilmot 10.5 (bow, strs); J.P. Dizer 10.12; H.W. Rushmere 13.2; P.C. Kirkpatrick 13.11 (stroke). Av: 12.0½
Heat: 1 TRC 2 Cesky Veslarsky Klub, Czechoslavakia. 1½ lengths, 8m 3s
Semi-final: 1 TRC 2 Leander Club. 2 lengths, 8m 1s
Final: 1 TRC 2 London RC. 2 lengths, 8m 4s

1948 A.S.F. Butcher 12.2 (bow, strs); T.H. Christie 13.7; H.W. Rushmere 13.7; P.C. Kirkpatrick 14.2 (stroke). Av: 13.4½
Heat: 1 TRC 2 Seeclub, Zurich, Switzerland. 2¼ lengths, 7m 17s
Semi-final: 1 TRC 2 Leander Club. 1¼ lengths, 7m 42s
Final: 1 TRC 2 Isis and Granta Clubs. 4 lengths, 7m 48s

1949 P.S. Pusey 11.1 (bow, strs); A.J.G. Wood 11.9; J.L. Sangster 12.10; P.C. Kirkpatrick 14.3 (stroke). Av: 12.5¾
Heat: 1 London RC 2 TRC. 2½ lengths, 7m 38s

1950 R.C. Morris 11.3 (bow, strs); J.B. Shaw 13.3; A.R. Watson 12.5; P.C. Kirkpatrick 14.0 (stroke). Av: 12.9¾
Heat: 1 Trinity College, Oxford 2 TRC. 3 lengths, 7m 52s

1951 J.P. Dizer 10.13 (bow, strs); A.J.R. Purssell 11.7; H.W. Rushmere 13.8; P.C. Kirkpatrick 13.13 (stroke). Av: 12.6¾
Heat: 1 TRC 2 Lady Margaret, Cambridge. 2 feet, 7m 21s
Heat: 1 TRC 2 New College, Oxford. Easily, 8m 13s
Semi-final: 1 TRC 2 Veslacki Klub Gusar, Jugoslavia. 1½ lengths, 8m 0s
Final: 1 TRC 2 Leander Club. 1½ lengths, 7m 53s

1952 P.A. de Giles 11.13 (bow); G.C. Fisk 11.9 (strs); R.A.F. Macmillan 13.6; P.M.O. Massey 13.8 (stroke). Av: 12.9
Heat: 1 TRC 2 Goldie BC, Cambridge. 3½ lengths, 7m 25s
Final: 1 TRC 2 London RC. 2 lengths, 7m 24s

1953 G.G.H. Page 11.3 (bow, strs); J. Pope 11.1; A.R. Watson 13.3; R.H. Nicholls 12.0 (stroke). Av: 11.12¼
Heat: 1 First and Third Trinity, Cambridge 2 TRC. ½ length, 7m 21s

1954 G.G.H. Page 11.4 (bow, strs); R.A.F. Macmillan 13.8; A.R. Davidson 12.13; M. Legg 12.11 (stroke). Av: 12.9
Heat: 1 Krylia Sovetov, USSR (winners) 2 TRC. 1¼ lengths, 7m 35s

Stewards' Challenge Cup

1956 M. Legg 12.8 (bow, strs); C.F. Porter 12.8; A.R. Davidson 13.0; J.M. Beresford 11.11 (stroke). Av: 12.6¾
R.A.F. Macmillan's crew: G.S. Dear 11.1 (bow, strs); H.G.V. Denning 12.4; D.H. McLellan 14.13; R.A.F. Macmillan 14.1 (stroke). Av: 13.1¼
Heat: 1 TRC 2 R.A.F. Macmillan's crew. 3 feet, 7m 48s
Semi-final: 1 TRC 2 Leander Club. 2½ lengths, 7m 45s
Final: 1 TRC 2 London RC. 3½ lengths, 8m 6s

1957 G.S. Dear 10.13 (bow, strs); J.N. Gladstone 13.3; D.R. Mount 13.2; A.R. Watson 12.8 (stroke). Av: 12.6½
Heat: 1 London RC 2 TRC. Easily, 7m 18s

1960 D.R. Mount 13.4 (bow, strs); P. Laws 13.6; W.J. Griffith 13.12; I. Wilson 12.12 (stroke). Av: 13.5
Heat: 1 Belvoir RC, Zurich, Switzerland 2 TRC. Easily, 7m 21s

1961 M.R. Woolner 12.10 (bow, strs); F.J. Lambert 12.13; J.A. Stephenson 14.0; J.F.C. Badcock 12.0 (stroke). Av: 12.12 ¾
Final: 1 Trud Club, Leningrad, USSR 2 TRC. 2 lengths, 7m 23s

1962 F.J. Lambert 13.7 (bow, strs); J.A. Stephenson 13.12; P. Laws 13.8; J.J. James 12.0 (stroke). Av: 13.3¼
Heat: 1 ASR Nereus, Holland 2 TRC. 2 lengths, 7m 11s

1963 A.C.W. Mills 11.6 (bow, strs); M.J. Lohnberg 12.5; J.A. Stephenson 13.13; J.F.C. Badcock 11.12 (stroke). Av: 12.5½
Heat: 1 TRC 2 The Skiff Club. 1 length, 7m 39s
Final 1 Molesey BC 2 TRC. ⅔ length, 7m 16s

1964 M.R. Woolner 13.1 (bow, strs); P.C. Allen 13.6; J.A. Stephenson 14.3; C.R. Barker 13.3 (stroke). Av: 13.6 ¾
Heat: 1 Molesey BC 2 TRC. 3⅓ lengths, 7m 42s

1965 I.A. MacRae 13.1 (bow,strs); P.D. Spatz 13.3; J.W. Fryer 13.9; F.J. Lambert 14.0 (stroke). Av: 13.6¾
Heat: 1 Quintin BC (winners) 2 TRC. 3¼ lengths, 7m 25s

WYFOLD CHALLENGE CUP

1870 W.H. Eyre 10.10 (bow); G.H. Vize 12.1; W.L. Slater 11.9; A.J. Lowe 11.1 (stroke); J. Shearman 8.0 (cox). Av: 10.12¼
Final: 1 TRC 2 Oxford Etonian Club 3 Oscillators Club, Kingston. Easily, 8m 34s

1871 W.H. Eyre 10.10 (bow); H.J. Smith 10.9; G.H. Vize 12.4; W.L. Slater 11.6 (stroke); J. Shearman 8.0 (cox). Av: 11.3 ¾
Final: 1 TRC; 2 Kingston RC. 1½ lengths, 9m 6s

1872 J. Hastie 10.12 (bow); J.A. Cameron 11.3; G.H. Vize 12.3; W.L. Slater 11.5 (stroke); A. Christie 8.0 (cox). Av: 11.5 ¾
Heat: 1 TRC 2 North London RC 3 Kingston RC. Easily, 8m 22s

1873 J. Hastie 11.5 (bow); A.C. Radmall 10.0; G.H. Vize 12.3; W.L. Slater 11.3 (stroke); H.R. Trehearne 8.0 (cox). Av: 11.2¾
Heat: 1 Kingstown Harbour BC, Ireland (winners) 2 TRC 3 North London RC. Easily.

1874 C. Russell 10.9 (bow); W.B. Giles 10.8; W. Page 11.6; J. Howell 10.8 (stroke). Av: 10.11¼
Heat: 1 Newcastle RC 2 Molesey BC 3 TRC. Easily.

1875 J.W. Hughes 10.4 (bow); W. Page 11.10; C.C. Cream 11.10; G.C. Gordon 11.5 (stroke). Av: 11.3¾
Final: 1 TRC 2 London RC 3 Molesey BC. 2½ lengths, 8m 10s

1876 J.W. Hughes 10.2 (bow); W.B. Giles 11.2; C.C. Cream 11.11; G.C. Gordon 11.4 (stroke). Av: 11.1¼
Final: 1 West London RC 2 London RC 3 TRC. 1 length, 8m 24s

1877 W.B. Giles 10.7 (bow); F. Canton 10.11; J.A.M. Robertson 11.2; S. Smelt 11.10 (stroke). Av: 11.0½
Heat: 1 Waldegrave RC 2 TRC. ¼ length.

1878 J.C. Sutherland 10.7 (bow); J.G. Jones 10.5; E.C. Otter 11.0; W. Nottebohm 10.7 (stroke). Av: 10.8¼
Final: 1 Kingston RC 2 London RC 3 TRC. 1½ lengths, 8m 44s

1879 J.C. Sutherland 10.6 (bow); E.C. Otter 10.12; W. Nottebohm 10.12; G. Smith 11.2 (stroke). Av: 10.11½
Heat: 1 TRC 2 Ino RC. Easily, 9m 52s
Final: 1 London RC 2 TRC. Easily, 9m 56s

1880 J.C. Sutherland 10.7 (bow); F. Fenner 10.10; W.A. Jenkin 11.11; W. Nottebohm 10.11 (stroke). Av: 10.13¼
Heat: 1 London RC (winners) 2 TRC 3 Kingston RC. Easily, 8m 14s

1881 J.C. Sutherland 10.10 (bow); W. Nottebohm 11.0; E.D. Johnson 11.5; H.J. Rust 12.0 (stroke). Av: 11.3¾
Heat: 1 London RC 2 TRC. Easily

1882 C. Dangerfield 10.1 (bow); W. Nottebohm 11.2; H.J. Rust 12.0; G. Smith 11.9 (stroke). Av: 11.3
Heat: 1 Jesus College, Cambridge (winners) 2 Reading RC 3 TRC. Easily.

1883 C. Dangerfield 10.2 (bow); W. Nottebohm
Heat: 1 (London RC (winners) 2 TRC 3 Kingston RC. Easily, 8m 14s
11.5; E.C. Otter 12.4; W. Liddle 11.13 (stroke). Av: 11.6
Heat: 1 Third Trinity, Cambridge 2 TRC 3 West London RC. Easily, 8m 6s

1884 B.W. Looker 10.3 (bow); W. Liddle 12.6; S. Fairbairn 13.4; A.M. Hutchinson 11.7 (stroke). Av: 11.12
Heat: 1 TRC 2 Royal Chester RC 3 Clare College, Cambridge. Easily.
Final: 1 TRC 2 Marlow RC 3 London RC. 3 lengths, 8m 58s

1885 F.W. Long 9.4 (bow); W. Nottebohm 11.9; P.S.G. Propert 11.9; B.E. Cole 10.10 (stroke). Av: 10.11½
Heat: 1 Kingston (winners) 2 TRC. Easily

1886 F.W. Long 9.3 (bow); S.M. Cooke 11.0; P.S.G. Propert 12.0; B.E. Cole 10.10 (stroke). Av: 10.9
Heat: 1 TRC 2 Kingston RC. 1½ lengths
Semi-final: 1 TRC 2 Twickenham RC. 1 length
Final: 1 TRC 2 Trinity College, Oxford. 2 lengths, 8m 4s

1887 F.W. Long 9.3 (bow); A.S. Falconer 11.13; R.J. Twyford 12.4; S.M. Cooke 11.1 (stroke). Av: 11.1
Heat: 1 Pembroke College, Cambridge (winners) 2 TRC. 4 lengths, 7m 58s

Wyfold Challenge Cup

1888 C.W. Hughes 10.2 (bow); A.S. Falconer 12.6; P.S.G. Propert 12.0; J.W. Fogg-Elliot 11.1 (stroke). Av: 11.5¾
Heat: TRC 2 Pembroke College, Cambridge. ½ length, 8m 8s
Semi-final: 1 TRC 2 Kingston RC. Easily, 8m 10s
Final: 1 TRC 2 London RC. 1 length, 7m 59s

1889 J.T. Musgrave 11.0 (bow); A.S. Falconer 12.3; P.S.G. Propert 11.10; B.E. Cole 10.12 (stroke). Av: 11.5¼
Heat: 1 TRC 2 Kingston RC. 1½ lengths, 7m 51s
Final: 1 London RC 2, TRC. 4 lengths, 7m 58s

1890 E.A. Staines 10.1 (bow); A.S. Falconer 12.7; W. Broughton 12.11; J.E. Spagnoletti 9.8 (stroke). Av: 11.3¼
Heat: 1 TRC 2 Royal Chester RC. 18 inches, 7m 54s
Final: 1 Kingston RC 2 TRC. 1 length, 7m 46s

1891 E.A. Staines 10.6 (bow); T.H. Burrows 11.12; W. Broughton 12.9; L.H.K. Bushe-Fox 10.12 (stroke). Av: 11.6¼
Heat: 1 Royal Chester RC (winners) 2 TRC. 1¾ lengths, 8m 17s

1892 R.H. Forster 10.10 (bow); T.H. Burrows 12.0; T. Young 13.6; L.H.K. Bushe-Fox 11.2 (stroke). Av: 11.11½
Heat: 1 Trinity College, Dublin 2 TRC. 2 lengths, 9m 16s

1893 E.A. Staines 10.1 (bow); T.H. Burrows 12.4; H.C. Arthur 12.3; L.H.K. Bushe-Fox 10.11 (stroke). Av: 11.4½
Heat: 1 Medway RC 2 TRC. Easily, 7m 25s

1894 G.G. Taylor 11.5 (bow); J.R. Orford 12.8; H.C. Arthur 11.13; A. Bogle 11.4 (stroke). Av: 11.11
Heat: 1 TRC 2 Kingston RC. Easily, 8m 22s
Final: 1 TRC 2 Balliol College, Oxford. 2¾ lengths, 8m 16s

1895 F. Stevenson 9.13 (bow); G. Hering 11.9; R.O. Atcherley 12.10; G.G. Taylor 11.2 (stroke). Av: 11.1½
Heat: 1 Molesey BC 2 TRC. Not rowed out, 8m 52s

1896 F. Stevenson 10.3 (bow); W.G. Ross 10.11; G.E. Gill 12.7; W.G. Stoffell 12.2 (stroke). Av: 11.5¾
Heat: 1 Trinity College, Oxford (winners) 2 TRC. Easily, 8m 10s

1897 J.M. Heath 9.12 (bow); G.E. Gill 11.3; C.H. Allin 11.10; A.F. Johnstone 12.8 (stroke). Av: 11.8¼
Heat: 1 Jesus College, Cambridge 2 TRC. Easily, 8m 3s

1898 R.C. Whiteing 10.8 (bow); G. Hering 11.9; S.C. Smith 11.9; W.G. Ross 10.9 (stroke). Av: 11.1¾
Heat: 1 Caius College, Cambridge 2 TRC. Easily, 8m 8s

1899 J.M. Heath 9.13 (bow); F.H. Harrison 11.5; S.C. Smith 11.13; R.H. Forster 11.6 (stroke). Av: 11.2¼
Heat: 1 London RC 2 TRC. Easily, 8m 13s

1901 R.C. Whiteing 10.8 (bow); C.F.H. Greenwood 11.0; S.C. Smith 12.8; H.G. Finch 11.4 (stroke). Av: 11.5
Heat: 1 TRC 2 London RC. 3 feet, 8m 0s
Semi-final: 1 Christ's College, Cambridge 2 TRC. 4 feet, 8m 13s

1906 R.A. Sparks 11.1 (bow, strs); H. Messom 11.8; H.C. Huxley 12.2; G.H. Kelly 10.12 (stroke). Av: 11.5¾
Heat: 1 TRC 2 St John's College, Oxford. 2 lengths, 8m 7s
Semi-final: 1 TRC 2 Royal Artillery BC. 2¼ lengths, 7m 56s
Final: 1 London RC 2 TRC. 2¼ lengths, 7m 58s

1907 S. Wood 10.8 (bow); H. Messom 11.6 (strs); J.S. Wilkes 12.10; C.G. Sprague 10.9 (stroke). Av: 11.4¾
Heat: 1 Jesus College, Cambridge A 2 TRC. 1 length, 8m 1s

1908 A.E. Snellgrove 9.11 (bow, strs); K. Doulton 12.6; J.S. Wilkes 12.7; C.G. Sprague 10.11 (stroke). Av: 11.5¼
Heat: 1 TRC 2 Worcester College, Oxford. 1 length, 8m 7s
Semi-final: 1 TRC 2 Molesey BC. 2 lengths, 7m 59s
Final: 1 TRC 2 London RC. 2 lengths, 7m 55s.

1909 A.E. Snellgrove 10.0 (bow, strs); H.G. Irwin 10.12; F. Trewby 11.8; H. Messom 11.10 (stroke). Av: 11.0½
Heat: 1 Molesey BC 2 TRC. 1 length, 8m 48s

1910 H. Green 11.0 (bow,strs); J.F.S. Hards 11.5; A. St G. Lyster 11.8; H. Thompson 10.1 (stroke). Av: 11.0
Heat: 1 Trinity Hall, Cambridge (winners) 2 TRC. 2½ lengths, 8m 20s

1911 G.H. Kelly 11.4 (bow,strs); H.G. Irwin 11.9; W.S. Douglas 13.1; C.M. Spielmann 12.12 (stroke). Av: 12.3
Heat: 1 Third Trinity, Cambridge 2 TRC. 2 lengths, 8m 2s

1912 D.F. Humphreys 10.3 (bow); G.A.L. Hatton 11.5; M.S. Gunn 11.8; H. Messom 11.11 (stroke). Av: 11.3¼
Heat: 1 London Hospital RC 2 TRC. Easily, 8m 36s

1913 R.W. Bennell 11.5 (bow,strs); G.T. Wilkes 11.8; L.P. Langton 12.4; R.S. Wilshire 11.1 (stroke). Av: 11.8
Heat: 1 Queens' College, Cambridge 2 TRC. 2 lengths, 8m 0s

1914 P. Beresford 9.2 (bow,strs); V.G. Teale 10.5; P. Rought 11.6; O.B. Wallis 11.10 (stroke). Av: 10.9¼
Heat: 1 TRC 2 London Hospital RC. 1¼ lengths, 8m 58s
Semi-final: 1 Lady Margaret, Cambridge 2 TRC. 3 lengths, 8m 9s

1920 K.C. Wilson 11.12 (bow,strs); Count S. Wachtmeister 12.0; S.I. Fairbairn 12.0; C.H. Rew 11.0 (stroke). Av: 11.10
Heat: 1 TRC 2 London RC. 3 lengths, 8m 30s
Semi-final: 1 TRC 2 Trinity Hall, Cambridge. Easily, 9m 0s
Final: 1 TRC 2 Vesta RC. Easily, 8m 10s

1921 H.L. Morphy 10.9 (bow,strs); H.A.A. Howell 12.0; H.M. Lane 12.11; A. Reymond 12.13 (stroke). Av: 12.1½
Heat: 1 TRC 2 Merton College, Oxford. 1¾ lengths, 7m 53s
Semi-final: 1 TRC 2 Hereford RC. 1 length, 7m 53s
Final: 1 Jesus College, Cambridge 2 TRC. Easily, 8m 22s

1922 H.L.Holman 10.6 (bow,strs); A.F. Long 11.4; C.T. Southgate 12.2; C.H. Rew 11.4 (stroke). Av: 11.5¼
Heat: 1 TRC 2 Vesta RC. Easily, 8m 54s
Semi-final: 1 TRC 2 Magdalen College, Oxford. Easily, 9m 6s

1923 G.C. Killick 11.13 (bow, strs); E.A. Pounds 11.11; C.T. Southgate 12.3; K.C. Wilson 11.12 (stroke). Av: 11.13¼
Heat: 1 Jesus College, Cambridge 2 TRC. Easily, 7m 50s (short course)

1924 A.F. Webber 9.8 (bow, strs); G.B. Hicks 11.4; H.C. Debenham 12.2; H.W. Dulley 11.0 (stroke). Av: 11.0
Heat:1 TRC 2 Broxbourne RC. ¾ length, 9m 12s
Heat: 1 Imperial College 2 TRC. 1½ lengths, 8m 26s

1925 G.C. Killick 12.4 (bow, strs); H.M. Lane 13.1; T.R.F. Barrett-Lennard 11.5; J.C. Badcock 12.4 (stroke). Av: 12.3½
Heat: 1 TRC 2 Edinburgh University. Easily, 7m 57s
Semi-final: 1 TRC 2 Royal Chester RC. Easily, 8m 4s
Final: 1 TRC 2 Selwyn College, Cambridge. 1¼ lengths, 7m 35s

1927 G.D. Smith 11.4 (bow, strs); D. Wheeler 12.10; G.C. Killick 12.2; W.S. Douglas 12.9 (stroke). Av: 12.3¼
Heat: 1 TRC 2 Worcester College, Oxford. Not rowed out
Heat: 1 TRC 2 Henley RC. 2 lengths, 8m 34s
Semi-final: 1 TRC 2 Maidenhead RC. 1¼ lengths, 8m 15s
Final: 1 TRC 2 Vesta RC. 2 lengths, 8m 23s

1928 E. Everest 10.4 (bow, strs); D.G. Newton 13.0; F.E.C. Cox 12.9; A.J. Gaul 11.7 (stroke). Av: 11.12
Heat: 1 TRC 2 Clare College, Cambridge. 1 length, 8m 23s
Heat: 1 Trinity Hall, Cambridge 2 TRC. Easily, 9m 7s

Wyfold Challenge Cup

1929 Hon C.R. Allanson-Winn 10.7 (bow, strs) H.W. Dulley 11.9; H.N. Sporborg 11.6; E.G. Beresford 11.1 (stroke). Av: 11.2 1/4
Heat: 1 TRC 2 Courtney Lodge. 2 lengths, 8m 21s
Heat: 1 TRC 2 Ibis RC. 2½ lengths, 8m 1s
Semi-final: 1 TRC 2 Pembroke College, Cambridge. 2 lengths, 9m 28s
Final: 1 TRC 2 Jesus College, Cambridge. 1 length, 7m 44s

1930 B.E.A. Joyner 9.13 (bow, strs); T.H. Tyler 11.13; R.D. George 12.8; F.G. Bunge 11.12 (stroke) Av: 11.8
Heat: 1 TRC 2 Balliol College, Oxford. Easily, 9m 3s
Semi-final: 1 London RC (winners) 2 TRC. 6 feet, 7m 48s

1931 B.E.A. Joyner 10.2 (bow, strs); T.H. Tyler 11.11; R.D. George 12.8; F.G. Bunge 11.9 (stroke). Av: 11.7½
Heat: 1 TRC 2 London RC. 1 length, 8m 14s
Semi-final: 1 TRC 2 First Trinity, Cambridge. 2 lengths, 8m 26s
Final: 1 TRC 2 Vesta RC. Easily, 9m 13s

1932 B.E.A. Joyner 10.6 (bow, strs); G. Hardwicke 12.9; J.H.M. Ward 12.10; D.C. Price 11.0 (stroke). Av: 11.9¾
Heat: 1 London RC (winners) 2 TRC. 2 lengths, 8m 12s

1933 G.E. Miller 11.1 (bow, strs); C.L. Champion 11.10; B.P. Drakeford 11.9; H.E.G. Watts 10.12 (stroke). Av: 11.4½
Heat: 1 Westminster Bank RC 2 TRC. 2½ lengths, 7m 58s

1934 H.E. Traylen 10.11 (bow, strs); J.N.L. Isaac 12.8; J. Schutter 11.7; C.E. Watson-Taylor 12.2 (stroke). Av: 11.10½
Heat: 1 London RC 2 TRC. 1¼ lengths, 8m 1s

1935 H.E. Traylen 11.3 (bow, strs); J.W.A. Winsor 12.4; G.E. Parlby 11.13; F.G. Bunge 11.11 (stroke). Av: 11.11¼
Heat: 1 TRC 2 Vesta RC. Easily, 8m 5s
Heat: 1 TRC 2 Auriol RC. Easily, 8m 24s
Semi-final: 1 TRC 2 First Trinity, Cambridge. Easily, 8m 1s
Final: 1 Reading RC 2 TRC. 2 lengths, 7m 39s

1936 H.E. Traylen 11.5 (bow, strs); K.A. Williams 12.10; J.T.M. O'Mara 13.8; H.E.G. Watts 11.5 (stroke). Av: 12.3½
Heat: 1 TRC 2 Guy's Hospital. ¾ length, 8m 40s
Heat: 1 London RC (winners) 2 TRC. 2 lengths, 8m 22s

1939 N.T. Taylor 12.0 (bow, strs); J.F.G. Sykes 12.6; D. Belson 12.4; J. March 11.2 (stroke). Av: 11.13½
Heat: 1 Brasenose College, Oxford 2 TRC. Easily, 8m 47s

1946 D.J. Cowan 10.12 (bow, strs); K.A. Williams 12.5; C.S. Windebank 11.12; J.E. MacIver 9.11 (stroke). Av: 11.3
Heat: 1 TRC 2 Royal Chester RC. 2 lengths, 8m 21s
Heat: 1 TRC 2 Reading RC. 2½ lengths, 9m 17s
Semi-final: 1 TRC 2 Marlow RC. 1¼ lengths, 8m 27s
Final: 1 King's College, London 2 TRC. 1¼ lengths, 7m 57s

1947 A.J. Edwards 9.13 (bow, strs); U. Burkhard 13.4; H.A.I. MacInnes 14.6; A.N. Watson 10.6 (stroke). Av: 12.3¾
Heat: 1 TRC 2 Oriel College, Oxford. 1¾ lengths, 8m 20s
Heat: 1 TRC 2 Edinburgh University. 3 lengths, 8m 24s
Heat: 1 TRC 2 Reading RC. Not rowed out, 8m 34s
Semi-final: 1 TRC 2 Twickenham RC. 4 lengths, 8m 40s
Final: 1 Quintin BC 2 TRC. 1½ lengths, 8m 19s

1948 C.M.E. Eugster 10.13 (bow, strs); V.C.N. Daniel 10.12; P.H.F. Andrew 11.13; F.L.A. de Marneffe 11.5 (stroke). Av: 11.3 ¾
Heat: 1 Victoria Lake RC, South Africa (winners) 2 TRC. 2¾ lengths, 7m 49s

1949 D. McCarraher 11.10 (bow, strs); R.H. Nicholls 12.2; G.P. Godenir 14.7; R.W. Brown 11.10 (stroke). Av: 12.7¼
Heat: 1 TRC 2 Middlesex and University College Hospital. 1 length, 7m 52s
Heat: 1 Lensbury RC (winners) 2 TRC. 3 lengths, 7m 42s

1950 A.C. Coates 12.0 (bow, strs); T.J.L. Alexander 10.9; A.C. Riemer 11.12; P.W.J. Simcox 10.6 (stroke). Av: 11.3¼
Heat: 1 Westminster Bank RC 2 TRC. 1¼ lengths, 8m 21s

1951 T.P. Wilson 9.9 (bow, strs); M.F. Alexander 10.6; P.G. Alliston 12.4; W. Bull 13.8 (stroke). Av: 11.6¾
Heat: 1 Trinity Hall, Cambridge 2 TRC. 1¼ lengths, 7m 50s

1952 P.S. Pusey 11.6 (bow, strs); R.C. Davie 11.5; J.C. Hyem 11.11; R.C. Wright 10.11 (stroke). Av: 11.4¾
Heat: 1 Worcester College, Oxford 2 TRC. 1 length, 8m 6s

1953 P.S. Pusey 11.3 (bow, strs); H.G.V. Denning 12.3; A.C. Riemer 11.11; K.J.S. Douglas-Mann 12.8 (stroke). Av: 11.13¼
Heat: 1 Royal Air Force (winners) 2 TRC. 2¼ lengths, 7m 20s

1954 P.S. Pusey 11.1 (bow, strs); H.G.V. Denning 12.1; A.C. Riemer 11.12; K.J.S. Douglas-Mann 12.9 (stroke). Av: 11.12¾
Heat: 1 Marlow RC 2 TRC. ¼ length, 7m 42s

1955 G.S. Dear 11.4 (bow, strs); J. Pope 11.5; A.C. Riemer 12.10; H.G.V. Denning 12.8 (stroke). Av: 11.13¾
Heat: 1 TRC 2 Trinity College, Oxford. 3 lengths, 8m 18s
Heat: 1 TRC 2 Jesus College, Cambridge. 2½ lengths, 7m 54s
Heat: 1 TRC 2 Bedford RC. 2½ lengths, 8m 17s
Semi-final: 1 TRC 2 Royal Air Force. 1¼ lengths, 8m 2s
Final: 1 TRC 2 Kettering RC. 1¼ lengths, 7m 51s

1956 P.S. Pusey 11.7 (bow, strs); R.C. Wright 11.0; D.R. Mount 13.1; D.A. Dunton 12.9 (stroke). Av: 12.0¾
Heat: 1 TRC 2 King's College, Cambridge. 1 length, 7m 53s
Heat: 1 TRC 2 Burway RC. 3 lengths, 8m 56s
Heat: 1 TRC 2 Royal Air Force, Cardington. 1¼ lengths, 7m 54s
Semi-final: 1 Brockville RC, Canada 2 TRC. 1¼ lengths, 7m 54s

1957 P.J.E. Dowden-Parker 12.6 (bow, strs); A.C.M. Provan 10.5; P.P. Doyle 11.8; L.E. Stevens 11.0 (stroke). Av: 11.4¾
Heat: 1 Royal Air Force, Cardington 2 TRC. 2 lengths, 7m 51s

1958 G.S. Dear 11.5 (bow, strs); A.B. Martin 11.9; J.R. Hegarty 12.0; R. Neale 11.12 (stroke). Av: 11.10
Heat: 1 Royal Engineers 2 TRC. 2½ lengths, 7m 45s

1959 D.P. Kelly 10.13 (bow, strs); H.S. Cochrane 11.6; C.G. Dean 11.9; A.J. Cooke 11.7 (stroke). Av: 11.5¼
Heat: 1 TRC 2 Trinity Hall, Cambridge. Easily, 8m 19s
Heat: 1 Walton RC 2 TRC. 2½ lengths, 8m 21s

1960 G.S. Dear 11.2 (bow, strs); M.J. Long 11.9; P. Bovet 12.13; A.J. Cooke 11.6 (stroke). Av: 11.11
Heat: 1 TRC 2 Pembroke College, Cambridge. 1⅔ lengths, 7m 30s
Heat: 1 Vesta RC 2 TRC. 1¾ lengths, 7m 34s

1961 R.A. Carr, 11.8 (bow, strs); R.H. Willett 11.9; I.A. MacRae 12.9; M.J. Lohnberg 11.10 (stroke). Av: 11.12½
Heat: 1 Nottingham City RC 2 TRC. ⅔ length, 7m 26s

1962 R. Hackford 11.0 (bow, strs); J.H.S. Sinclair 12.12; M.E.C. Joyner 14.2; G.W.J. Bridge 11.5 (stroke). Av: 12.4¾
Heat: 1 TRC 2 Westminster Bank RC. 2½ lengths, 7m 44s
Heat: 1 University of London 2 TRC. 3⅔ lengths, 7m 29s

Wyfold Challenge Cup

1963 J.R. Buzeman 11.8 (bow, strs); C. Clifford 11.13; A.A. Reader 12.8; T.R.I. Haynes 10.9 (stroke). Av: 11.9½
Heat: 1 London RC 2 TRC. 2⅓ lengths, 8m 19s

1964 W.H. Needham 11.6 (bow, strs); R.M. Telling 11.8; I.A. MacRae 13.0; J.P.M. Thomson 12.4 (stroke) Av: 12.1
Heat: 1 TRC 2 Downing College, Cambridge. ⅓ length, 7m 43s
Heat: 1 Weybridge RC 2 TRC. Easily, 7m 54s

1965 M.H. Garrett-Cox 11.9 (bow, strs); F.D.L. Wilmot 12.6; D.R. Allen 13.2; J.J. Mills 11.13 (stroke). Av: 12.4
Heat: 1 TRC 2 Downing College, Cambridge. Easily, 7m 32s
Heat: 1 Christiania Roklub, Norway 2 TRC. 3 lengths, 7m 16s

1967 V.B.A. Temple 11.0 (bow, strs); D.J. Pedraza 11.13; T.A. Bakiewicz 12.3 B.R. Hanham 12.11 (stroke). Av: 11.13¾
Heat: 1 Quintin BC 2 TRC. Easily, 8m 20s

1968 R. Hackford 11.10 (bow, strs); V.B.A. Temple 11.2; J.S. Stephenson 12.12; D.F. Hanham 12.11 (stroke). Av: 12.1¾
Heat: 1 Quintin BC 2 TRC. 2 lengths, 8m 34s

1969 N.S. Read 11.2 (bow, strs); M.H. Rowlatt 12.5; M.D. Amor 11.11; G.E. Lee 11.2 (stroke). Av: 11.8¼
Heat: 1 TRC 2 Kingston RC. 1⅔ lengths, 7m 51s
Heat: 1 Trident RC, South Africa 2 TRC. Easily, 7m 29s

1970 N.S. Read 11.2 (bow, strs); P.J. Norman 11.7; P.W.H. Rushmere 11.11; J.R. Lester 12.1 (stroke). Av: 11.8¾
Heat: 1 TRC 2 Hereford RC. ⅔ length, 7m 48s
Heat: 1 Trident RC, South Africa (winners) 2 TRC. Easily, 7m 55s

1971 V.B.A. Temple 11.7 (bow, strs); T.A. Bakiewicz 12.8; D.L. Cruttenden 16.2; S.A. Slee 12.10 (stroke). Av: 13.3
Heat: 1 TRC 2 Spuyten Duyvil RC of New York, USA. 4 lengths, 8m 9s
Heat: 1 TRC 2 Vesta RC. 3¾ lengths, 7m 50s
Heat: 1 TRC 2 Burway RC. 1⅓ lengths, 7m 55s
Semi-final: 1 Marlow RC 2 TRC. 1⅓ lengths, 7m 42s

1972 J.D. Davidson 11.0 (bow, strs); N. Rudd 11.3; S.J. Barber 12.0; G.A. Hodson 11.9 (stroke). Av: 11.7
Heat: 1 Trident RC, South Africa 2 TRC. Easily, 8m 9s

1973 A.G. Taylor 11.8 (bow); S.P.C.H. Woods 10.4 (strs); N.S. Read 10.12; A.G. Bingham 10.9 (stroke). Av: 10.12
Heat: 1 TRC 2 Selwyn College, Cambridge. Easily, 7m 56s
Heat: 1 Molesey BC 2 TRC. 3 feet, 7m 21s

1974 A.G. Bingham 10.9 (bow); N.S. Read 10.6; C.J.D. George 11.3 (strs); A.J.H. Stocking 11.2 (stroke). Av: 10.12
Heat: 1 TRC 2 Twickenham RC. Easily, 8m 14s
Heat: 1 TRC 2 Henley RC. 4 lengths, 7m 55s
Heat: 1 Porcellian Club, USA (winners) 2 TRC. ¾ length, 7m 22s

1976 S.L. Jones 10.3 (bow, strs); S.J. Macartney 10.7; M.R. McGowan 11.5; A.G. Bingham 11.0 (stroke). Av: 10.11
Heat: 1 Potomac BC, USA 2 TRC. Easily, 7m 16s

1977 T.J.S. Levy 9.7 (bow, strs); A. Thomson 10.10; S.L. Jones 10.7; P.W.H. Rushmere 12.12 (stroke). Av: 10.12
Heat: 1 Tideway Scullers School 2 TRC. 2½ lengths, 8m 5s

1978 S.P.C.H. Woods 10.5 (bow, strs); S.J. Wise 13.0; M.J.S. Levy 13.0; R.J. Macartney 11.1 (stroke). Av: 11.13
Heat: 1 TRC 2 Midland Bank RC. Easily, 8m 3s
Heat: 1 University of London 2 TRC. 1¾ lengths, 7m 34s

1979 R.F. Kenyon 11.1 (bow, strs); M.P. Kaminski 12.9; W.G. Sandifer 13.1; A.G. Rankine 14.1 (stroke). Av: 12.10
Heat: 1 Nottingham and Union RC 2 TRC. 2⅓ lengths, 7m 45s

1980 R.F. Kenyon 11.8 (bow, strs); A. Hill 13.4; P.N. Davis 10.12; M.P. Kaminski 12.10 (stroke). Av: 12.2
Heat: 1 Horseferry RC 2 TRC. Easily, 8m 19s

1981 M.J.S. Levy 11.6 (bow, strs); T.Kirby 11.8; S.J. Crump 13.1; T.J.S. Levy 10.5 (stroke). Av: 11.8½
Heat: 1 TRC 2 Argonaut RC, Canada. 3⅔ lengths, 8m 28s
Heat: 1 Kew Meadows BC 2 TRC. 2 lengths, 7m 48s

1982 P.M. Davis 11.6 (bow, strs); T. Kirby 13.5; T.J.S. Levy 10.8; S.P.K. Austin 9.8 (stroke). Av: 11.3
Heat: 1 TRC 2 London RC B disqualified.
Heat: 1 TRC 2 Barclay's Bank RC. 1½ lengths, 7m 26s
Heat: 1 London RC A 2 TRC. 1½ lengths, 7m 25s

1983 P.N. Davis 12.0 (bow, strs); C.R. Jones 13.3; M. Urry 14.4; G. Spice 12.3 (stroke). Av: 12.13
Heat: 1 Leander Club 2 TRC. 1¾ lengths, 7m 26s

1984 S.P. Bowden 11.8 (bow, strs); G.P.R. Reddin 12.12; W. Dunnet 12.4; M.R. Thomas 11.7 (stroke). Av: 12.5
Heat: 1 Reading University 2 TRC. 1½ lengths, 7m 28s

1985 W.J. Baker 11.9 (Bow, strs); A.T. Smith 11.12; S.P. Bowden 11.5; T.J.S. Levy 10.0 (stroke). Av: 11.3
Heat: 1 TRC 2 Vesta RC. Easily, 7m 41s
Heat: 1 Stirling Amateur Boating and Swimming Club 2 TRC. 3 lengths, 7m 31s

1986 W.J. Baker 11.10 (bow, strs); A.M. Ward 14.0; S.P. Bowden 11.7; S.P.K. Austin 10.7 (stroke). Av: 11.13
Heat: 1 TRC 2 City of Oxford RC. Easily, 7m 53s
Heat: 1 Nottingham County RA A 2 TRC. Easily, 7m 24s

1987 A: M.P. Clark 11.12 (bow, strs); J.W.P. Chalmers 12.6; A. Seddon 12.13; G.J. Elkington 12.13 (stroke). Av: 12.4
Heat: 1 Bedford Star RC 2 TRC A. Easily, 7m 35s
B: W.J. Baker 11.5 (bow); A.M. Ward 12.10; S.P. Bowden 11.5 (strs); D.P. McDonald 11.2 (stroke). Av: 11.9
Heat: 1 TRC 2 Army RC. 3⅔ lengths, 7m 42s
Heat: 1 Nautilus RC 2 TRC B. 1¾ lengths, 7m 16s

1990 S.L. Jones 11.0 (bow, strs); R.J. Moon 12.9; D.B. Gates 14.4; A.A. Dodd 11.13 (stroke). Av: 12.7
Heat: 1 TRC 2 Sons of the Thames RC A. 2¾ lengths, 8m 10s
Heat: 1 London RC A 2 TRC. Easily, 7m 36s

PRINCE PHILIP CHALLENGE CUP

1963 C.R. Barker 13.0 (bow); C.J.F.S. Rowley 12.3; J.E.Taylor 12.10; S.F.A. Miskin 12.11 (stroke); J.R. Winner 8.5 (cox). Av: 12.9½
Heat: 1 TRC 2 Melbourne University, Australia. 4 feet, 8m 8s
Final: 1 Auckland RC, New Zealand 2 TRC. Easily, 7m 32s

1965 B.R. Hanham 12.4 (bow); C.R. Barker 13.8; C.D. Barrett 14.4; D.W. Gramolt 12.13 (stroke); P.G. Bailey 8.0 (cox). Av: 13.3¾
Heat: 1 TRC 2 City Orient RC. Easily, 7m 26s
Heat: 1 TRC 2 St Mark's School, USA. Easily, 7m 23s
Semi-final: 1 Leander Club (winners) 2 TRC. 1¾ lengths, 7m 16s

1966 B.R. Hanham 12.7 (bow); C.R. Barker 13.7; C.D. Barrett 15.2; D.W. Gramolt 13.2 (stroke); P.G. Bailey 8.0 (cox). Av: 13.8
Heat: 1 SG Dynamo, Potsdam, East Germany (winners) 2 TRC. Easily, 7m 38s

HENLEY PRIZE

1968 T.A. Bakiewicz 12.6 (bow); P.C. Allen 13.6; D.W. Gramolt 13.1; B.R. Hanham 12.9 (stroke); P.G. Bailey 8.3 (cox). Av: 12.8
Heat: 1 TRC 2 Scottish Argonauts BC. 3¾ lengths, 7m 34s
Heat: 1 TRC 2 Nautilus (Midlands) Club. Easily, 8m 29s
Semi-final: 1 TRC 2 Trinity College, Dublin. Easily, 9m 40s
Final: 1 Crowland RC 2 TRC. 2 lengths, 9m 32s

BRITANNIA CHALLENGE CUP

1969 P.M.G. Meagher 12.5 (bow); A.G. Bingham 10.5; J.A. Friend 11.13; D.C. Pollard 12.5 (stroke); L.W. Taylor 8.3 (cox). Av: 11.10
Heat: 1 London RC 2 TRC. Easily, 7m 54s

1970 T.A. Bakiewicz 12.11 (bow); D.F. Hanham 12.8; J.S. Stephenson 12.12; B.R. Hanham 12.8 (stroke); L.W. Taylor 8.11 (cox). Av: 12.10
Heat: 1 TRC 2 Scottish Argonauts BC. 2½ lengths, 8m 5s
Heat: 1 Nottingham and Union RC 2 TRC. 1¾ lengths, 7m 57s

1974 G.D.St J. Bagnall 11.3 (bow); T. Clarke 10.5; G.J.E. Jack 12.6; N. Greenwood 11.7 (stroke); N. Scriven 8.0 (cox). Av: 11.5
Heat: 1 Worcester RC 2 TRC. 3⅓ lengths, 8m 18s

1976 P.W.H. Rushmere 12.7 (bow); J.P. Kelly 14.4; G.J.E. Jack 13.4; J.P. Pritchard 13.10 (stroke); A.W.N. Probert 8.1 (cox). Av: 13.6
Heat: 1 TRC 2 Worcester RC. 1⅔ lengths, 7m 24s
Heat: 1 Wallingford Schools 2 TRC. 1½ lengths, 7m 25s

1977 D.G. Shove 11.2 (bow); W.G. Sandifer 12.7; G.D. St J. Bagnall 11.7; H.S. Brass 12.10 (stroke); P.J.S. Burnett 6.7 (cox). Av: 11.13
Heat: 1 Rob Roy BC 2 TRC. 1¾ lengths, 8m 22s

1983 S.L. Jones 12.7 (bow); D.J. Badcock 13.0; C.V. Hughes 13.0; J.T. Hopkins 13.0 (stroke); R. Barlow 7.4 (cox). Av: 12.12
Heat: 1 Kingston RC 2 TRC. 1⅓ lengths, 7m 36s

1987 A.L. Slemeck 13.1 (bow); M. Urry 15.5; R.H.B. Thain 14.2; X.V.J. Calamita 14.2 (stroke); G.G.P. Herbert 7.12 (cox). Av: 12.10
Heat: 1 TRC 2 Nottingham BC. 1¾ lengths, 7m 25s
Heat: 1 TRC 2 Tideway Scullers' School. 2 lengths, 7m 16s
Semi-final: 1 Lea RC 2 TRC. 2½ lengths, 7m 14s

1989 A.L. Slemeck 13.4 (bow); C.J. Slemeck 13.3; N.B. Copley 14.0; B.D. Crawford 14.2 (stroke); N.G. Powell 8.0 (cox). Av: 13.9
Heat: 1 TRC 2 Baltimore RC, USA. Easily, 8m 3s.
Heat: 1 Lea RC A 2 TRC. 2¾ lengths, 7m 6s

1990 C.J. Slemeck 13.5 (bow); S.R. Allpass 12.7; M.A. Urry 14.6; N.B. Copley 13.13 (stroke); I. Grindal 7.7 (cox). Av: 13.8
Heat: 1 TRC 2 Royal Chester RC. 3¾ lengths, 7m 55s
Heat: 1 University College, Galway (winners) 2 TRC. 2¼ lengths, 7m 21s

SILVER GOBLETS AND NICKALLS' CHALLENGE CUP

1877 W.H. Eyre 10.12 (bow); J. Hastie 11.3 (stroke).
Heat: 1 TRC 2 A de L. Long & F.S. Gulston (London RC); 3 W. Chillingworth & C. Herbert (Ino RC). Easily
Final: 1 TRC 2 S.Le B. Smith & F.L. Playford (London RC). Easily

1878 W.H. Eyre 11.0 (bow); J. Hastie 11.8 (stroke).
Heat: 1 T.C. Edwards-Moss & W.A. Ellison (Oxford Etonian Club) (winners) 2 TRC. 2½ lengths, 8m 33s

1879 W.H. Eyre 10.11 (bow); J. Hastie 11.7 (stroke).
Final: 1 R.H. Labat & F.S. Gulston (London RC) 2 TRC. Easily, 11m 16s

1880 W.H. Eyre 11.0 (bow); J. Hastie 11.8 (stroke).
Final: 1 TRC 2 A. Payne & F.D. Leader (Molesey BC) 3 R.H. Labat & F.S. Gulston (London RC). 5 lengths, 8m 45s

1881 W.H. Eyre 10.7 (bow); J. Hastie 11.6 (stroke).
Heat: 1 TRC 2 A. Payne & F.D. Leader (Molesey BC). Easily
Final: 1 TRC 2 P. Adcock & F.L. Playford (London RC). 3 lengths, 9m 4s

1883 H.B. Tween 10.5 (bow); J. Hastie 11.9 (stroke).
Final: 1 G.Q. Roberts & D.E. Brown (Twickenham RC) 2 TRC. Easily, 9m 22s

1885 J.A. Drake-Smith 10.8 (bow); J. Hastie 12.3 (stroke).
Heat: 1 G.R.B. Earnshaw & C.E. Earnshaw (London RC) 2 TRC. L. Frere & D.E. Brown (Twickenham RC) disqualified. Not rowed out

1886 A.M. Hutchinson 11.10 (bow); S. Fairbairn 13.10 (stroke).
Heat: 1 F.E. Churchill & S.D. Muttlebury (Third Trinity, Cambridge) (winners) TRC disqualified.

1889 B.W. Looker 11.2 (bow); F.E.C. Clark 12.11 (stroke).
Heat: 1 J.C. Gardner & S.D. Muttlebury (CUBC) (winners) 2 TRC. Easily, 8m 31s

1891 A.M. Hutchinson 12.3 (bow); F.E.C. Clark 12.12 (stroke).
Heat: 1 Lord Ampthill & G. Nickalls (Leander Club) (winners) 2 TRC. ½ length, 9m 7s

1892 F.E.C. Clark 13.1 (bow); S.D. Muttlebury 13.7 (stroke).
Heat: 1 TRC 2 F.E. Thorn & P.A.N. Thorn (London RC). Easily, 10m 11s
Final: 1 V. Nickalls & W.A.L. Fletcher (OUBC) 2 TRC. Easily, 9m 7s

1895 W. Broughton 12.13 (bow); S.D. Muttlebury 13.9 (stroke).
Heat: 1 TRC 2 A.J. Davis & L.H.K. Bushe-Fox (Lady Margaret, Cambridge). Not rowed out.
Final: 1 V. Nickalls & G. Nickalls (London RC) 2 TRC. Not rowed out, 9m 11s

1898 A. Bogle 11.5 (bow); W.J. Fernie 12.0 (stroke).
Heat: 1 TRC 2 H.W. Stout & F.S. Lowe (London RC). Easily, 8m 47s
Final: 1 TRC 2 A.M. Hutchinson & S. Fairbairn (Jesus College, Cambridge). Easily, 8m 41s

1899 D.E. Campbell-Muir (bow); J.A. Rennie (stroke).
Heat: 1 G.E. Orme & D. Pennington (St George's Hospital) 2 TRC. Easily, 9m 11s

1906 J. Beresford 10.2 (bow); K. Vernon 10.12 (stroke).
Heat: 1 V. Molmans & G. Visser (SN de Gand, Belgium) 2 TRC. Easily, 8m 46s

1907 J. Beresford 10.2 (bow); K. Vernon 11.3 (stroke).
Final: 1 B.C. Johnstone & R.V. Powell (Leander Club) 2 TRC. Easily, 8m 52s

1908 J. Beresford 10.2 (bow); K. Vernon 11.3 (stroke).
Final: 1 H.R. Barker & A.C. Gladstone (Christ Church, Oxford) 2 TRC. 4 lengths, 8m 26s

1909 J. Beresford 10.3 (bow); K. Vernon 11.4 (stroke).
Heat: 1 TRC 2 Sir W.L. Parker, Bart & E.V. Culme-Seymour (New College, Oxford). Easily, 9m 13s
Final: 1 B.C. Johnstone & E.G. Williams (Leander Club) 2 TRC. 3 lengths, 8m 30s

1910 A.C. Richardson 9.13 (bow); T.D. Richardson 9.10 (stroke).
Heat: 1 G.W.H. Walker & G.C. Drinkwater (Wadham College, Oxford) 2 TRC. Not rowed out, 9m 31s

1911 J. Beresford 10.3 (bow); A.H. Cloutte 12.6 (stroke). B. Logan 12.8 (bow); C.G. Rought 13.1 (stroke).
Heat: 1 TRC (J. Beresford & A.H. Cloutte) 2 A.S. Garton & D. Mackinnon (Magdalen College, Oxford). 2½ lengths, 8m 27s
Heat: TRC (J. Beresford & A.H. Cloutte) and TRC (B. Logan & G.G. Rought), dead heat, 8m 8s (record) J. Beresford & A.H. Cloutte won toss to go to final.
Final: 1 TRC (J. Beresford & A.H. Cloutte) 2 N.M. Bruce & C.A. Gladstone (Christ Church, Oxford). 1½ lengths, 8m 15s

1912 B. Logan 12.10 (bow); C.G. Rought 13.0 (stroke). J. Beresford 10.2 (bow); A.H. Cloutte 12.2 (stroke).
Heat: 1 TRC (B. Logan & A.H. Cloutte) 2 C.G. Barton & J.G. Madden (Pembroke College, Cambridge). 1½ lengths, 8m 27s
Heat: 1 TRC (J. Beresford & A.H. Cloutte) 2 L.J. Cadbury & F.E. Hellyer (First Trinity, Cambridge). 1¼ lengths, 8m 42s
Final: 1 TRC (B. Logan & C.G. Rought) 2 TRC (J. Beresford & A.H. Cloutte). 1¼ lengths, 8m 36s

1920 S. Fairbairn 12.0 (bow); B. Logan 12.13 (stroke).
J. Beresford 8.13 (bow); A.M. Harding 9.1 (stroke).
Heat: 1 H. Peake & R.I.L. MacEwen (Third Trinity, Cambridge) 2 TRC (J. Beresford & A.M. Harding). Easily, 9m 40s
Heat: 1 TRC (S. Fairbairn & B. Logan) 2 A.E.C. Tennyson-d'Eyncourt & W.L.F. Tennyson-d'Eyncourt (Household Brigade BC). 1 length, 10m 6s
Semi-final: 1 TRC (S. Fairbairn & B. Logan) 2 H.W.B. Cairns & A.S. MacIver (Balliol College and Christ Church, Oxford). Easily, 10m 10s
Final: 1 G.O. Nickalls & R.S.C. Lucas (Magdalen College, Oxford) 2 TRC (S.I. Fairbairn & B. Logan). Easily, 8m 53s

1922 H.E. West 10.13 (bow); K. Vernon 11.3 (stroke).
C.G. Chandler 11.0 (bow); S.I. Fairbairn 12.0 (stroke).
Heat: 1 TRC (H.E. West & K. Vernon) 2 B.J.C. te Hennepe & J.A. van der Vegte (Holland). Easily, 9.52
Semi-final: 1 G.O. Nickalls & R.S.C. Lucas (Magdalen College, Oxford) 2 TRC (C.G. Chandler & S.I. Fairbairn). Easily, 9m 8s
Semi-final: 1 TRC (H.E. West & S.I. Fairbairn) 2 K.N. Craig & B.G. Ivory (Pembroke College, Cambridge). Easily, 9m 29s
Final: 1 G.D. Nickalls & R.S.C. Lucas 2 TRC (H.E. West & K. Vernon). Easily, 9m 19s

1923 H.E. West 11.3 (bow); H.M. Lane 13.2 (stroke).
Heat: 1 W.G. Godden & R.E. Eason (Trinity College, Oxford) (winners) 2 TRC. 1½ lengths, 8m 15s

1924 G.C. Killick 11.12 (bow); C.T. Southgate 12.11 (stroke).
C.G. Chandler 11.1 (bow); C.H. Rew 11.4 (stroke).
Heat: 1 TRC (G.C. Killick & C.T. Southgate) 2 TRC (C.G. Chandler & C.H. Rew). 3 lengths, 9m 51s
Heat: 1 C.R.M. Eley & J.A. Macnabb (Third Trinity, Cambridge) (winners) 2 TRC (G.C. Killick & C.T. Southgate). Easily, 10m 52s

Silver Goblets and Nickalls' Challenge Cup

1926 K. Vernon 11.6 (bow); W.S. Douglas 12.10 (stroke).
Heat: 1 H.R. Carver & E.C. Hamilton-Russell (Third Trinity, Cambridge) (winners) 2 TRC. 2 lengths, 8m 42s

1927 K. Vernon 11.8 (bow); W.S. Douglas 12.9 (stroke).
Heat: 1 R.A. Nisbet & T.N. O'Brien (London RC) (winners) 2 TRC. Easily, 9m 9s

1928 G.C. Killick 12.2 (bow); J. Beresford Jnr 11.4 (stroke).
Heat: 1 TRC 2 R.A. Nisbet & T.N. O'Brien (London RC). 5 lengths, 8m 49s
Final: 1 TRC 2 C. Daniel & J. London (Quintin BC). Easily, 9m 57s

1929 G.C. Killick 12.2 (bow); J. Beresford Jnr 11.1 (stroke).
Heat: 1 TRC 2 H.R. Carver & T.R.B. Sanders (Third Trinity, Cambridge). 2½ lengths, 8m 52s after dead-heat in 8m 39s
Final: 1 TRC 2 A. Graham & H.C. Morphett (Brasenose College, Oxford). 1¾ lengths, 8m 32s

1933 A.P. Brown 12.9 (bow); J.H.M. Ward 12.8 (stroke).
Heat: 1 H.R.A. Edwards & L. Clive (Christ Church, Oxford) (winners) 2 TRC. ½ length, 8m 50s

1935 B.S. Fidler 12.5 (bow); D.G. Newton 13.8 (stroke).
Heat: 1 TRC 2 V.A.C. Wood & D.A. Bond (Maidenhead RC). 2½ lengths, 9m 13s
Heat: 1 TRC 2 R.G. Rowe & E.E.D. Tomlin (University College, Oxford). Easily, 8m 53s
Final: 1 T.S. Cree & D.W. Burnford (Jesus College, Cambridge) 2 TRC. 2½ lengths, 8m 20s

1936 C.H. van Dam 11.7 (bow); B.S. Fidler 12.1 (stroke)
Heat: 1 T.S. Cree & D.W. Burnford (Jesus College, Cambridge) 2 TRC. Easily, 9m 15s

1939 J.T.M. O'Mara 13.0 (bow); P.C. Kirkpatrick 14.1 (stroke).
Heat: 1 TRC; 2 E.F. Bigland & T.S. Bigland (Royal Chester RC). Easily, 9m 47s
Heat: 1 C.B. Sanford & H. Parker (Trinity Hall, Cambridge) (winners) 2 TRC. Easily, 9m 20s

1947 R.C. Morris 11.2 (bow); A. Burrough 11.7 (stroke).
Heat: 1 TRC 2 R.R. Swatton & R.S. Hollom (Walton RC). Easily, 8m 30s
Semi-final: 1 J.H. Pinches & E.M. Sturges (London RC) (winners) 2 TRC. 6 feet, 8m 42s

1948 J.A. Wilmot 10.7 (bow); J.P. Dizer 10.13 (stroke).
Heat: 1 TRC 2 R.R. Swatton & R.S. Hollom (Walton RC). 1¼ lengths, 8m 51s
Heat: 1 J.R.W. Gleave & D.G. Jamison (Radcliffe Infirmary BC) 2 TRC. 1¼ lengths, 8m 42s

1949 A.S.F. Butcher 11.11 (bow); T.H. Christie 13.3 (stroke).
R.C. Morris 11.6 (bow); A. Burrough 12.5 (stroke).
Heat: 1 TRC (R.C. Morris & A. Burrough) 2 R. Hylton-Smith & W. Skelton (Quintin BC). Easily, 9m 14s
Heat: 1 TRC (A.S.F. Butcher & T.H. Christie) 2 A.M. Gray & B.D. Murphy (Kingston RC). Easily, 8m 46s
Semi-final: 1 TRC (R.C. Morris & A. Burrough) 2 P.G.F. Henderson & R.L. Arundel (Merton College, Oxford). 1½ lengths, 8m 11s
Semi-final: 1 TRC (A.S.F. Butcher & T.H. Christie) 2 J.A. Iliffe & D.O'R. Dickey (Exeter College, Oxford). Easily, 8m 28s
Final: 1 TRC (A.S.F. Butcher & T.H. Christie) 2 TRC (R.C. Morris & A. Burrough). 2½ lengths, 8m 20s

1952 A.S.F. Butcher 12.5 (bow); P.C. Kirkpatrick 14.0 (stroke).
Heat: 1 TRC 2 A.M. Clay & J.D.S. Hester (Marlow RC). 1½ lengths, 8m 21s
Semi-final: 1 D.A.T. Leadley & J.N. King (Emmanuel College, Cambridge) 2 TRC. 2½ lengths, 8m 23s

1953 G.C. Fisk 11.9 (bow); M. Legg 11.13 (stroke).
Heat: 1 TRC 2 F.M. St L. Bircher & E.A.P. Bircher (Old Radleian BC). 1½ lengths, 8m 10s

Semi-final: 1 R. Baetens & M. Knuysen (Antwerp Sculling Club, Belgium) (winners) 2 TRC. Easily, 7m 51s

1956 M.S. Atkins 12.3 (bow); A.C. Riemer 12.3 (stroke).
Heat: 1 A.M. Clay & W.H. Findlay (Marlow RC) 2 TRC. 2 lengths, 9m 23s

1962 R.D.F. Anderson 13.4 (bow); S.F.A. Miskin 12.13 (stroke).
Heat: 1 S. Farquharson & J.D. Lee-Nicholson (University of London) 2 TRC. Easily, 8m 9s

1986 P. Dominey 12.10 (bow); M. Johnson 13.1 (stroke).
Heat: 1 TRC 2 R.M. Owen & J.H. Richards (Isis BC). 1 length, 8m 41s
Heat: 1 A.M. Peach & C. Guppy (Leander Club) 2 TRC. Easily, 8m 49s

QUEEN MOTHER CHALLENGE CUP

1987 G.D. St J. Bagnall 11.7 (bow); W. Dunnet 12.0; I.G.P. Pritchard 13.1; G.P.R. Reddin 12.10 (stroke).
Av: 12.5
Heat: 1 Soviet Army, USSR 2 TRC. Easily, 6m 52s.

CENTENARY DOUBLE SCULLS

1939 J. Beresford 11.9 (bow); L.F. Southwood 13.6 (stroke).
Heat: 1 TRC 2 C.P. Revell & E.G. Cooper (Yare RC). Easily, 9m 29s
Semi-final: 1 TRC 2 H. Andersen & B. Piessens (SRN Anversoise, Belgium). 4 lengths, 8m 35s
Final: TRC and G. Scherli & E. Broschi (SCN di Trieste, Italy), dead heat, 8m 35s. No re-row.

DOUBLE SCULLS CHALLENGE CUP

1969 D.J. Pedraza 11.13 (bow); D.W. Gramolt 13.5 (stroke).
Heat: 1 D. Oswald & M. Burgin (SN de Neuchatel and Grasshopper Club, Zurich, Switzerland) 2 TRC. Easily, 7m 29s

1988 G.P.R. Reddin 13.0 (bow); I.G.P. Pritchard 13.0 (stroke).
Heat: 1 TRC 2 D. Cave & H.A.J. Maltby (Bedford RC). Easily, 8m 2s
Heat: 1 J.D.M. Scrivener & R. Henderson (Lea RC) 2 TRC. Easily, 7m 56s

DIAMOND CHALLENGE SCULLS

1877 W.L. Slater 11.8
Heat: 1 W.L. Slater 2 J.T. Bucknill (Royal Engineers BC) 3 P.J. Maloney (Dublin University BC). 2 lengths, 9m 23s
Semi-final: 1 A.V. Frere (Kingston RC) 2 W.L. Slater. 3 lengths

1884 E. St J. Christophers
Heat: 1 J. Farrell (London RC) 2 E. St J. Christophers 3 J. Bungert (Mannheim). Easily

1885 R.H. Smith
Heat: 1 F.I. Pitman (Third Trinity, Cambridge) 2 R.H. Smith. Easily

1886 C.W. Hughes 9.13
Heat: 1 F.I. Pitman (Third Trinity, Cambridge) (winner) 2 C.W. Hughes. Easily

1887 C.W. Hughes 9.13
Heat: 1 C.W. Hughes 2 J. Cowen (Ryton-on-Tyne). Easily, 10m 9s
Semi-final: 1 J.C. Gardner (Emmanuel College, Cambridge) (winner) 2 C.W. Hughes. Easily

1893 G. McHenry
F. Beddington
Heat: 1 G. McHenry 2 C. Fenwick (Société d'Encouragement du Sport Nautique, Paris, France). Easily, 9m 6s
Heat: 1 F. Beddington 2 G. McHenry. Not rowed out, 9m 24s
Semi-final: 1 G.E.B. Kennedy (Kingston RC) 2 F. Beddington. Easily, 9m 39s

1896 Hon E.A. Guinness
Heat: 1 W.S. McDowell (Delaware BC, Chicago, USA) 2 E.A. Guinness. ¾ length, 9m 36s

1897 Hon E.A. Guinness
G. McHenry
Heat: 1 W.S. McDowell (Delaware BC, USA) 2 E.A. Guinness. Easily, 9m 45s
Heat: 1 B.H. Howell (Trinity Hall, Cambridge) 2 G. McHenry. Easily, 8m 58s

1898 R.K. Beaumont
Heat: 1 R.K. Beaumont 2 E.W. Bell (Rifle Brigade). Easily, 9m 8s
Semi-final: 1 H.T. Blackstaffe (Vesta RC) 2 R.K. Beaumont. Easily, 8m 37s

1899 B.H. Howell
St G. Ashe
Heat: 1 St G. Ashe E.A. Thompson (Argonaut RC, Toronto) disqualified.
Semi-final: 1 H.T. Blackstaffe (Vesta RC) 2 St G. Ashe. Easily, 8m 41s
Heat: 1 B.H. Howell 2 W.M. Bright (Argonaut RC, Toronto, Canada). Easily, 8m 45s
Semi-final: 1 B.H. Howell 2 E.G. Hemmerde (University College, Oxford). Easily, 8m 34s
Final: 1 B.H. Howell 2 H.T. Blackstaffe (Vesta RC). 4 lengths, 8m 38s

1900 B.H. Howell
St G. Ashe
Heat: 1 C.V. Fox (Guards Brigade RC) 2 St G. Ashe. Easily, 9m 7s
Heat: 1 B.H. Howell 2 F.A. Boynton (London RC). Easily, 9m 28s
Semi-final: 1 B.H. Howell 2 C.V. Fox (Guards Brigade RC). 2 lengths, 9m 1s
Final: 1 E.G. Hemmerde (University College, Oxford) 2 B.H. Howell. ¾ length, 8m 42s

1901 St G. Ashe
Heat: 1 St G. Ashe 2, W.C. Bond (London RC). Easily, 8m 58s
Semi-final: 1 St G. Ashe 2 K. Johnson (Twickenham RC). 2¾ lengths, 8m 53s
Final: 1 C.V. Fox (Guards Brigade RC) 2 St G. Ashe. Easily, 8m 52s

1902 St G. Ashe
Heat: 1 J. Beresford (Kensington RC) 2 St G. Ashe. Easily, 9m 0s

1904 St G. Ashe
Heat: 1 G. Rixon (Kingston RC) 2 St G. Ashe. Easily, 9m 18s

1905 J. Beresford 10.12
St G. Ashe 10.9
Heat: 1 G. Rixon (Kingston RC) 2 St G. Ashe. Easily, 9m 5s
Heat: 1 J. Beresford 2 D. Fitte (Vesta RC). Easily, 9m 9s
Heat: 1 H.T. Blackstaffe (Vesta RC) 2 J. Beresford. 1½ lengths, 8m 32s

1906 St G. Ashe 11.1
Heat: 1 D.C.R. Stuart (Trinity Hall, Cambridge) 2 St G. Ashe. Easily, 9m 8s

Diamond Challenge Sculls

1912 R.W. Bennell 11.6
Heat: 1 E.W. Powell (Vikings Club) (winner) 2 R.W. Bennell. 4 lengths, 9m 14s

1913 E.L. Watts 12.3
Heat: 1 E.L. Watts 2, H.M. Kusik (St Petersburg RC, Russia). 3 lengths, 8m 44s
Heat: 1 E.D.P. Pinks (London RC) 2 E.L. Watts. 4 lengths, 8m 54s

1914 D.H.L. Gollan 11.12
J.L. Tann 11.11
Heat: 1 D.H.L. Gollan 2 R.W.M. Arbuthnot (Third Trinity, Cambridge). ¾ length, 8m 40s
Heat: 1 C.M. Stuart (Trinity Hall, Cambridge) 2 D.H.L. Gollan. 1 length, 9m 23s
Heat: 1 J.L. Tann 2 P.Withington (Union BC, Boston, USA). 1½ lengths, 9m 24s
Heat: 1 R. Dibble (Don RC, Toronto, Canada) 2 J.L. Tann. 1 length, 8m 58s

1920 J. Beresford Jnr 11.4
Heat: 1 J. Beresford Jnr 2 The Hon The Master of Gray (Vikings RC). Easily, 9m 36s
Heat: 1 J. Beresford Jnr 2 O.B. Wallis (Hereford RC). 1 length, 10m 19s
Semi-final: 1 J. Beresford Jnr 2 T.M. Nussey (King's College, Cambridge). Easily, 8m 48s
Final: 1 J. Beresford Jnr 2 D.H.L. Gollan (First Trinity, Cambridge). 3 lengths, 8m 57s

1921 J. Beresford Jnr 11.6
Heat: 1 J. Beresford Jnr 2 I.P.Muller (Vesta RC). Easily, 8m 55s
Semi-final: 1 J. Beresford Jnr 2 J.W. Shaw (Marlow RC). Easily, 9m 48s
Final: 1 F.E. Eyken (Delftsche Studenten Roeivereeniging Laga) 2 J. Beresford Jnr. 1½ lengths, 8m 26s

1922 J. Beresford Jnr 11.5
D.N. Ciclitira 9.11
Heat: 1 S.Earl (Magdalen College, Oxford) 2 D.N. Ciclitira. Easily, 9m 40s
Heat: 1 J. Beresford Jnr 2 J.E. Pedder (Worcester College, Oxford). 2 lengths, 9m 17s
Heat: 1 J. Beresford Jnr 2 D.H.L. Gollan (Leander Club). Easily, 9m 32s
Semi-final: 1 J. Beresford Jnr 2 R. Blyth (Christ's College, Cambridge). Easily, 10m 23s
Final: 1 W.M. Hoover (Duluth BC, Minnesota, USA) (winner) 2 J. Beresford Jnr. Easily, 9m 32s

1923 J. Beresford Jnr 11.6
Heat: 1 J. Beresford Jnr 2 R. Blyth (Vesta RC). Easily, 8m 55s (short course)
Heat: 1 J. Beresford Jnr 2 K.A.B. Wilson (Royal Chester RC). Easily, 8m 30s
Semi-final: 1 M.K. Morris (London RC) (winner) 2 J. Beresford Jnr. 3 lengths, 8m 5s

1924 J. Beresford Jnr 11.5
Heat: 1 J. Beresford Jnr 2 D.H.L. Gollan (Leander Club). 2½ lengths, 10m 16s
Heat: 1 J. Beresford Jnr 2 S. Earl (Leander Club). Not rowed out.
Semi-final: 1 J. Beresford Jnr 2 R.S. Muttlebury (Third Trinity, Cambridge). Easily, 11m 48s
Final: 1 J. Beresford Jnr 2 K.N. Craig (Pembroke College, Cambridge). Easily, 10m 32s

1925 J. Beresford Jnr 11.8
Heat: 1 J. Beresford Jnr 2 S.E.J. Hart (Quintin BC). Easily, 8m 57s
Semi-final: 1 J. Beresford Jnr 2 W.M. Hoover (Undine Barge Club, USA). 3 lengths, 8m 27s
Final: 1 J. Beresford Jnr 2 D.H.L. Gollan (Leander Club). Easily, 8m 28s

1926 J. Beresford Jnr 11.6
Heat: 1 J. Beresford Jnr 2 D.H.L. Gollan (Leander Club). Easily, 8m 32s
Heat: 1 J. Beresford Jnr 2 E.J. de Lotbiniere (Third Trinity, Cambridge). Easily, 9m 2s
Semi-final: 1 J. Beresford Jnr 2 T.D.A. Collet (Pembroke College, Cambridge). Easily, 8m 37s
Final: 1 J. Beresford Jnr 2 G.E.G. Goddard (Jesus College, Cambridge). Easily, 8m 45s

1927 J. Beresford Jnr 11.7
Heat: 1 J. Beresford Jnr 2 H. Boulton (Maidenhead RC). Easily, 9m 22s
Semi-final: 1 R.T. Lee (Worcester College, Oxford) (winner) 2 J. Beresford Jnr. 3 lengths, 9m 4s

1930 J. Beresford Jnr 11.6
Heat: 1 J. Wright (Argonaut RC, Canada) 2 J. Beresford Jnr. 2½ lengths, 9m 35s

1931 L.F. Southwood 12.10
Heat: 1 L.F. Southwood 2 F.R. Stephen (London RC). Easily, 9m 10s
Heat: 1 L.F. Southwood 2 D. Guye (London RC). 2 lengths, 9m 38s
Semi-final: 1 R. Pearce (Leander BC, Hamilton, Canada) (winner) 2 L.F. Southwood. Easily, 9m 11s

1932 L.F. Southwood 12.12
G. von Opel 12.4
Heat: 1 J.L. West (London RC) 2 G. von Opel. Not rowed out.
Heat: 1 L.F. Southwood 2 L. Clive (Christ Church, Oxford). Easily, 9m 28s
Heat: H. Buhtz (Berliner RC, Germany) (winner) 2 L.F. Southwood. 2 lengths, 9m 5s

1933 B.S. Fidler 12.10
G. von Opel 12.8
Heat: 1 G. von Opel 2 B.S. Fidler. Easily, 8m 45s
Heat: 1 G. von Opel 2 V. Saurin (SN de Lagny, France). ⅓ length, 8m 31s
Semi-final: 1 H.L. Warren (Trinity Hall, Cambridge) 2 G. von Opel. Easily, 9m 46s

1934 L.F. Southwood 12.10
B.S. Fidler 12.7
Heat: 1 E.W. Wingate (Vesta RC) 2 B.S. Fidler. 2 lengths, 8m 36s
Heat: 1 L.F. Southwood 2 C.A.S. Ross (Exeter College, Oxford). Easily, 8m 39s
Heat: 1 J. Zavrel (Veslarsky Club, Czechoslovakia) 2 L.F. Southwood. Easily, 8m 21s

1935 T.H. Tyler 11.8
Heat: 1 T.H. Tyler 2 E.C. Branco (Club de Regattas Boqueirao do Passeio, Brazil). 2 lengths, 9m 11s
Heat: 1 E. Rufli (Zurich RC, Switzerland) (winner) 2 T.H. Tyler. Easily, 8m 45s

1936 T.H. Tyler 11.12
Heat: 1 T.H. Tyler 2 M.O. Palmer (Lady Margaret, Cambridge). Easily, 9m 28s
Heat: 1 T.H. Tyler 2 J.F. Coulson (Argonaut RC, Canada). Not rowed out.
Semi-final: 1 T.H. Tyler 2 R.F. Winstone (Molesey BC). Easily, 9m 32s
Final: 1 E. Rufli (Zurich RC, Switzerland) 2 T.H. Tyler. 3 lengths, 9m 22s

1937 T.H. Tyler 11.12
Heat: 1 G. von Opel (RV Russelsheim, Germany) 2 T.H. Tyler. 6 feet, 9m 13s

1938 T.H. Tyler 11.11
Heat: 1 T.H. Tyler 2 R. Hope (Leander Club). Easily, 8m 58s
Semi-final: 1 J.W. Burk (Penn Athletic Club, USA) (winner) 2 T.H. Tyler. Easily, 9m 0s

1952 S.C. Rand 11.11
Heat: 1 S.C. Rand 2 R.E. Bowles (Barnes RC). 2 lengths, 9m 7s
Heat: 1 S.C. Rand 2 R.M. Martin (Marlow RC). 1 length, 8m 29s
Semi-final: 1 M.T. Wood (Sydney RC, Australia) (winner) 2 S.C. Rand. 4 lengths, 8m 23s

1961 J.R. Buzeman 10.8
Heat: 1 S.A. Mackenzie (Mosman RC, Australia) (winner) 2 J.R. Buzeman. ½ length, 8m 38s

1962 J.R. Buzeman 11.2
Heat: 1 J.R. Buzeman 2 J.H. Libby (Abingdon RC). Easily, 8m 38s
Heat: 1 W.L. Barry (Quintin BC) 2 J.R. Buzeman. Easily, 8m 10s

1970 D.W. Gramolt 12.13
Heat: 1 J.T. McCarthy (Poplar, Blackwall and District RC) 2 D.W. Gramolt. Easily, 8m 47s

Diamond Challenge Sculls

1980 A.J. Ross 12.10
Heat: 1 A.J. Ross 2 A. Gilje (Stavanger Roklub, Norway). 1½ lengths, 8m 37s
Heat: 1 B. Lewis (University of California, Irvine, USA) 2 A.J. Ross. ½ length, 8m 36s

1983 A.J. Ross 12.10
Heat: 1 A.J. Ross 2 A.C. Rudkin (Bewl Bridge RC). Easily, 8m 29s
Heat: 1 A.J. Ross 2 S.J. McCarthy (Lea RC). 3½ lengths, 8m 40s
Semi-final: 1 T.J. Crooks (Kingston RC) 2 A.J. Ross. 4 lengths, 8m 32s

1984 A.J. Ross 12.10
Heat: 1 A.J. Ross 2 T.J. Crooks (Kingston RC). Easily, 8m 16s
Heat: 1 A.J. Ross 2 B.S. Cooper (New Zealand Sports Union). 3¼ lengths, 8m 22s
Semi-final: 1 B. Eltang (Danske Studenten Roklub, Denmark) 2 A.J. Ross. 1¾ lengths, 8m 2s

1987 I.G.P. Pritchard 13.1
G.P.R. Reddin 12.10
Heat: 1 L. Fletcher (Hollingworth Lake RC) 2 I.G.P. Pritchard. 4¼ lengths, 8m 26s
Heat: 1 P.H. Ashmore (St Ives RC) 2 G.P.R. Reddin. 2⅔ lengths, 8m 48s

1989 I.G.P. Pritchard 13.0
G.P.R. Reddin 12.13
W. Baker 11.7
Heat: 1 B.S. Ford (Burnaby Lake RC, Canada) 2 I.G.P. Pritchard. 4 lengths, 8m 39s
Heat: 1 H.W. Kelderman (Zutphense RZ 'Isala', Holland) 2 G.P.R. Reddin. 1⅓ lengths, 8m 52s
Heat: 1 B.S. Ford 2 W. Baker. 4⅓ lengths, 8m 0s

ROYAL HENLEY PEACE REGATTA, 1919

Fawley Cup
V.G. Teale 10.10 (bow); G.H. Kelly 11.5; J.L. Tann 11.2; K. Vernon 11.5; C.K. Roylance 12.8; B. Logan 12.7; S.I. Fairbairn 12.0; J. Beresford Snr 10.0 (stroke); C.A.A. Robertson 8.5 (cox). Av: 11.6¼
Heat: 1 TRC 2 Marlow RC. ¾ length, 7m 45s
Semi-final: 1 TRC 2 Kingston RC. 1¼ lengths, 7m 48s
Final: 1 TRC 2 Christ Church, Oxford. 1 length, 7m 18s

Wargrave Manor Cup
J. Beresford Snr 10.0 (bow, strs); K. Vernon 11.5; J.L. Tann 11.2; B. Logan 12.7 (stroke). Av: 11.3½
Heat: 1 Leander Club (winners) 2 TRC. Easily, 8m 13s

Hambleden Pairs
S.I. Fairbairn 12.5 (bow); I.P.R.Napier 13.0 (stroke).
Heat: 1 C.E.V. Buxton & M.V. Buxton (Third Trinity, Cambridge) (winners) 2 TRC. Easily, 9m 11s

HENLEY ONE-DAY REGATTA 1945 (Short course)

Danesfield Cup (Open Eights)
A.J. Crosbie-Browne (bow); P.F. Whalley; H.A.I. MacInness; K.A. Williams; C.S. Windebank; A.E. Shave; R.C. Morris; J.A.E. Cutler (stroke); J.F. Levy (cox).
Heat: 1 TRC 2 Guy's Hospital 3 Pembroke College, Cambridge. 1¾ lengths, 4m 58s
Semi-final: 1 Jesus College, Cambridge 2 Oriel College, Oxford 3 TRC. ½ length, 4.49

Index

This index does not include trophies at Henley Royal Regatta, references to which appear frequently in the text.